ALSO AVAILABLE FROM TOKYOPOP®

PLANET LADDER
PLANETES
PRIEST
PRINCESS AI
PSYCHIC ACADEMY
QUEEN'S KNIGHT, THE
RAGNAROK
RAVE MASTER
REALITY CHECK
REBIRTH
REBOUND
REMOTE
RISING STARS OF MANGA
SABER MARIONETTE J
SAILOR MOON
SAINT TAIL
SAIYUKI
SAMURAI DEEPER KYO
SAMURAI GIRL REAL BOUT HIGH SCHOOL
SCRYED
SEIKAI TRILOGY, THE
SGT. FROG
SHAOLIN SISTERS
SHIRAHIME-SYO: SNOW GODDESS TALES
SHUTTERBOX
SKULL MAN, THE
SNOW DROP
SORCERER HUNTERS
STONE
SUIKODEN III
SUKI
THREADS OF TIME
TOKYO BABYLON
TOKYO MEW MEW
TOKYO TRIBES
TRAMPS LIKE US
UNDER THE GLASS MOON
VAMPIRE GAME
VISION OF ESCAFLOWNE, THE
WARRIORS OF TAO
WILD ACT
WISH
WORLD OF HARTZ
X-DAY
ZODIAC P.I.

NOVELS

CLAMP SCHOOL PARANORMAL INVESTIGATORS
KARMA CLUB
SAILOR MOON
SLAYERS

ART BOOKS

ART OF CARDCAPTOR SAKURA
ART OF MAGIC KNIGHT RAYEARTH, THE
PEACH: MIWA UEDA ILLUSTRATIONS

ANIME GUIDES

COWBOY BEBOP
GUNDAM TECHNICAL MANUALS
SAILOR MOON SCOUT GUIDES

TOKYOPOP KIDS

STRAY SHEEP

CINE-MANGA™

ALADDIN
CARDCAPTORS
DUEL MASTERS
FAIRLY ODDPARENTS, THE
FAMILY GUY
FINDING NEMO
G.I. JOE SPY TROOPS
GREATEST STARS OF THE NBA
JACKIE CHAN ADVENTURES
JIMMY NEUTRON: BOY GENIUS, THE ADVENTURES OF
KIM POSSIBLE
LILO & STITCH: THE SERIES
LIZZIE MCGUIRE
LIZZIE MCGUIRE MOVIE, THE
MALCOLM IN THE MIDDLE
POWER RANGERS: DINO THUNDER
POWER RANGERS: NINJA STORM
PRINCESS DIARIES 2
RAVE MASTER
SHREK 2
SIMPLE LIFE, THE
SPONGEBOB SQUAREPANTS
SPY KIDS 2
SPY KIDS 3-D: GAME OVER
THAT'S SO RAVEN
TOTALLY SPIES
TRANSFORMERS: ARMADA
TRANSFORMERS: ENERGON

**You want it? We got it!
A full range of TOKYOPOP
products are available now at:
www.TOKYOPOP.com/shop**

05.11.04T

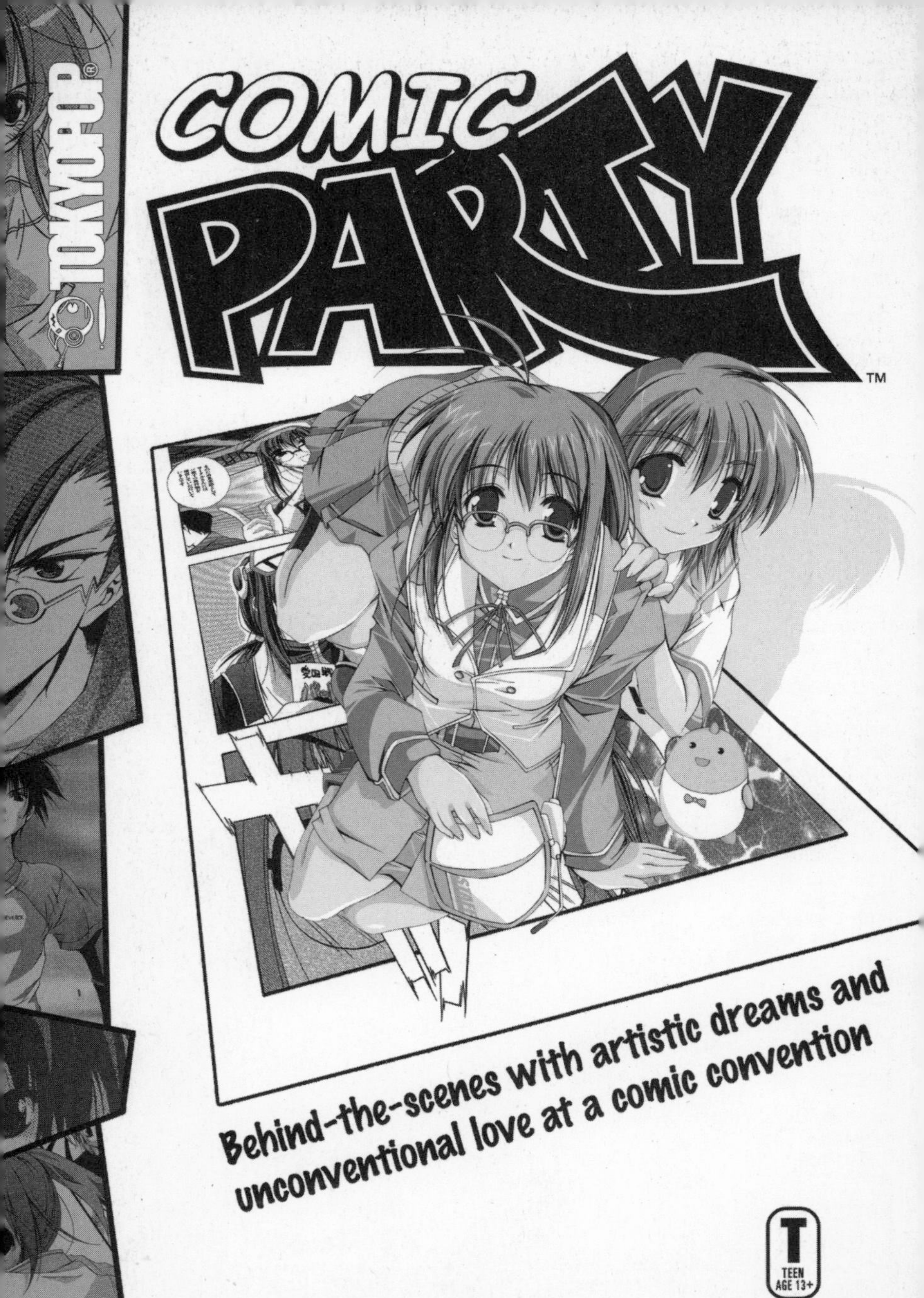
TOKYOPOP
COMIC PARTY
Behind-the-scenes with artistic dreams and unconventional love at a comic convention
T
TEEN
AGE 13+

ing!

T ... t-to-left
fo ... ders
ge ... en
as ... ss,
ar

s

... s a

4
2
8
7
6
5
10
9

... op right panel and follow the numbers. Have fun, and look for more 100% authentic manga from TOKYOPOP®!

100% AUTHENTIC MANGA

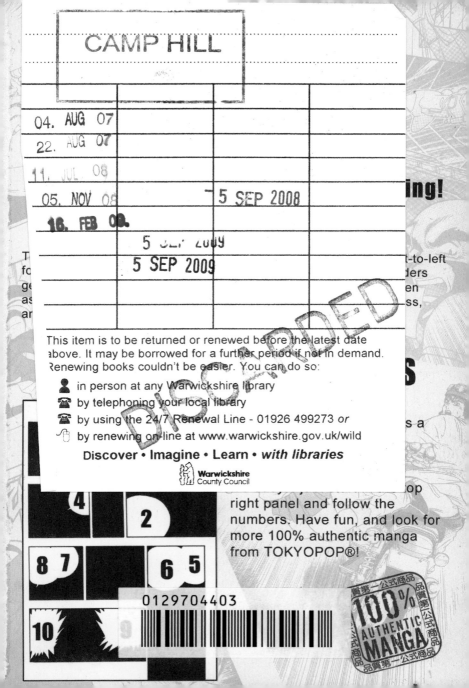

ALSO AVAILABLE FROM  TOKYOPOP®

MANGA

.HACK//LEGEND OF THE TWILIGHT
@LARGE
ABENOBASHI: MAGICAL SHOPPING ARCADE
A.I. LOVE YOU
AI YORI AOSHI
ANGELIC LAYER
ARM OF KANNON
BABY BIRTH
BATTLE ROYALE
BATTLE VIXENS
BRAIN POWERED
BRIGADOON
B'TX
CANDIDATE FOR GODDESS, THE
CARDCAPTOR SAKURA
CARDCAPTOR SAKURA - MASTER OF THE CLOW
CHOBITS
CHRONICLES OF THE CURSED SWORD
CLAMP SCHOOL DETECTIVES
CLOVER
COMIC PARTY
CONFIDENTIAL CONFESSIONS
CORRECTOR YUI
COWBOY BEBOP
COWBOY BEBOP: SHOOTING STAR
CRAZY LOVE STORY
CRESCENT MOON
CROSS
CULDCEPT
CYBORG 009
D•N•ANGEL
DEMON DIARY
DEMON ORORON, THE
DEUS VITAE
DIABOLO
DIGIMON
DIGIMON TAMERS
DIGIMON ZERO TWO
DOLL
DRAGON HUNTER
DRAGON KNIGHTS
DRAGON VOICE
DREAM SAGA
DUKLYON: CLAMP SCHOOL DEFENDERS
EERIE QUEERIE!
ERICA SAKURAZAWA: COLLECTED WORKS
ET CETERA
ETERNITY
EVIL'S RETURN
FAERIES' LANDING
FAKE
FLCL
FLOWER OF THE DEEP SLEEP
FORBIDDEN DANCE
FRUITS BASKET
G GUNDAM

GATEKEEPERS
GETBACKERS
GIRL GOT GAME
GIRLS' EDUCATIONAL CHARTER
GRAVITATION
GTO
GUNDAM BLUE DESTINY
GUNDAM SEED ASTRAY
GUNDAM WING
GUNDAM WING: BATTLEFIELD OF PACIFISTS
GUNDAM WING: ENDLESS WALTZ
GUNDAM WING: THE LAST OUTPOST (G-UNIT)
GUYS' GUIDE TO GIRLS
HANDS OFF!
HAPPY MANIA
HARLEM BEAT
I.N.V.U.
IMMORTAL RAIN
INITIAL D
INSTANT TEEN: JUST ADD NUTS
ISLAND
JING: KING OF BANDITS
JING: KING OF BANDITS - TWILIGHT TALES
JULINE
KARE KANO
KILL ME, KISS ME
KINDAICHI CASE FILES, THE
KING OF HELL
KODOCHA: SANA'S STAGE
LAMENT OF THE LAMB
LEGAL DRUG
LEGEND OF CHUN HYANG, THE
LES BIJOUX
LOVE HINA
LUPIN III
LUPIN III: WORLD'S MOST WANTED
MAGIC KNIGHT RAYEARTH I
MAGIC KNIGHT RAYEARTH II
MAHOROMATIC: AUTOMATIC MAIDEN
MAN OF MANY FACES
MARMALADE BOY
MARS
MARS: HORSE WITH NO NAME
MINK
MIRACLE GIRLS
MIYUKI-CHAN IN WONDERLAND
MODEL
MY LOVE
NECK AND NECK
ONE
ONE I LOVE, THE
PARADISE KISS
PARASYTE
PASSION FRUIT
PEACH GIRL
PEACH GIRL: CHANGE OF HEART
PET SHOP OF HORRORS
PITA-TEN

05.11.04T

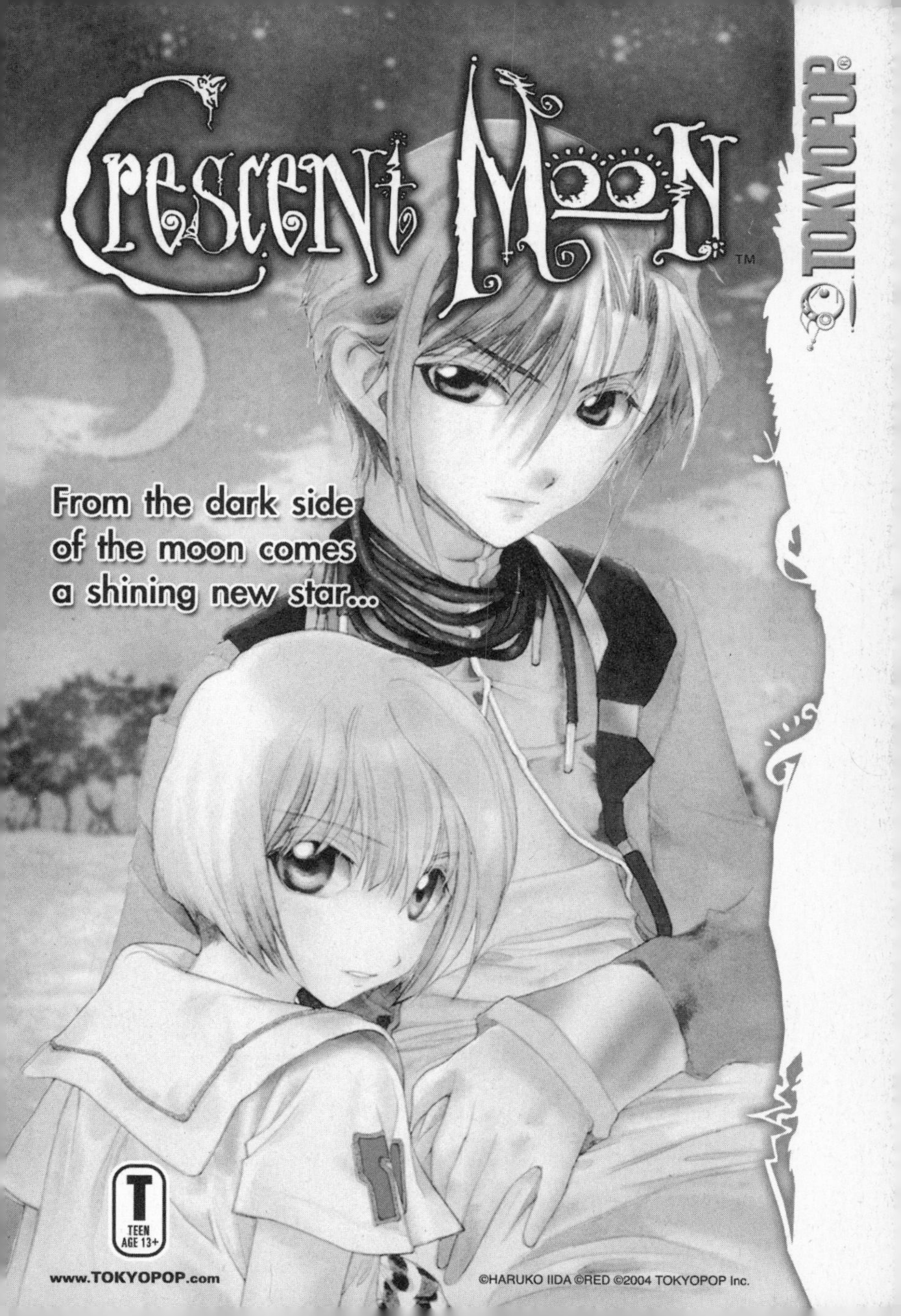
Crescent Moon™
TOKYOPOP®
From the dark side of the moon comes a shining new star...
T TEEN AGE 13+
www.TOKYOPOP.com
©HARUKO IIDA ©RED ©2004 TOKYOPOP Inc.

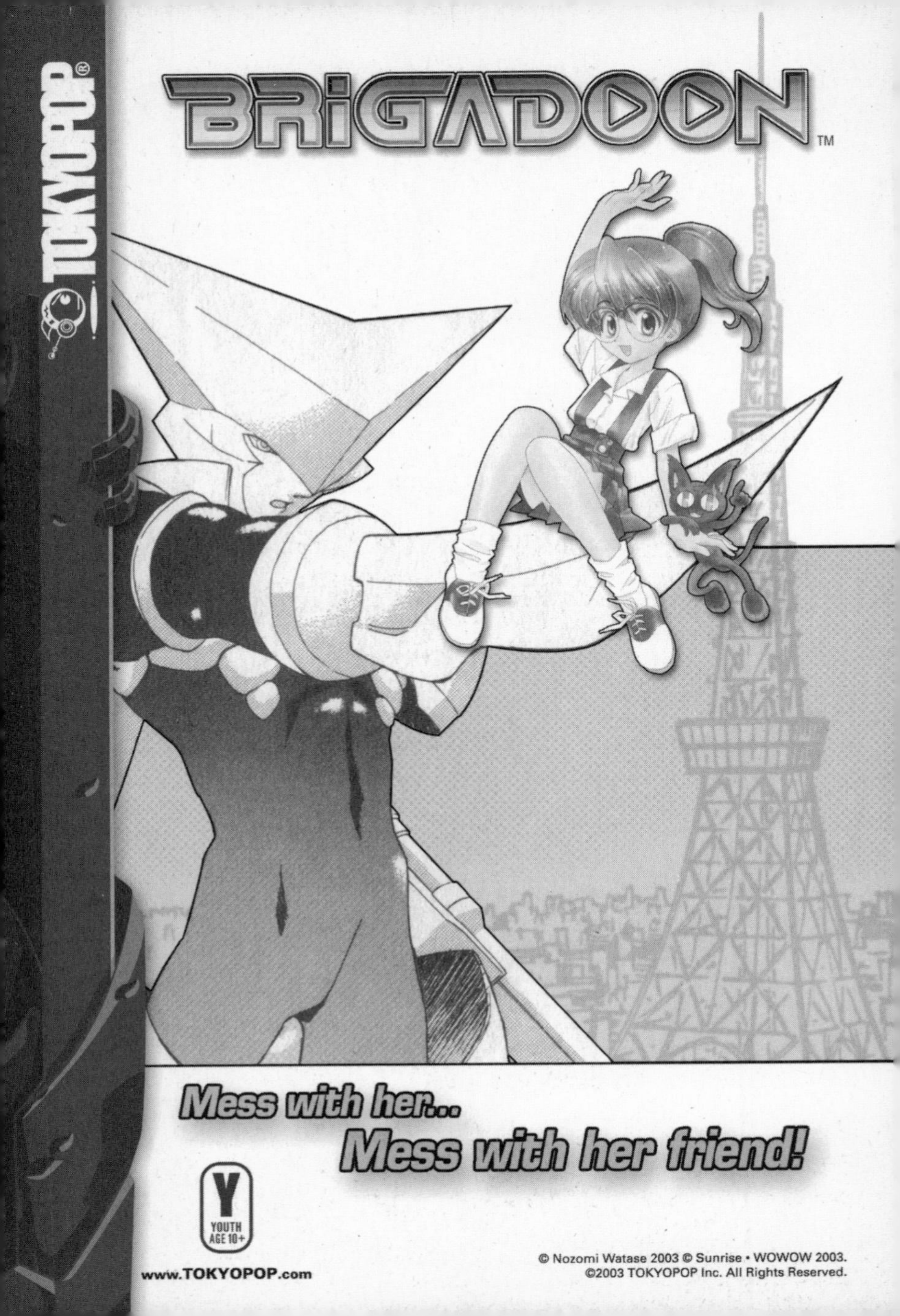
TOKYOPOP
BRIGADOON™
Mess with her...
Mess with her friend!
Y YOUTH AGE 10+
www.TOKYOPOP.com
© Nozomi Watase 2003 © Sunrise • WOWOW 2003.
©2003 TOKYOPOP Inc. All Rights Reserved.

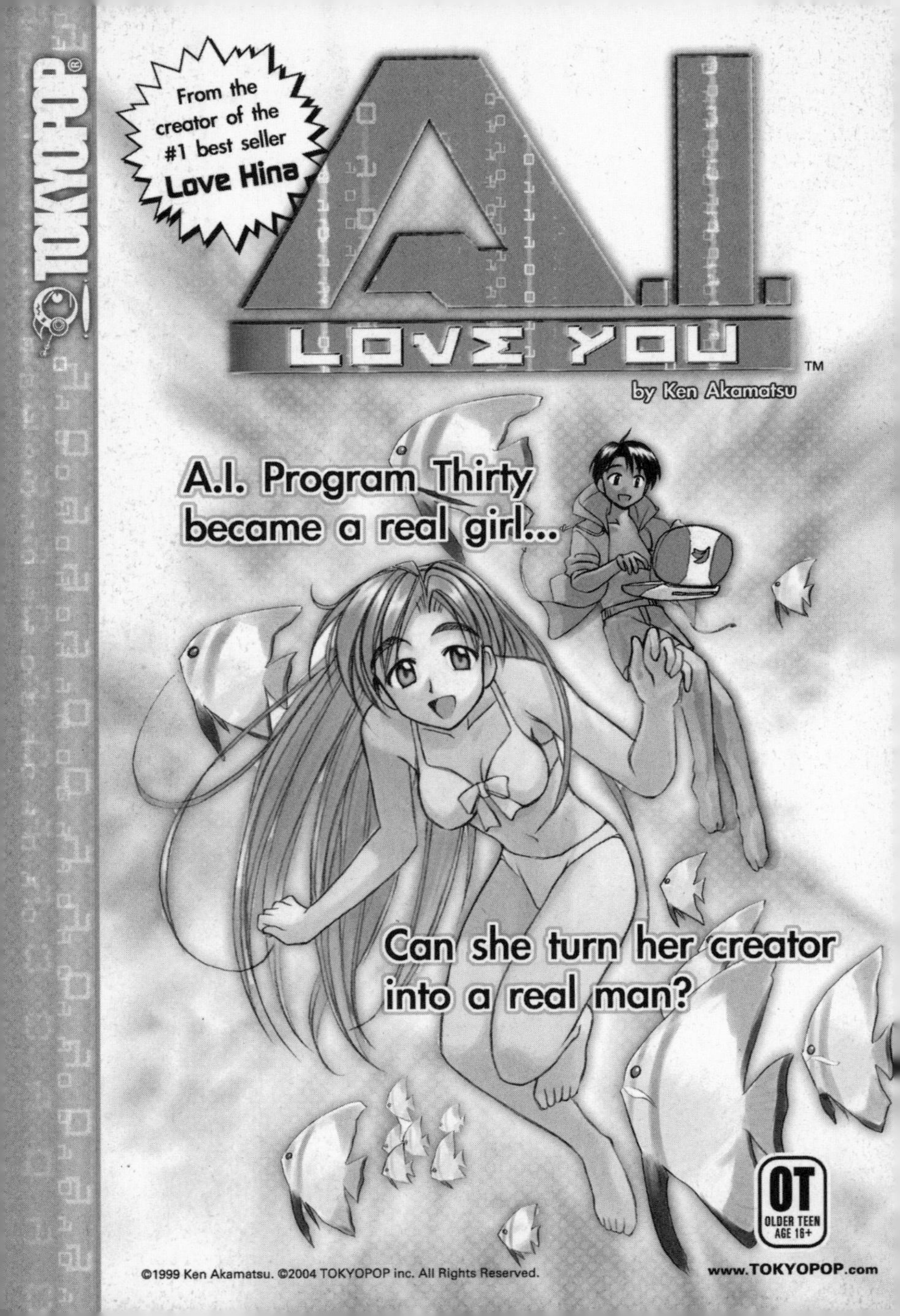
TOKYOPOP
From the creator of the #1 best seller Love Hina
A.I. LOVE YOU
by Ken Akamatsu
A.I. Program Thirty became a real girl...
Can she turn her creator into a real man?
OT OLDER TEEN AGE 16+
©1999 Ken Akamatsu. ©2004 TOKYOPOP inc. All Rights Reserved.
www.TOKYOPOP.com

D•N•ANGEL

BY YUKIRU SUGISAKI

VOLUME 3

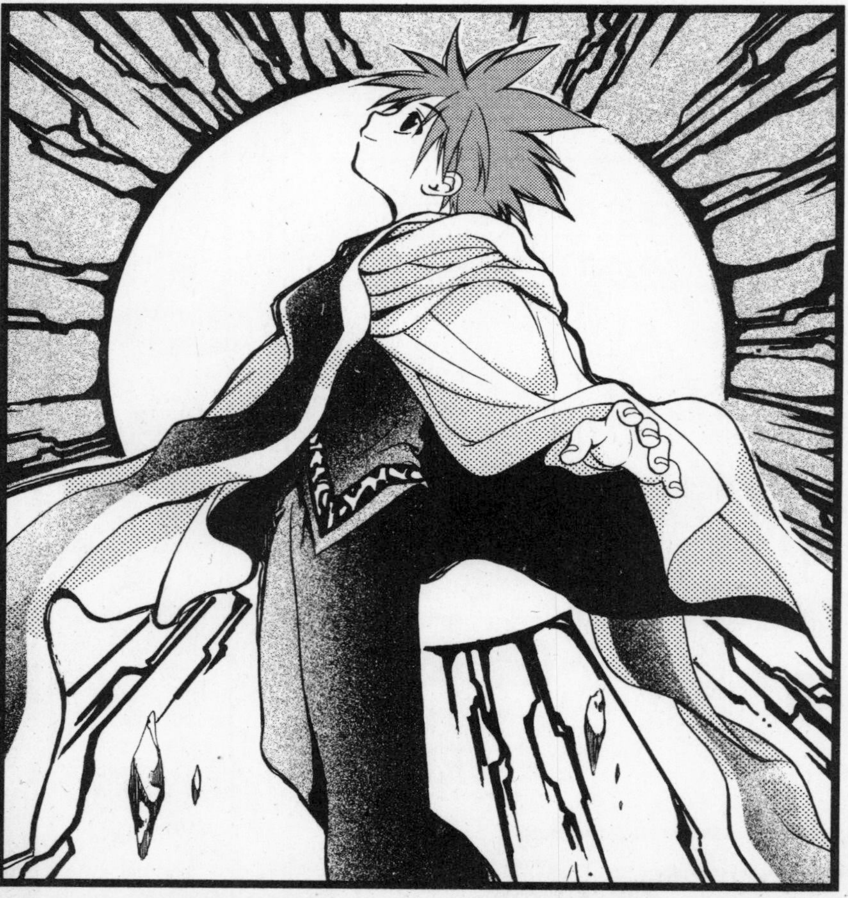

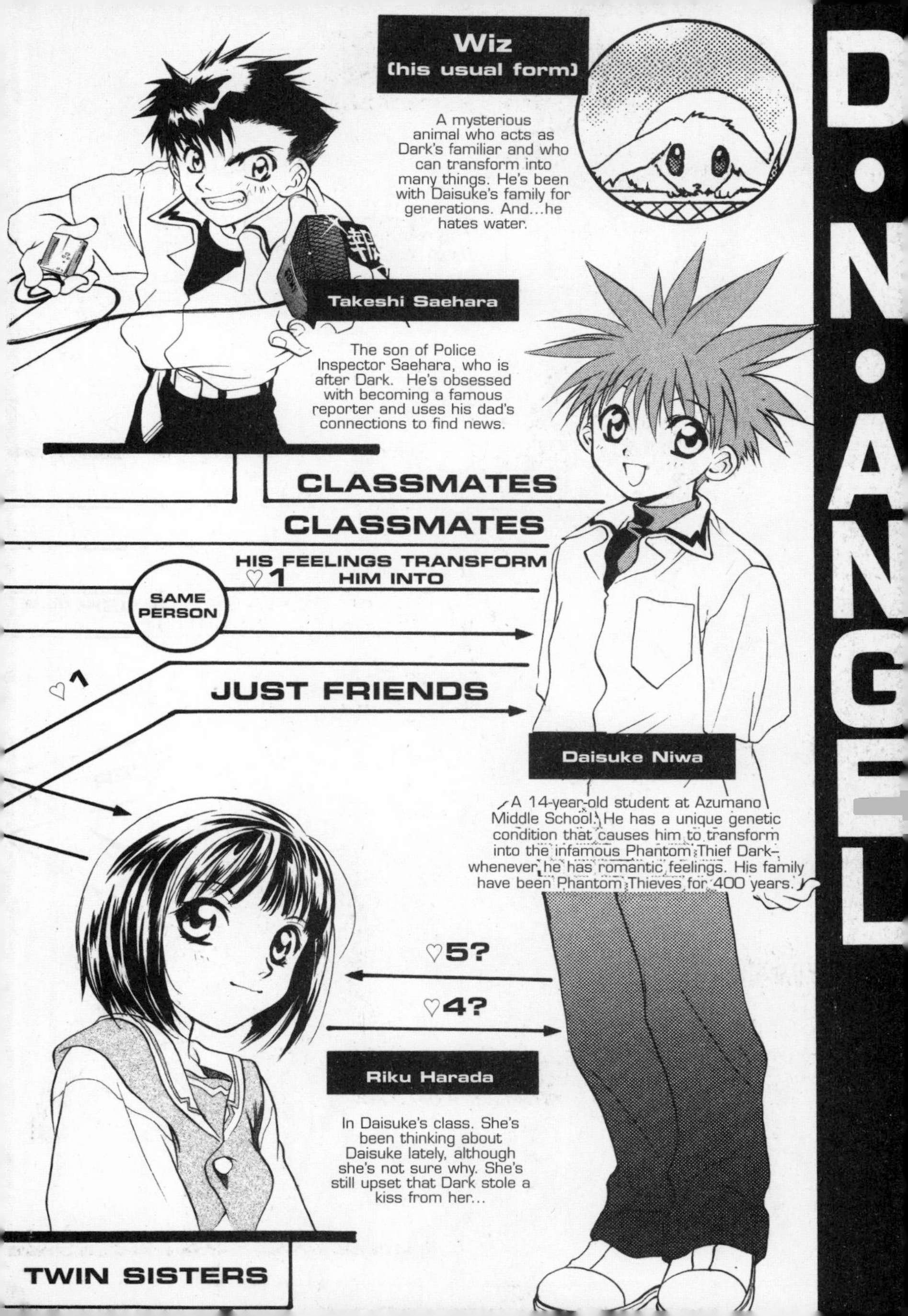
D•N•ANGEL
Wiz
(his usual form)
A mysterious animal who acts as Dark's familiar and who can transform into many things. He's been with Daisuke's family for generations. And...he hates water.
Takeshi Saehara
The son of Police Inspector Saehara, who is after Dark. He's obsessed with becoming a famous reporter and uses his dad's connections to find news.
CLASSMATES
CLASSMATES
HIS FEELINGS TRANSFORM HIM INTO
♡1
SAME PERSON
♡1
JUST FRIENDS
Daisuke Niwa
A 14-year-old student at Azumano Middle School. He has a unique genetic condition that causes him to transform into the infamous Phantom Thief Dark—whenever he has romantic feelings. His family have been Phantom Thieves for 400 years.
♡5?
♡4?
Riku Harada
In Daisuke's class. She's been thinking about Daisuke lately, although she's not sure why. She's still upset that Dark stole a kiss from her...
TWIN SISTERS

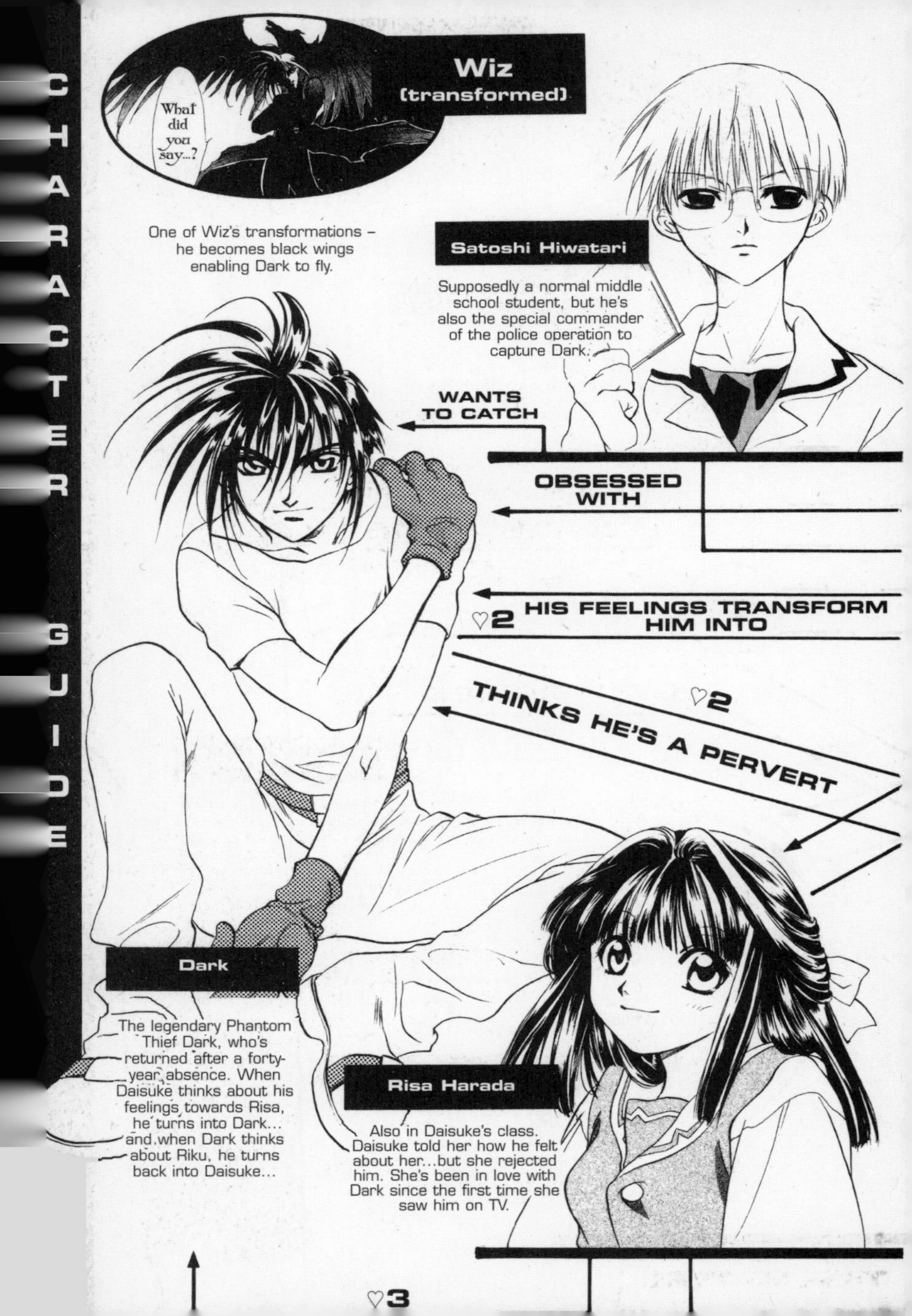

CHARACTER GUIDE
Wiz (transformed)
What did you say...?
One of Wiz's transformations – he becomes black wings enabling Dark to fly.
Satoshi Hiwatari
Supposedly a normal middle school student, but he's also the special commander of the police operation to capture Dark.
WANTS TO CATCH
OBSESSED WITH
♡2 HIS FEELINGS TRANSFORM HIM INTO
♡2
THINKS HE'S A PERVERT
Dark
The legendary Phantom Thief Dark, who's returned after a forty-year absence. When Daisuke thinks about his feelings towards Risa, he turns into Dark... and when Dark thinks about Riku, he turns back into Daisuke...
Risa Harada
Also in Daisuke's class. Daisuke told her how he felt about her...but she rejected him. She's been in love with Dark since the first time she saw him on TV.
♡3

D•N•ANGEL Vol. 3
Created by Yukiru Sugisaki

Translation - Alethea Nibley, Athena Nibley
English Adaptation - Sarah Dyer
Copy Editors - Troy Lewter, Hope Donovan
Retouch and Lettering - Paul Tanck
Production Artist - Vicente Rivera, Jr.
Cover Layout - Gary Shum

Editor - Bryce P. Coleman
Digital Imaging Manager - Chris Buford
Pre-Press Manager - Antonio DePietro
Production Managers - Jennifer Miller and Mutsumi Miyazaki
Art Director - Matt Alford
Managing Editor - Jill Freshney
VP of Production - Ron Klamert
President and C.O.O. - John Parker
Publisher and C.E.O. - Stuart Levy

A  Manga

TOKYOPOP Inc.
5900 Wilshire Blvd. Suite 2000
Los Angeles, CA 90036

E-mail: info@TOKYOPOP.com
Come visit us online at www.TOKYOPOP.com

ISBN: 1-59182-801-5

First TOKYOPOP printing: August 2004
10 9 8
Printed in the USA

Volume 3

By

Yukiru Sugisaki

HAMBURG // LONDON // LOS ANGELES // TOKYO

CONTENTS

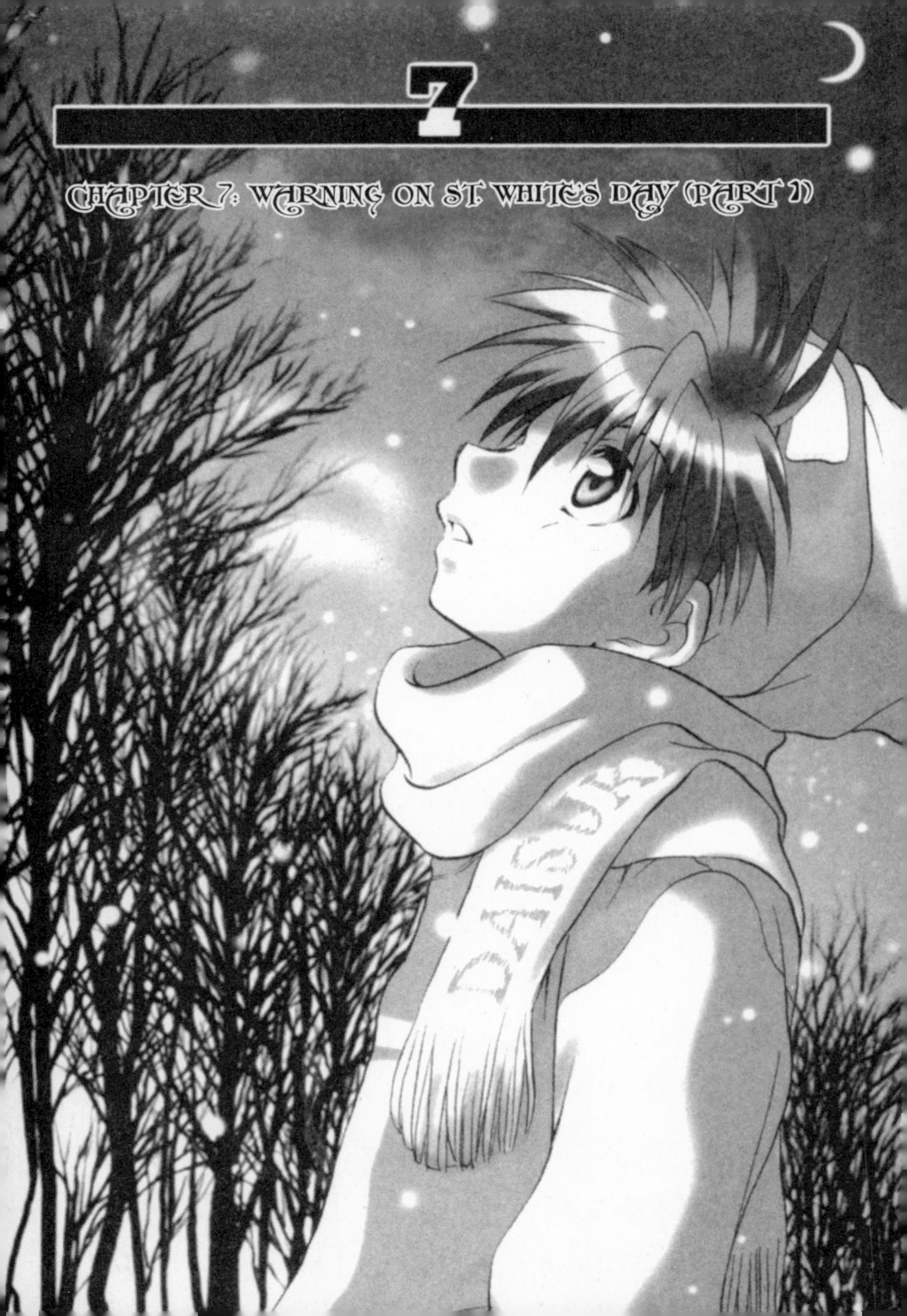
7
CHAPTER 7: WARNING ON ST. WHITE'S DAY (PART 1)

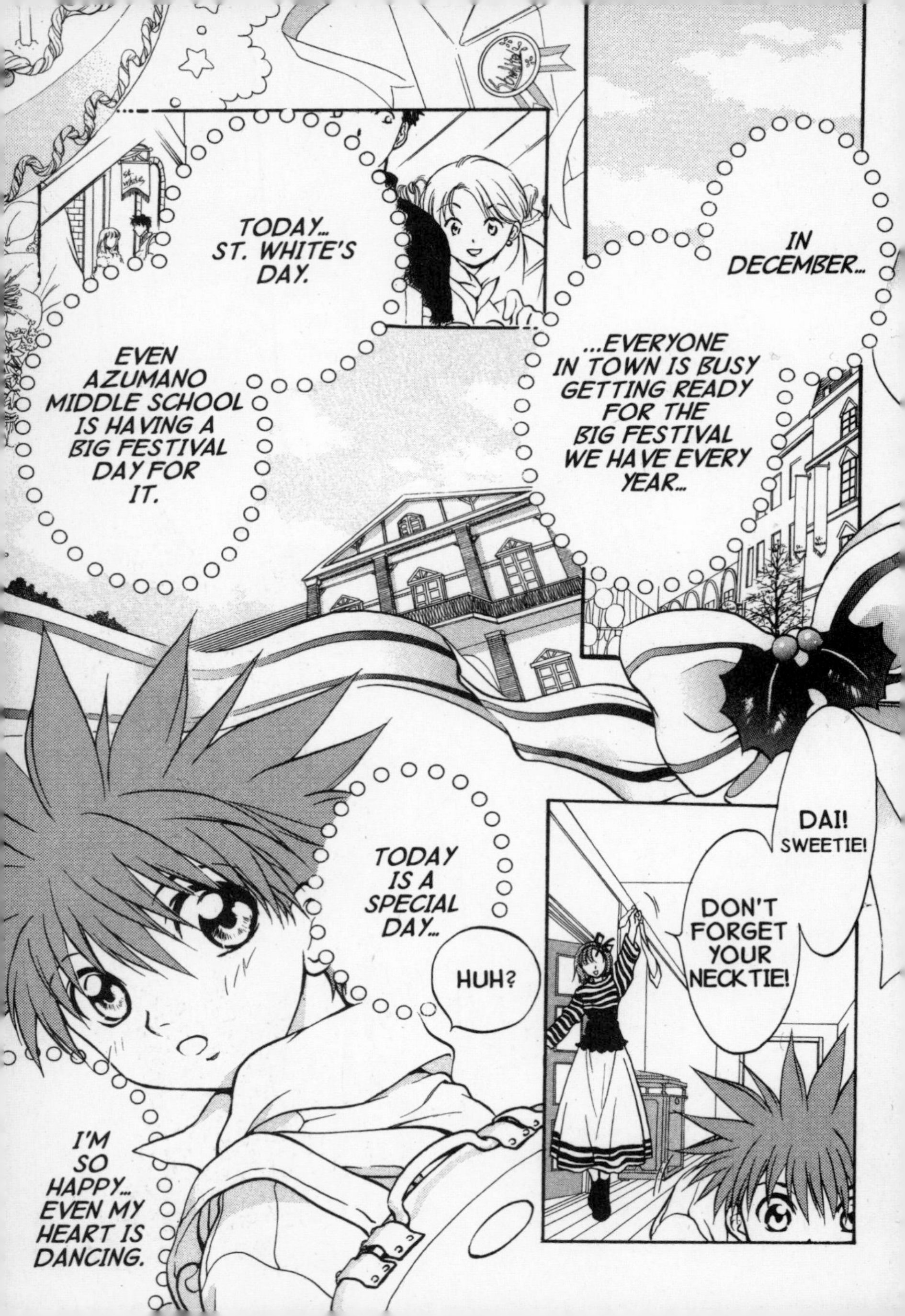
IN DECEMBER...
TODAY... ST. WHITE'S DAY.
...EVERYONE IN TOWN IS BUSY GETTING READY FOR THE BIG FESTIVAL WE HAVE EVERY YEAR...
EVEN AZUMANO MIDDLE SCHOOL IS HAVING A BIG FESTIVAL DAY FOR IT.
DAI! SWEETIE!
DON'T FORGET YOUR NECKTIE!
TODAY IS A SPECIAL DAY...
HUH?
I'M SO HAPPY... EVEN MY HEART IS DANCING.

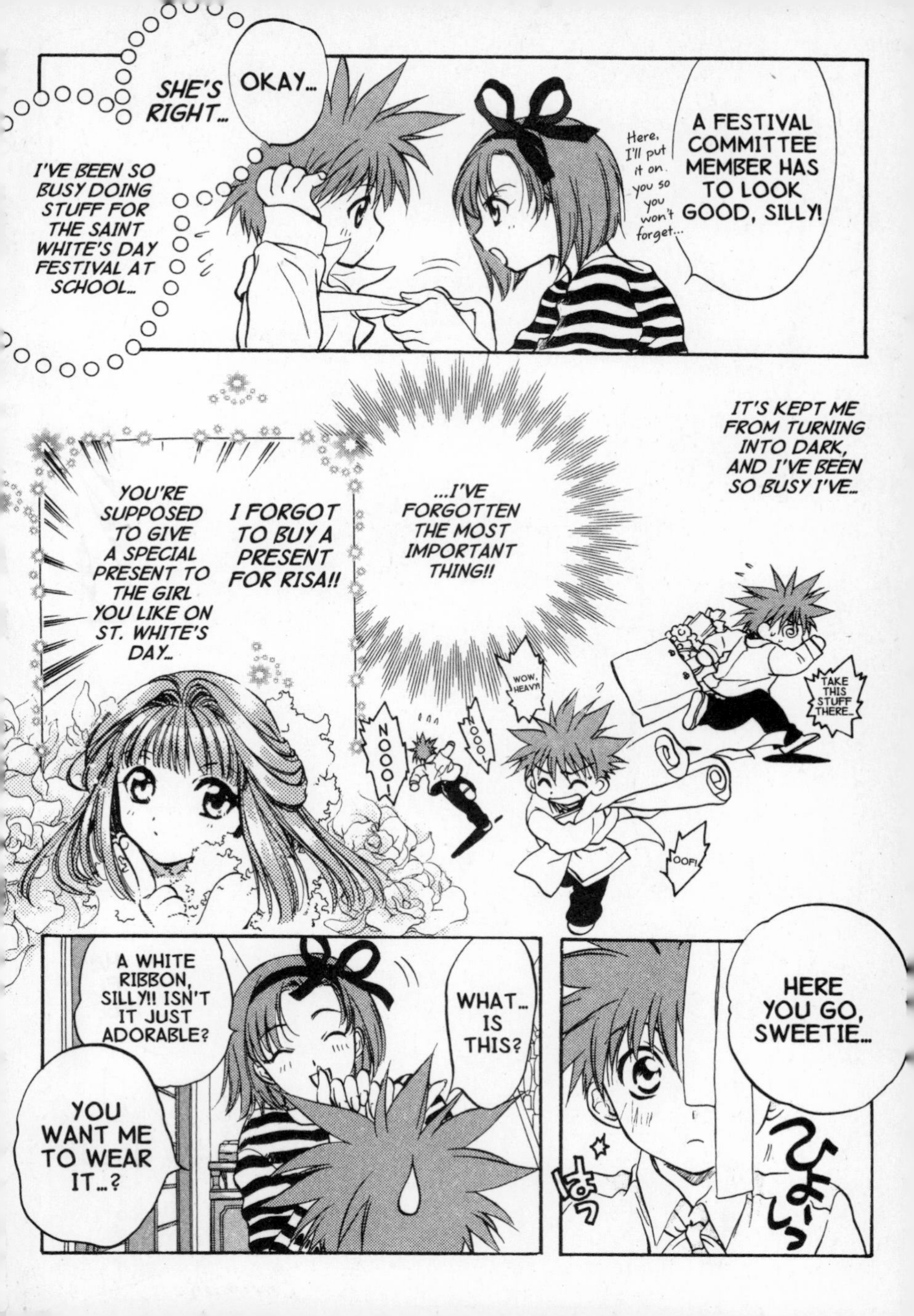
A FESTIVAL COMMITTEE MEMBER HAS TO LOOK GOOD, SILLY!
Here, I'll put it on. you so you won't forget...
OKAY...
SHE'S RIGHT...
I'VE BEEN SO BUSY DOING STUFF FOR THE SAINT WHITE'S DAY FESTIVAL AT SCHOOL...
IT'S KEPT ME FROM TURNING INTO DARK, AND I'VE BEEN SO BUSY I'VE...
TAKE THIS STUFF THERE...
WOW, HEAVY!
NOOO!
NOOO!
OOF!
...I'VE FORGOTTEN THE MOST IMPORTANT THING!!
I FORGOT TO BUY A PRESENT FOR RISA!!
YOU'RE SUPPOSED TO GIVE A SPECIAL PRESENT TO THE GIRL YOU LIKE ON ST. WHITE'S DAY...
HERE YOU GO, SWEETIE...
ひょいっ
はっ
WHAT... IS THIS?
A WHITE RIBBON, SILLY!! ISN'T IT JUST ADORABLE?
YOU WANT ME TO WEAR IT...?

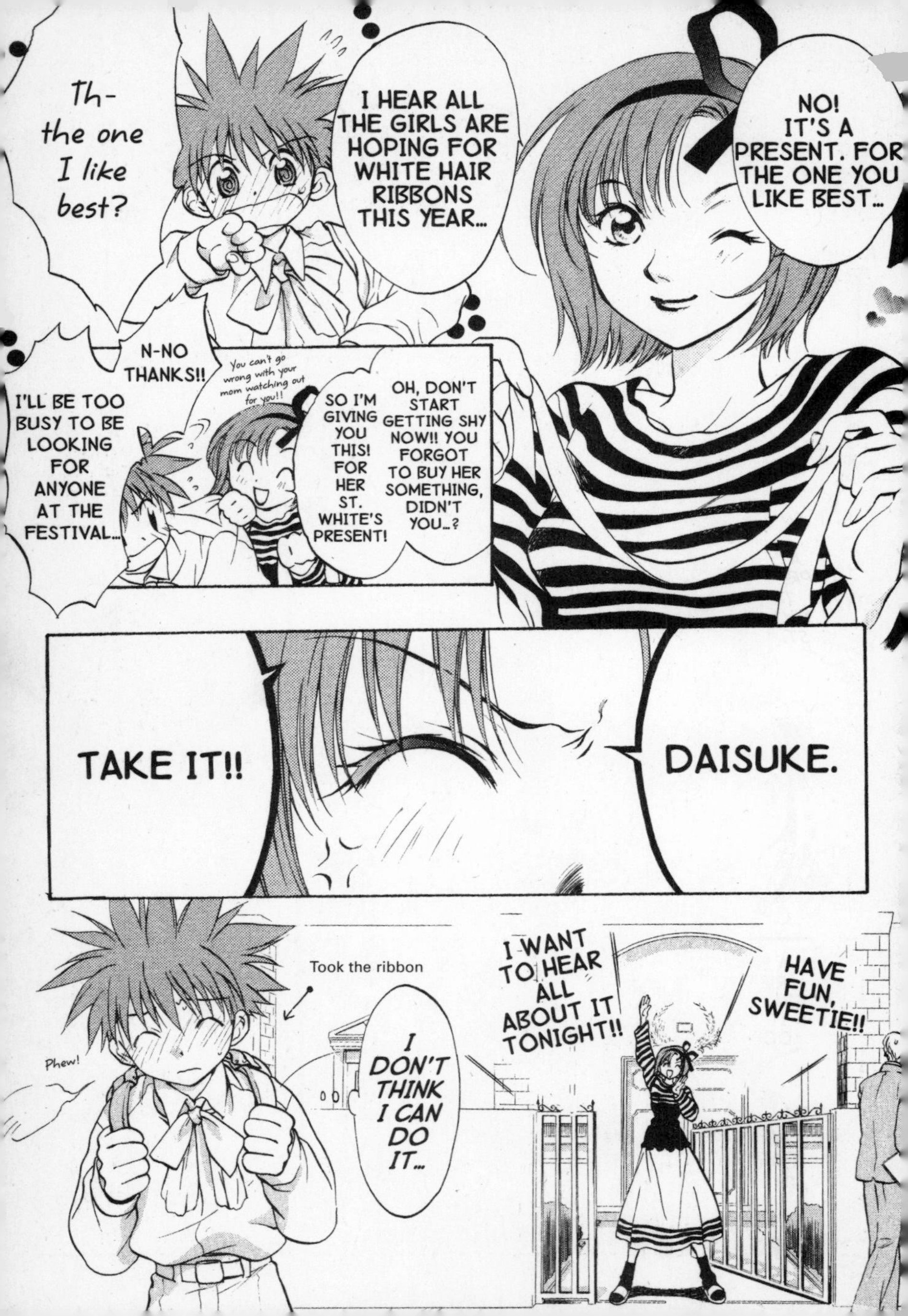
NO! IT'S A PRESENT. FOR THE ONE YOU LIKE BEST...
I HEAR ALL THE GIRLS ARE HOPING FOR WHITE HAIR RIBBONS THIS YEAR...
Th- the one I like best?
OH, DON'T START GETTING SHY NOW!! YOU FORGOT TO BUY HER SOMETHING, DIDN'T YOU..?
SO I'M GIVING YOU THIS! FOR HER ST. WHITE'S PRESENT!
You can't go wrong with your mom watching out for you!!
N-NO THANKS!!
I'LL BE TOO BUSY TO BE LOOKING FOR ANYONE AT THE FESTIVAL...
DAISUKE.
TAKE IT!!
HAVE FUN, SWEETIE!!
I WANT TO HEAR ALL ABOUT IT TONIGHT!!
I DON'T THINK I CAN DO IT...
Took the ribbon
Phew!

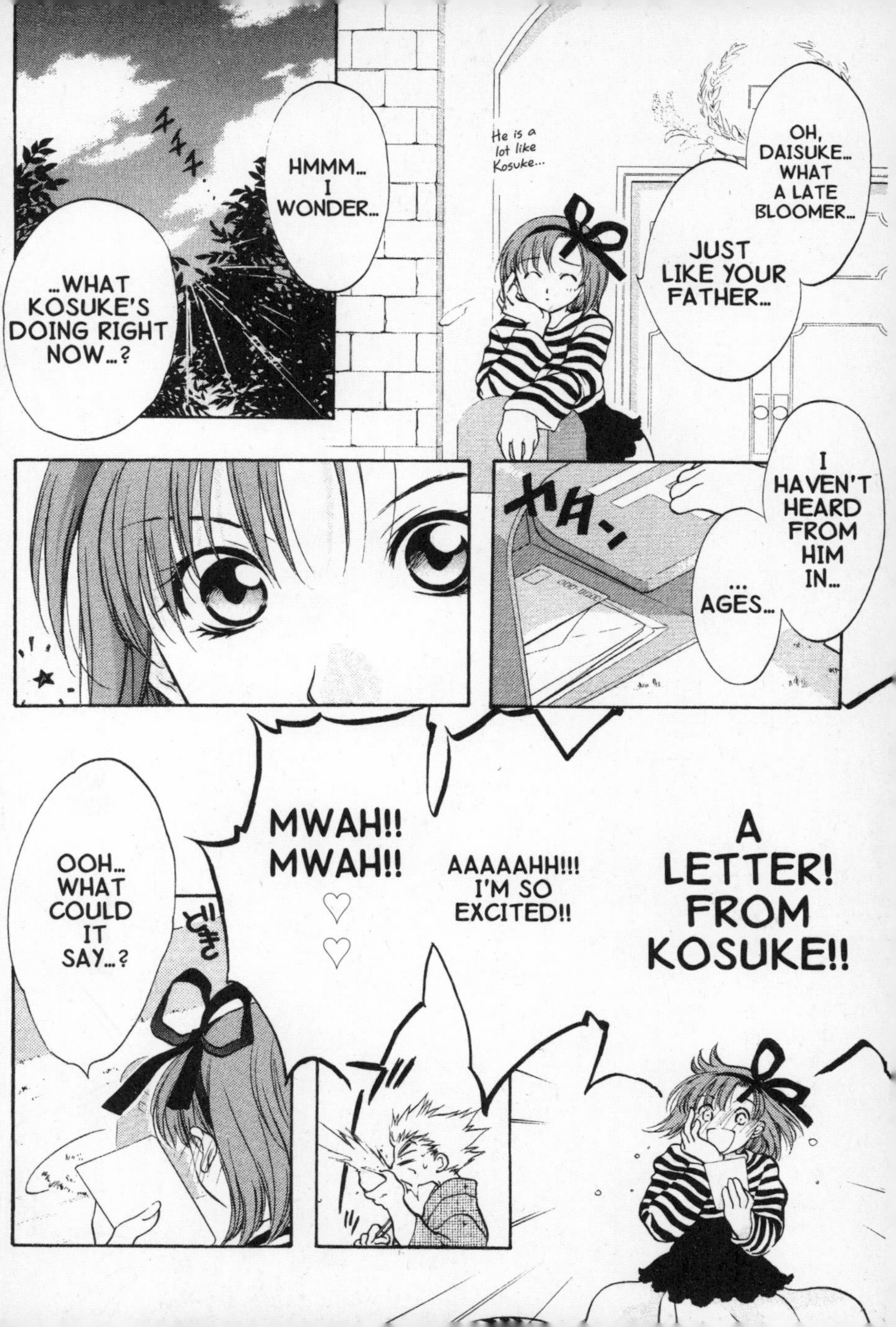
He is a lot like Kosuke...
OH, DAISUKE... WHAT A LATE BLOOMER...
JUST LIKE YOUR FATHER...
HMMM... I WONDER...
...WHAT KOSUKE'S DOING RIGHT NOW...?
I HAVEN'T HEARD FROM HIM IN...
...AGES...
A LETTER! FROM KOSUKE!!
AAAAAHH!!! I'M SO EXCITED!!
MWAH!! MWAH!! ♡ ♡
OOH... WHAT COULD IT SAY...?

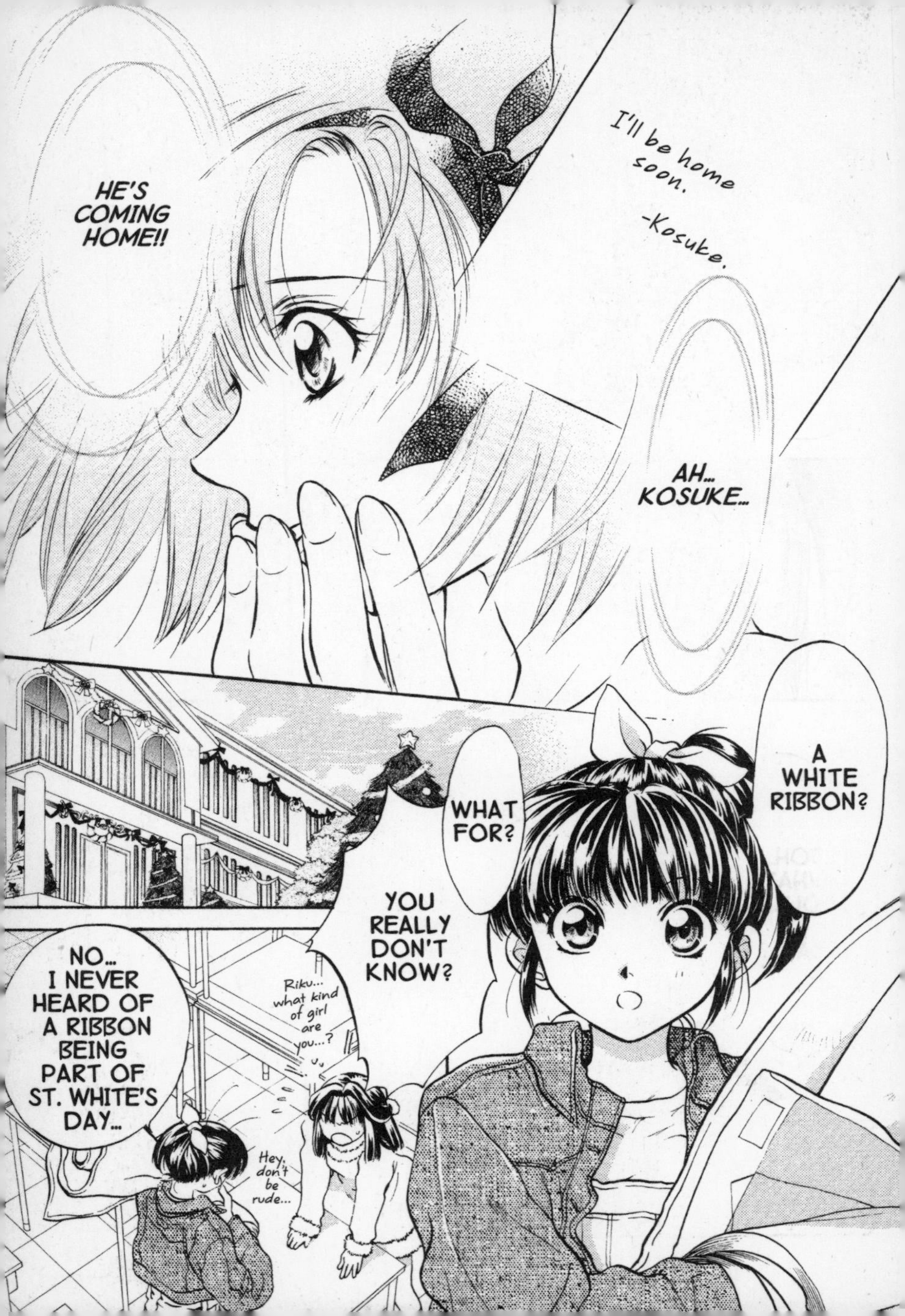
I'll be home soon.
-Kosuke.
HE'S COMING HOME!!
AH... KOSUKE...
A WHITE RIBBON?
WHAT FOR?
YOU REALLY DON'T KNOW?
Riku... what kind of girl are you...?
NO... I NEVER HEARD OF A RIBBON BEING PART OF ST. WHITE'S DAY...
Hey, don't be rude...

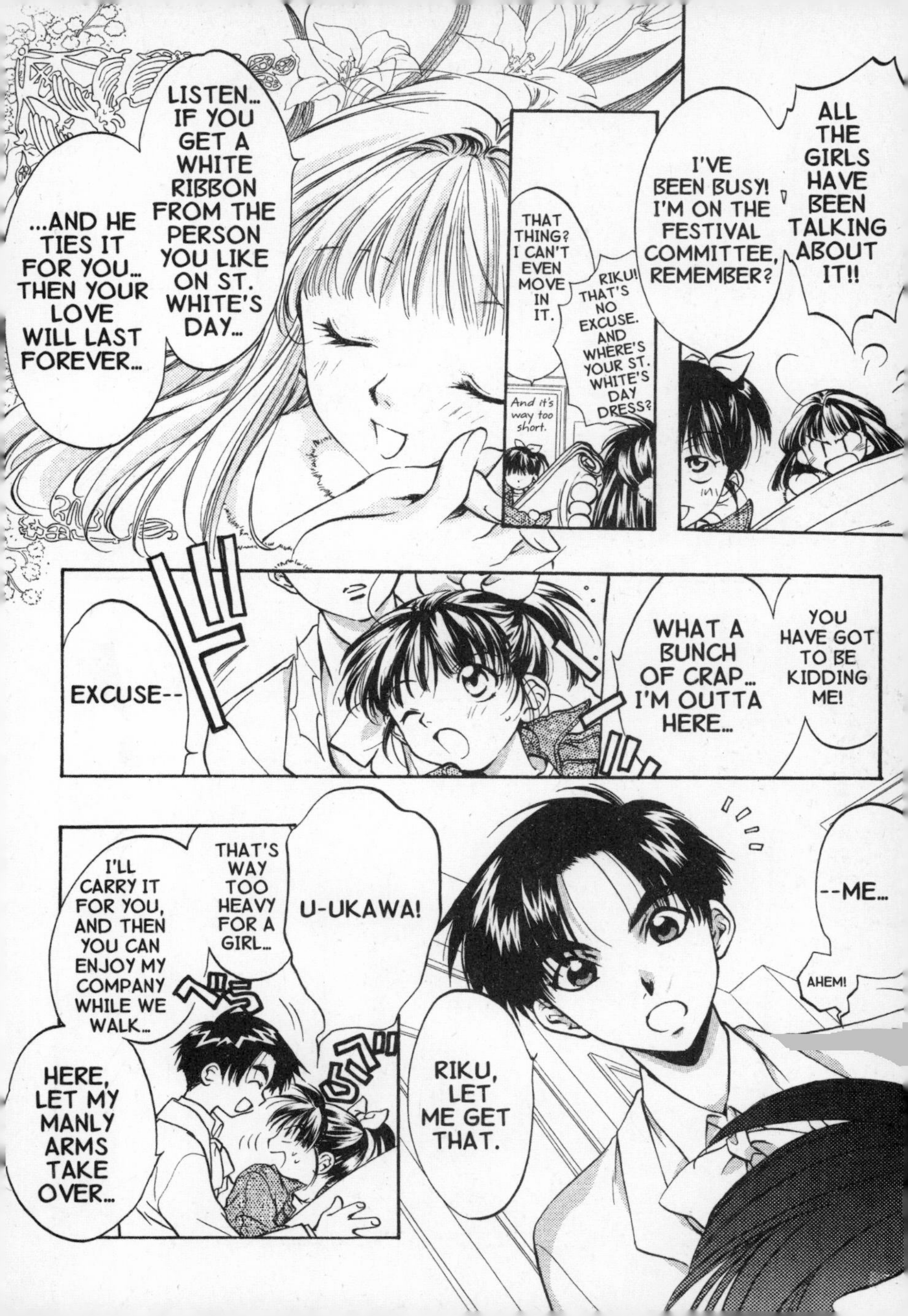
ALL THE GIRLS HAVE BEEN TALKING ABOUT IT!!
I'VE BEEN BUSY! I'M ON THE FESTIVAL COMMITTEE, REMEMBER?
RIKU! THAT'S NO EXCUSE. AND WHERE'S YOUR ST. WHITE'S DAY DRESS?
THAT THING? I CAN'T EVEN MOVE IN IT.
And it's way too short.
LISTEN... IF YOU GET A WHITE RIBBON FROM THE PERSON YOU LIKE ON ST. WHITE'S DAY...
...AND HE TIES IT FOR YOU... THEN YOUR LOVE WILL LAST FOREVER...
YOU HAVE GOT TO BE KIDDING ME!
WHAT A BUNCH OF CRAP... I'M OUTTA HERE...
EXCUSE--
--ME...
AHEM!
RIKU, LET ME GET THAT.
U-UKAWA!
THAT'S WAY TOO HEAVY FOR A GIRL...
I'LL CARRY IT FOR YOU, AND THEN YOU CAN ENJOY MY COMPANY WHILE WE WALK...
HERE, LET MY MANLY ARMS TAKE OVER...

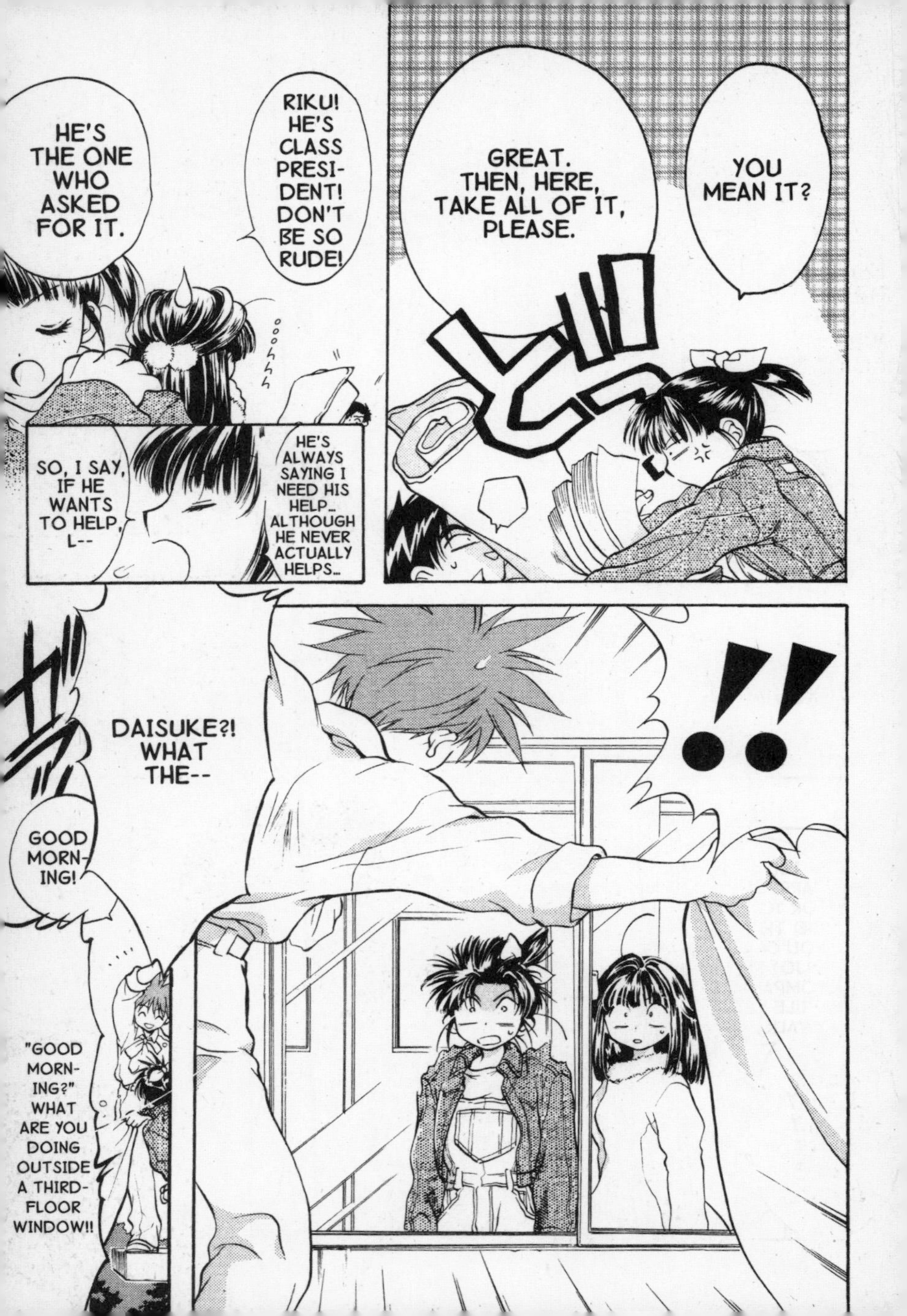

YOU MEAN IT?
GREAT. THEN, HERE, TAKE ALL OF IT, PLEASE.
RIKU! HE'S CLASS PRESI-DENT! DON'T BE SO RUDE!
HE'S THE ONE WHO ASKED FOR IT.
HE'S ALWAYS SAYING I NEED HIS HELP... ALTHOUGH HE NEVER ACTUALLY HELPS...
SO, I SAY, IF HE WANTS TO HELP, I--
!!
DAISUKE?! WHAT THE--
GOOD MORN-ING!
"GOOD MORN-ING?" WHAT ARE YOU DOING OUTSIDE A THIRD-FLOOR WINDOW!!

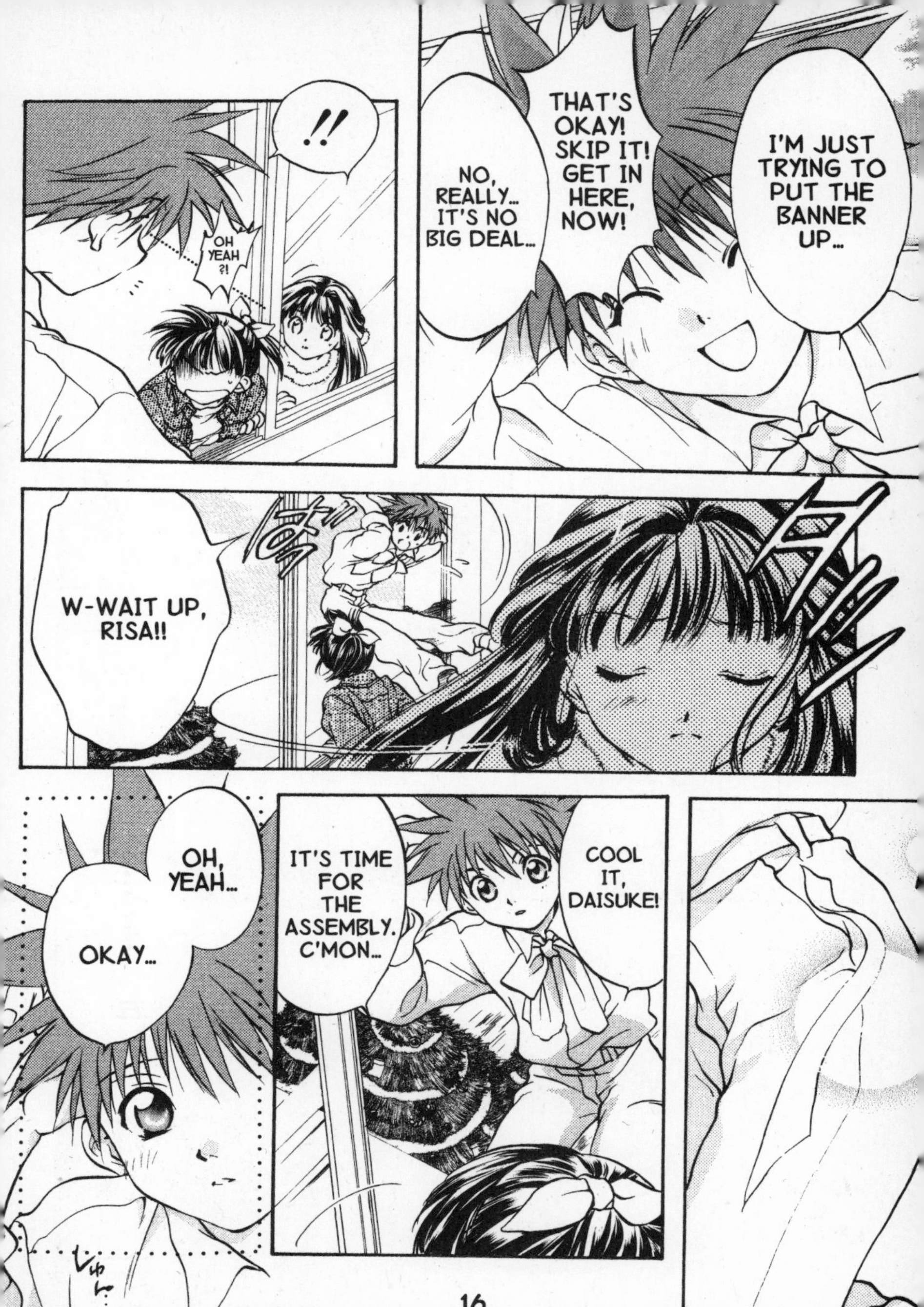

I'M JUST TRYING TO PUT THE BANNER UP...
THAT'S OKAY! SKIP IT! GET IN HERE, NOW!
NO, REALLY... IT'S NO BIG DEAL...
!!
OH YEAH ?!
W-WAIT UP, RISA!!
COOL IT, DAISUKE!
IT'S TIME FOR THE ASSEMBLY. C'MON...
OH, YEAH...
OKAY...

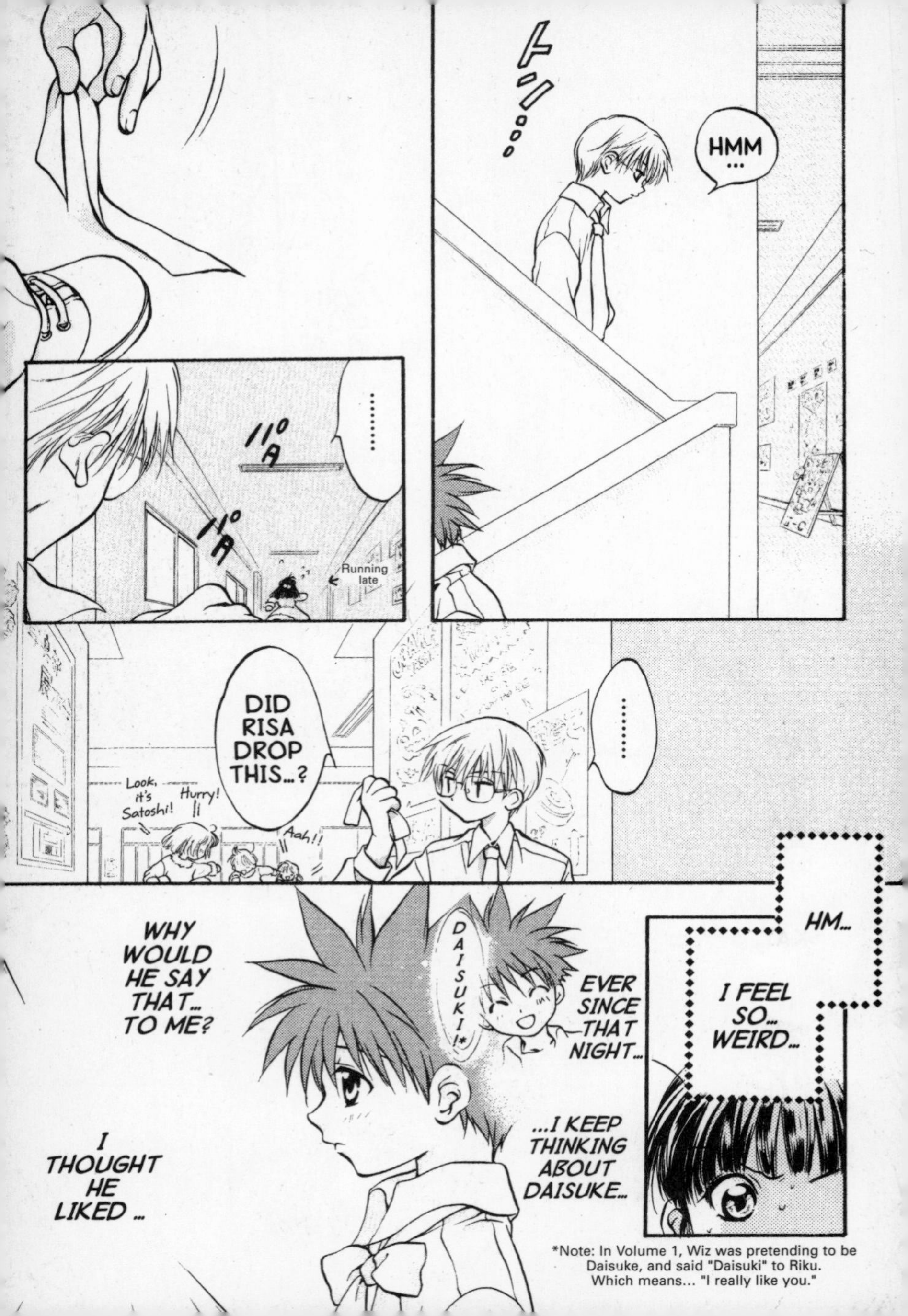
HMM ...
......
Running late
......
DID RISA DROP THIS...?
Hurry!
Look, it's Satoshi!
Aah!!
HM...
I FEEL SO... WEIRD...
EVER SINCE THAT NIGHT...
...I KEEP THINKING ABOUT DAISUKE...
DAISUKI!*
WHY WOULD HE SAY THAT... TO ME?
I THOUGHT HE LIKED ...

*Note: In Volume 1, Wiz was pretending to be Daisuke, and said "Daisuki" to Riku. Which means... "I really like you."

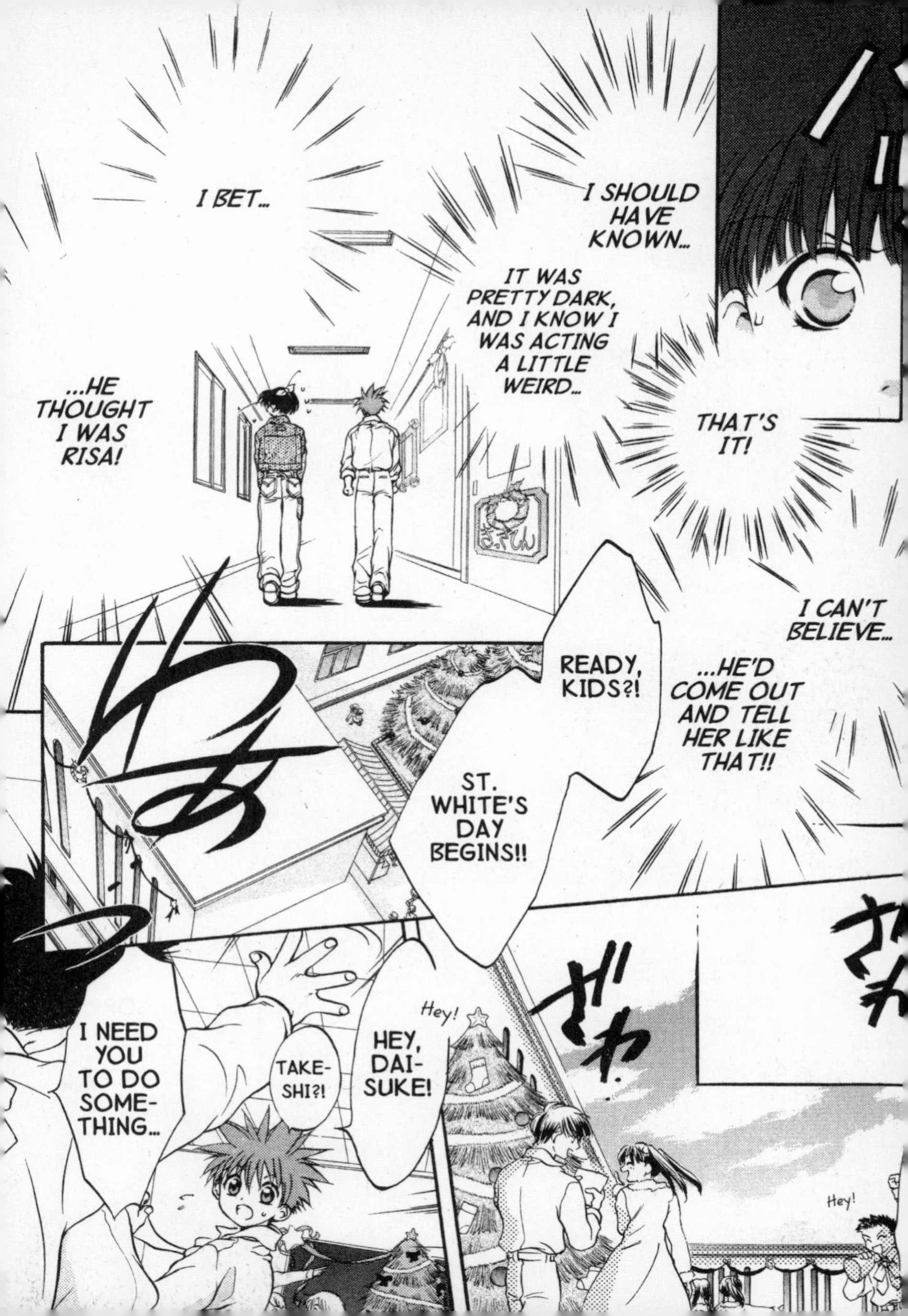
I SHOULD HAVE KNOWN...
IT WAS PRETTY DARK, AND I KNOW I WAS ACTING A LITTLE WEIRD...
THAT'S IT!
I BET...
...HE THOUGHT I WAS RISA!
I CAN'T BELIEVE...
...HE'D COME OUT AND TELL HER LIKE THAT!!
READY, KIDS?!
ST. WHITE'S DAY BEGINS!!
Hey!
Hey!
HEY, DAI-SUKE!
TAKE-SHI?!
I NEED YOU TO DO SOME-THING...

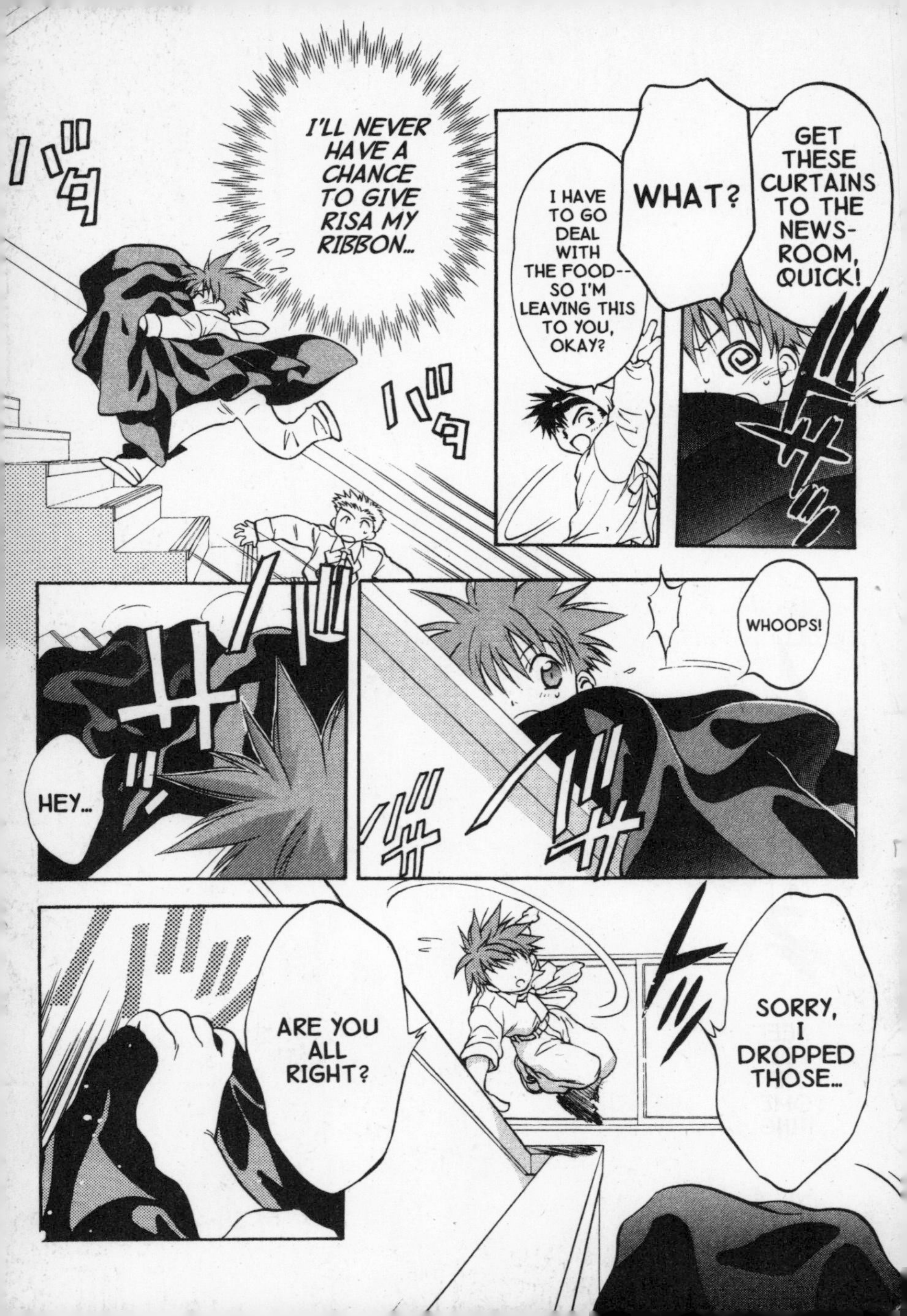
GET THESE CURTAINS TO THE NEWS-ROOM, QUICK!
WHAT?
I HAVE TO GO DEAL WITH THE FOOD--SO I'M LEAVING THIS TO YOU, OKAY?
I'LL NEVER HAVE A CHANCE TO GIVE RISA MY RIBBON...
WHOOPS!
HEY...
SORRY, I DROPPED THOSE...
ARE YOU ALL RIGHT?

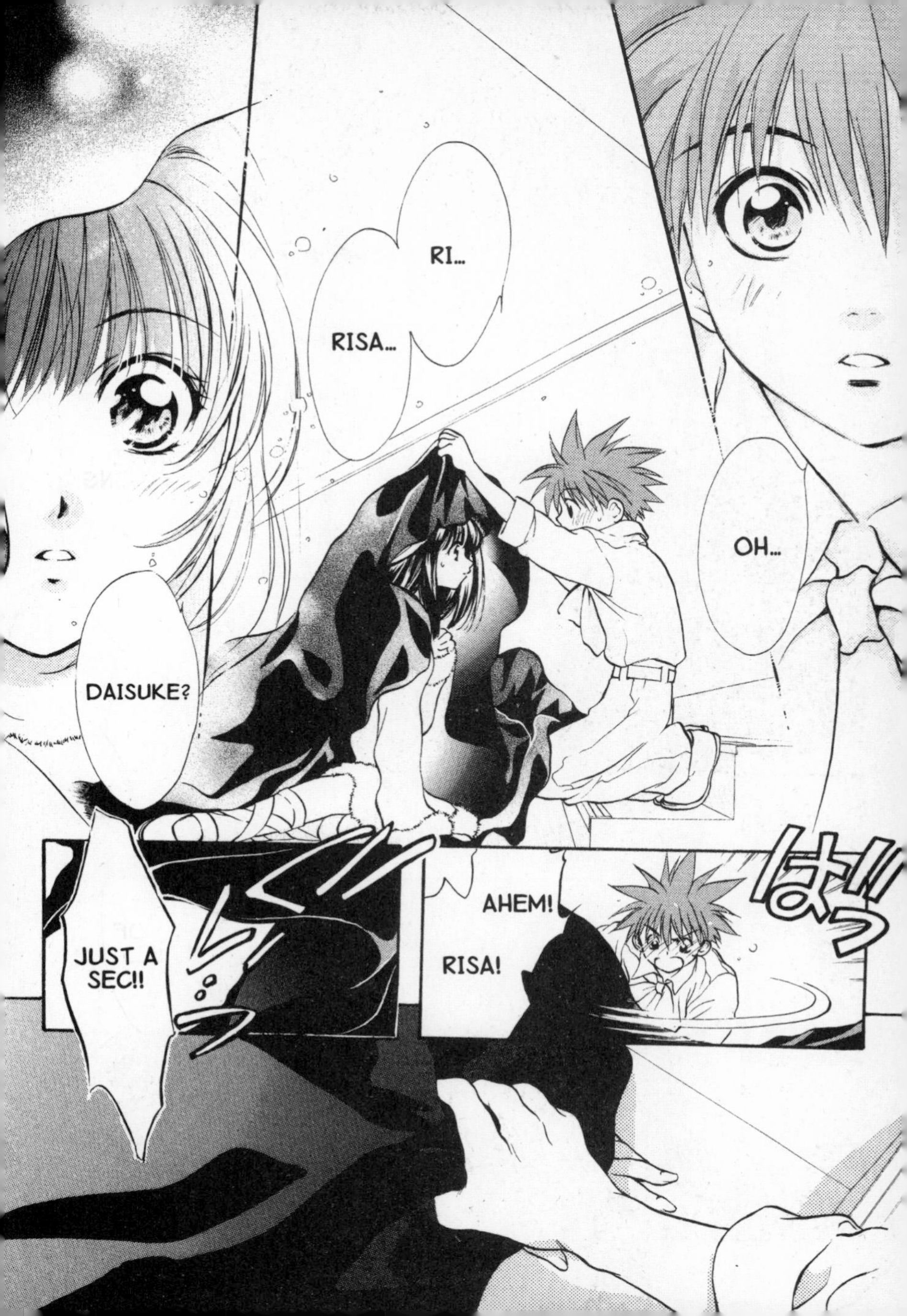
OH...
RI... RISA...
DAISUKE?
はっ!!
AHEM! RISA!
JUST A SEC!!

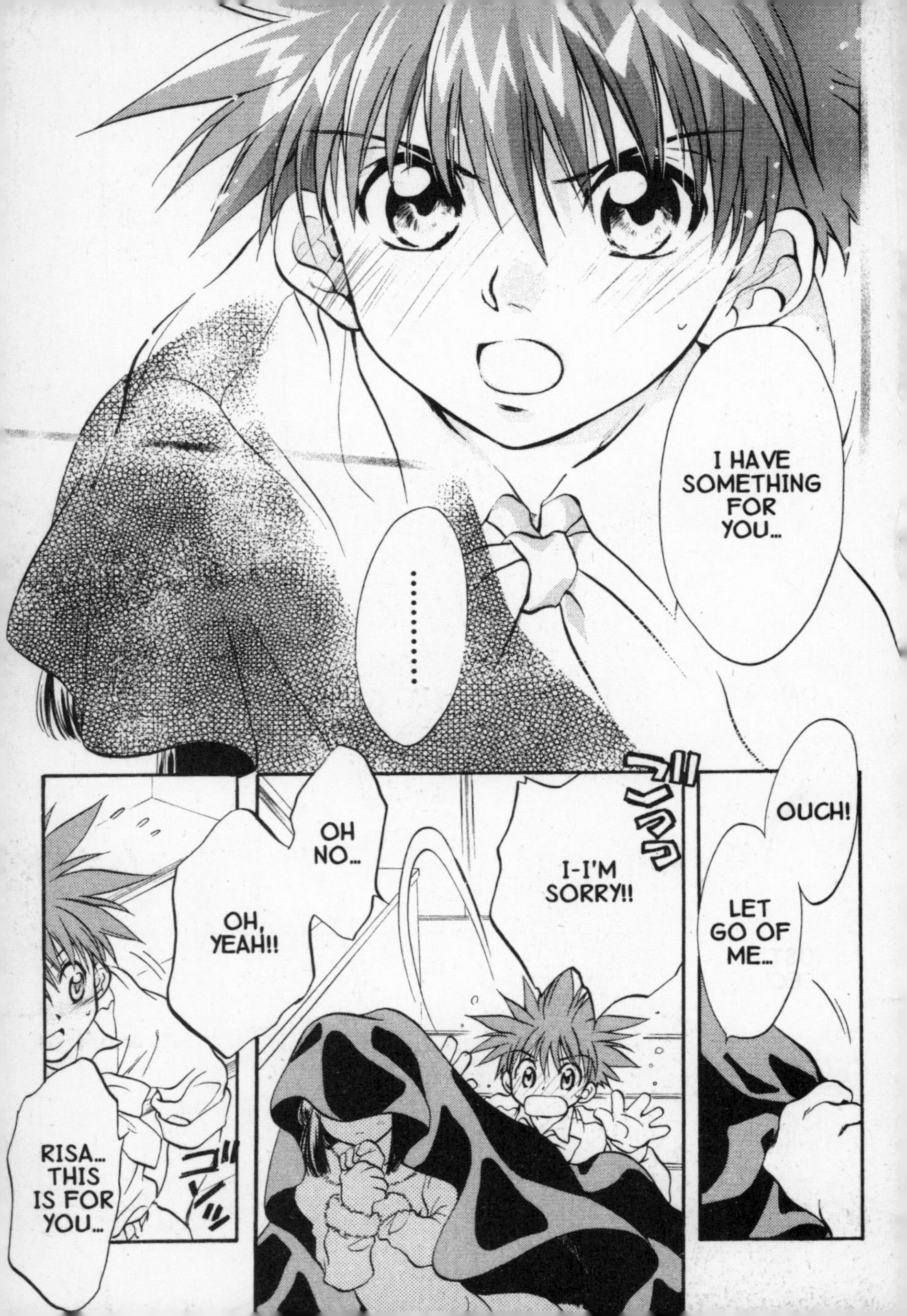
I HAVE SOMETHING FOR YOU...
....
OUCH!
LET GO OF ME...
I-I'M SORRY!!
OH NO...
OH, YEAH!!
RISA... THIS IS FOR YOU...

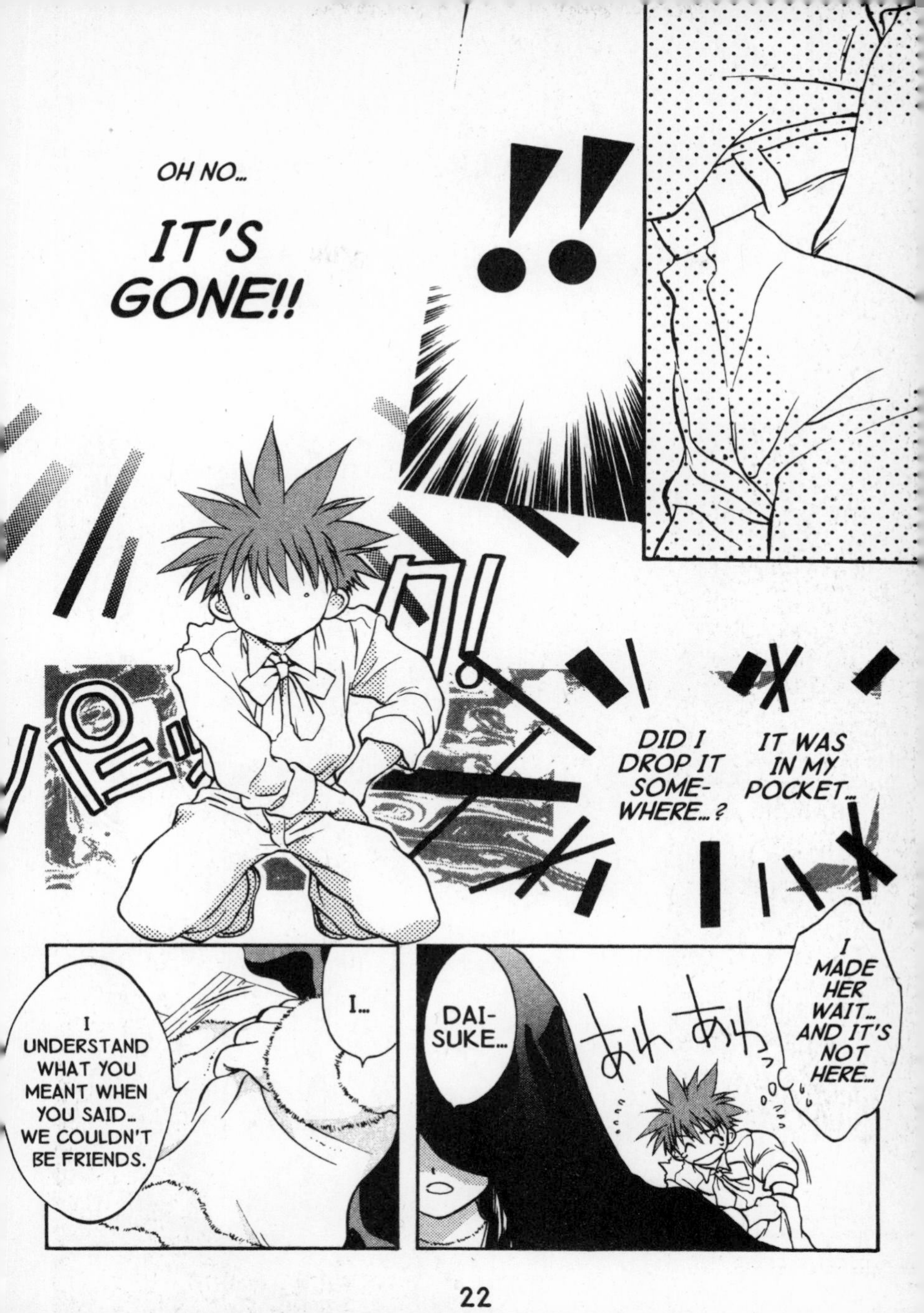
OH NO...
IT'S GONE!!
IT WAS IN MY POCKET...
DID I DROP IT SOME- WHERE...?
I MADE HER WAIT... AND IT'S NOT HERE...
あれ あれっ
DAI- SUKE...
I...
I UNDERSTAND WHAT YOU MEANT WHEN YOU SAID... WE COULDN'T BE FRIENDS.

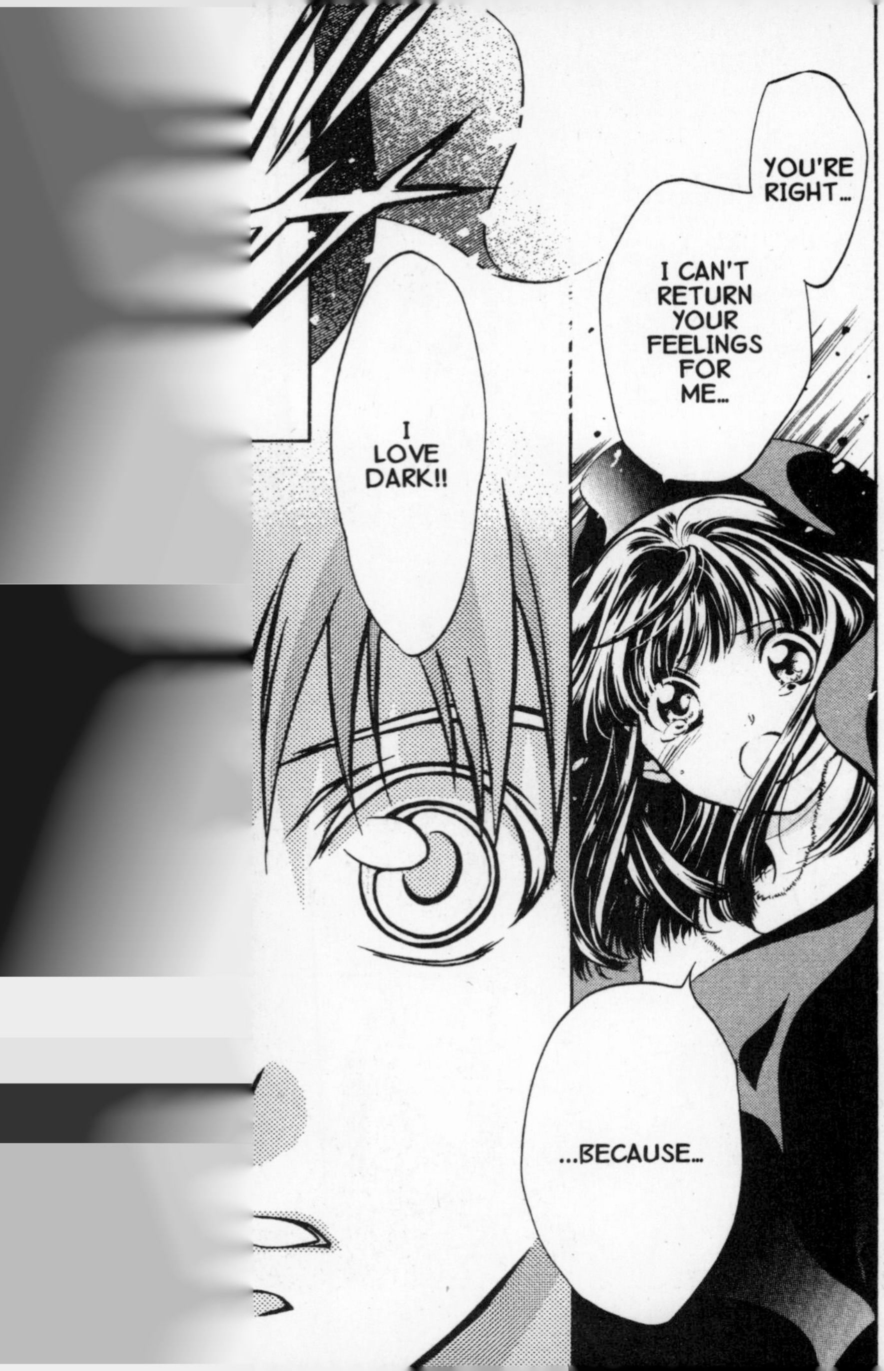
YOU'RE RIGHT...
I CAN'T RETURN YOUR FEELINGS FOR ME...
...BECAUSE...
I LOVE DARK!!

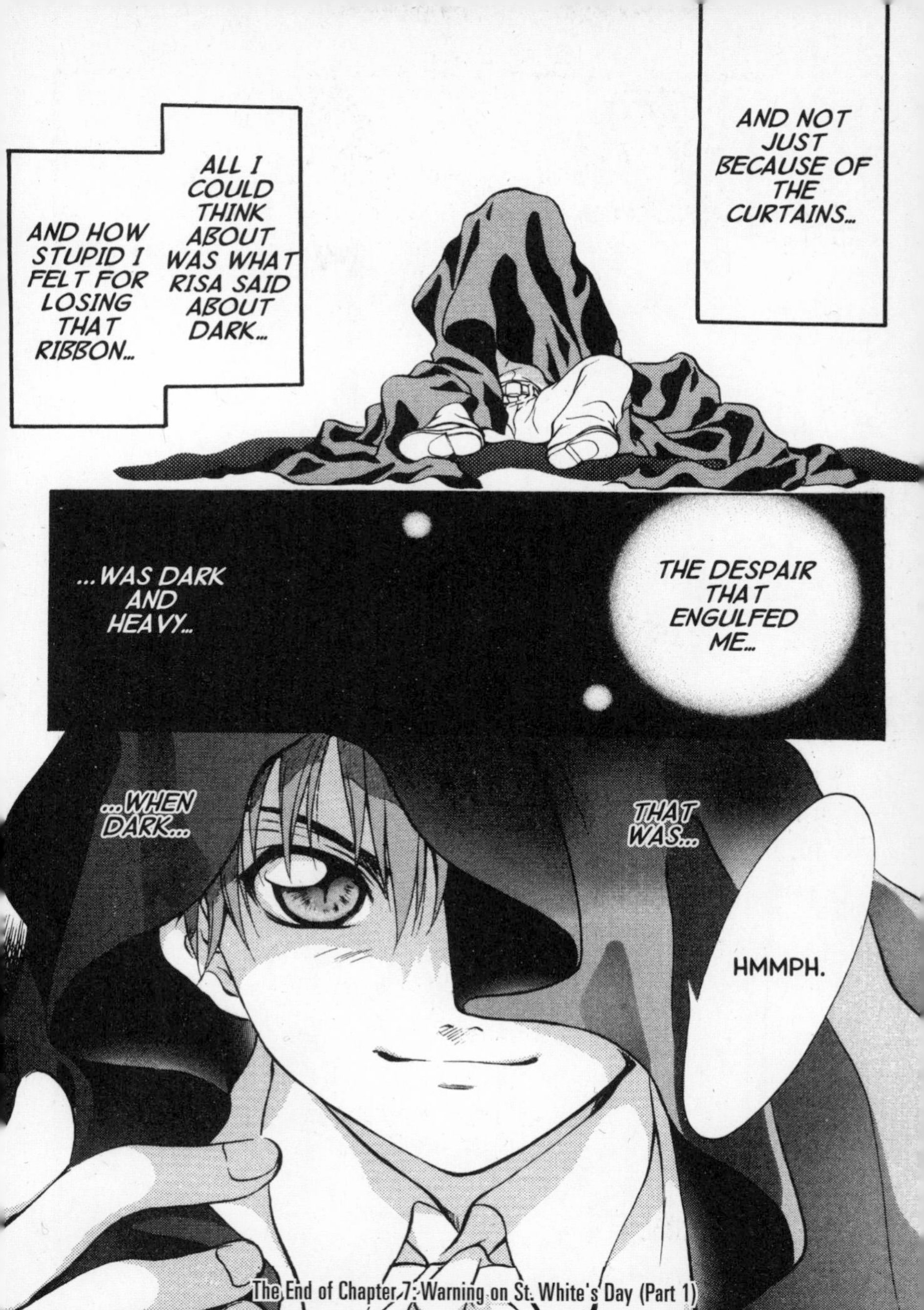
AND NOT JUST BECAUSE OF THE CURTAINS...
ALL I COULD THINK ABOUT WAS WHAT RISA SAID ABOUT DARK...
AND HOW STUPID I FELT FOR LOSING THAT RIBBON...
THE DESPAIR THAT ENGULFED ME...
...WAS DARK AND HEAVY...
THAT WAS...
...WHEN DARK...
HMMPH.

The End of Chapter 7: Warning on St. White's Day (Part 1)

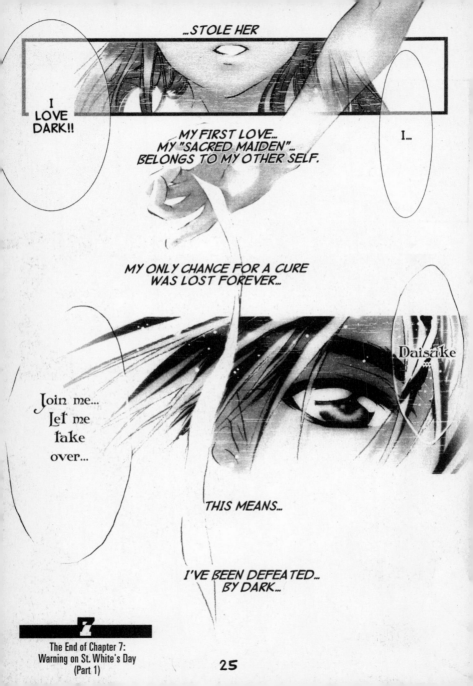

...STOLE HER

I LOVE DARK!!

MY FIRST LOVE...
MY "SACRED MAIDEN"...
BELONGS TO MY OTHER SELF.

I...

MY ONLY CHANCE FOR A CURE
WAS LOST FOREVER...

Daisuke

Join me...
Let me
take
over...

THIS MEANS...

I'VE BEEN DEFEATED...
BY DARK...

The End of Chapter 7:
Warning on St. White's Day
(Part 1)

25

7

CHAPTER 7: WARNING ON ST. WHITE'S DAY (PART 2)

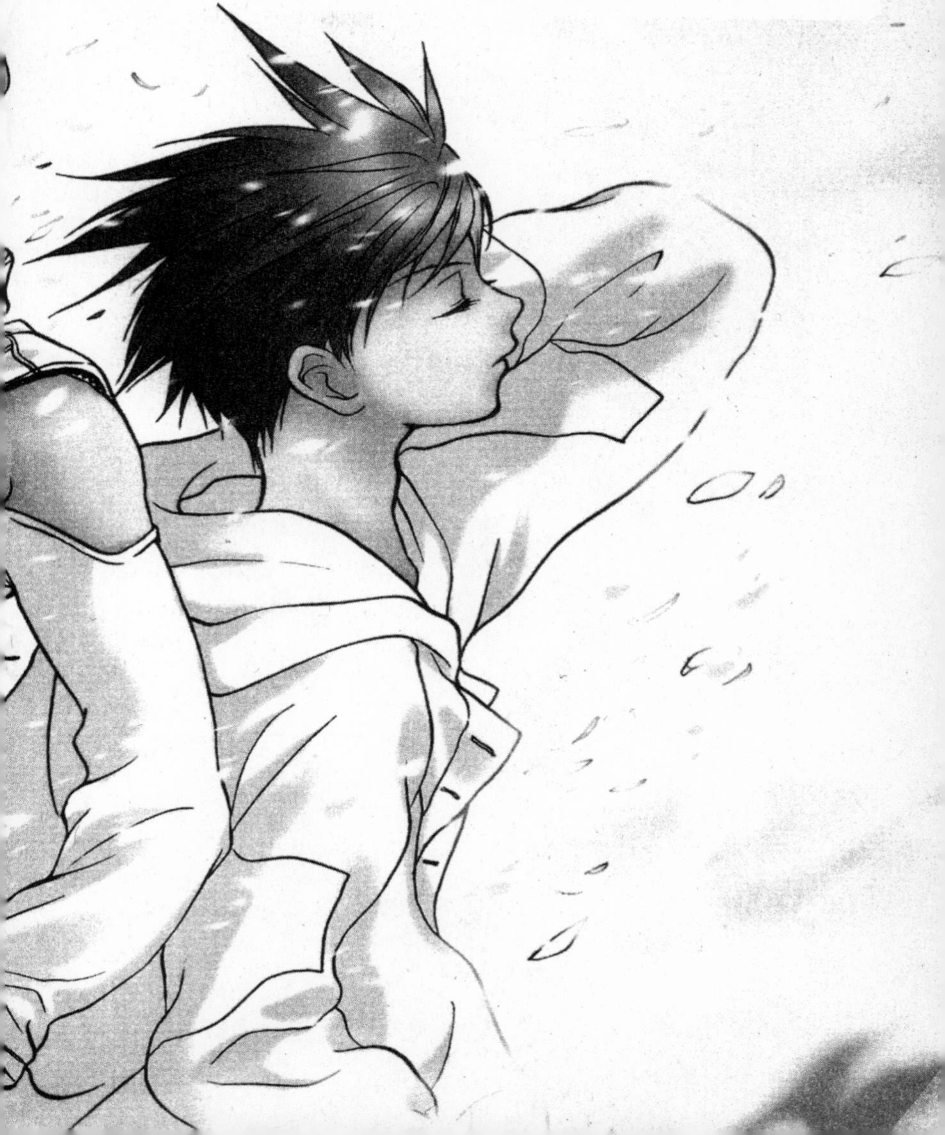

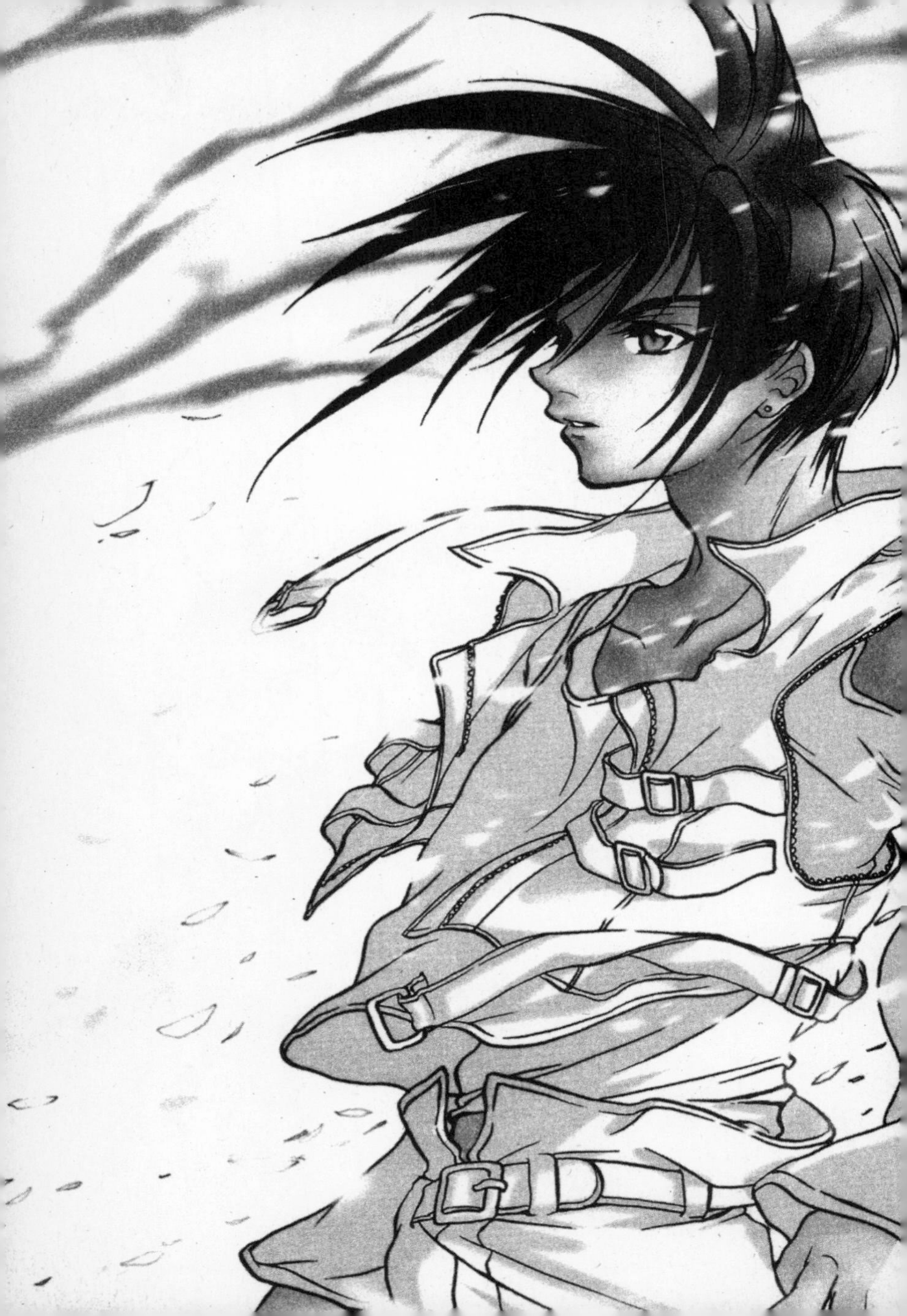

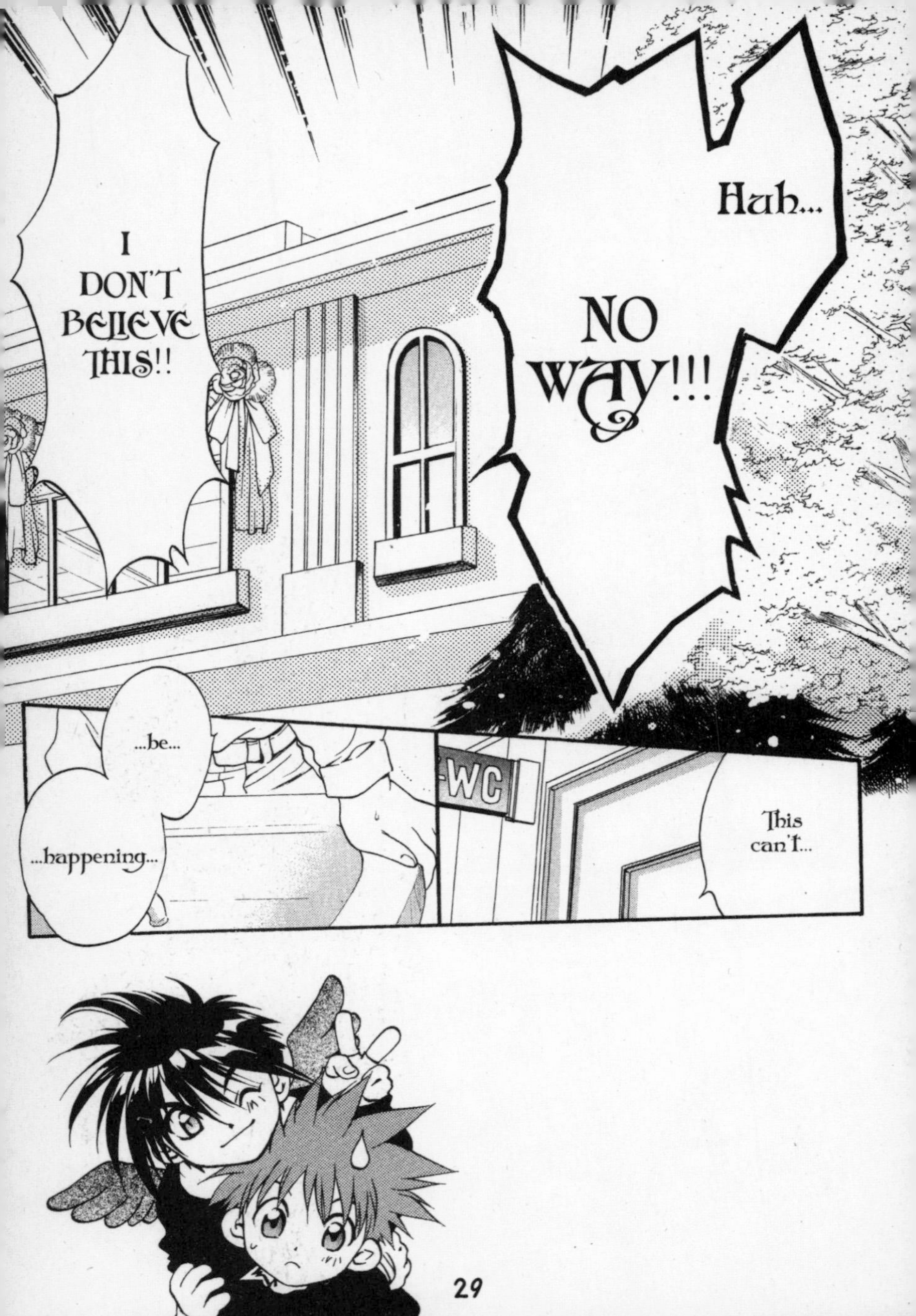
Huh... NO WAY!!!
I DON'T BELIEVE THIS!!
WC
This can't...
...be...
...happening...

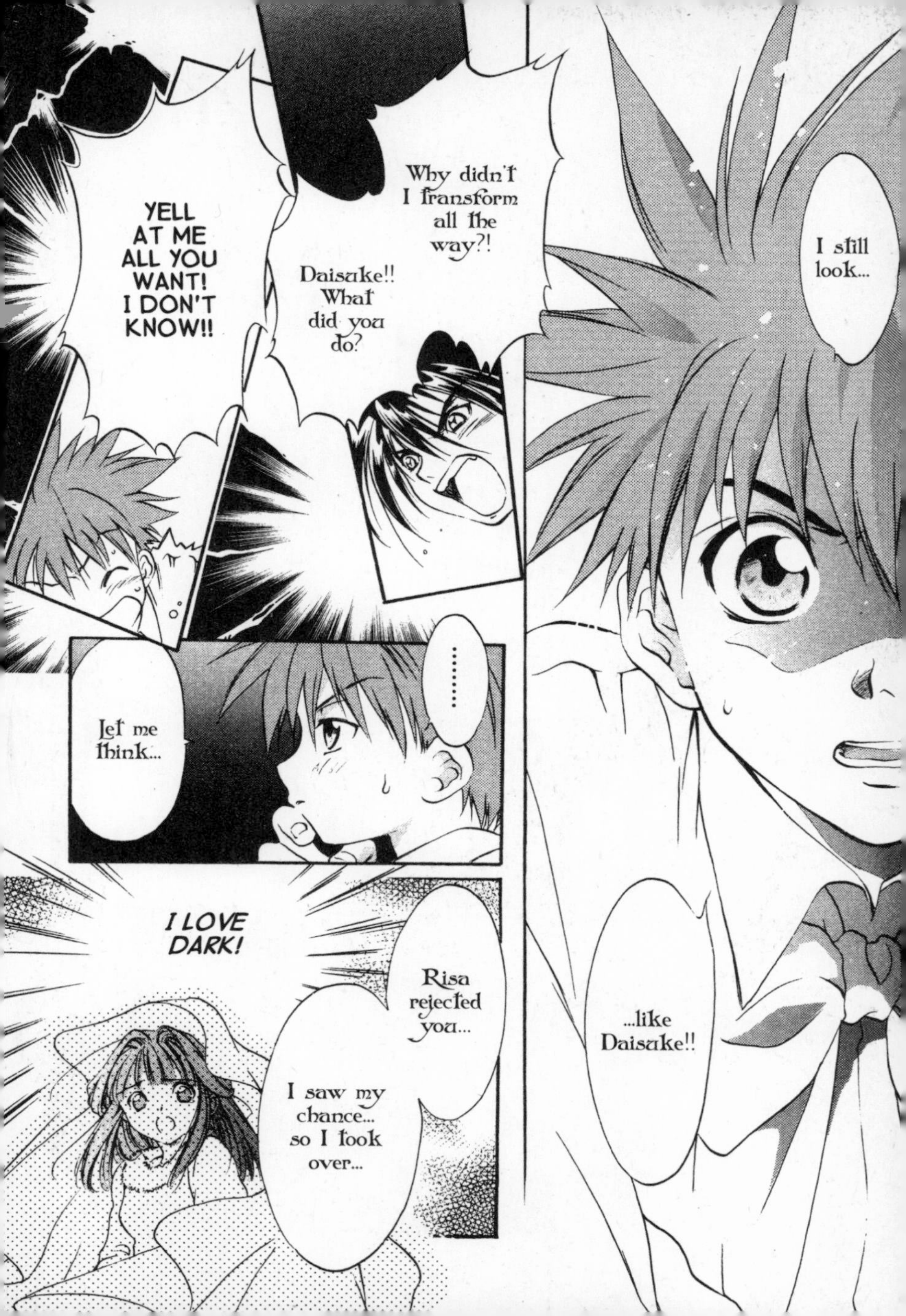
Why didn't I transform all the way?!
Daisuke!! What did you do?
YELL AT ME ALL YOU WANT! I DON'T KNOW!!
......
Let me think...
Risa rejected you...
I saw my chance... so I took over...
I LOVE DARK!
I still look...
...like Daisuke!!

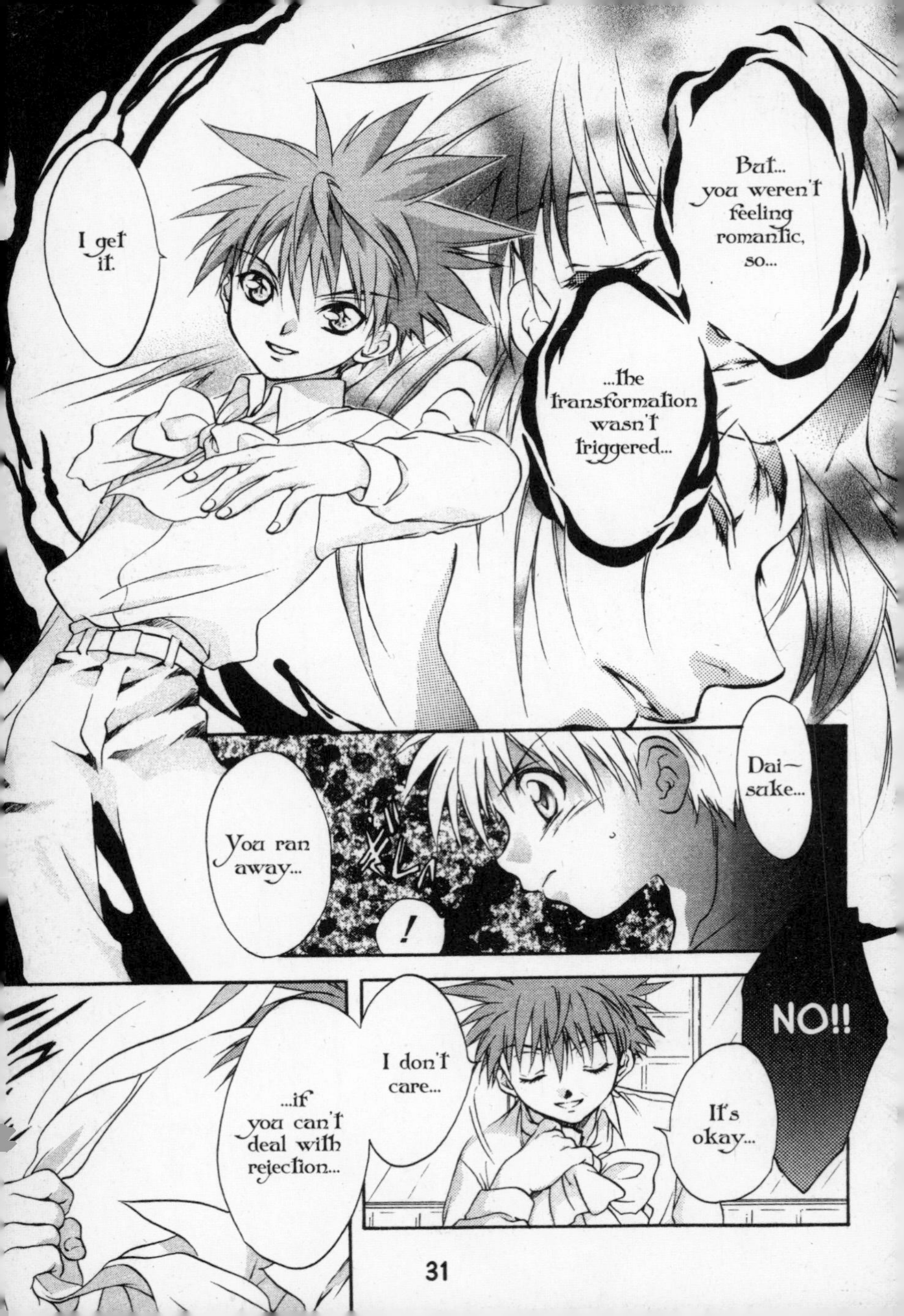
But... you weren't feeling romantic, so...
...the transformation wasn't triggered...
I get it.
Dai-suke...
!
You ran away...
NO!!
It's okay...
I don't care...
...if you can't deal with rejection...

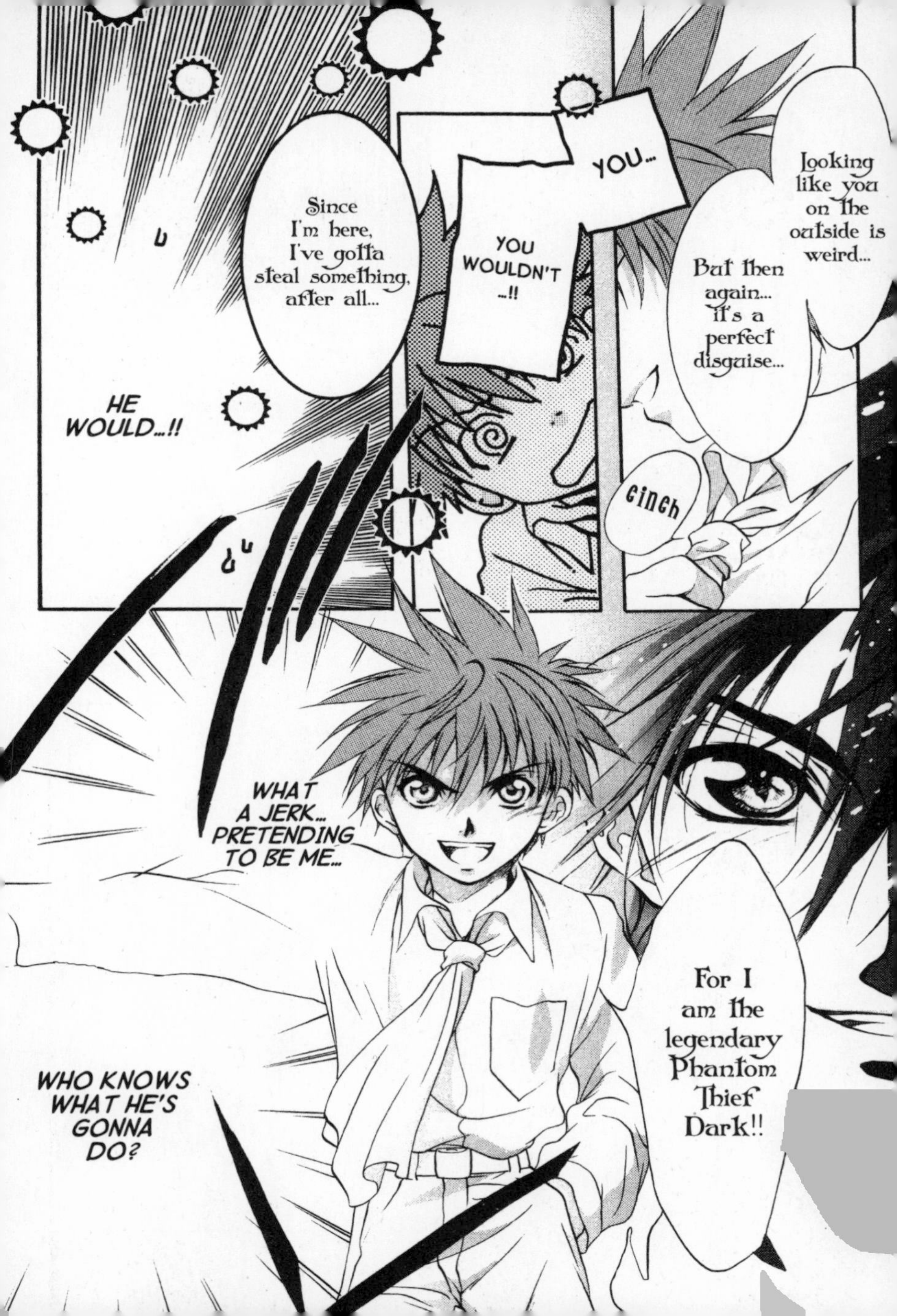
Looking like you on the outside is weird...
But then again... it's a perfect disguise...
Cinch
YOU...
YOU WOULDN'T ...!!
Since I'm here, I've gotta steal something, after all...
HE WOULD...!!
For I am the legendary Phantom Thief Dark!!
WHAT A JERK... PRETENDING TO BE ME...
WHO KNOWS WHAT HE'S GONNA DO?

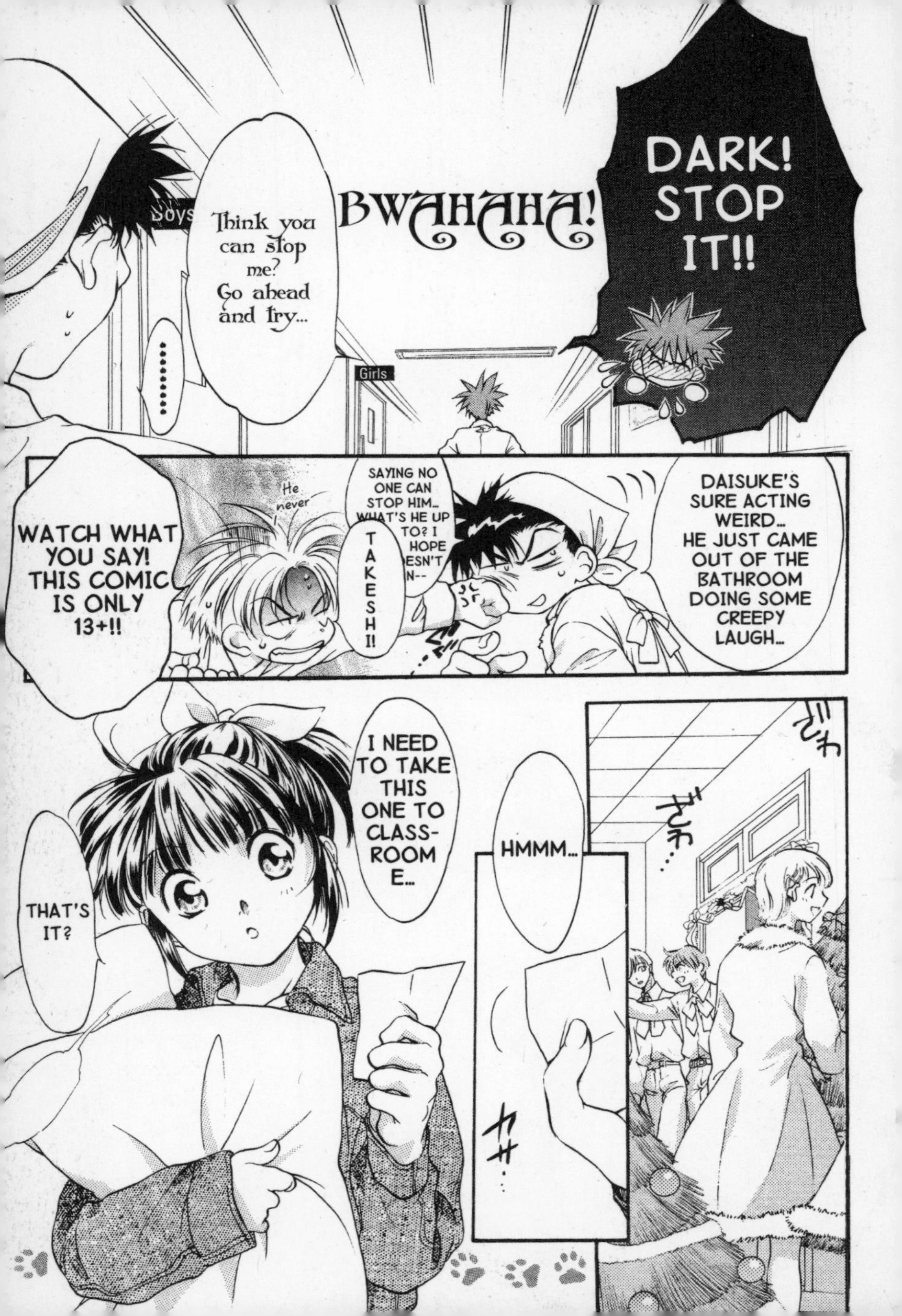

DARK! STOP IT!!
BWAHAHA!
Think you can stop me? Go ahead and try...
....
Boys
Girls
DAISUKE'S SURE ACTING WEIRD... HE JUST CAME OUT OF THE BATHROOM DOING SOME CREEPY LAUGH...
SAYING NO ONE CAN STOP HIM... WHAT'S HE UP TO? I HOPE
TAKESHI!
He never
WATCH WHAT YOU SAY! THIS COMIC IS ONLY 13+!!
HMMM...
I NEED TO TAKE THIS ONE TO CLASSROOM E...
THAT'S IT?

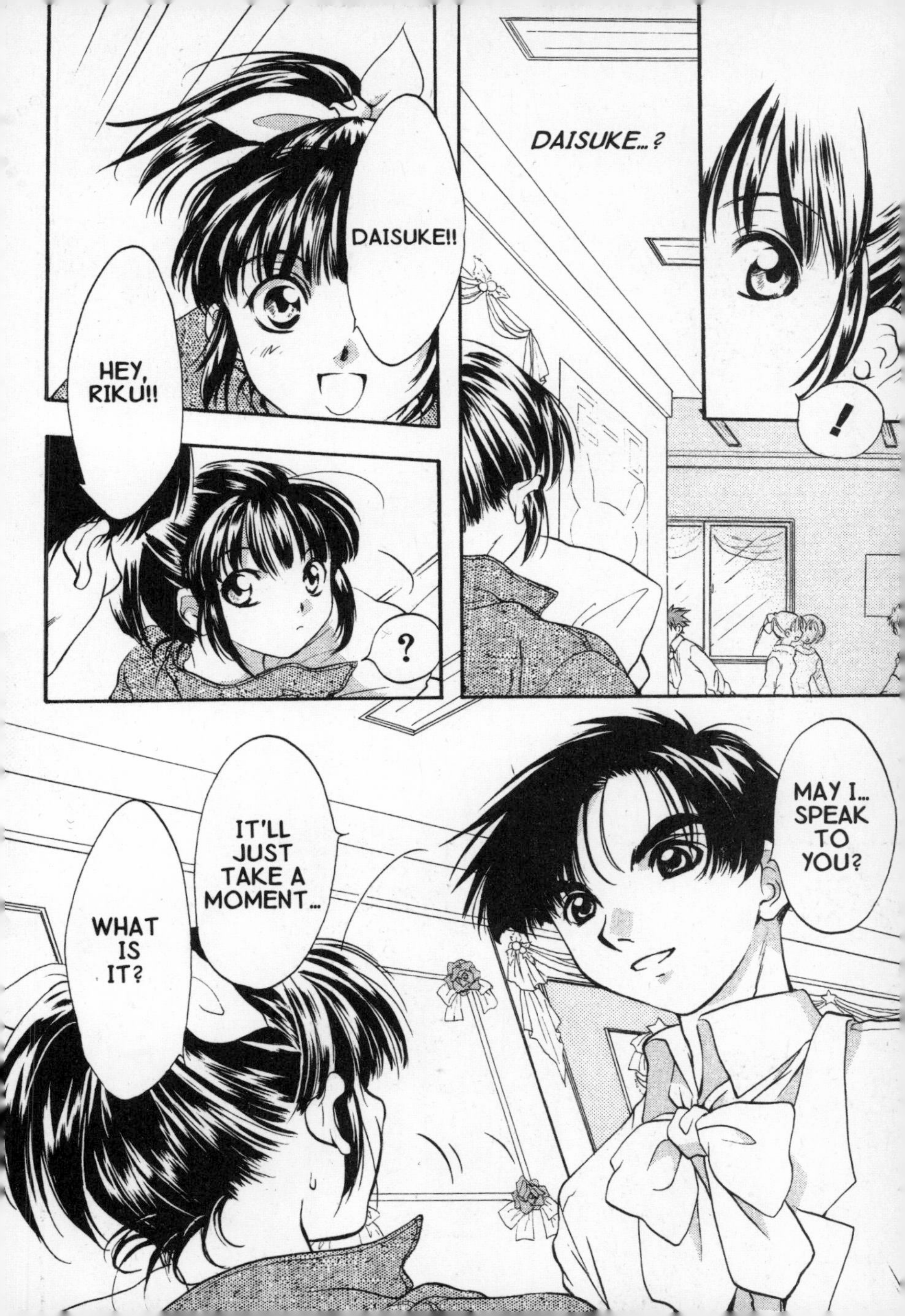
DAISUKE...?
!
DAISUKE!!
HEY, RIKU!!
?
MAY I... SPEAK TO YOU?
IT'LL JUST TAKE A MOMENT...
WHAT IS IT?

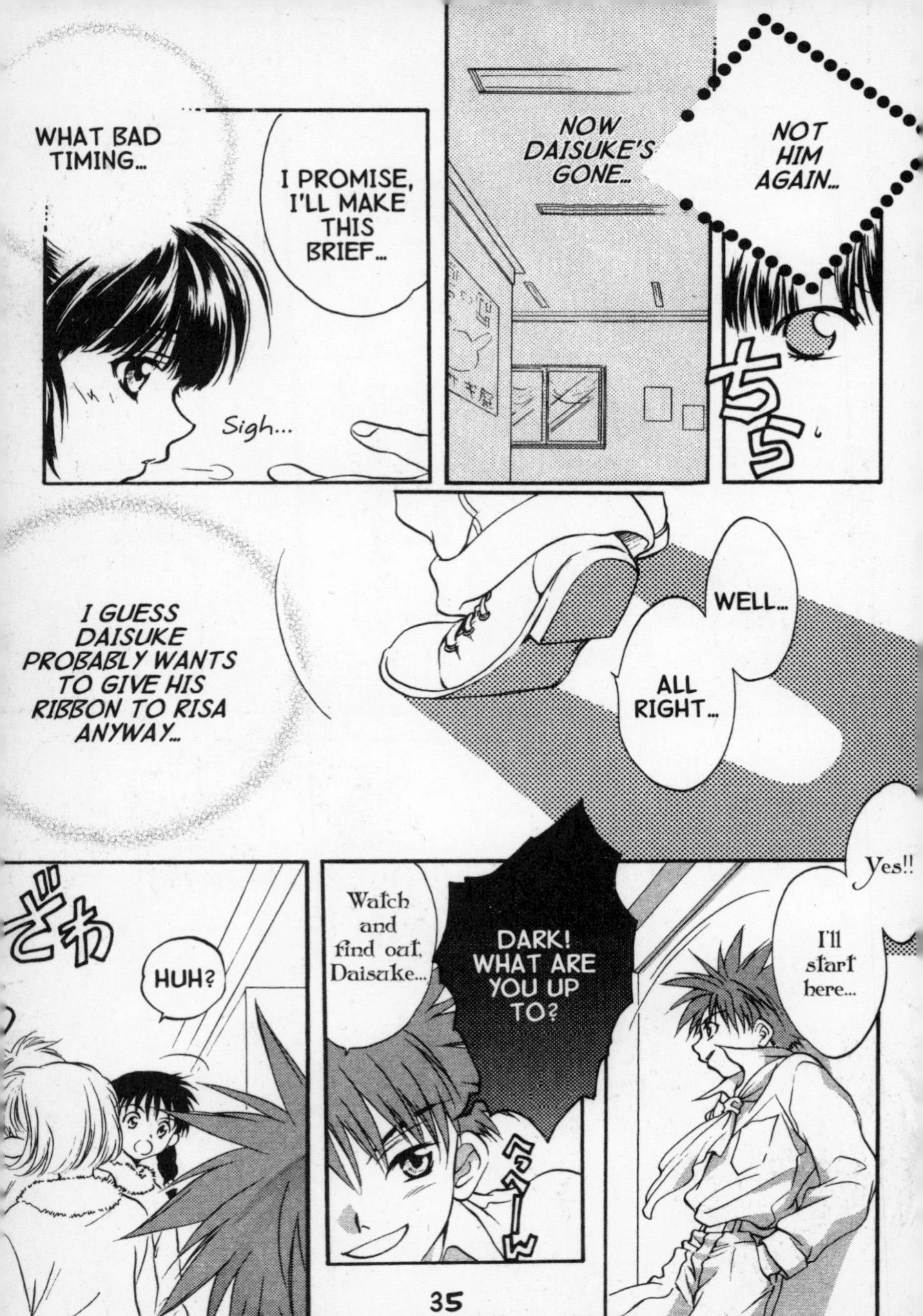
NOT HIM AGAIN...
ちら
NOW DAISUKE'S GONE...
I PROMISE, I'LL MAKE THIS BRIEF...
WHAT BAD TIMING...
Sigh...
WELL...
ALL RIGHT...
I GUESS DAISUKE PROBABLY WANTS TO GIVE HIS RIBBON TO RISA ANYWAY...
Yes!!
I'll start here...
DARK! WHAT ARE YOU UP TO?
Watch and find out, Daisuke...
ざわ
HUH?

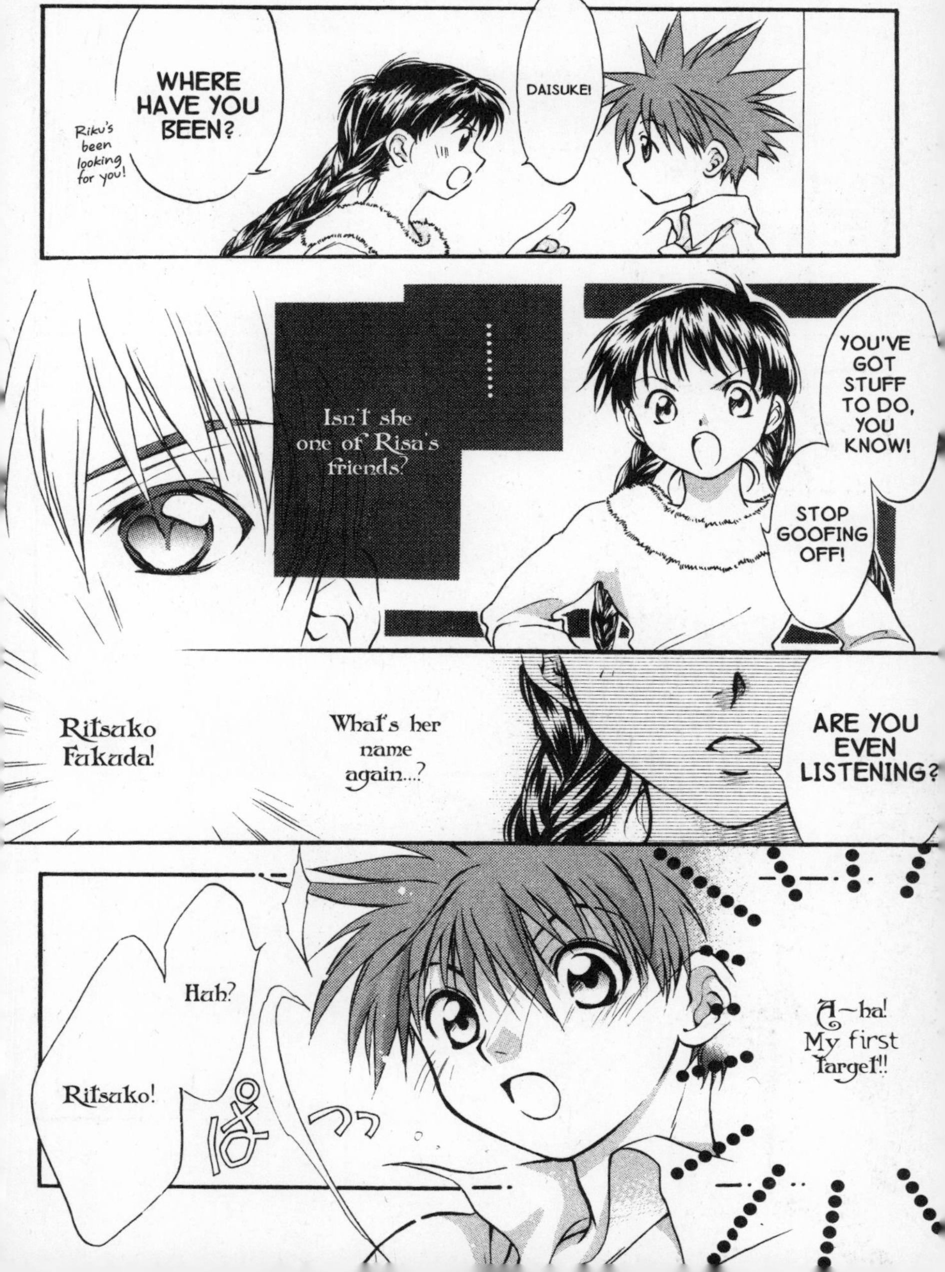
DAISUKE!
WHERE HAVE YOU BEEN?
Riku's been looking for you!
YOU'VE GOT STUFF TO DO, YOU KNOW!
STOP GOOFING OFF!
......
Isn't she one of Risa's friends?
ARE YOU EVEN LISTENING?
What's her name again...?
Ritsuko Fukuda!
A~ha! My first target!!
Huh?
Ritsuko!

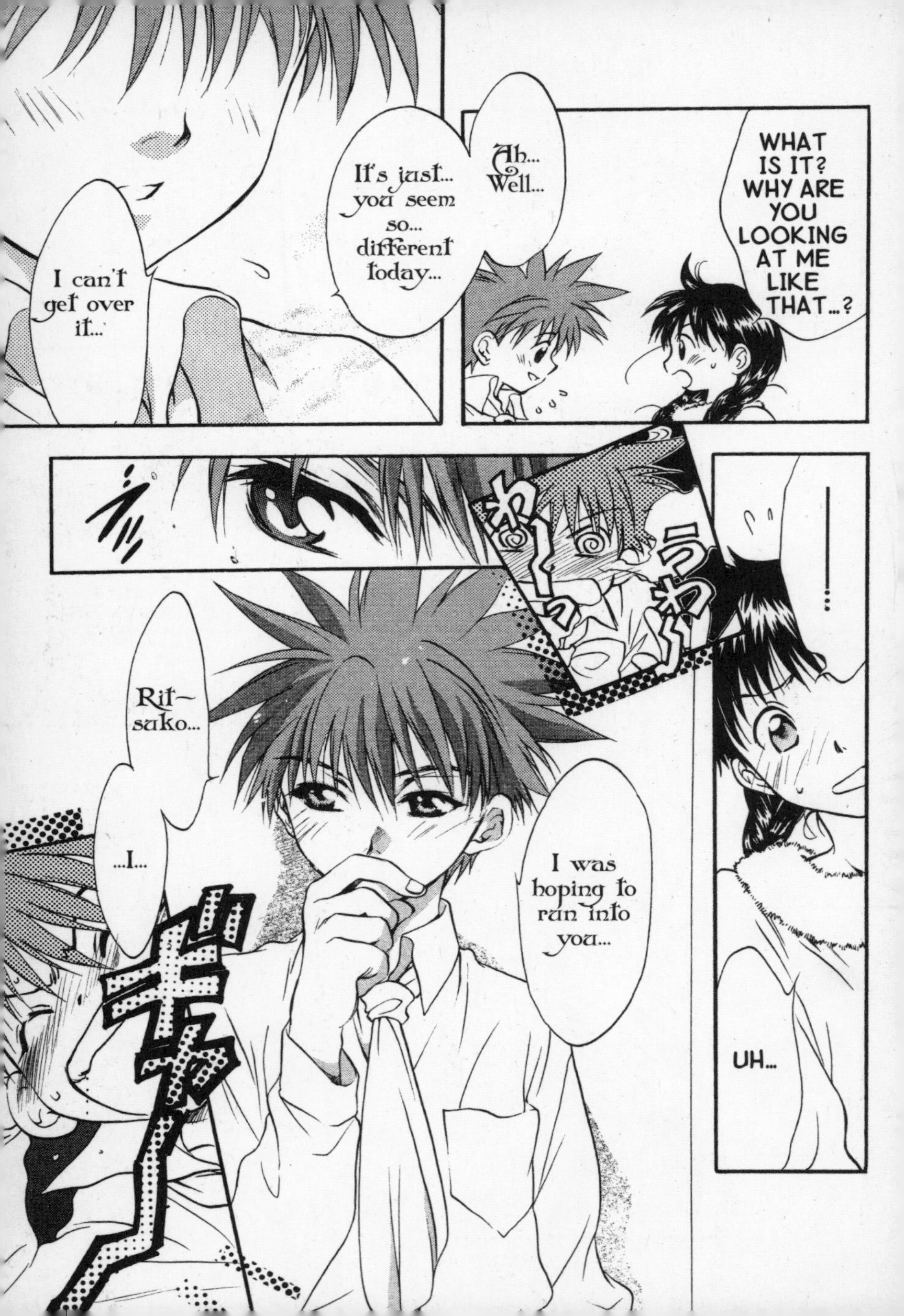
WHAT IS IT? WHY ARE YOU LOOKING AT ME LIKE THAT...?
Ah... Well...
It's just... you seem so... different today...
I can't get over it...
—...!
UH...
Rit-suko...
...I...
I was hoping to run into you...

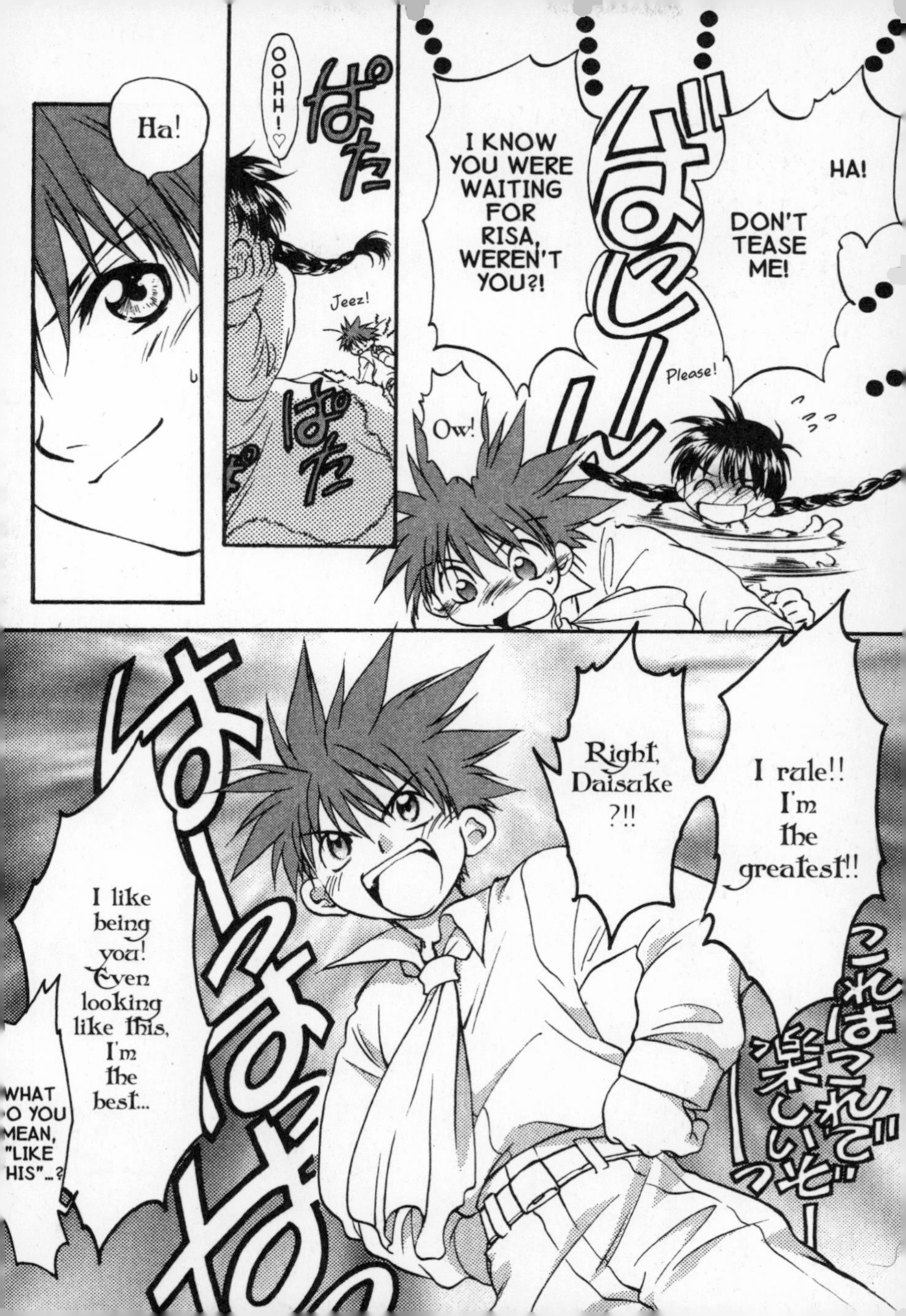
HA!
DON'T TEASE ME!
I KNOW YOU WERE WAITING FOR RISA, WEREN'T YOU?!
ばこーん
Please!
Ow!
ぱた
OOHH!♡
Jeez!
ぱた
Ha!
I rule!! I'm the greatest!!
Right, Daisuke ?!!
これはこれで楽しいぞーっ
はーっはっはっ
I like being you! Even looking like this, I'm the best...
WHAT O YOU MEAN, "LIKE HIS"...?

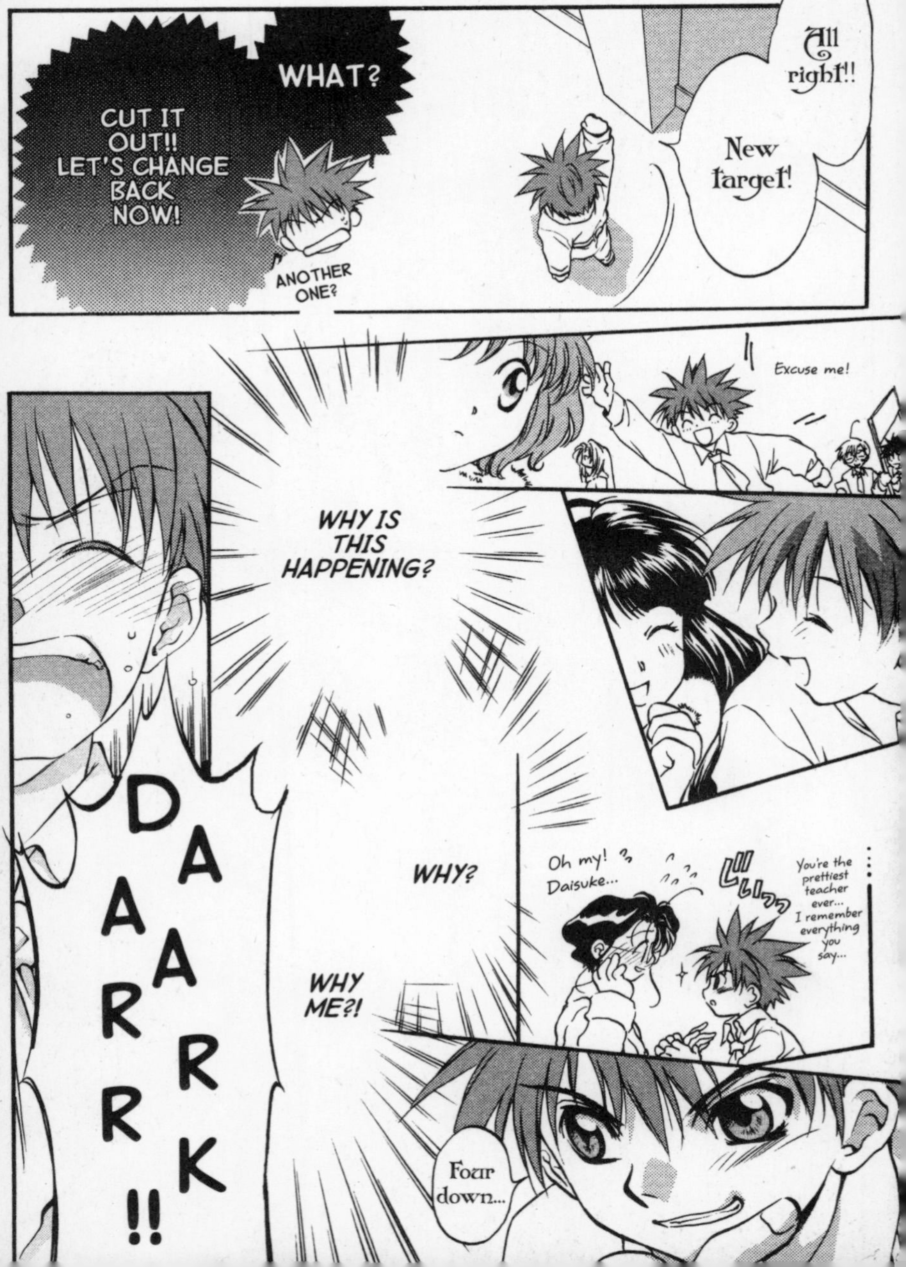
All right!!
New target!
WHAT?
CUT IT OUT!! LET'S CHANGE BACK NOW!
ANOTHER ONE?
Excuse me!
WHY IS THIS HAPPENING?
You're the prettiest teacher ever... I remember everything you say...
Oh my! Daisuke...
WHY?
WHY ME?!
DAARRRK!!
Four down...

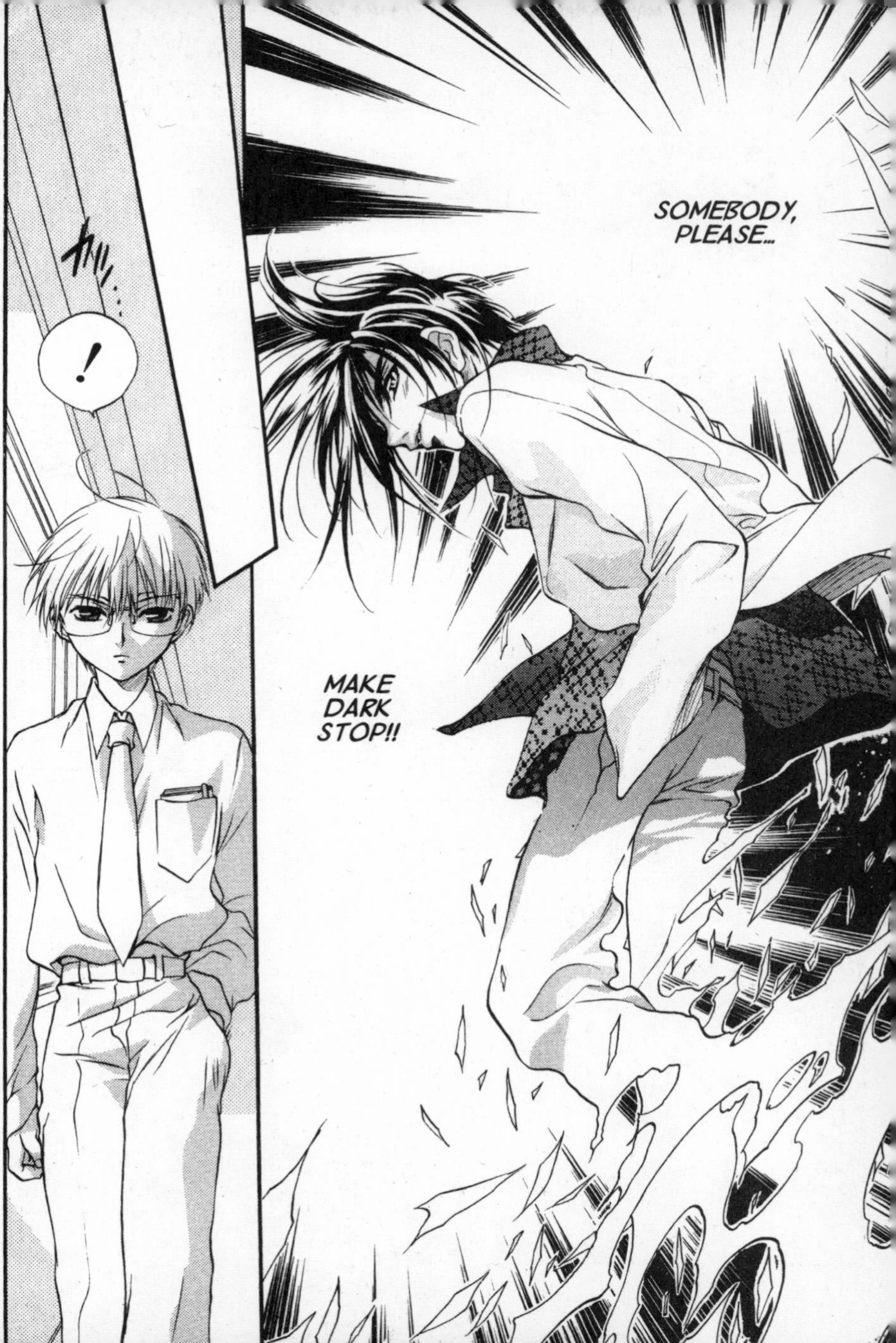
SOMEBODY, PLEASE...
MAKE DARK STOP!!
!

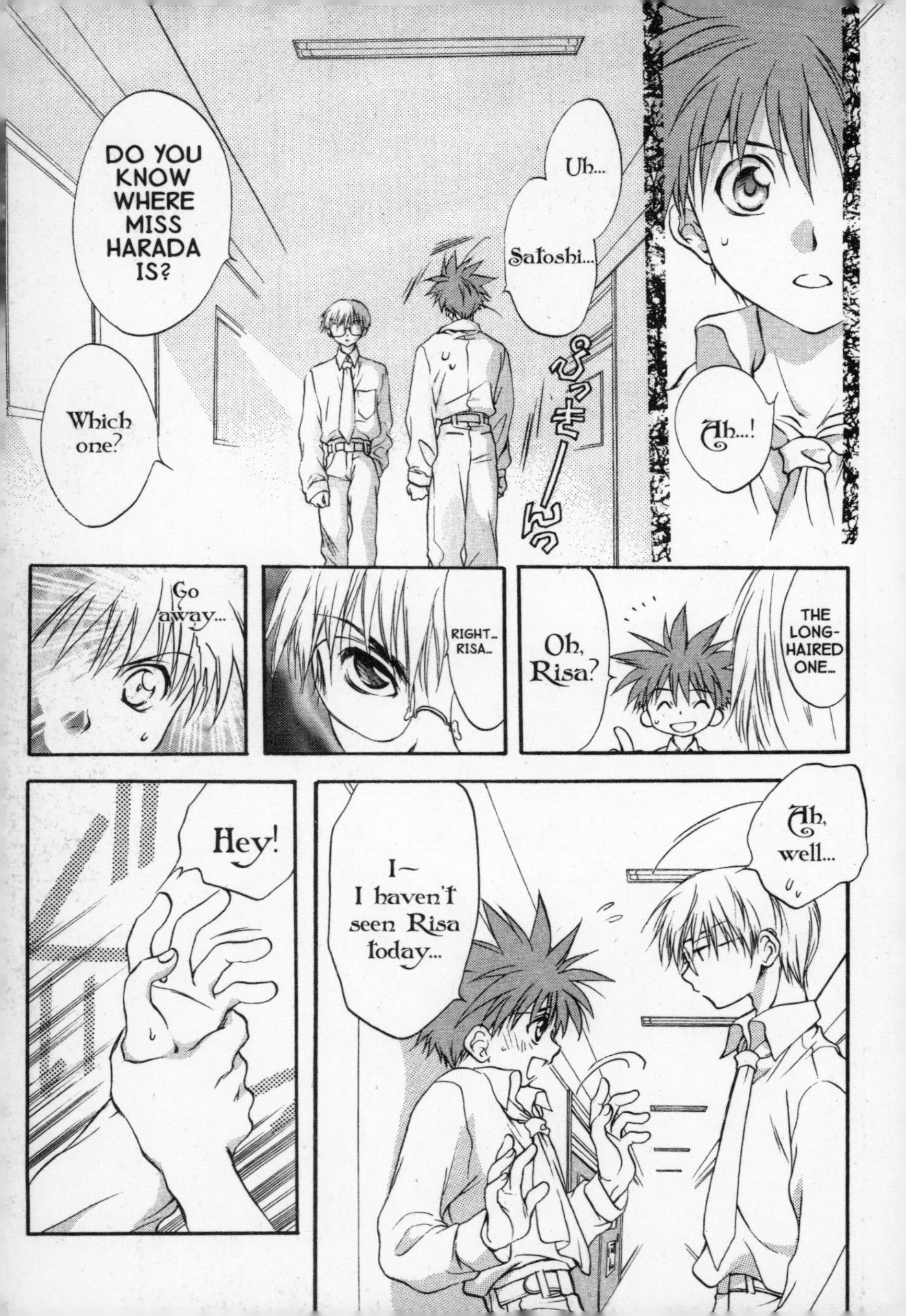
Ah...!
Uh...
Satoshi...
ぴっきーんっ
DO YOU KNOW WHERE MISS HARADA IS?
Which one?
THE LONG-HAIRED ONE...
Oh, Risa?
RIGHT... RISA...
Go away...
Ah, well...
I~ I haven't seen Risa today...
Hey!

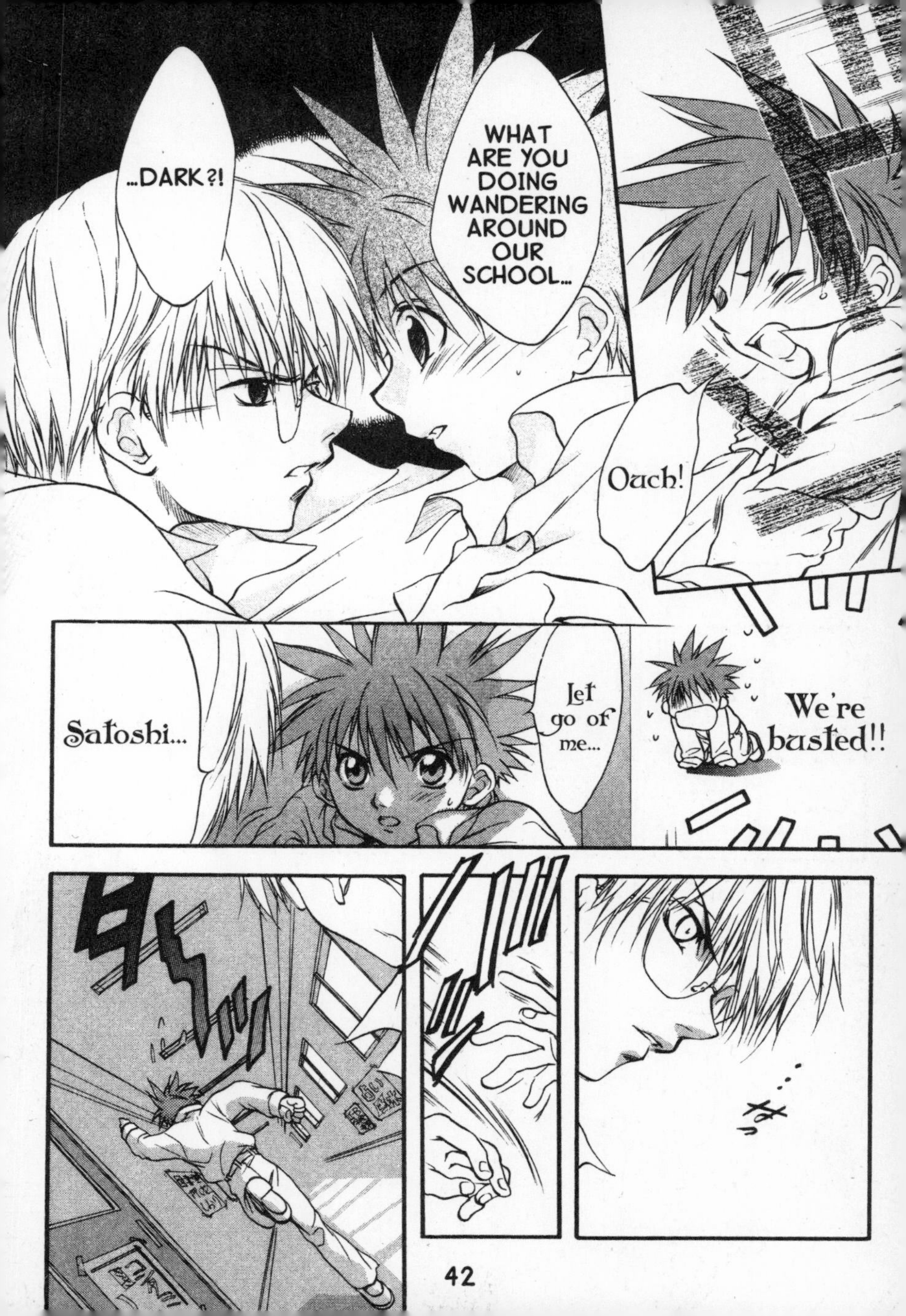
Ouch!
WHAT ARE YOU DOING WANDERING AROUND OUR SCHOOL...
...DARK?!
We're busted!!
Let go of me...
Satoshi...

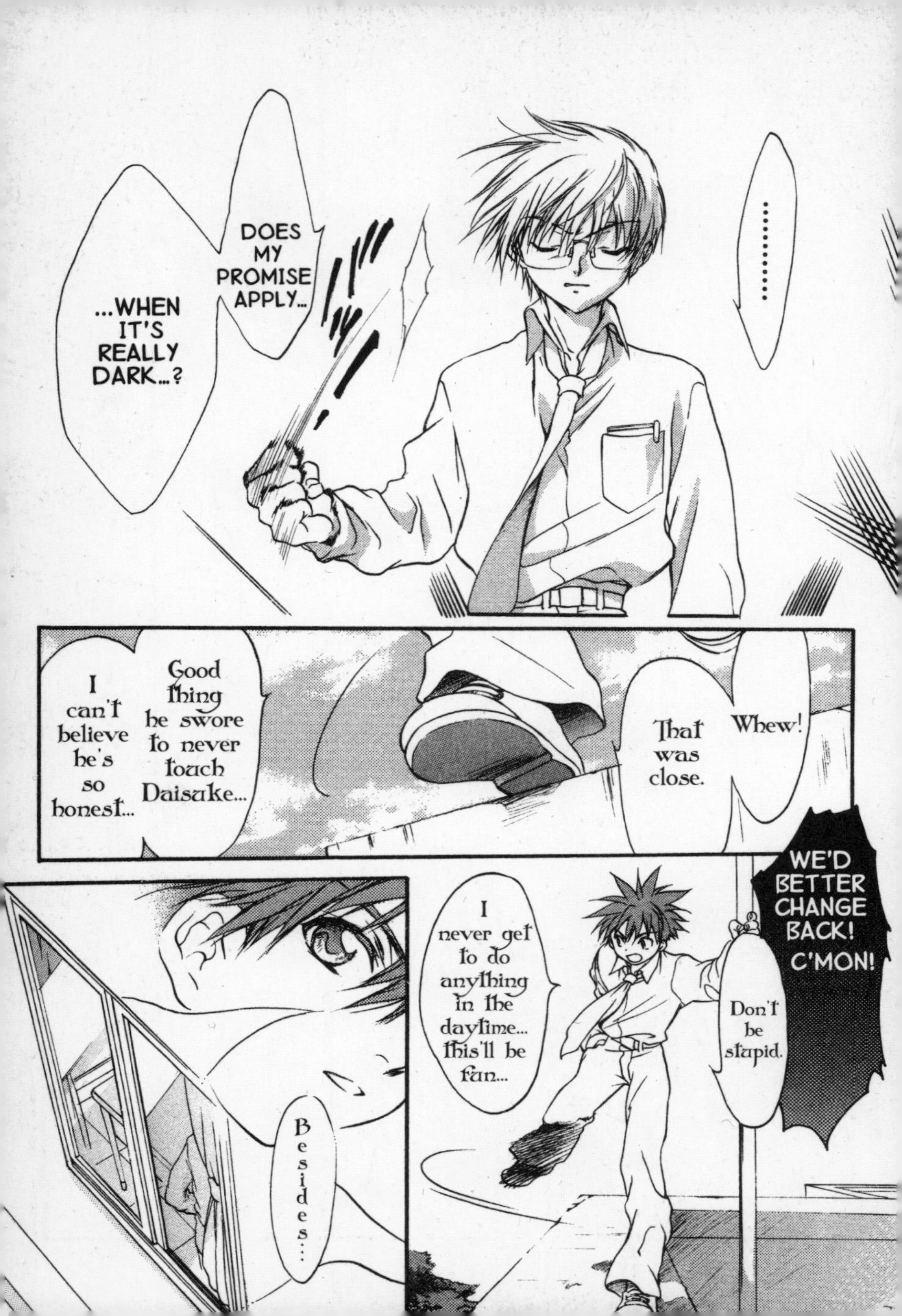
....
DOES MY PROMISE APPLY...
...WHEN IT'S REALLY DARK...?
Whew!
That was close.
Good thing he swore to never touch Daisuke...
I can't believe he's so honest...
WE'D BETTER CHANGE BACK! C'MON!
Don't be stupid.
I never get to do anything in the daytime... this'll be fun...
Besides...

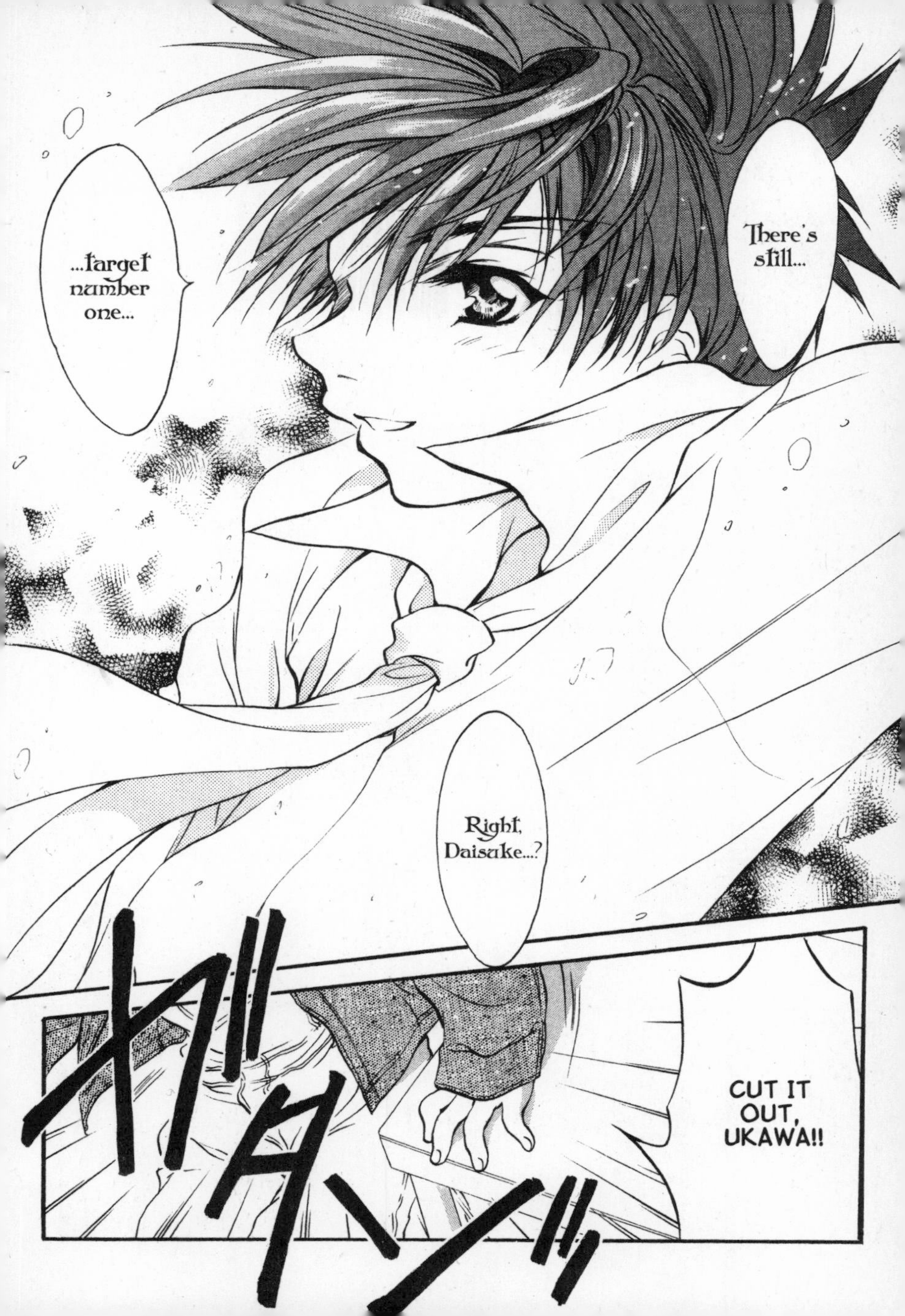
There's still...
...target number one...
Right, Daisuke...?
CUT IT OUT, UKAWA!!

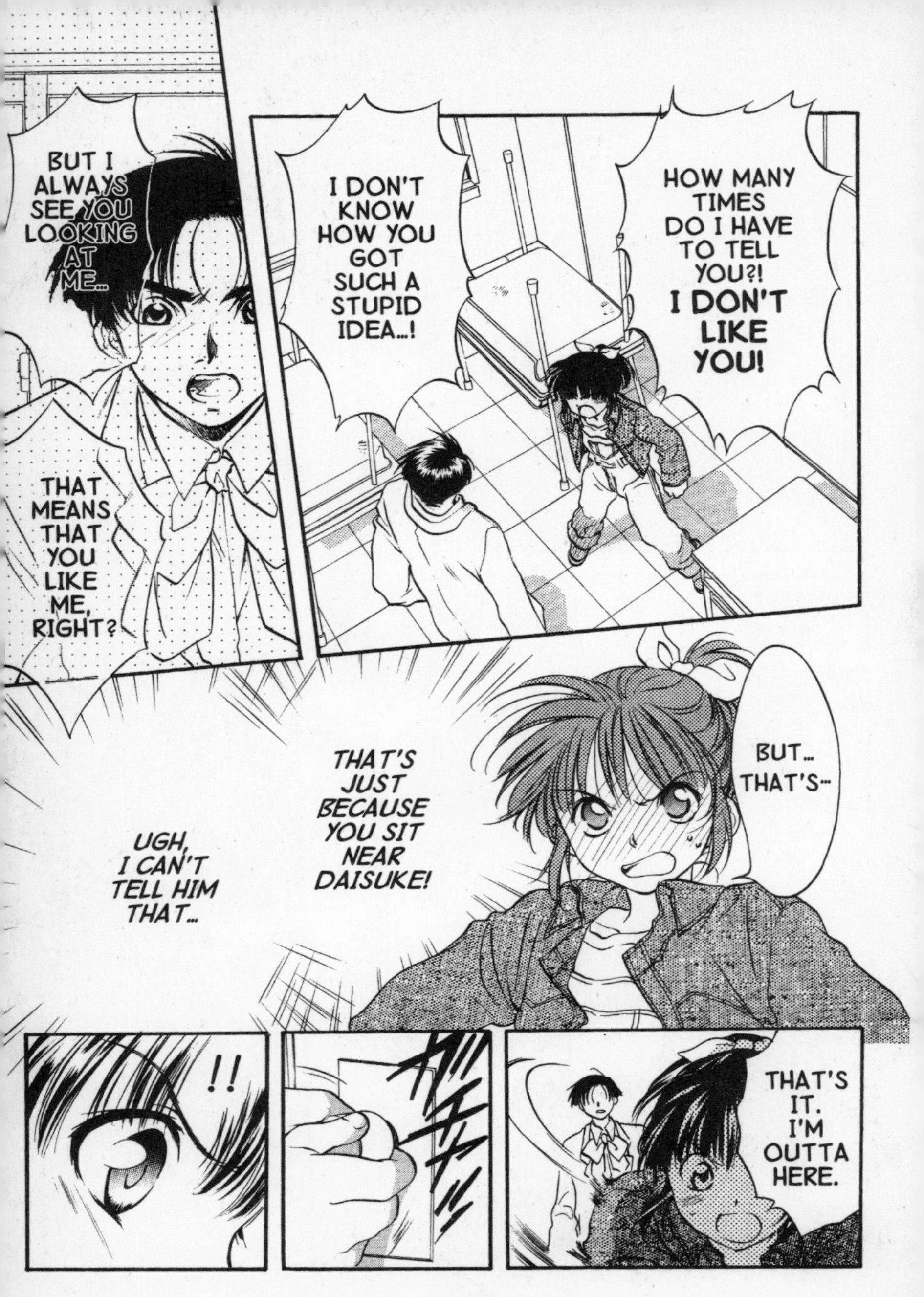
HOW MANY TIMES DO I HAVE TO TELL YOU?! I DON'T LIKE YOU!
I DON'T KNOW HOW YOU GOT SUCH A STUPID IDEA...!
BUT I ALWAYS SEE YOU LOOKING AT ME...
THAT MEANS THAT YOU LIKE ME, RIGHT?
BUT... THAT'S—
THAT'S JUST BECAUSE YOU SIT NEAR DAISUKE!
UGH, I CAN'T TELL HIM THAT...
THAT'S IT. I'M OUTTA HERE.
!!

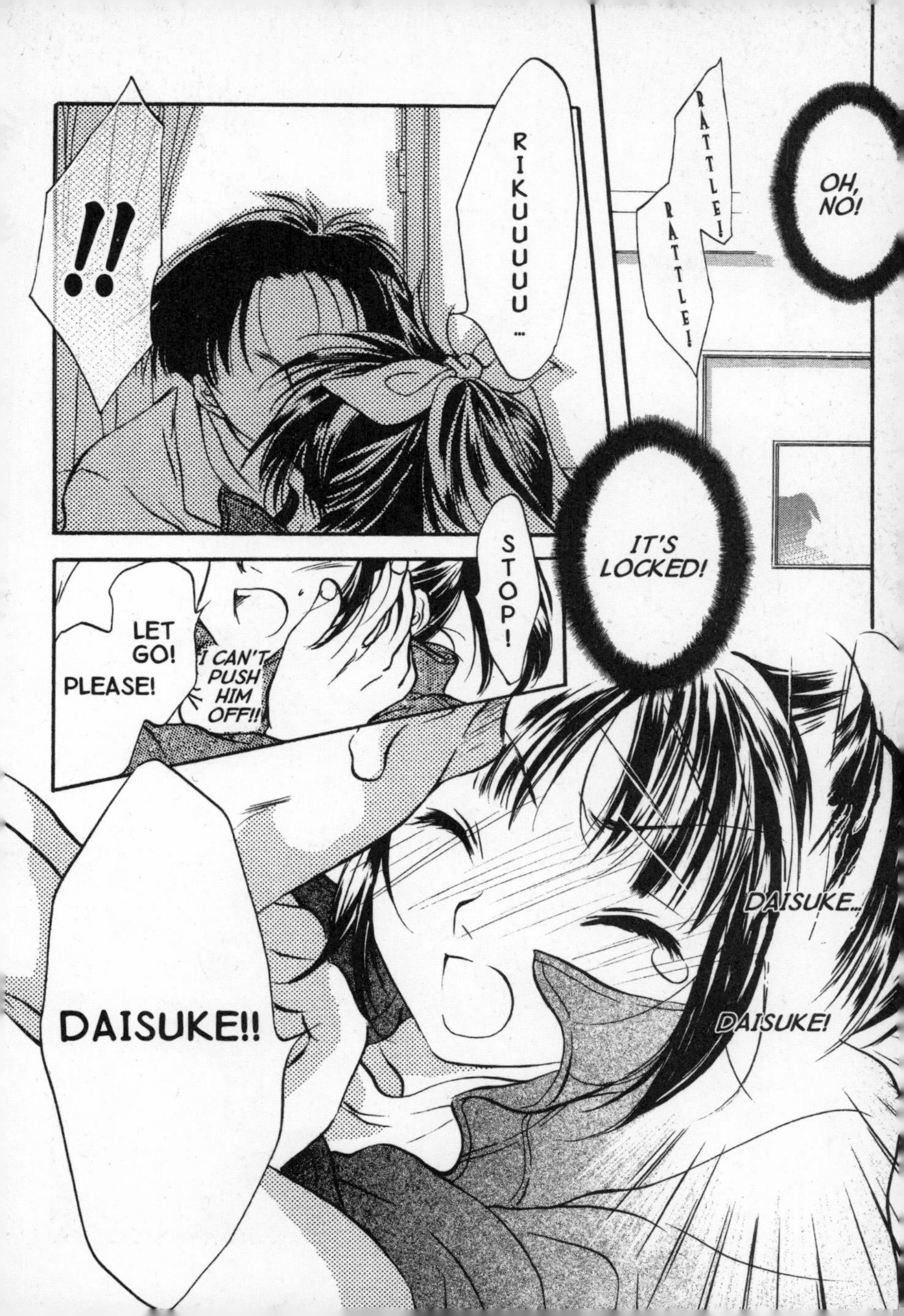
OH, NO!
RATTLE!
RATTLE!
RIKUUUUU...
!!
IT'S LOCKED!
STOP!
I CAN'T PUSH HIM OFF!!
LET GO!
PLEASE!
DAISUKE...
DAISUKE!
DAISUKE!!

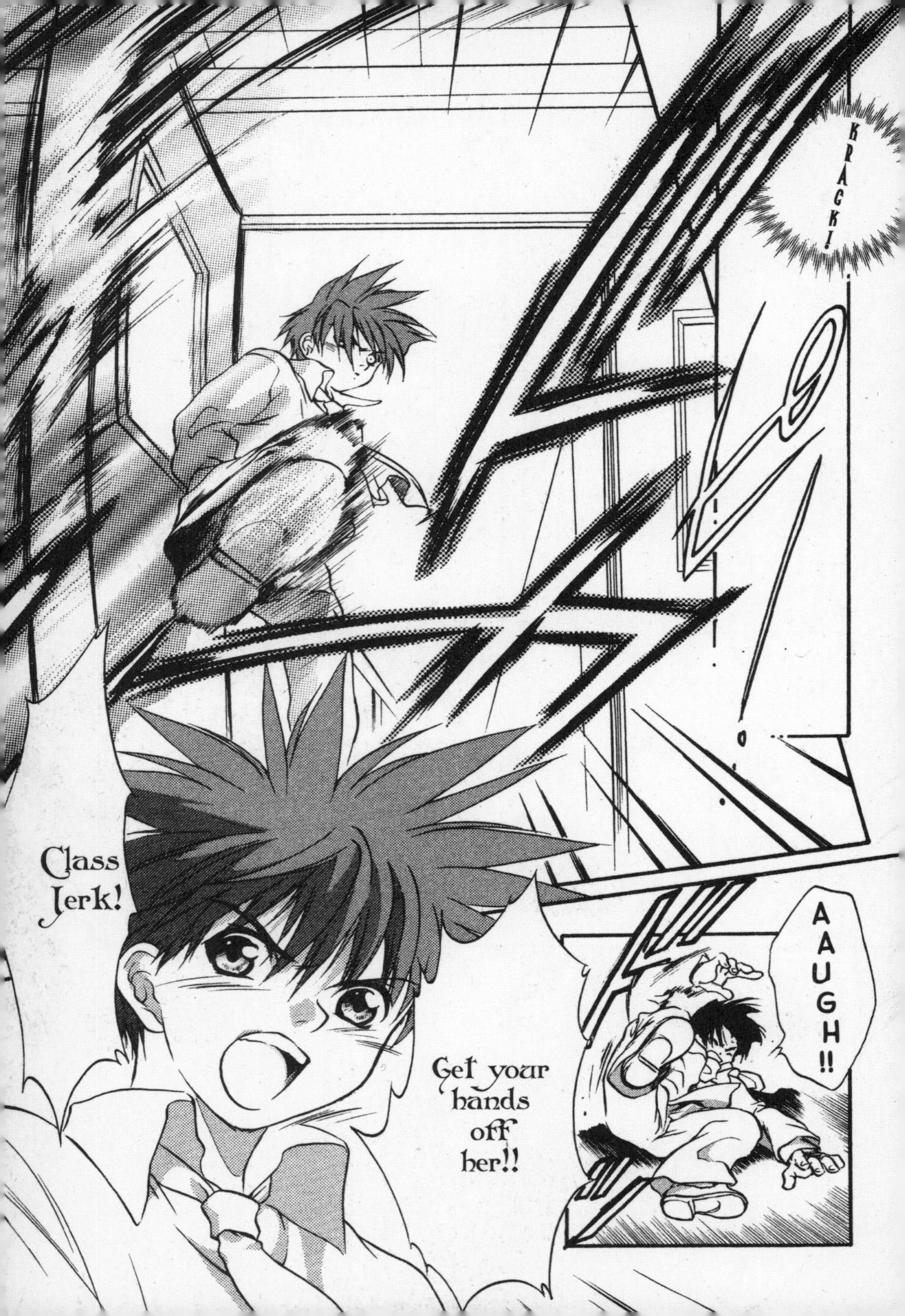
KRAGK!
AAUGH!!
Get your hands off her!!
Class Jerk!

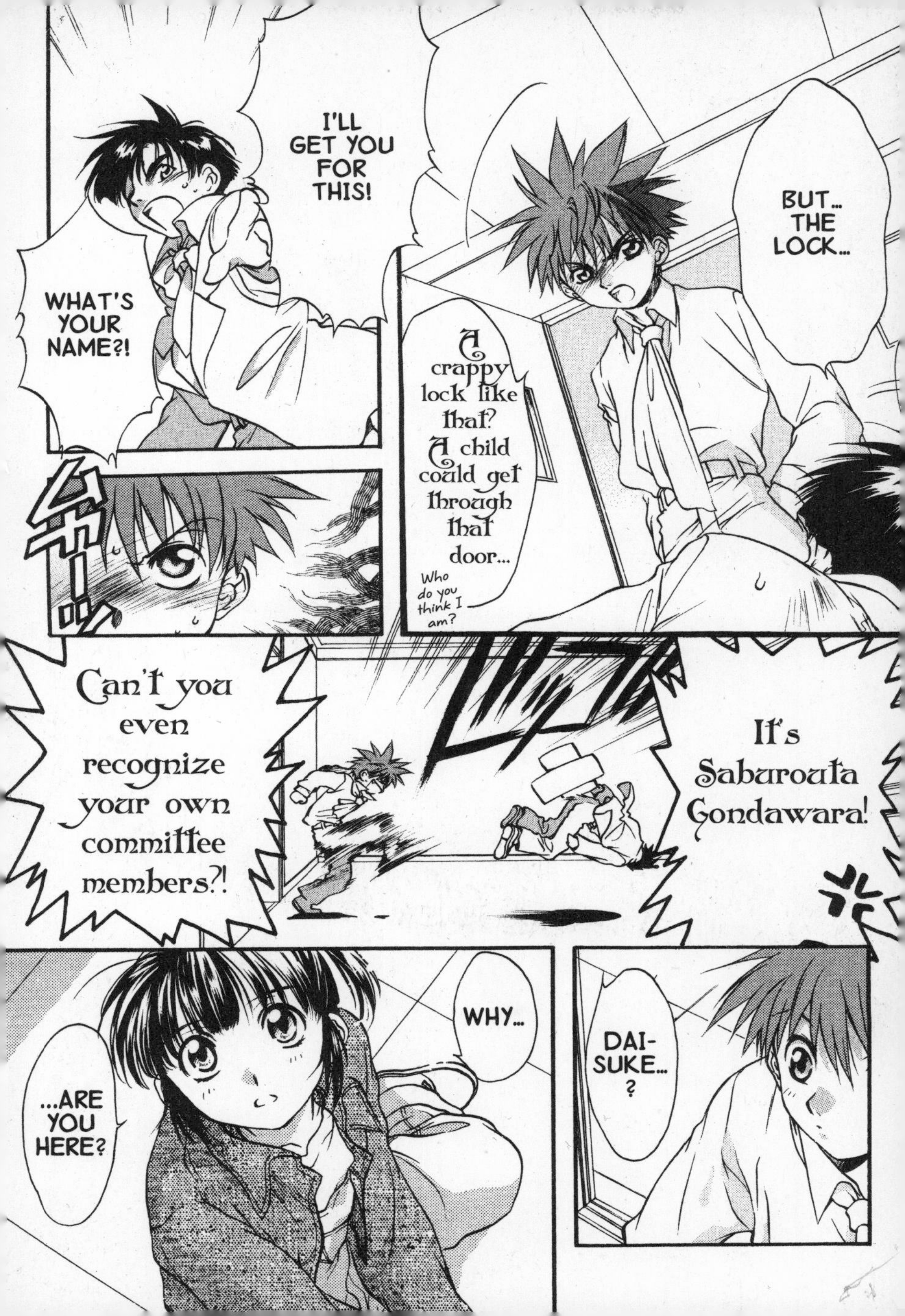

BUT... THE LOCK...
A crappy lock like that? A child could get through that door...
Who do you think I am?
I'LL GET YOU FOR THIS!
WHAT'S YOUR NAME?!
It's Saburouta Gondawara!
Can't you even recognize your own committee members?!
DAI-SUKE...?
WHY...
...ARE YOU HERE?

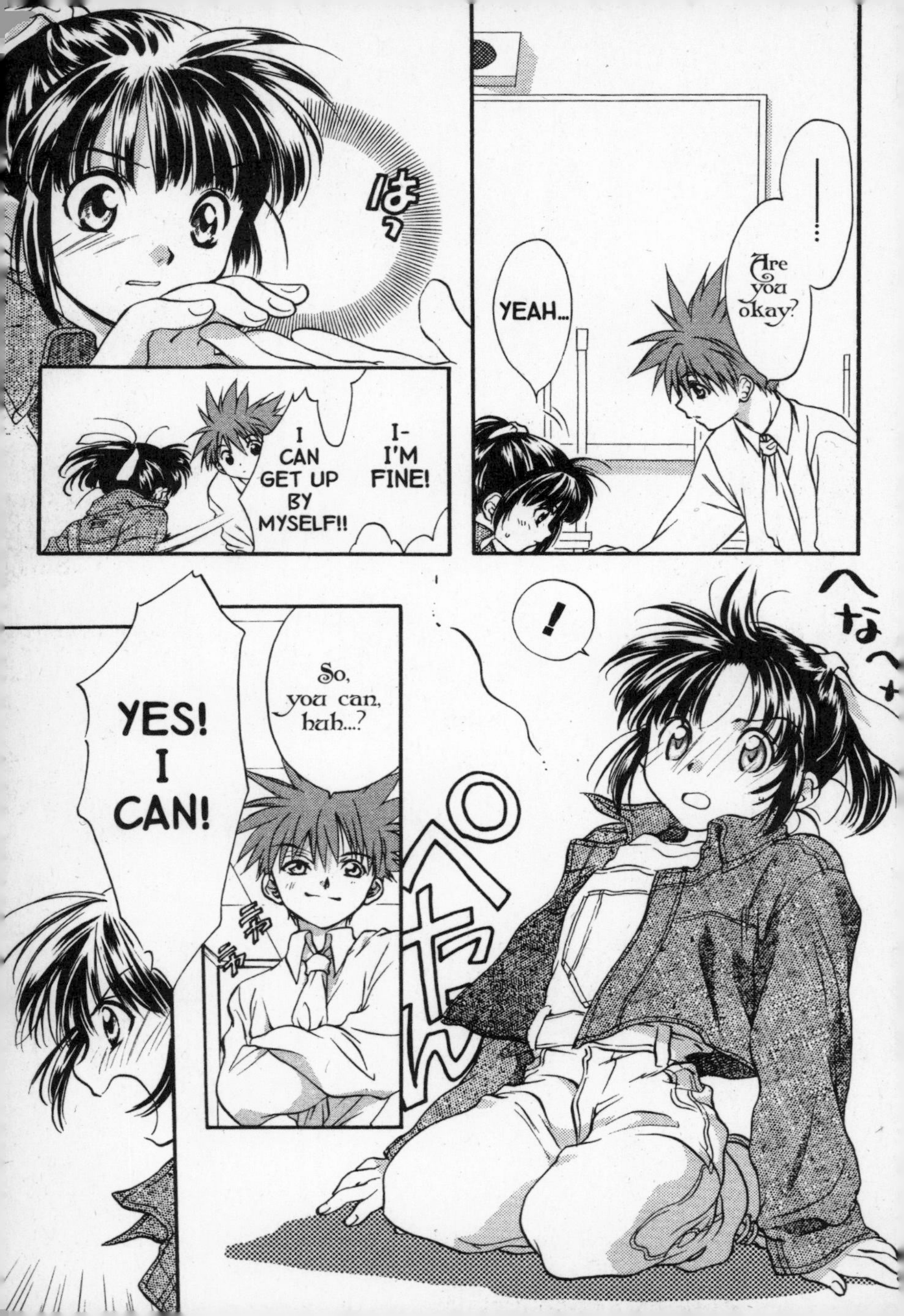
Are you okay?
YEAH...
はっ
I-I'M FINE!
I CAN GET UP BY MYSELF!!
へなへ
!
ぺたん
So, you can, huh...?
YES! I CAN!

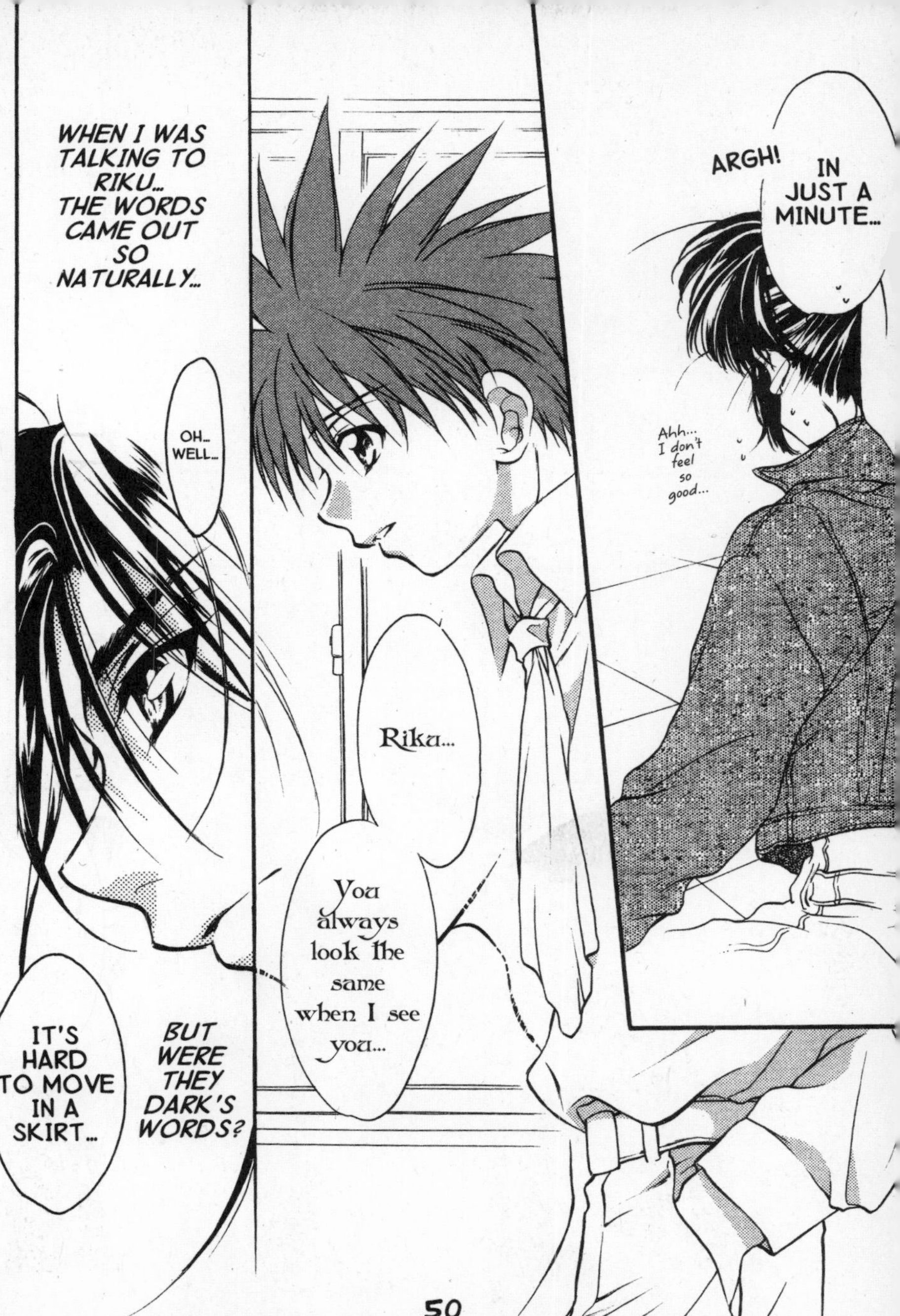

IN JUST A MINUTE...
ARGH!
Ahh... I don't feel so good...
Riku...
You always look the same when I see you...
WHEN I WAS TALKING TO RIKU... THE WORDS CAME OUT SO NATURALLY...
OH... WELL...
BUT WERE THEY DARK'S WORDS?
IT'S HARD TO MOVE IN A SKIRT...

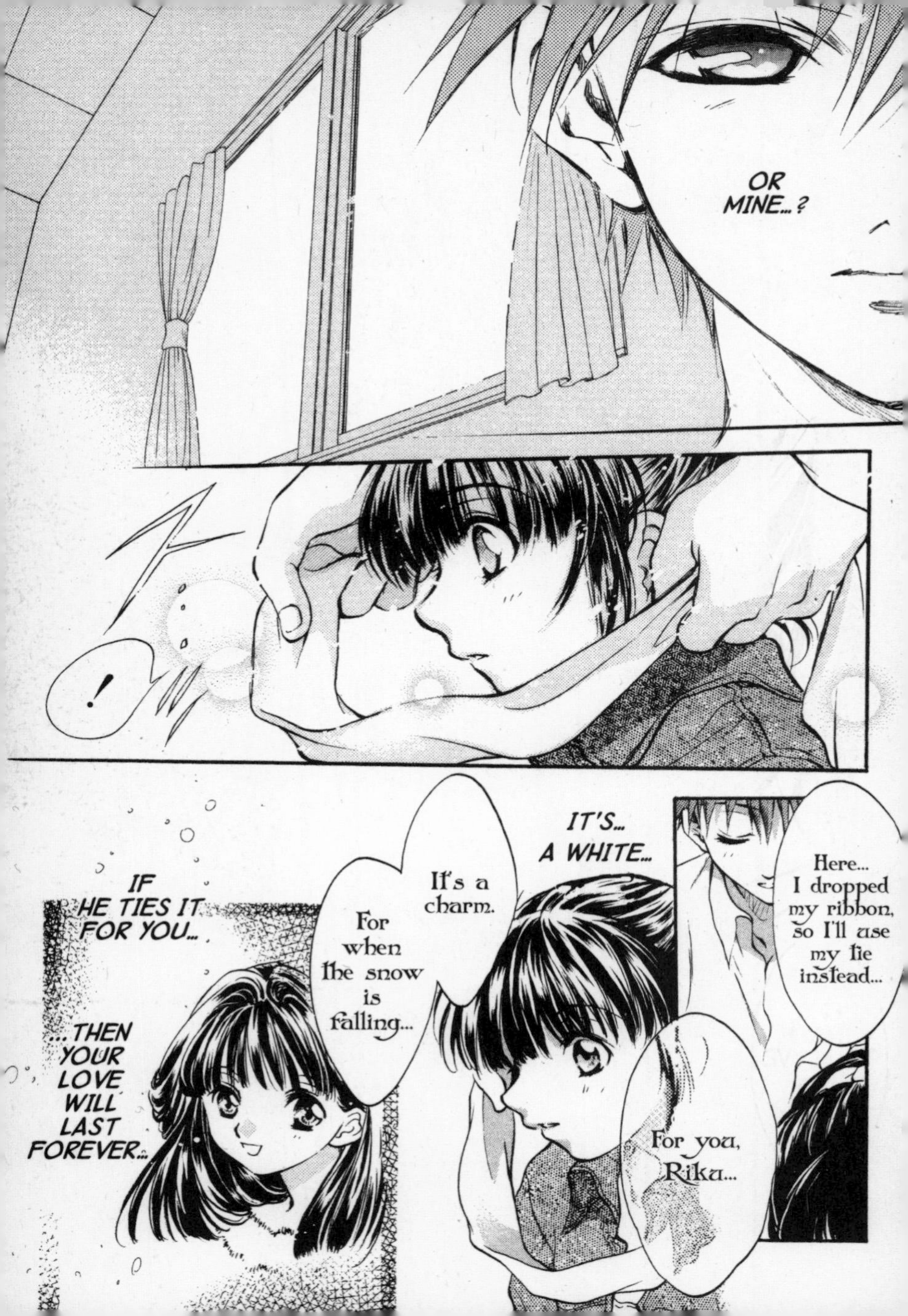
OR MINE...?
!
Here... I dropped my ribbon, so I'll use my tie instead...
For you, Riku...
IT'S... A WHITE...
It's a charm.
For when the snow is falling...
IF HE TIES IT FOR YOU...
...THEN YOUR LOVE WILL LAST FOREVER...

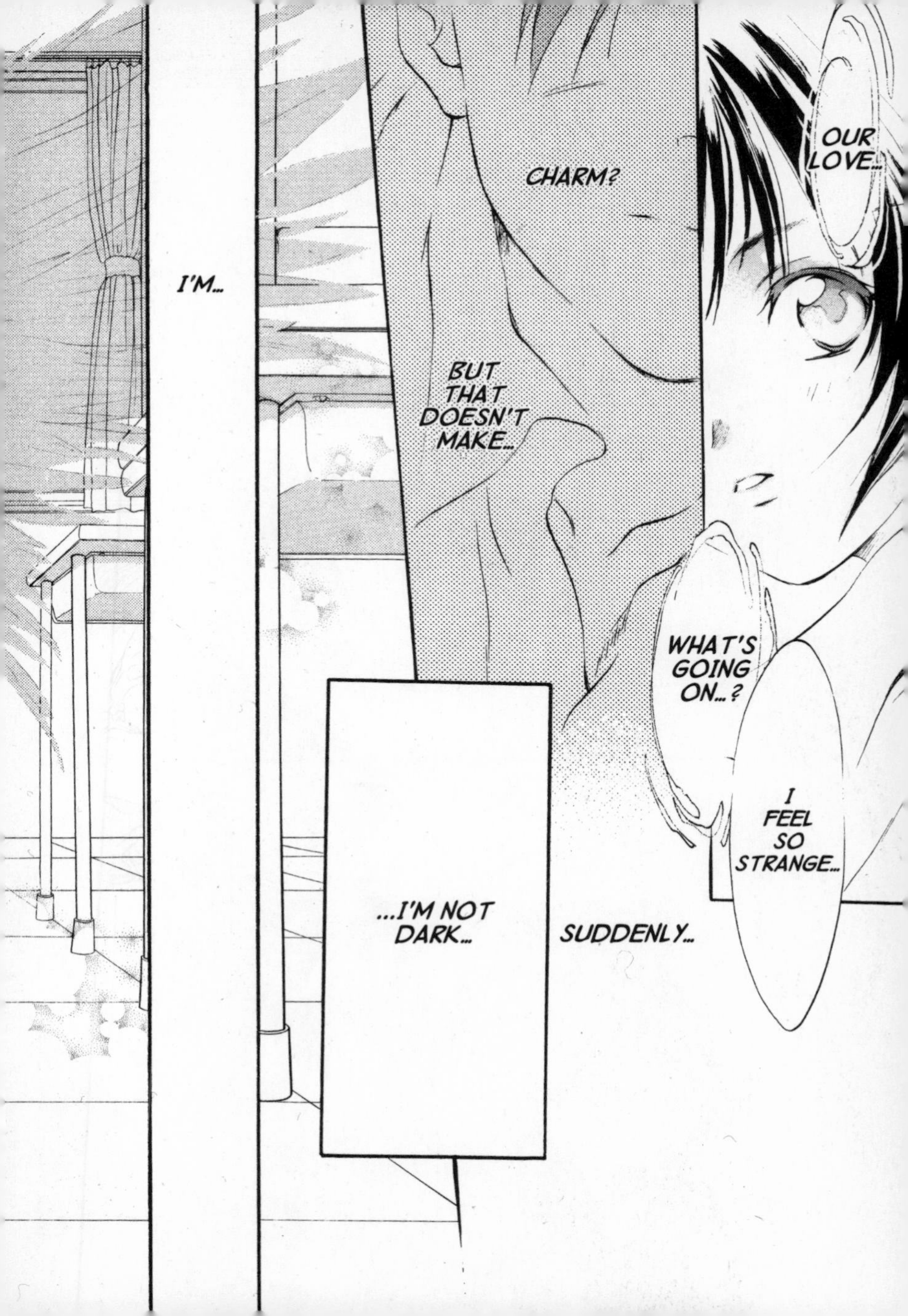
OUR LOVE...
CHARM?
BUT THAT DOESN'T MAKE...
WHAT'S GOING ON...?
I FEEL SO STRANGE...
SUDDENLY...
...I'M NOT DARK...
I'M...

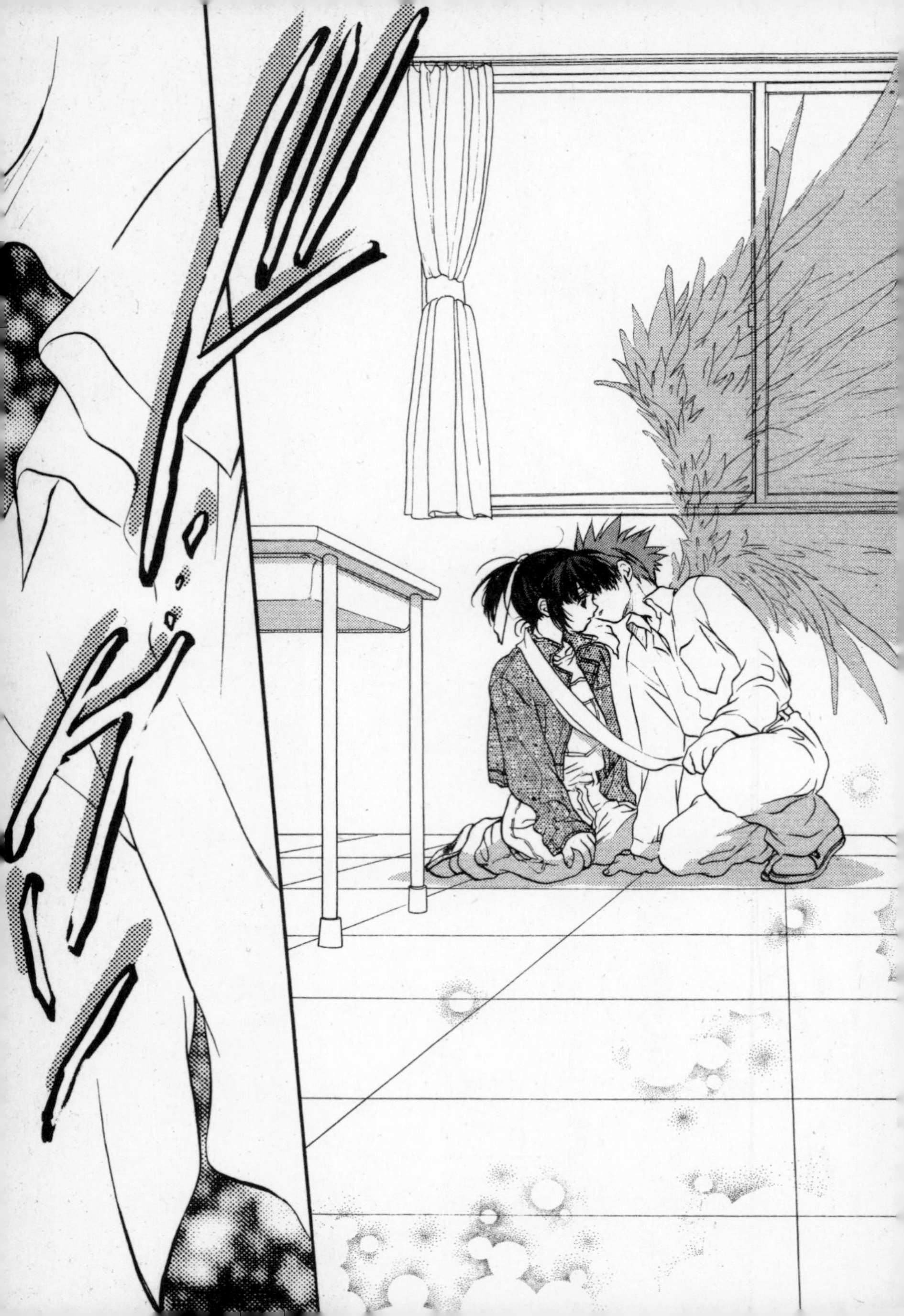

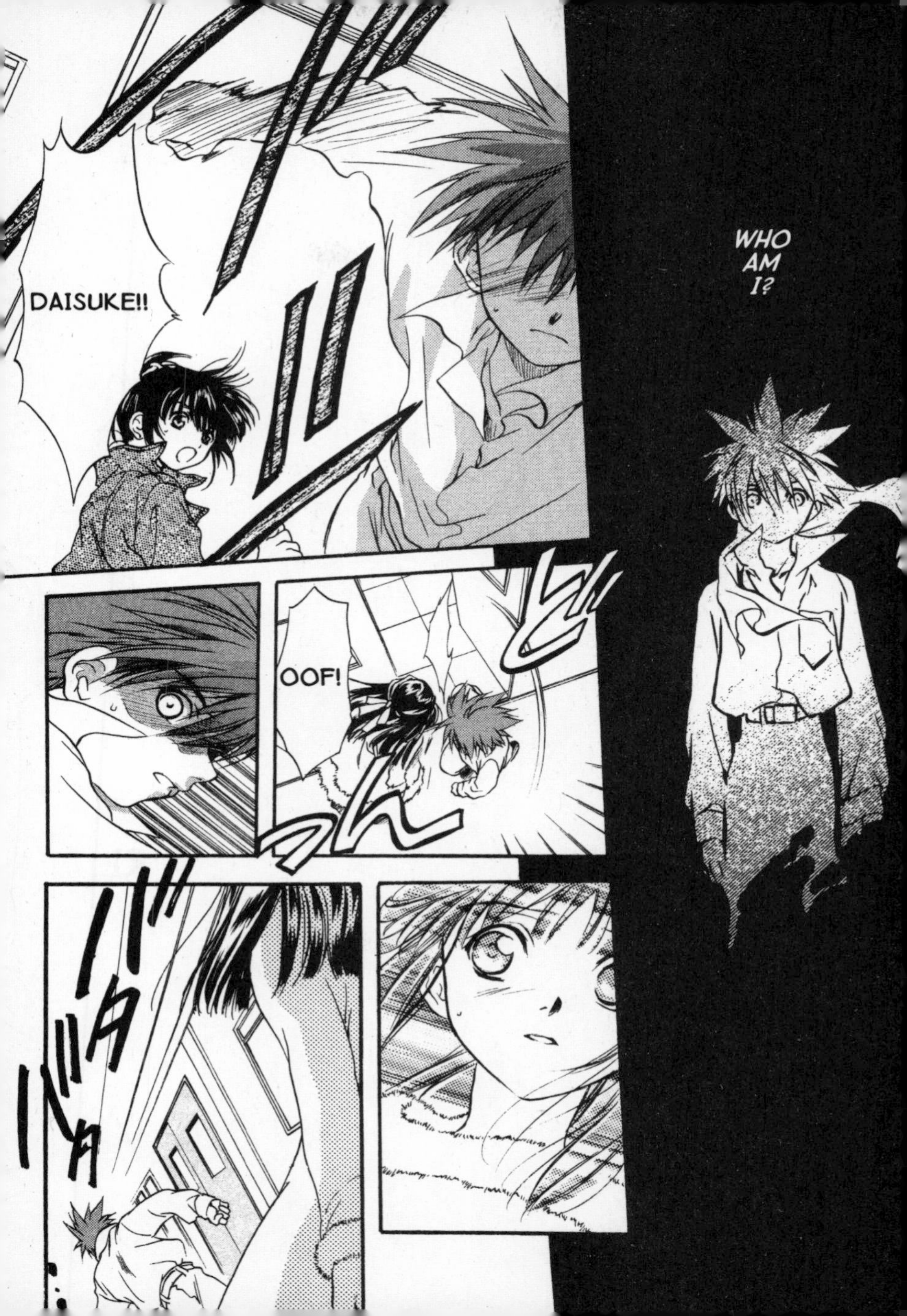
WHO AM I?
DAISUKE!!
OOF!

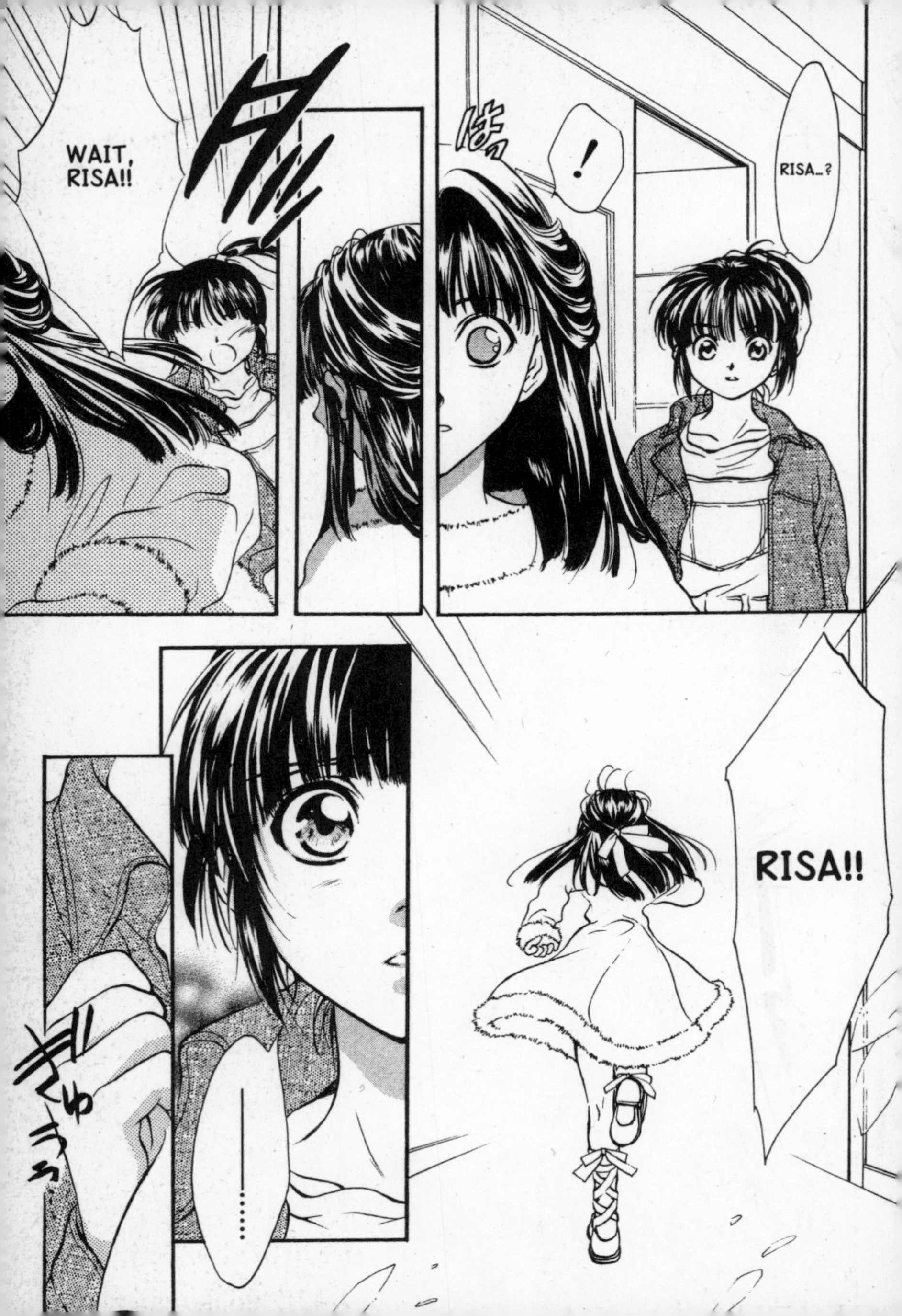
RISA...?
!
はっ
WAIT, RISA!!
RISA!!
......

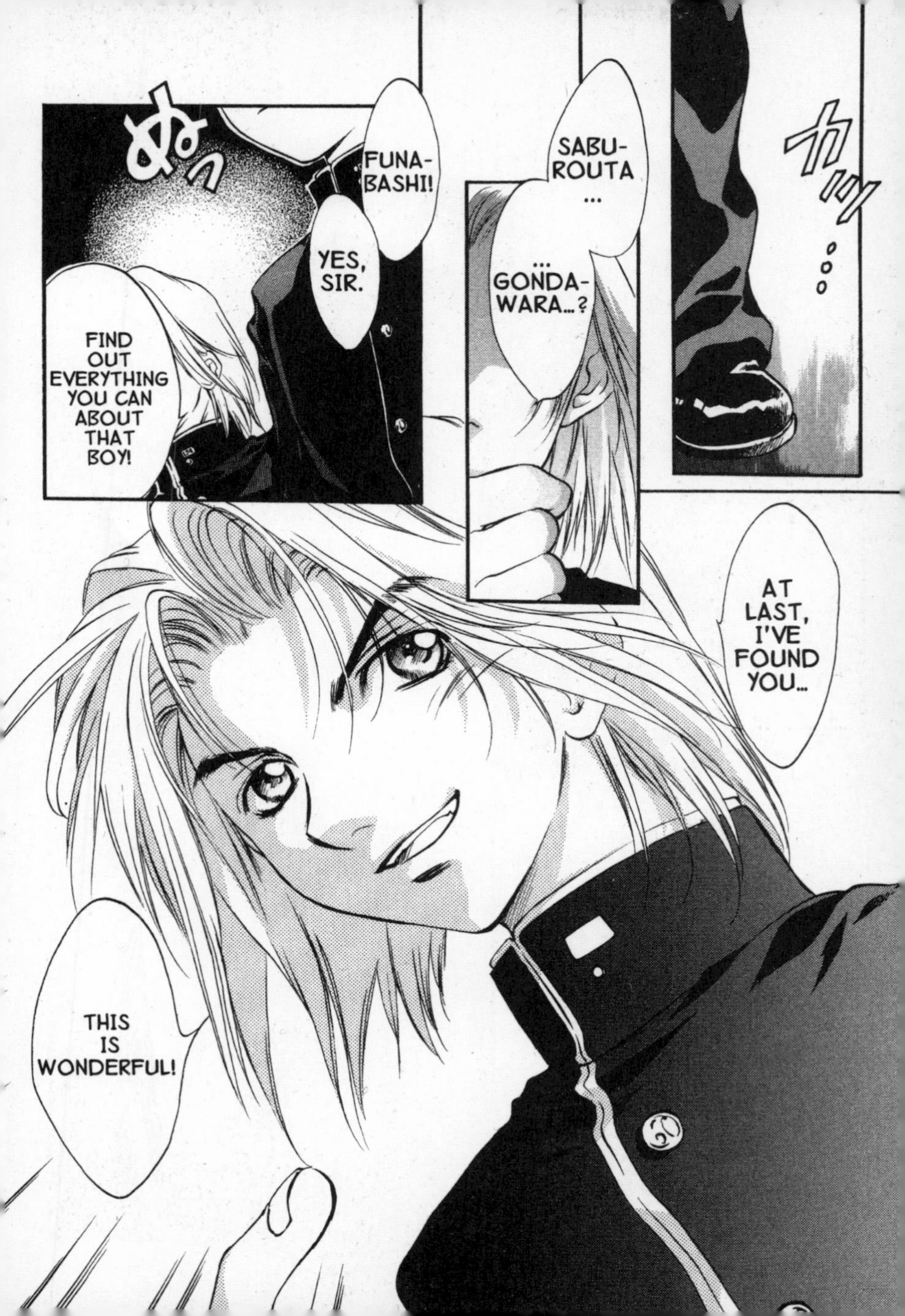
カッ
SABU-ROUTA ...
... GONDA-WARA...?
ぬっ
FUNA-BASHI!
YES, SIR.
FIND OUT EVERYTHING YOU CAN ABOUT THAT BOY!
AT LAST, I'VE FOUND YOU...
THIS IS WONDERFUL!

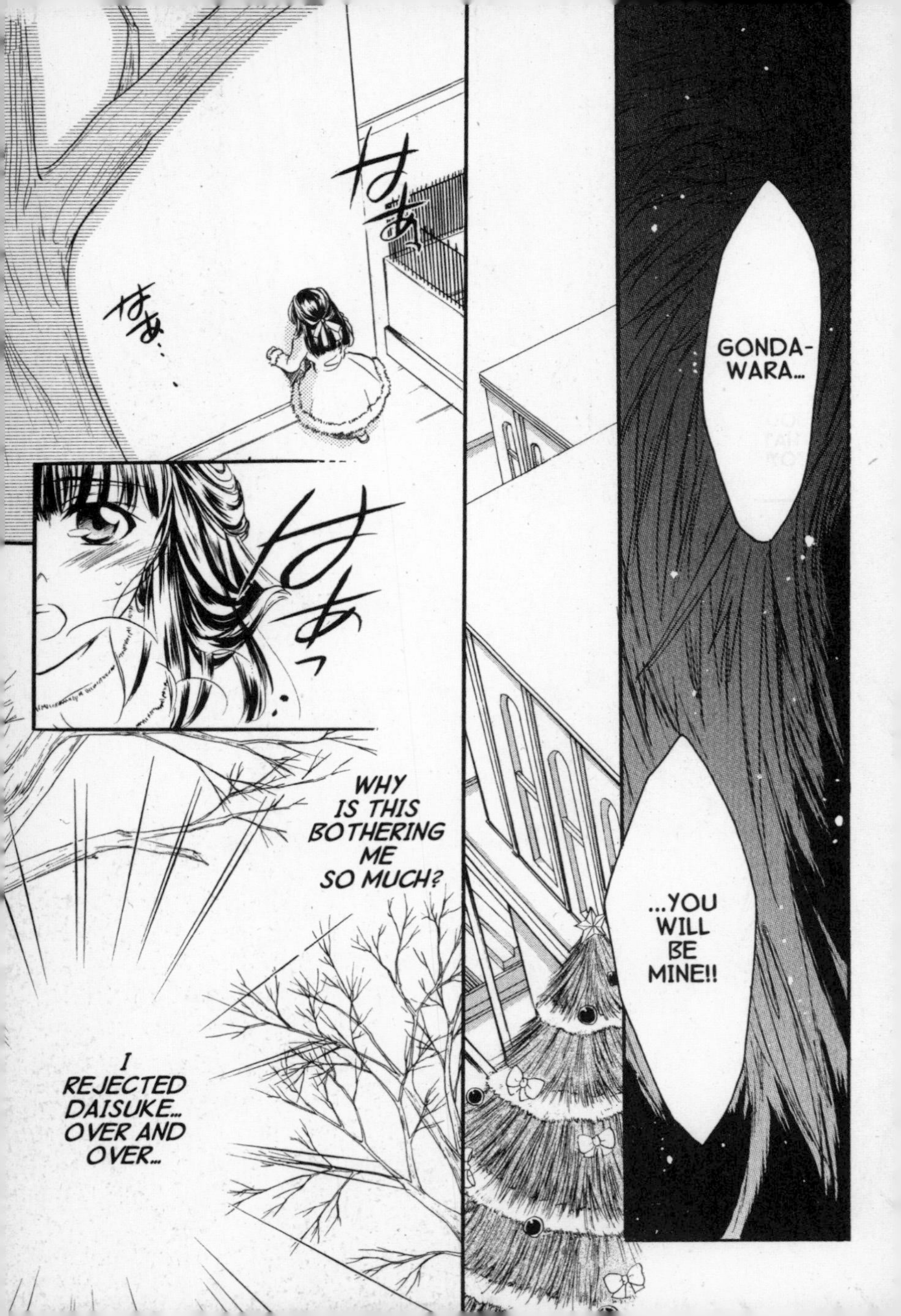
GONDA-WARA...
...YOU WILL BE MINE!!
はぁ
はぁ・・
はぁっ
WHY IS THIS BOTHERING ME SO MUCH?
I REJECTED DAISUKE... OVER AND OVER...

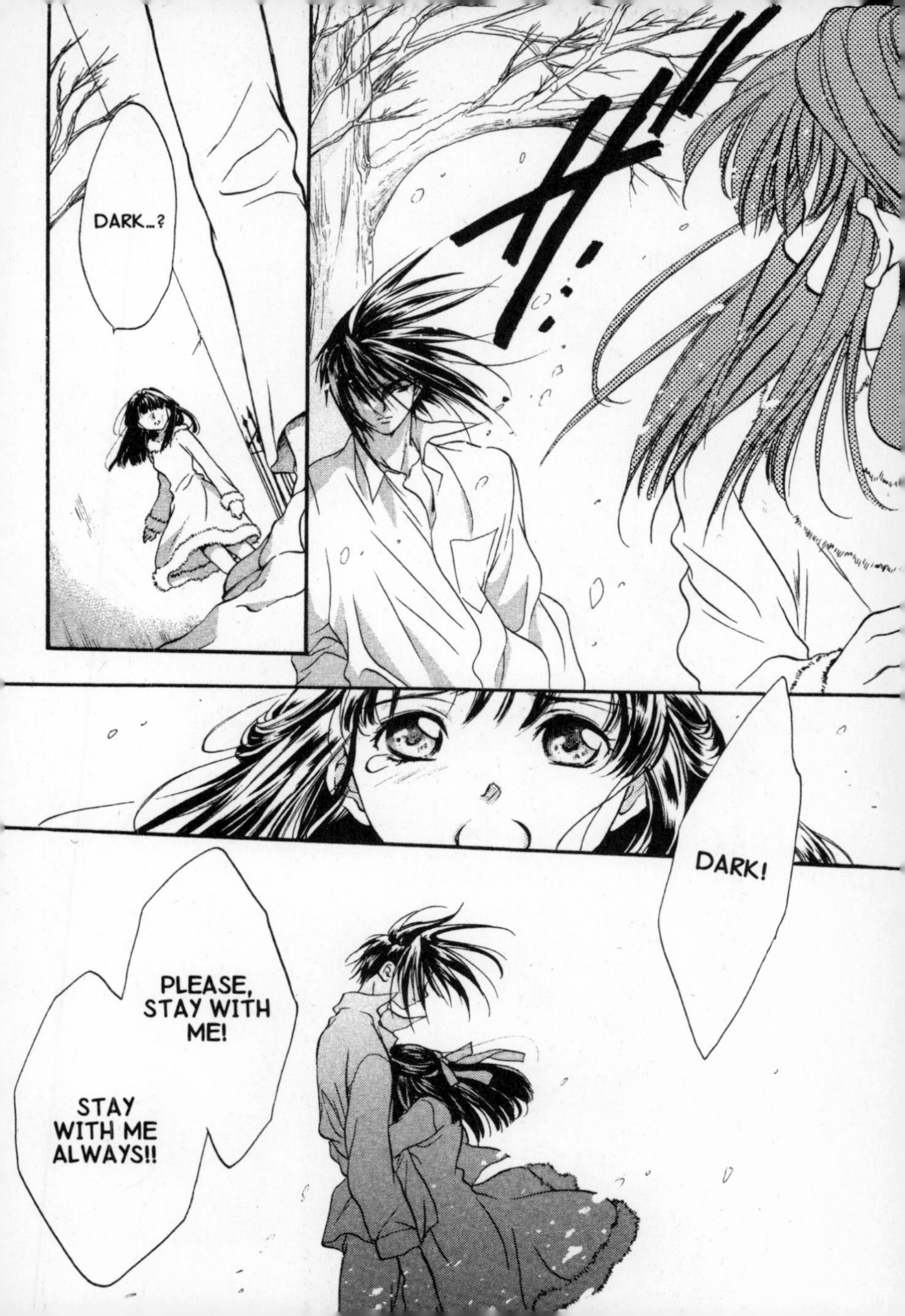
DARK...?
DARK!
PLEASE, STAY WITH ME!
STAY WITH ME ALWAYS!!

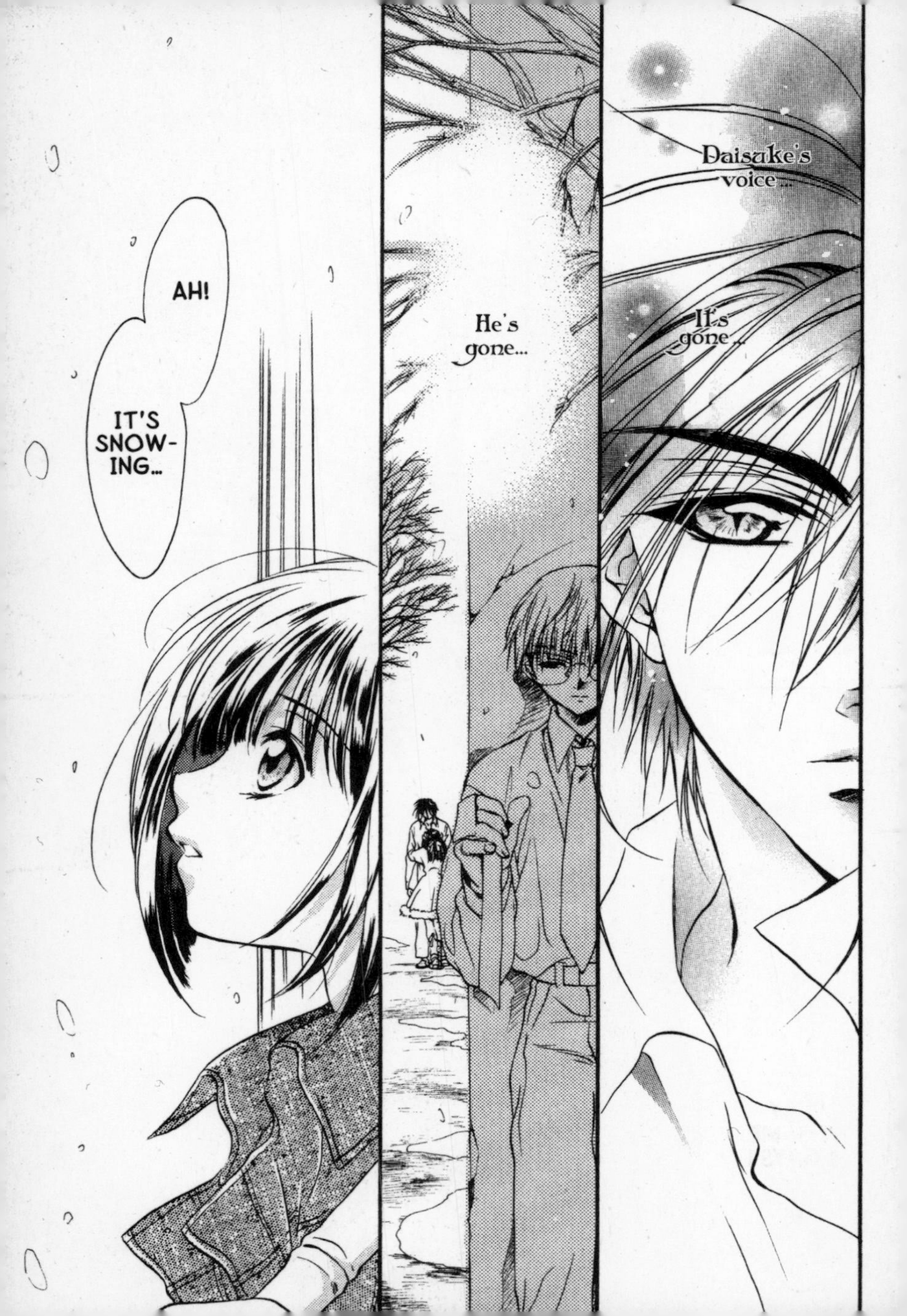
Daisuke's voice...
It's gone...
He's gone...
AH!
IT'S SNOWING...

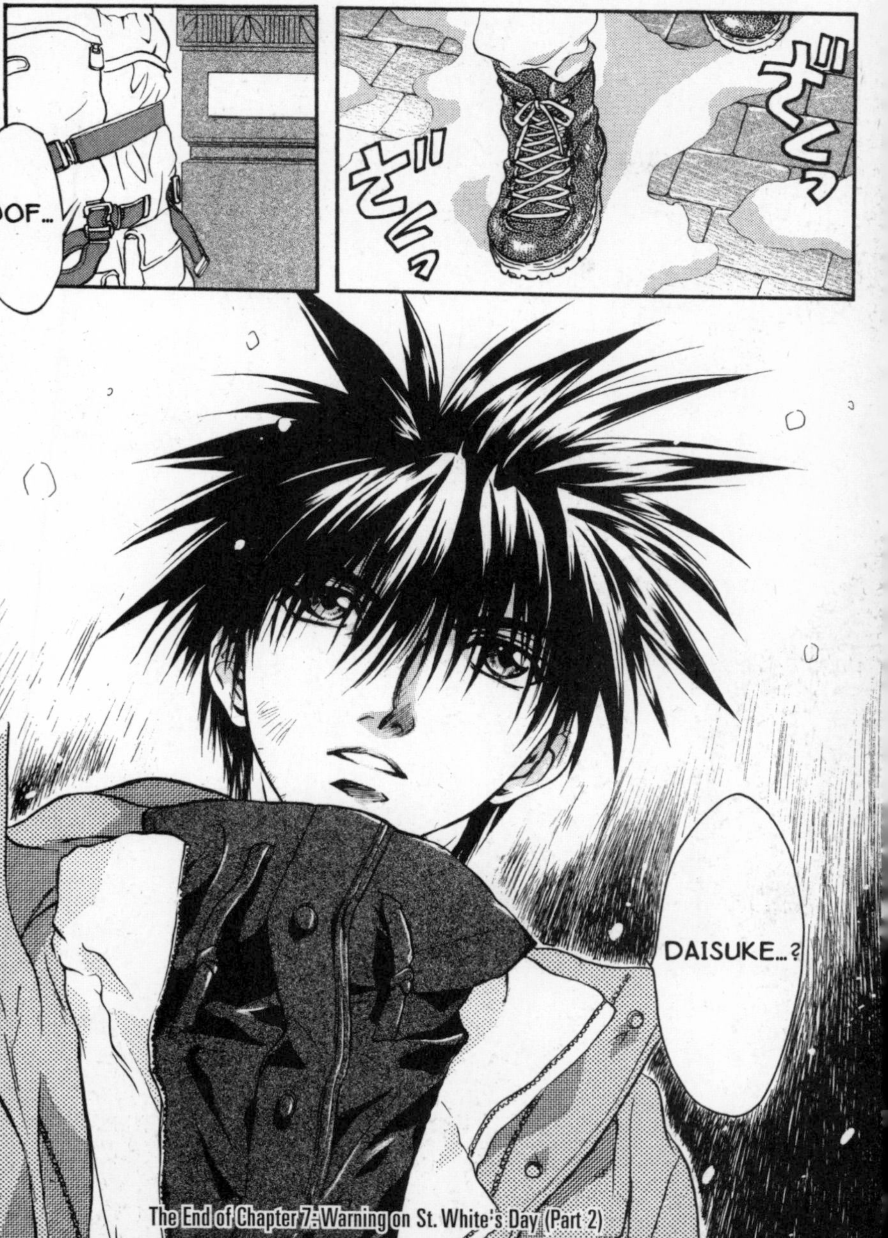
ざくっ
ざくっ
OOF...
DAISUKE...?

The End of Chapter 7: Warning on St. White's Day (Part 2)

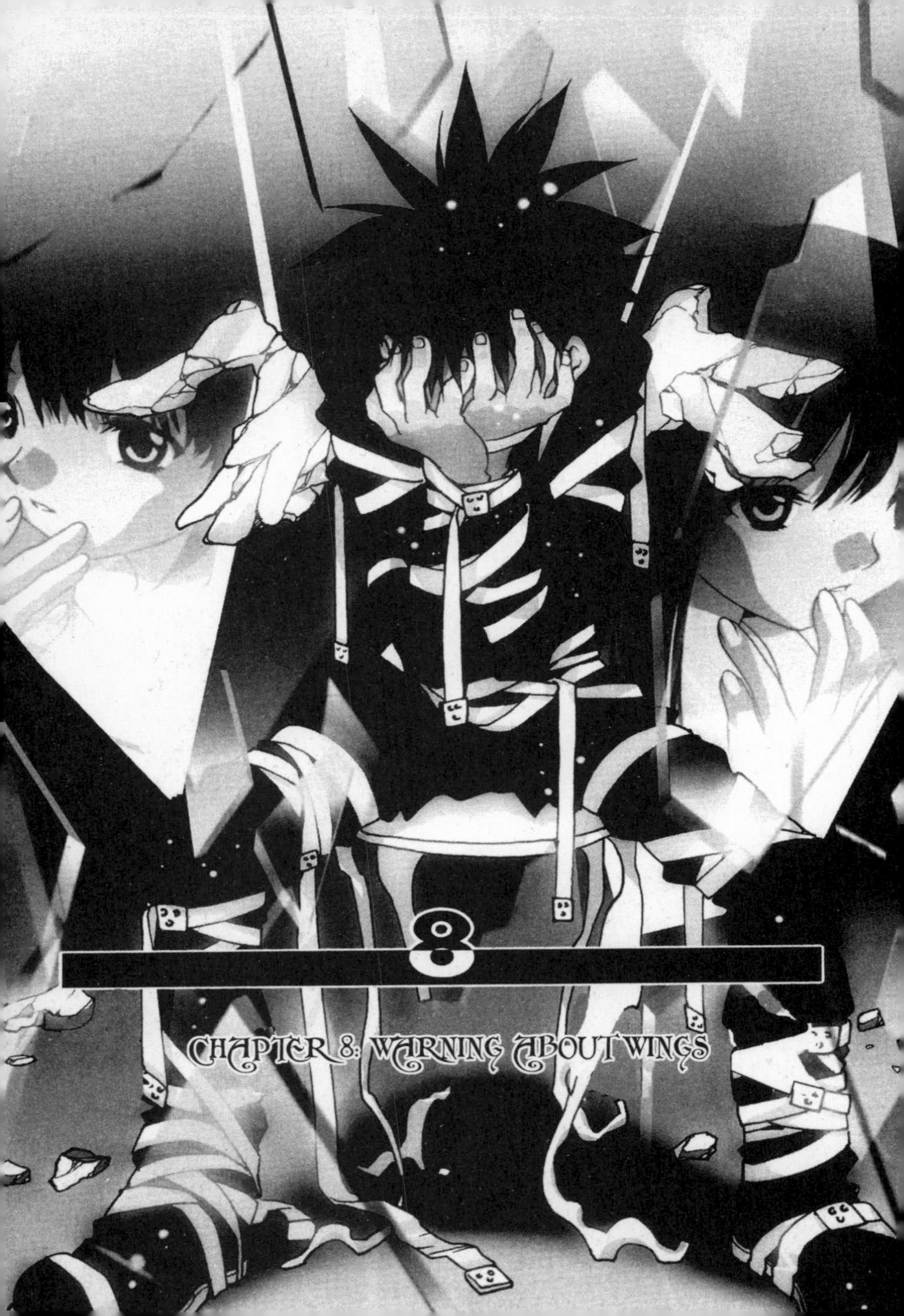
8
CHAPTER 8: WARNING ABOUT WINGS

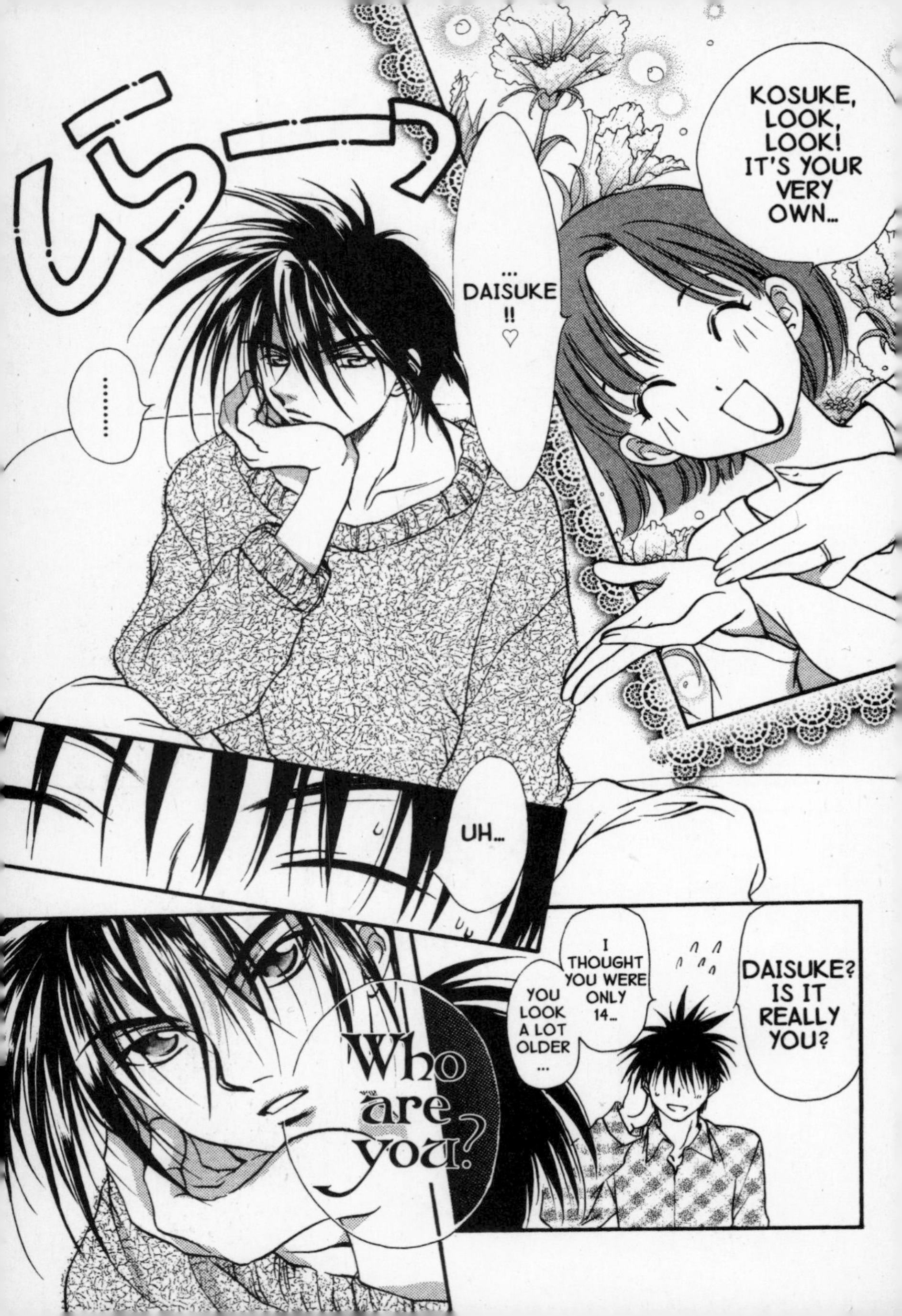

KOSUKE, LOOK, LOOK! IT'S YOUR VERY OWN...
...DAISUKE!! ♡
......
じろーっ
UH...
DAISUKE? IS IT REALLY YOU?
I THOUGHT YOU WERE ONLY 14...
YOU LOOK A LOT OLDER ...
Who are you?

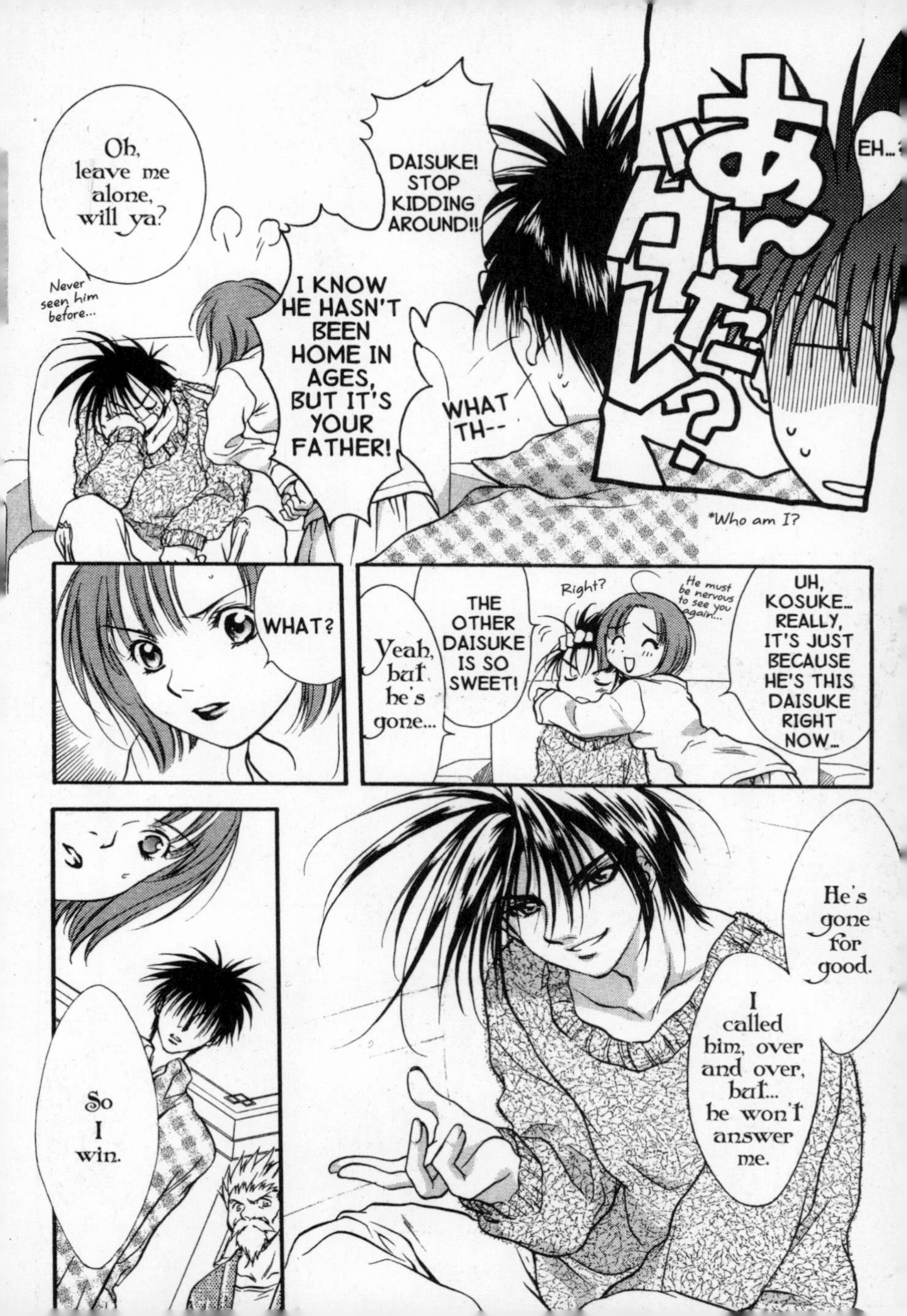
EH...?
あんただれ?
*Who am I?
WHAT TH--
DAISUKE! STOP KIDDING AROUND!!
I KNOW HE HASN'T BEEN HOME IN AGES, BUT IT'S YOUR FATHER!
Oh, leave me alone, will ya?
Never seen him before...
UH, KOSUKE... REALLY, IT'S JUST BECAUSE HE'S THIS DAISUKE RIGHT NOW...
He must be nervous to see you again...
Right?
THE OTHER DAISUKE IS SO SWEET!
Yeah, but he's gone...
WHAT?
He's gone for good.
I called him, over and over, but... he won't answer me.
So I win.

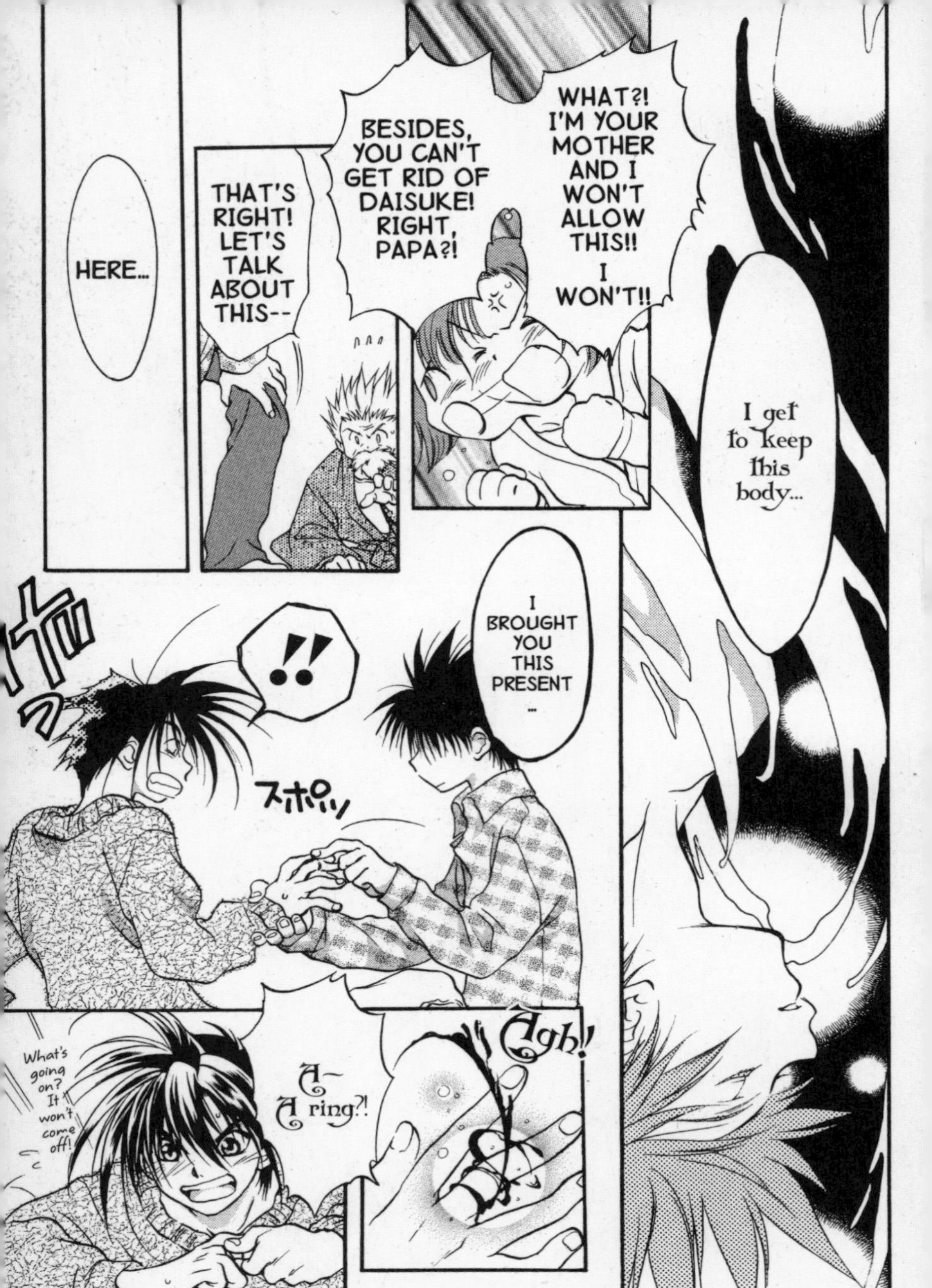
I get to keep this body...
WHAT?! I'M YOUR MOTHER AND I WON'T ALLOW THIS!! I WON'T!!
BESIDES, YOU CAN'T GET RID OF DAISUKE! RIGHT, PAPA?!
THAT'S RIGHT! LET'S TALK ABOUT THIS--
HERE...
I BROUGHT YOU THIS PRESENT...
!!
スポッ
Agh!
A-A ring?!
What's going on? It won't come off!

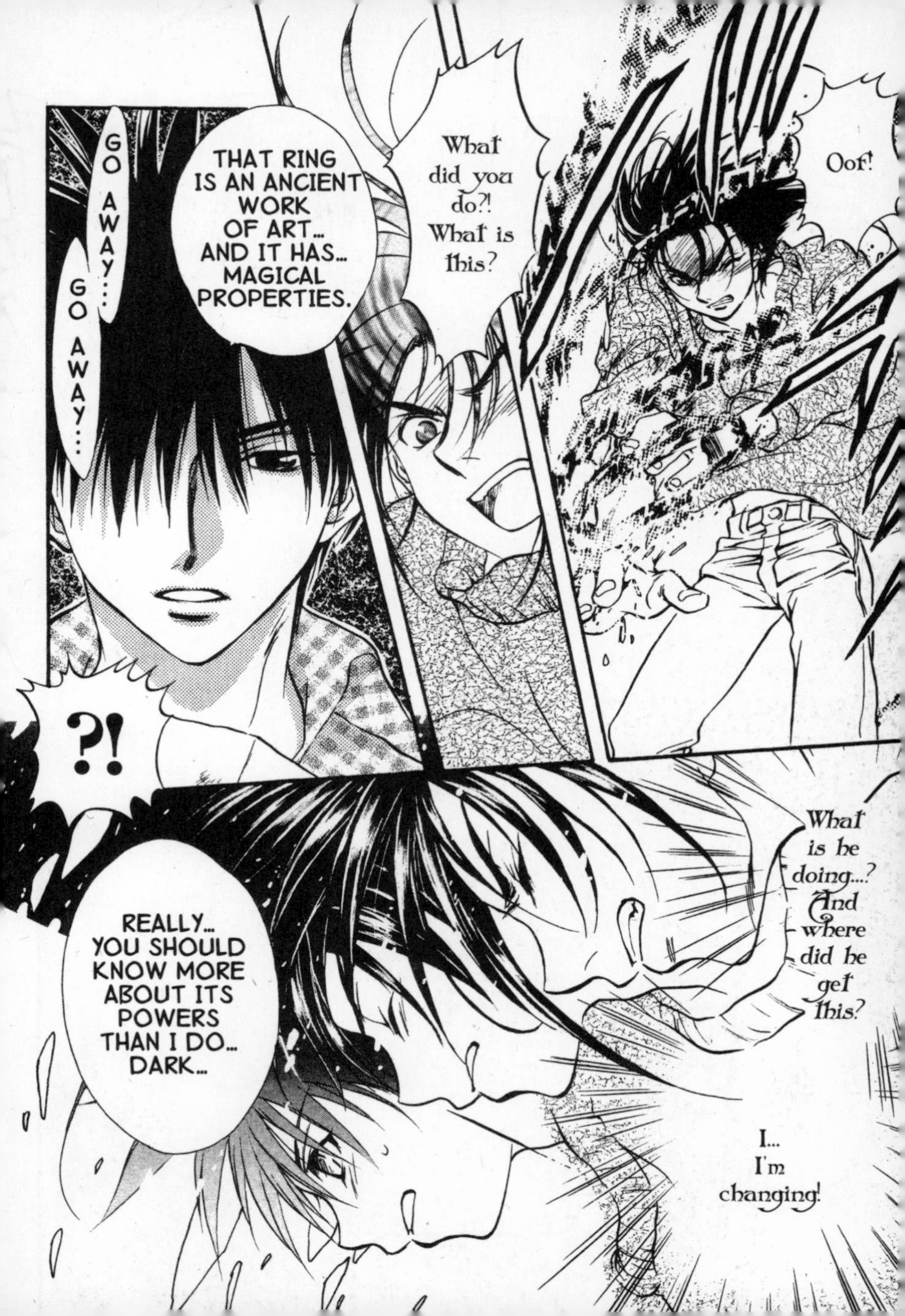

Oof!
What did you do?! What is this?
THAT RING IS AN ANCIENT WORK OF ART... AND IT HAS... MAGICAL PROPERTIES.
GO AWAY...
GO AWAY...
?!
What is he doing...? And where did he get this?
I... I'm changing!
REALLY... YOU SHOULD KNOW MORE ABOUT ITS POWERS THAN I DO... DARK...

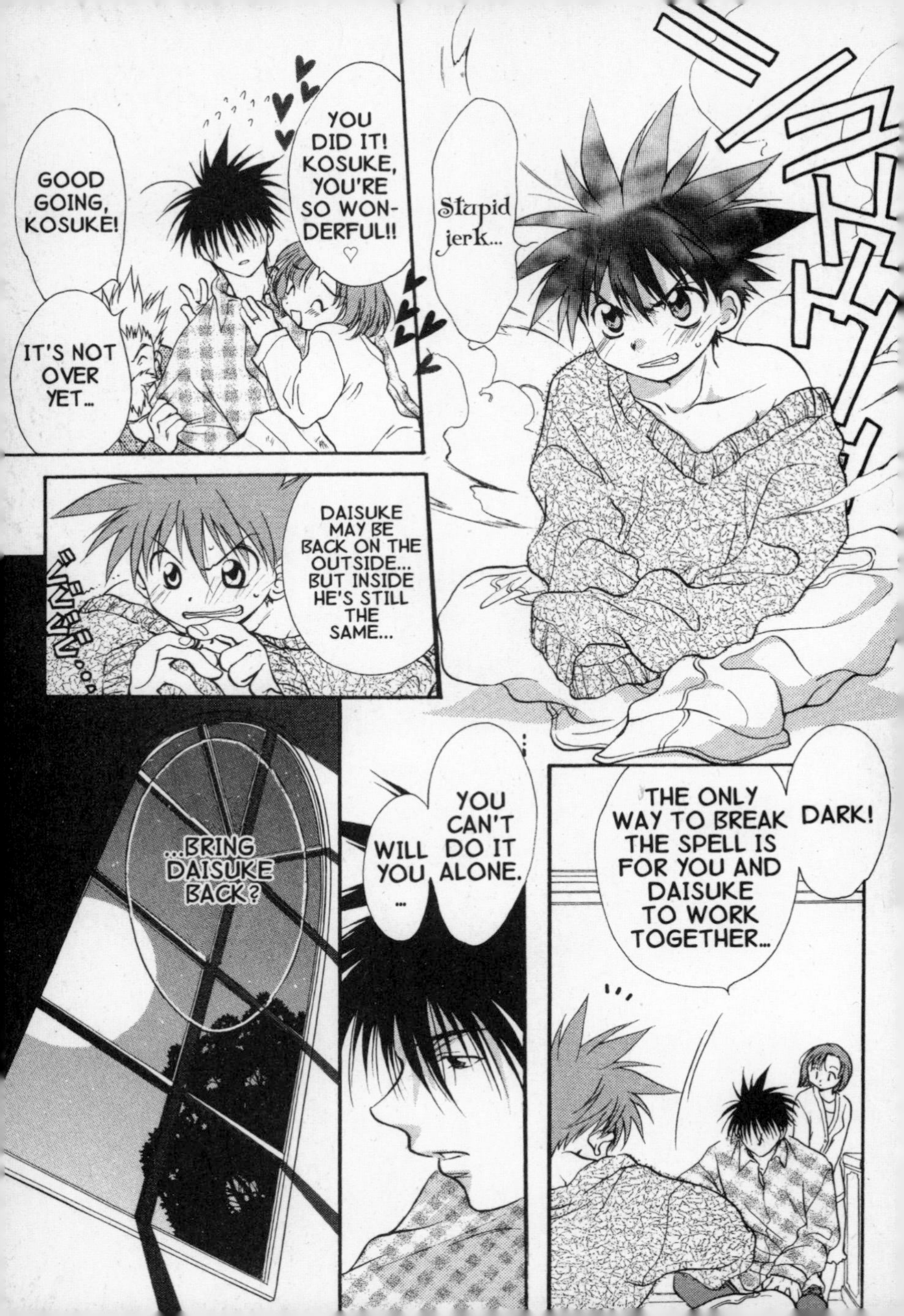

Stupid jerk...
YOU DID IT! KOSUKE, YOU'RE SO WONDERFUL!! ♡
GOOD GOING, KOSUKE!
IT'S NOT OVER YET...
DAISUKE MAY BE BACK ON THE OUTSIDE... BUT INSIDE HE'S STILL THE SAME...
DARK!
THE ONLY WAY TO BREAK THE SPELL IS FOR YOU AND DAISUKE TO WORK TOGETHER...
...
YOU CAN'T DO IT ALONE.
WILL YOU ...
...BRING DAISUKE BACK?

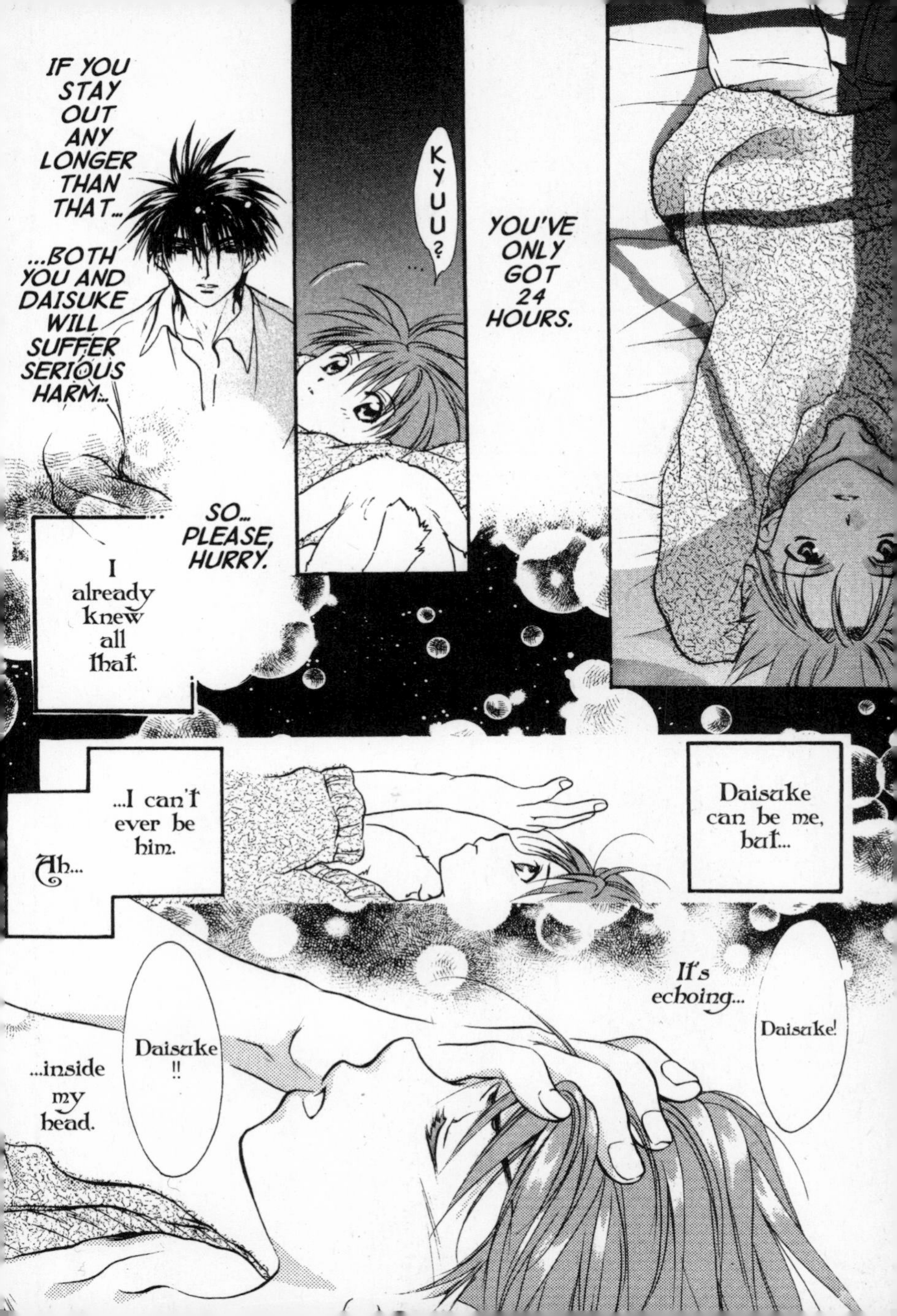

YOU'VE ONLY GOT 24 HOURS.
KYUU?
...
IF YOU STAY OUT ANY LONGER THAN THAT...
...BOTH YOU AND DAISUKE WILL SUFFER SERIOUS HARM...
SO... PLEASE, HURRY.
I already knew all that.
Daisuke can be me, but...
...I can't ever be him.
Ah...
It's echoing...
Daisuke!
Daisuke !!
...inside my head.

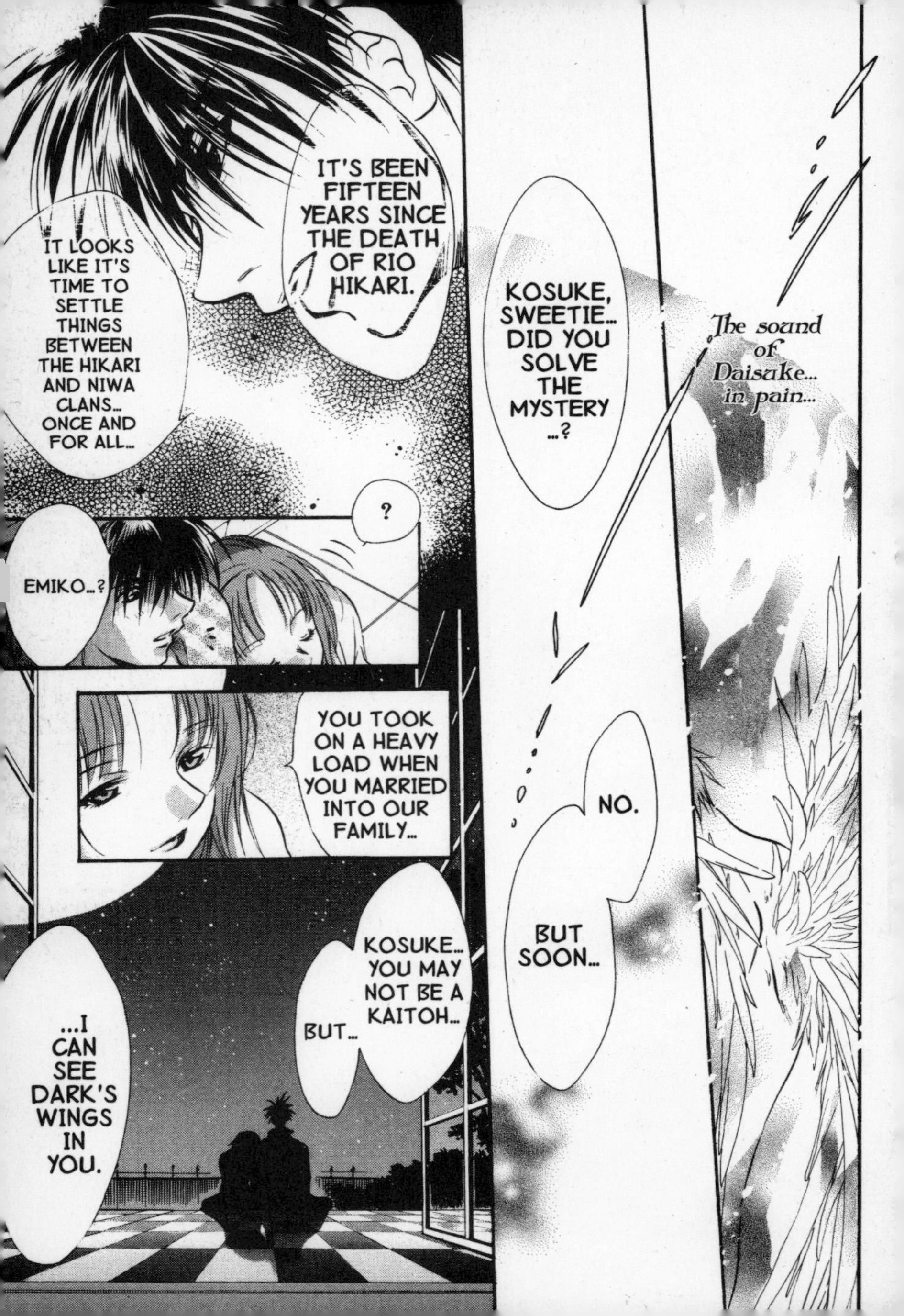
The sound of Daisuke... in pain...
KOSUKE, SWEETIE... DID YOU SOLVE THE MYSTERY ...?
NO.
BUT SOON...
IT'S BEEN FIFTEEN YEARS SINCE THE DEATH OF RIO HIKARI.
IT LOOKS LIKE IT'S TIME TO SETTLE THINGS BETWEEN THE HIKARI AND NIWA CLANS... ONCE AND FOR ALL...
?
EMIKO...?
YOU TOOK ON A HEAVY LOAD WHEN YOU MARRIED INTO OUR FAMILY...
KOSUKE... YOU MAY NOT BE A KAITOH...
BUT...
...I CAN SEE DARK'S WINGS IN YOU.

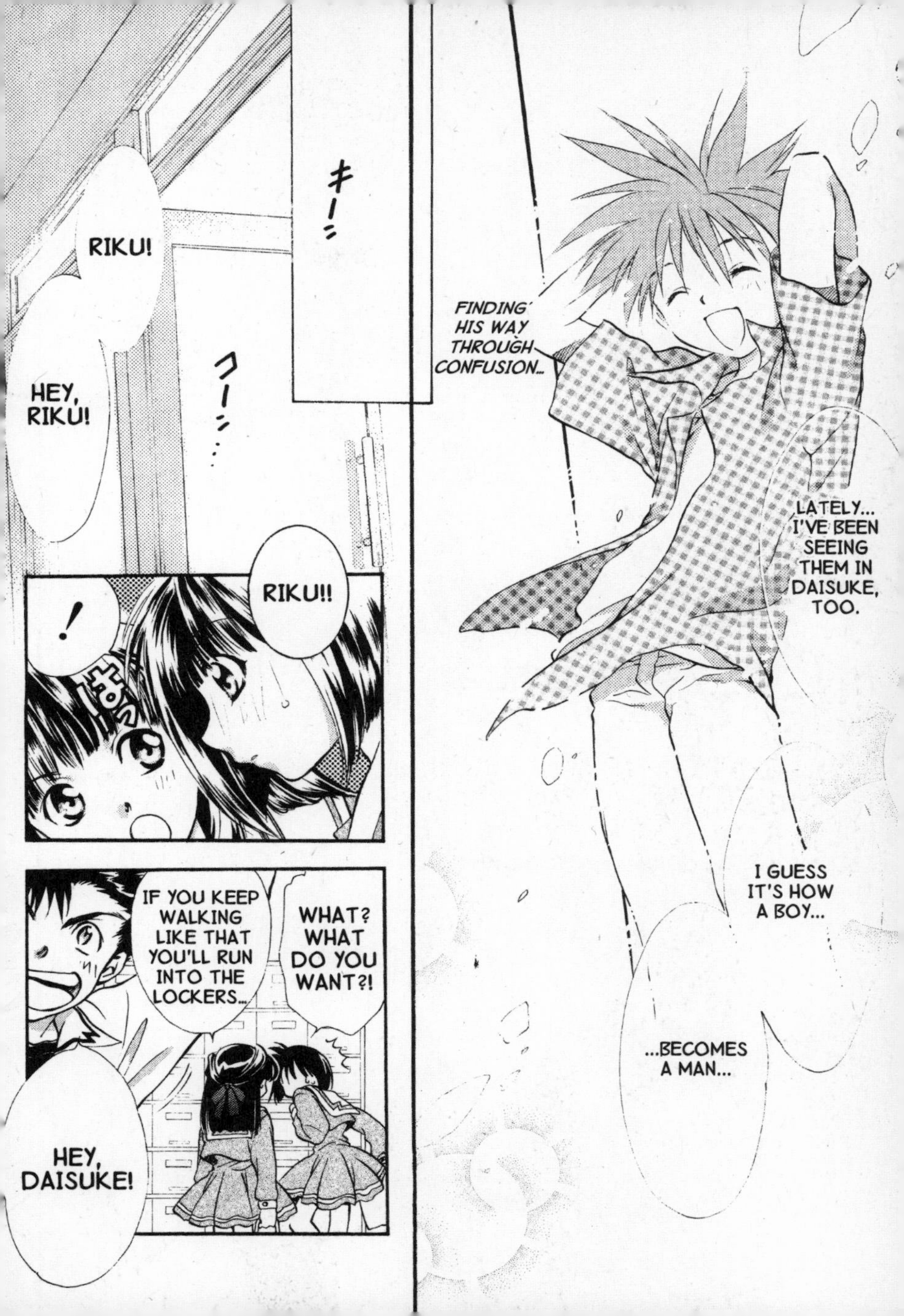
FINDING HIS WAY THROUGH CONFUSION...
LATELY... I'VE BEEN SEEING THEM IN DAISUKE, TOO.
I GUESS IT'S HOW A BOY...
...BECOMES A MAN...
RIKU!
HEY, RIKU!
RIKU!!
!
WHAT? WHAT DO YOU WANT?!
IF YOU KEEP WALKING LIKE THAT YOU'LL RUN INTO THE LOCKERS...
HEY, DAISUKE!

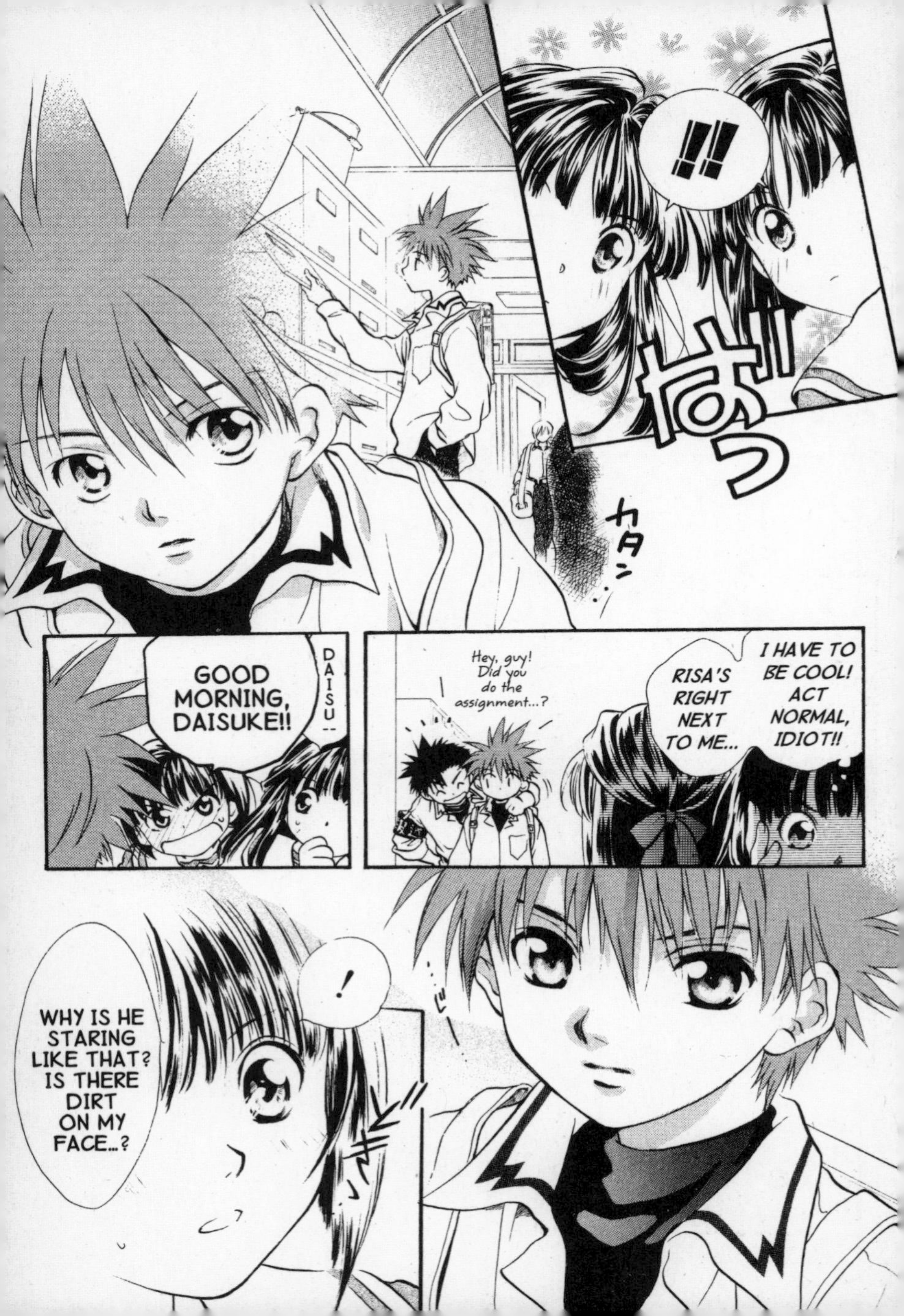
!!
はっ
カタン…
I HAVE TO BE COOL! ACT NORMAL, IDIOT!!
RISA'S RIGHT NEXT TO ME...
Hey, guy! Did you do the assignment...?
DAISU--
GOOD MORNING, DAISUKE!!
!
WHY IS HE STARING LIKE THAT? IS THERE DIRT ON MY FACE...?

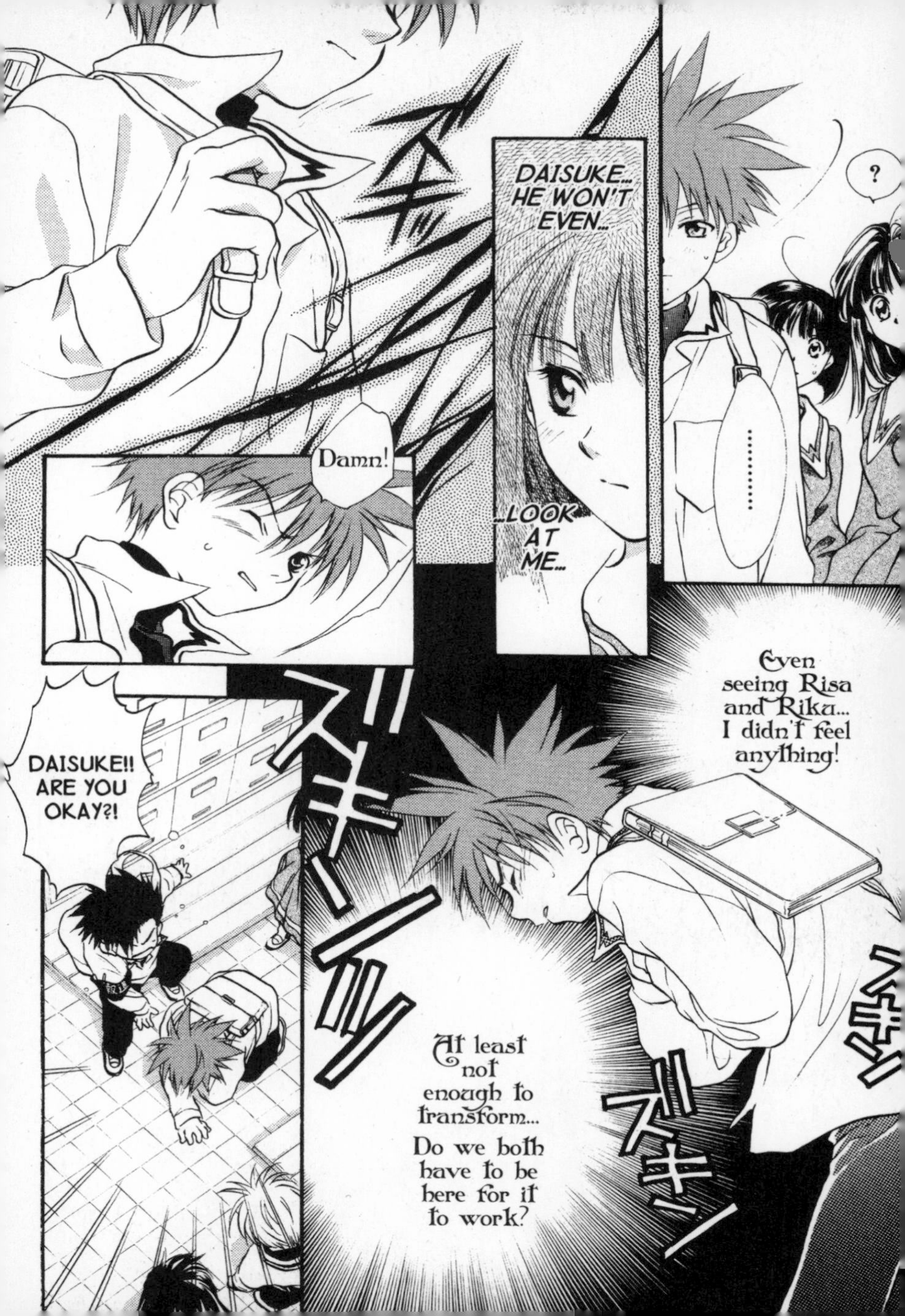
?
DAISUKE... HE WON'T EVEN...
...LOOK AT ME...
Damn!
Even seeing Risa and Riku... I didn't feel anything!
At least not enough to transform... Do we both have to be here for it to work?
DAISUKE!! ARE YOU OKAY?!

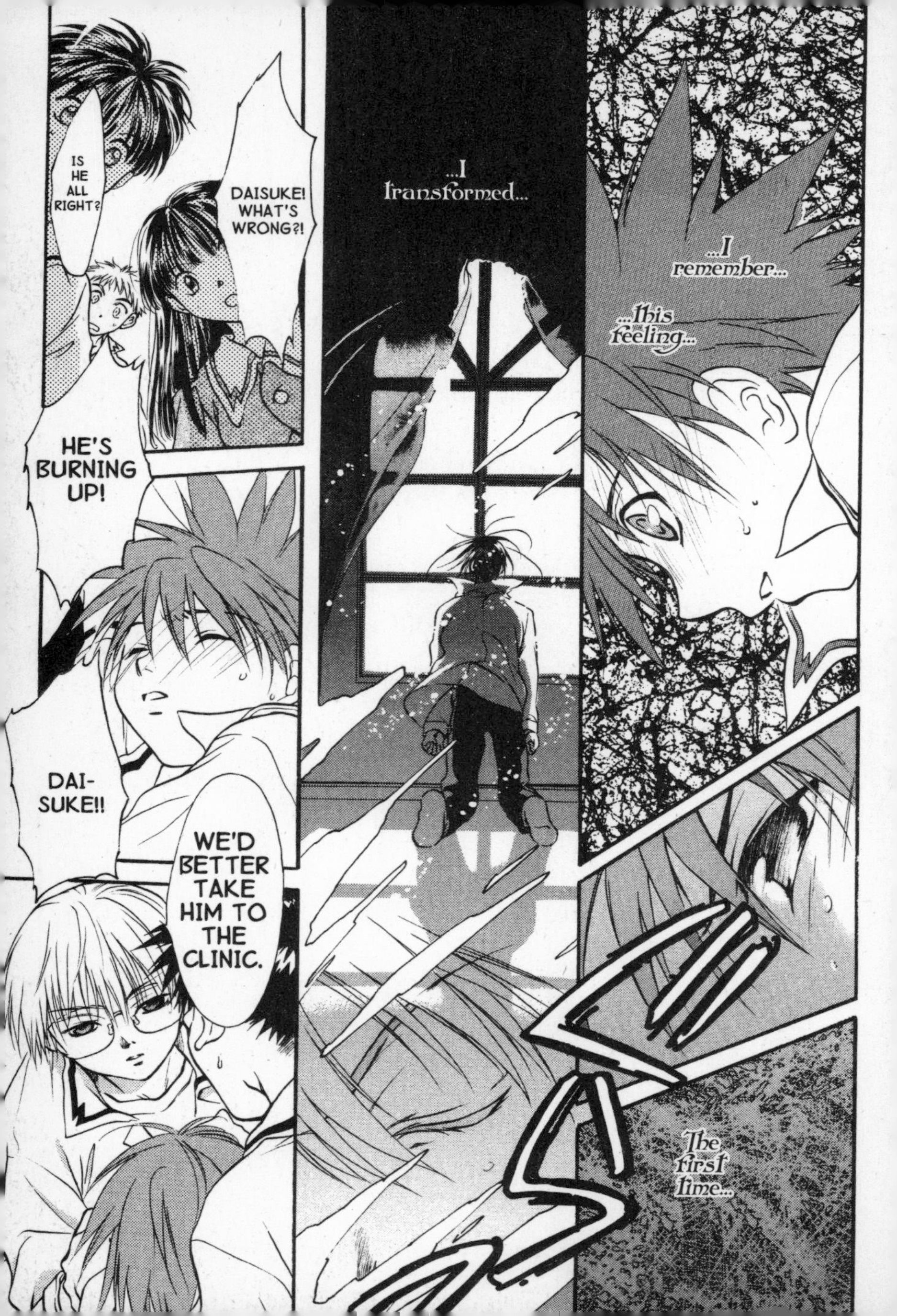

...I remember...
...this feeling...
The first time...
...I transformed...
DAISUKE! WHAT'S WRONG?!
IS HE ALL RIGHT?
HE'S BURNING UP!
DAI-SUKE!!
WE'D BETTER TAKE HIM TO THE CLINIC.

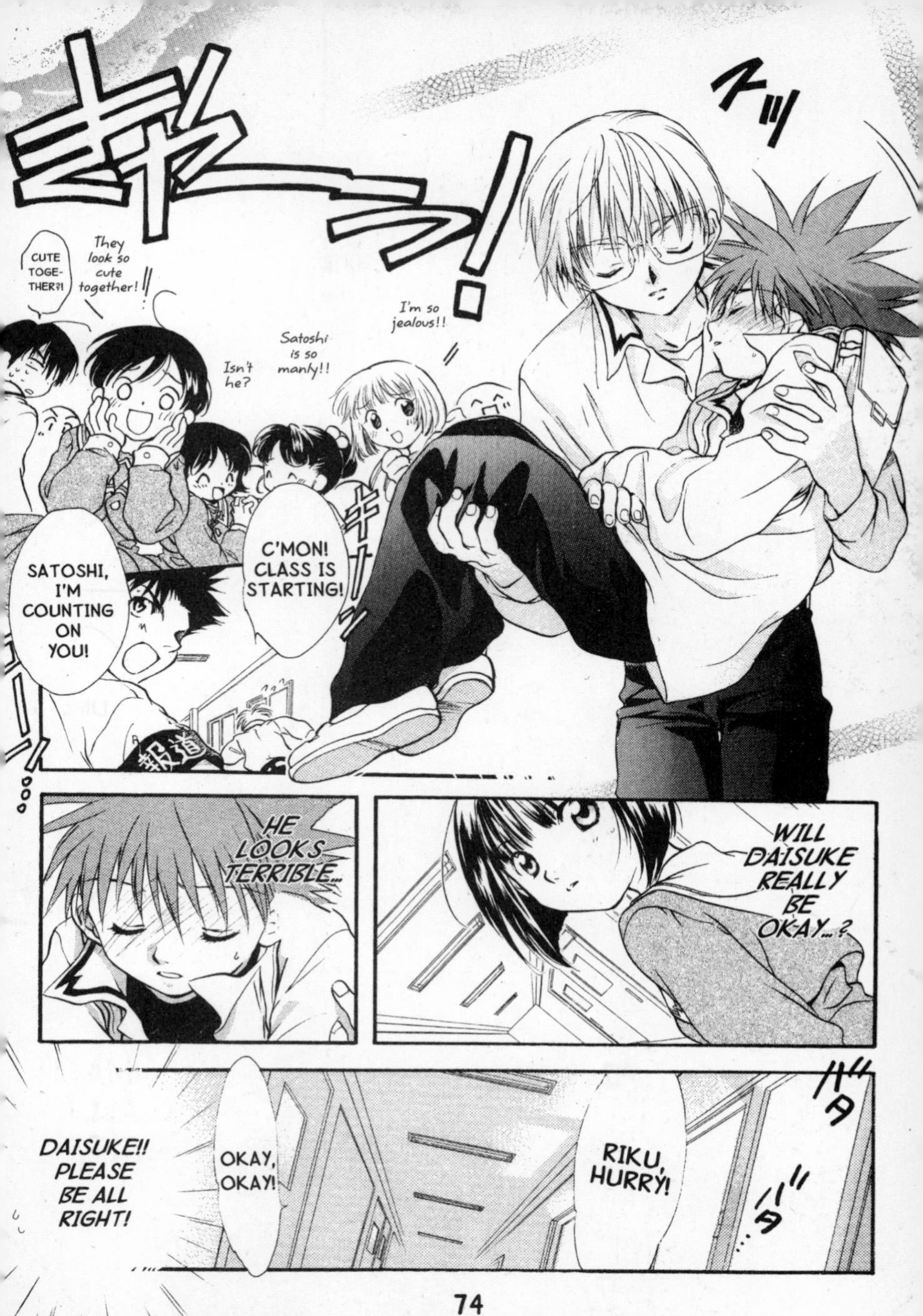

They look so cute together!
CUTE TOGE-THER?!
I'm so jealous!!
Satoshi is so manly!!
Isn't he?
C'MON! CLASS IS STARTING!
SATOSHI, I'M COUNTING ON YOU!
WILL DAISUKE REALLY BE OKAY...?
HE LOOKS TERRIBLE...
RIKU, HURRY!
OKAY, OKAY!
DAISUKE!! PLEASE BE ALL RIGHT!

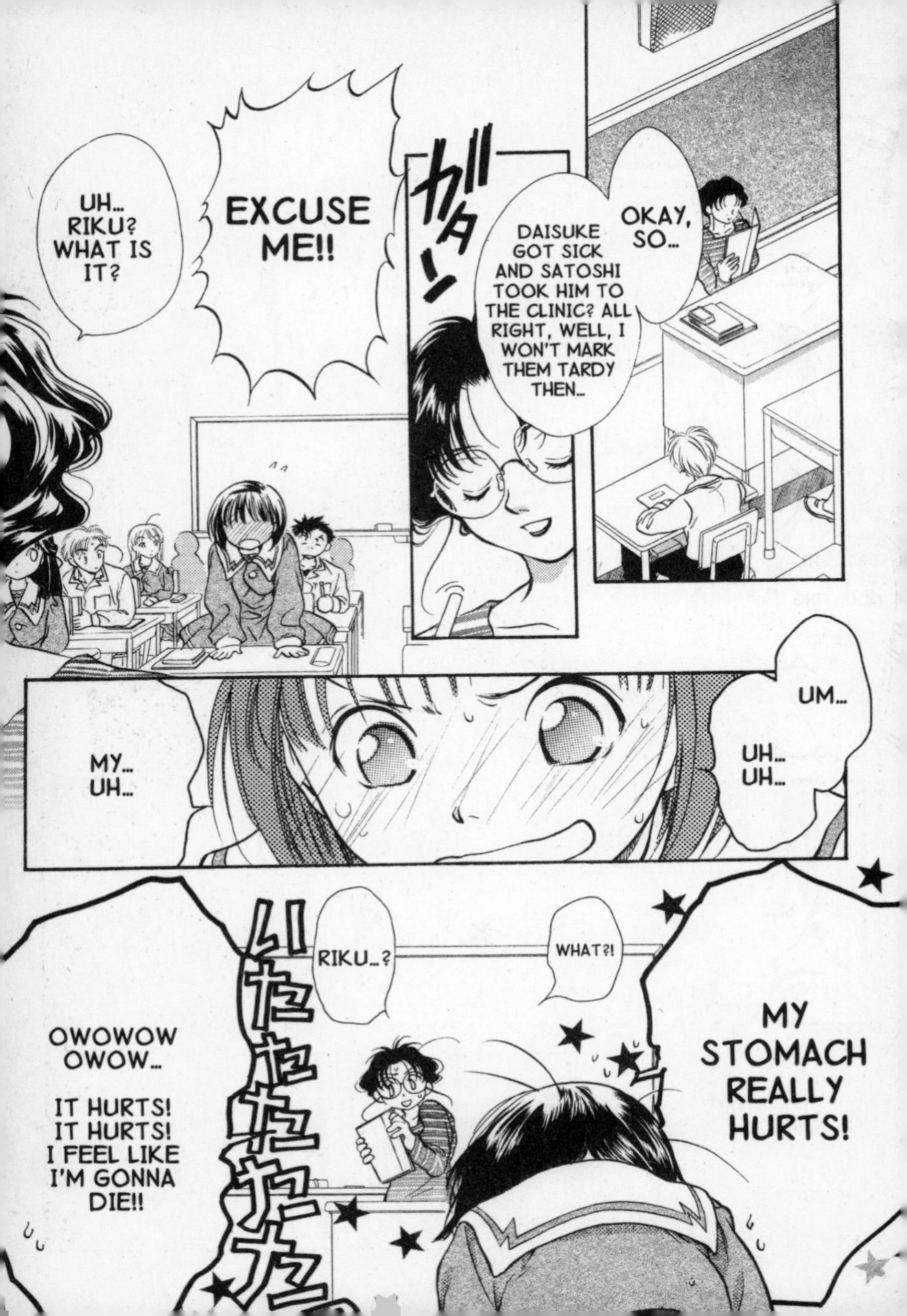
OKAY, SO...
DAISUKE GOT SICK AND SATOSHI TOOK HIM TO THE CLINIC? ALL RIGHT, WELL, I WON'T MARK THEM TARDY THEN...
EXCUSE ME!!
UH... RIKU? WHAT IS IT?
UM...
UH... UH...
MY... UH...
MY STOMACH REALLY HURTS!
WHAT?!
RIKU...?
OWOWOW OWOW...
IT HURTS! IT HURTS! I FEEL LIKE I'M GONNA DIE!!

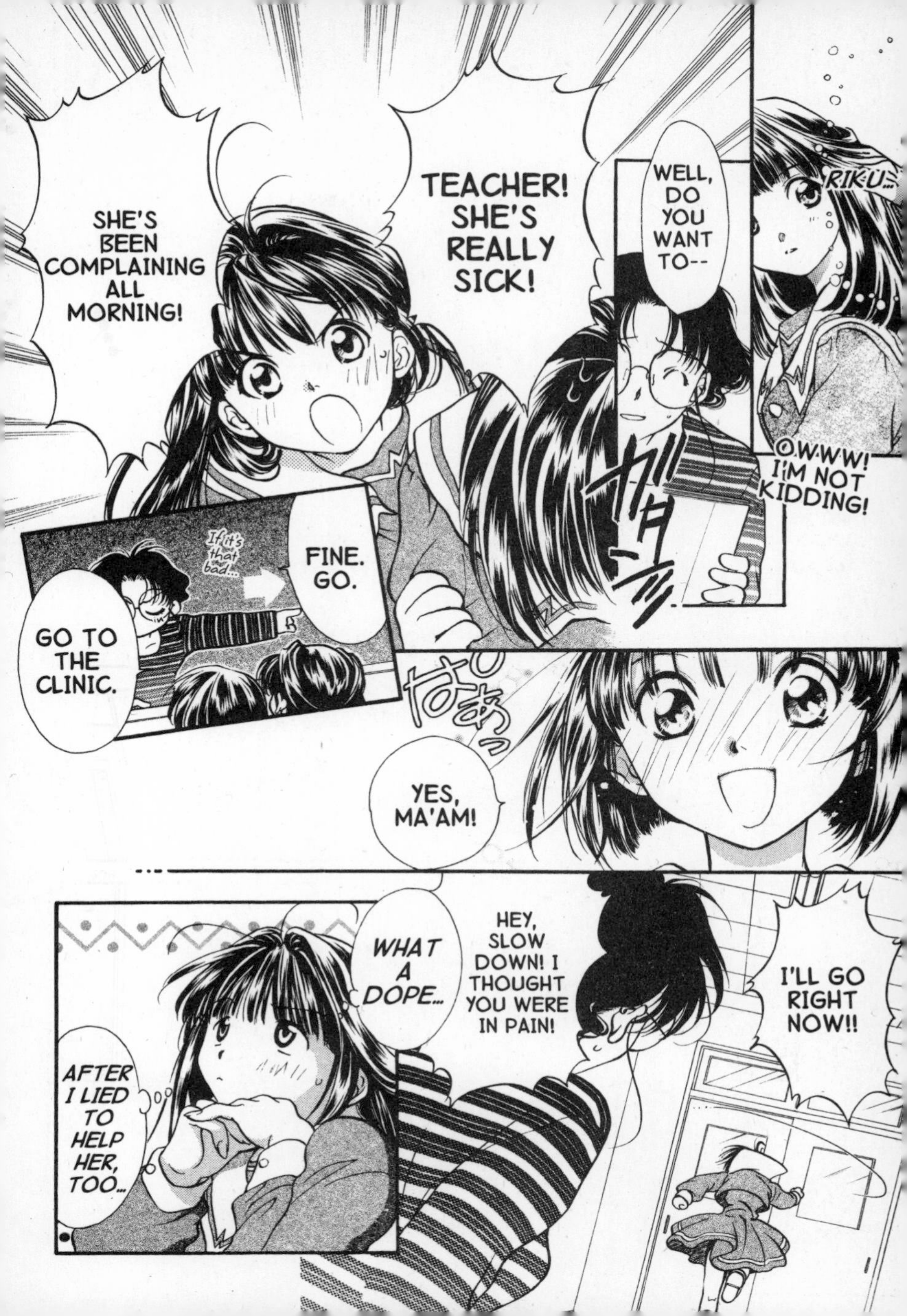
RIKU...
OWWW! I'M NOT KIDDING!
WELL, DO YOU WANT TO--
TEACHER! SHE'S REALLY SICK!
SHE'S BEEN COMPLAINING ALL MORNING!
If it's that bad...
FINE. GO.
GO TO THE CLINIC.
YES, MA'AM!
I'LL GO RIGHT NOW!!
HEY, SLOW DOWN! I THOUGHT YOU WERE IN PAIN!
WHAT A DOPE...
AFTER I LIED TO HELP HER, TOO...

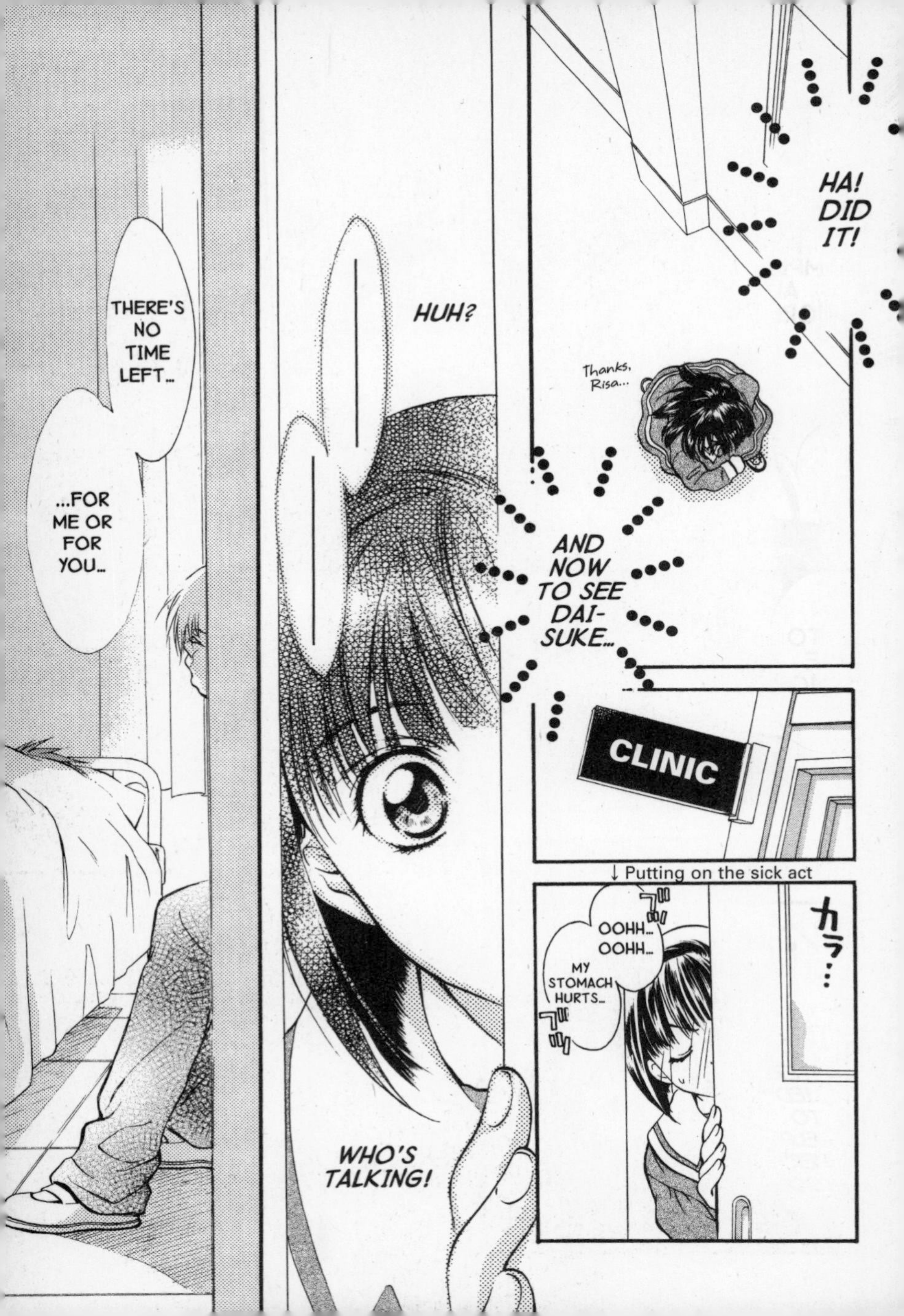
HA! DID IT!
Thanks, Risa...
AND NOW TO SEE DAI-SUKE...
CLINIC
↓ Putting on the sick act
カラ...
OOHH... OOHH... MY STOMACH HURTS...
HUH?
WHO'S TALKING!
THERE'S NO TIME LEFT...
...FOR ME OR FOR YOU...

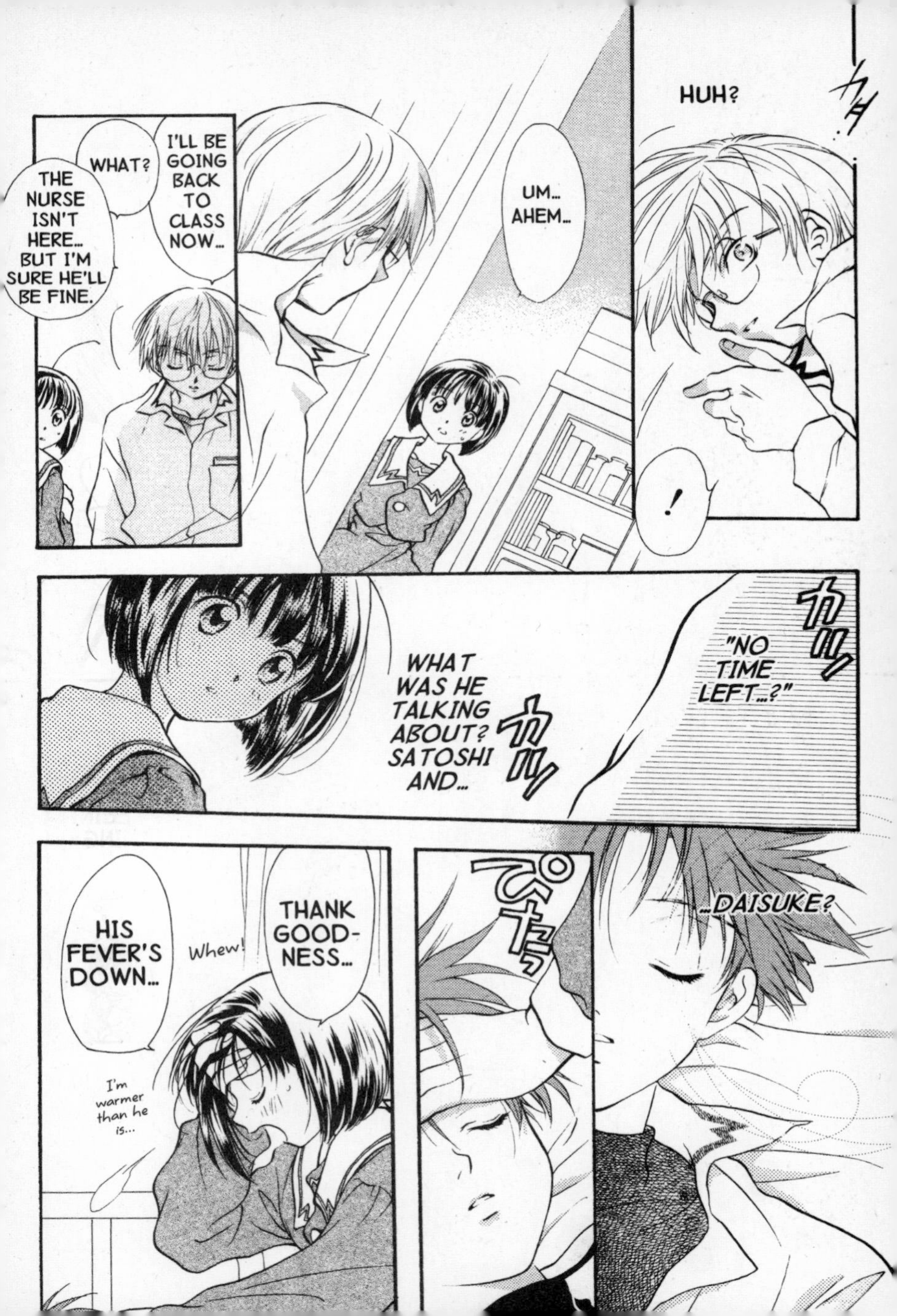

HUH?
!
UM... AHEM...
I'LL BE GOING BACK TO CLASS NOW...
WHAT?
THE NURSE ISN'T HERE... BUT I'M SURE HE'LL BE FINE.
"NO TIME LEFT...?"
WHAT WAS HE TALKING ABOUT? SATOSHI AND...
...DAISUKE?
THANK GOODNESS...
Whew!
HIS FEVER'S DOWN...
I'm warmer than he is...

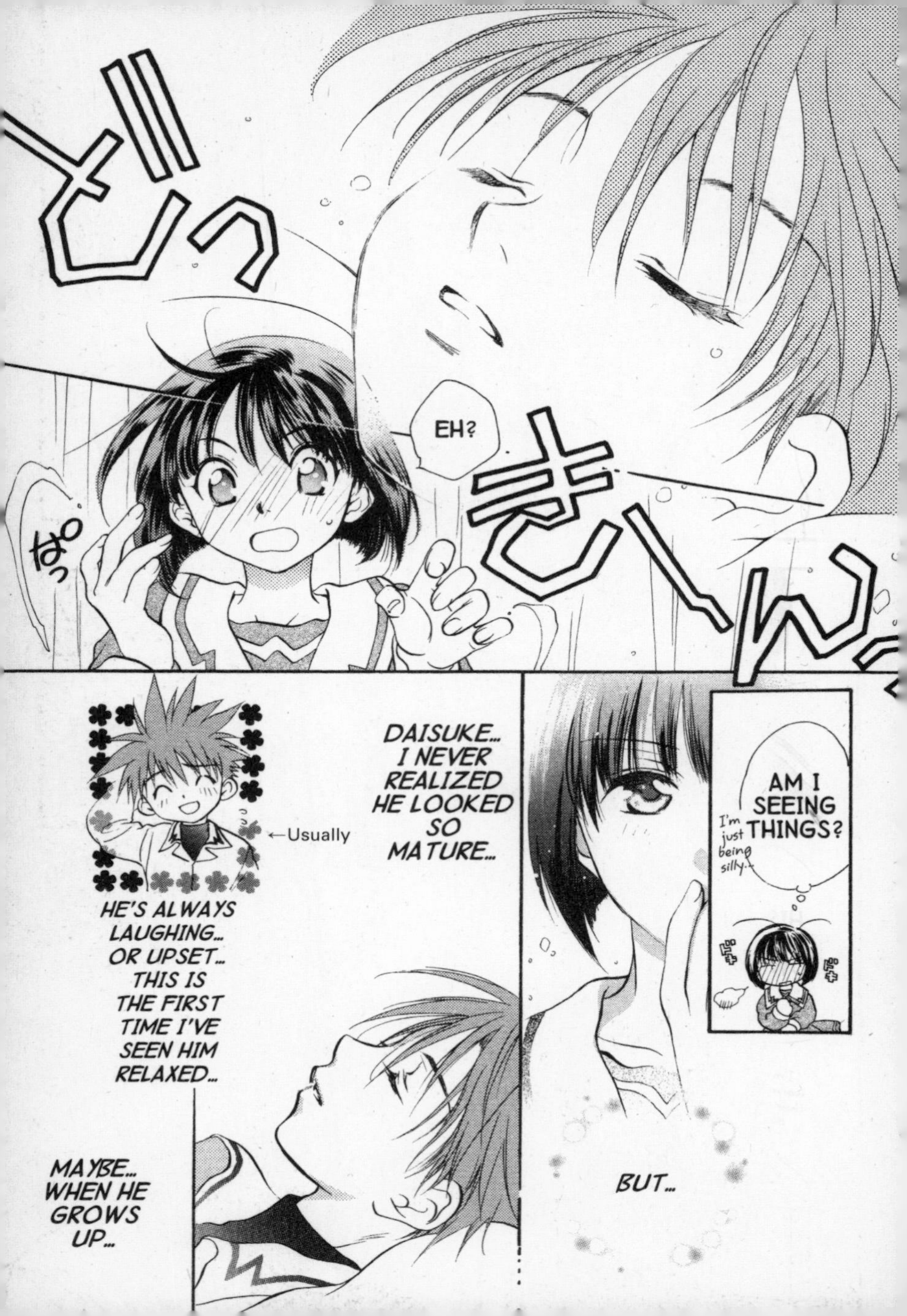
EH?
ぱっ
AM I SEEING THINGS?
I'm just being silly...
BUT...
DAISUKE... I NEVER REALIZED HE LOOKED SO MATURE...
←Usually
HE'S ALWAYS LAUGHING... OR UPSET... THIS IS THE FIRST TIME I'VE SEEN HIM RELAXED...
MAYBE... WHEN HE GROWS UP...

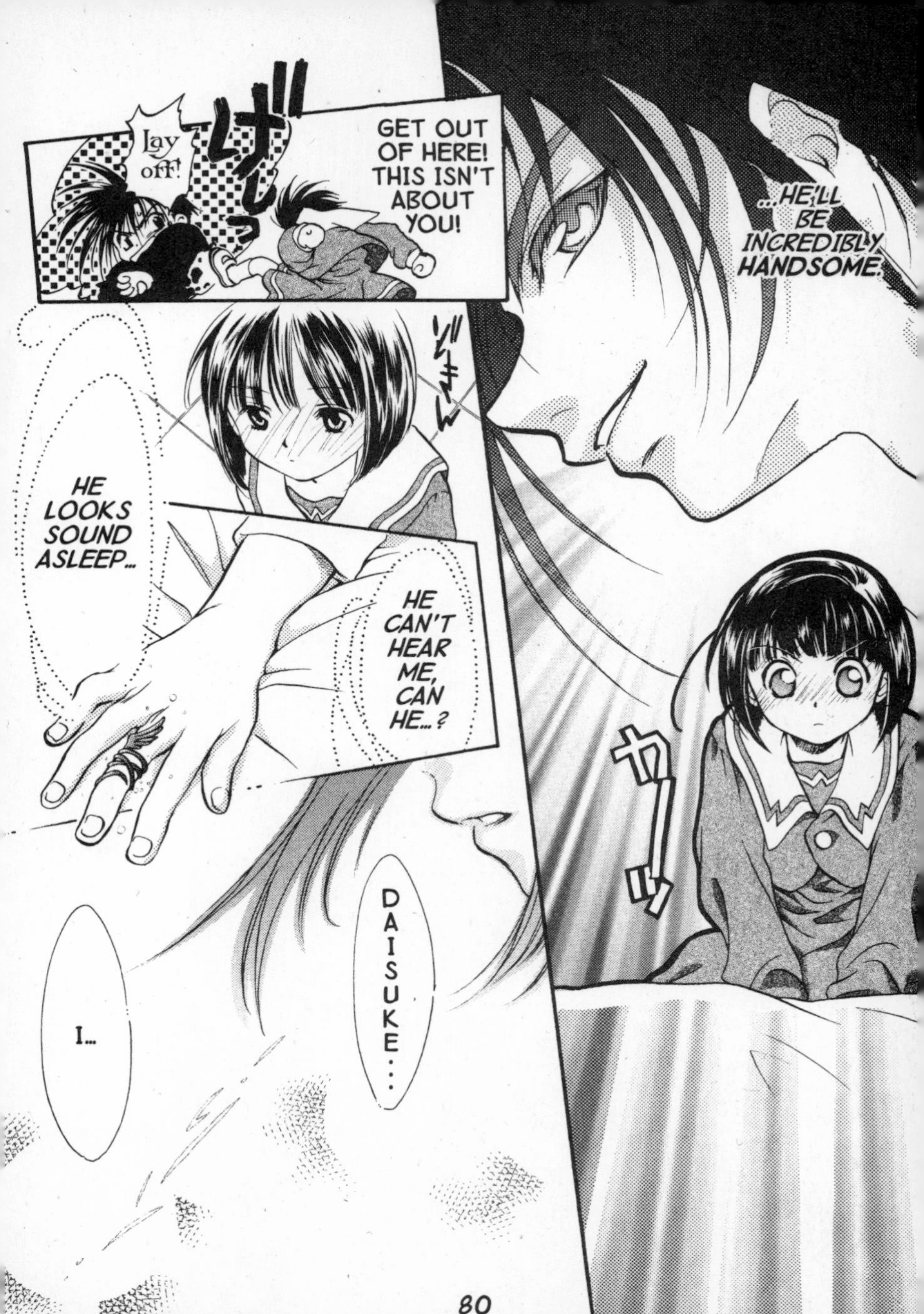
...HE'LL BE INCREDIBLY HANDSOME.
GET OUT OF HERE! THIS ISN'T ABOUT YOU!
Lay off!
HE LOOKS SOUND ASLEEP...
HE CAN'T HEAR ME, CAN HE...?
DAISUKE...
I...

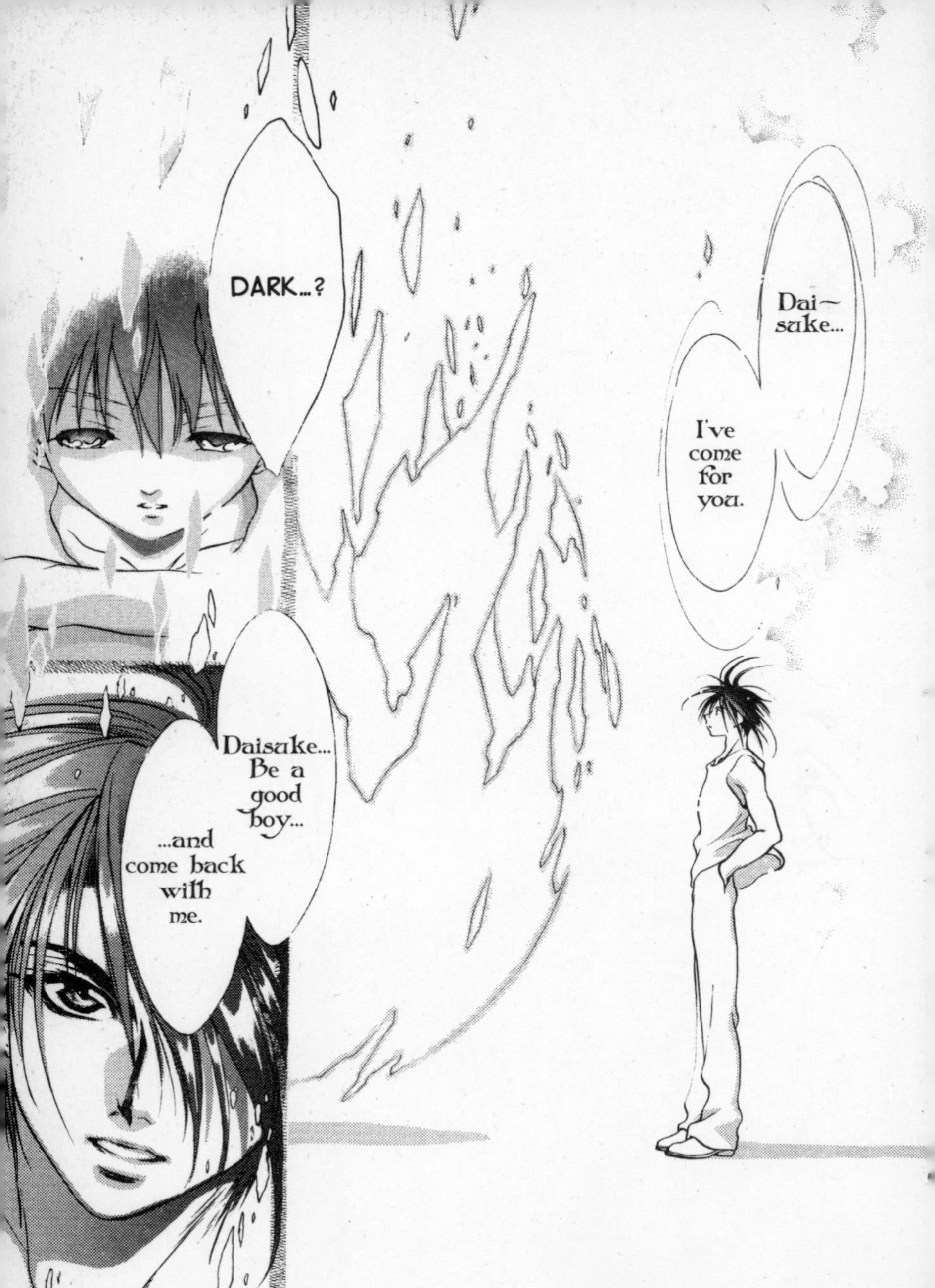
Dai-suke...
I've come for you.
DARK...?
Daisuke... Be a good boy...
...and come back with me.

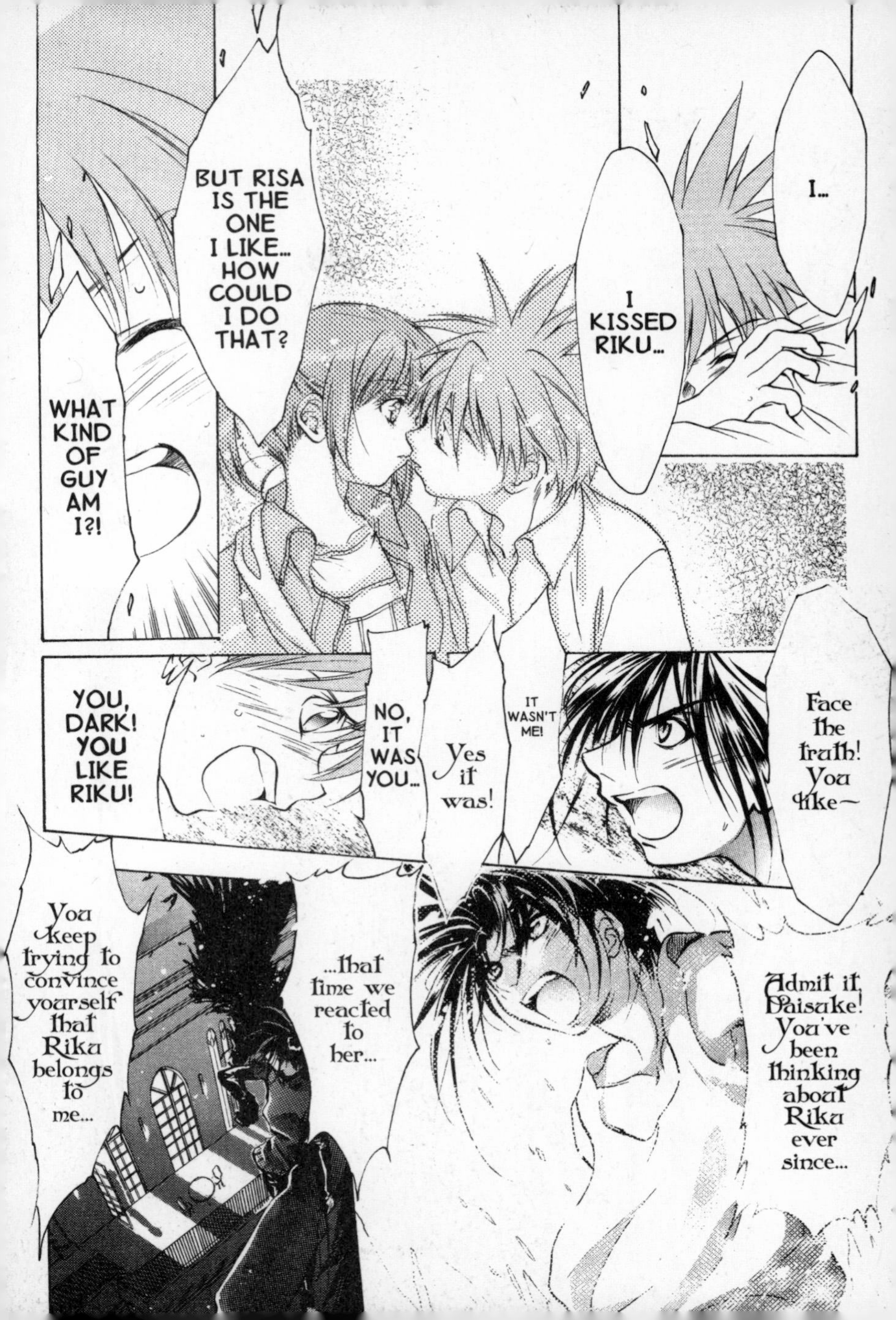
I...
I KISSED RIKU...
BUT RISA IS THE ONE I LIKE... HOW COULD I DO THAT?
WHAT KIND OF GUY AM I?!
Face the truth! You like~
IT WASN'T ME!
Yes it was!
NO, IT WAS YOU...
YOU, DARK! YOU LIKE RIKU!
Admit it, Daisuke! You've been thinking about Riku ever since...
...that time we reacted to her...
You keep trying to convince yourself that Riku belongs to me...

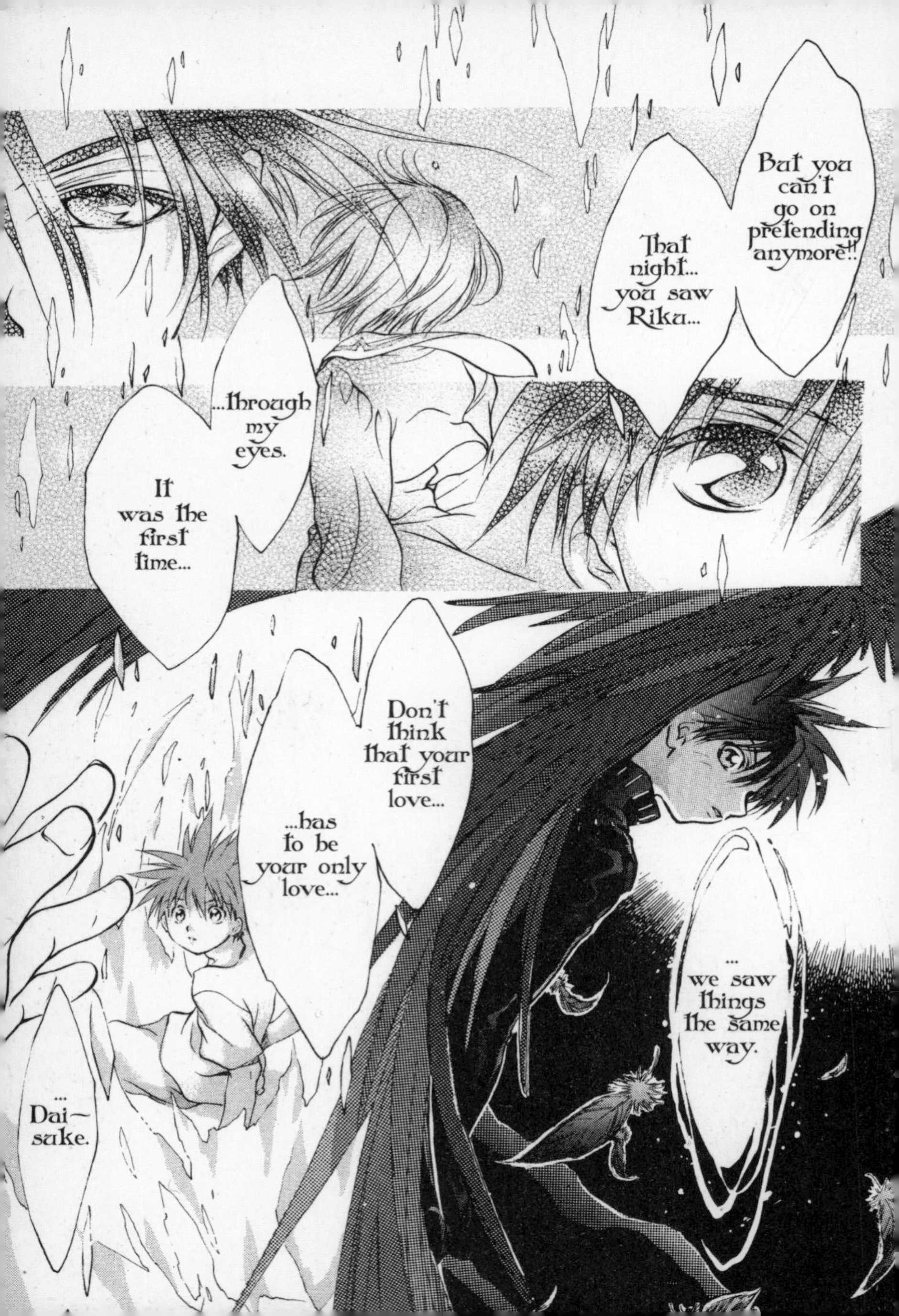
But you can't go on pretending anymore!!
That night... you saw Riku...
...through my eyes.
It was the first time...
...we saw things the same way.
Don't think that your first love...
...has to be your only love...
...Dai-suke.

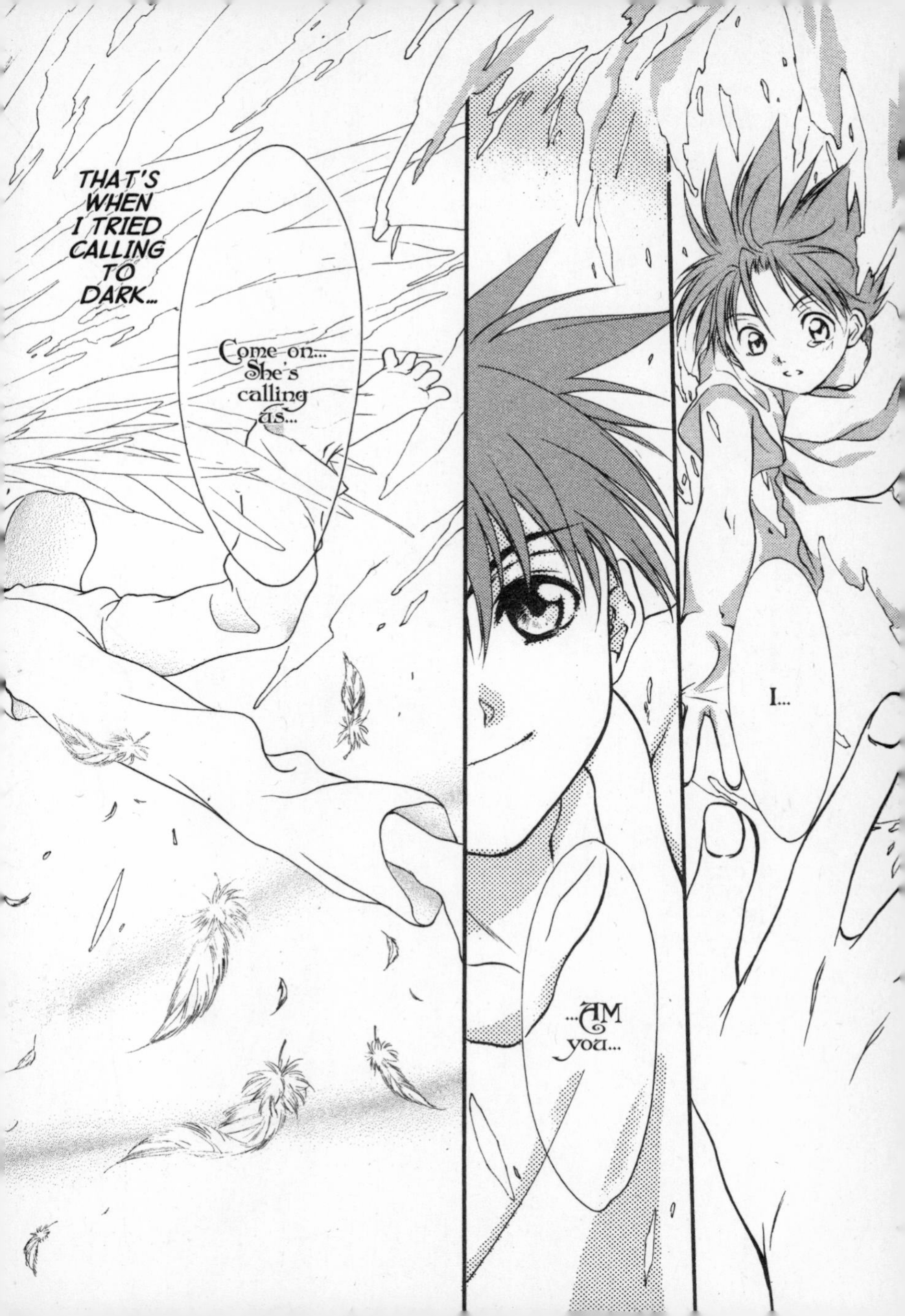
THAT'S WHEN I TRIED CALLING TO DARK...
Come on... She's calling us...
I...
...AM you...

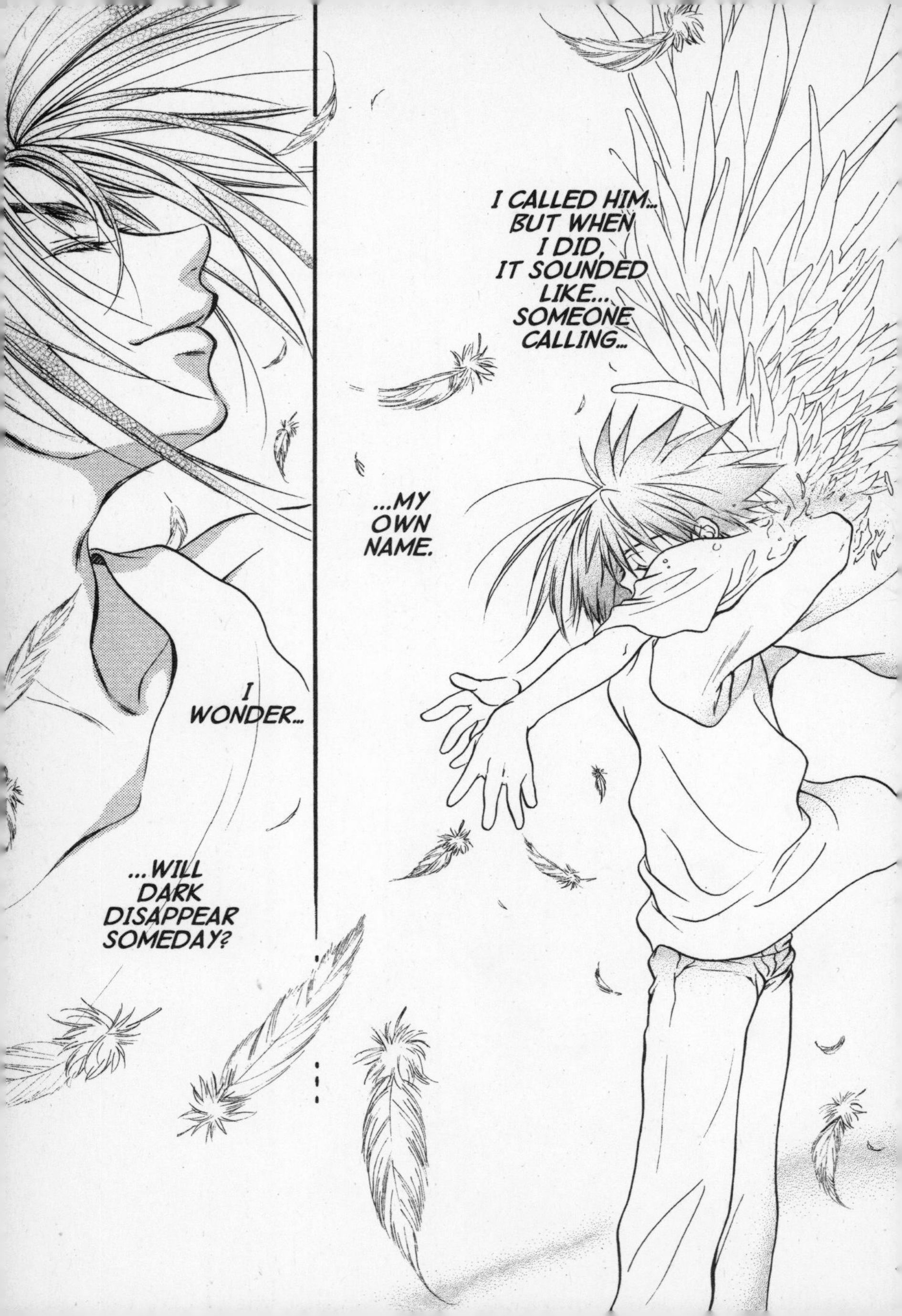
I CALLED HIM... BUT WHEN I DID, IT SOUNDED LIKE... SOMEONE CALLING...
...MY OWN NAME.
I WONDER...
...WILL DARK DISAPPEAR SOMEDAY?

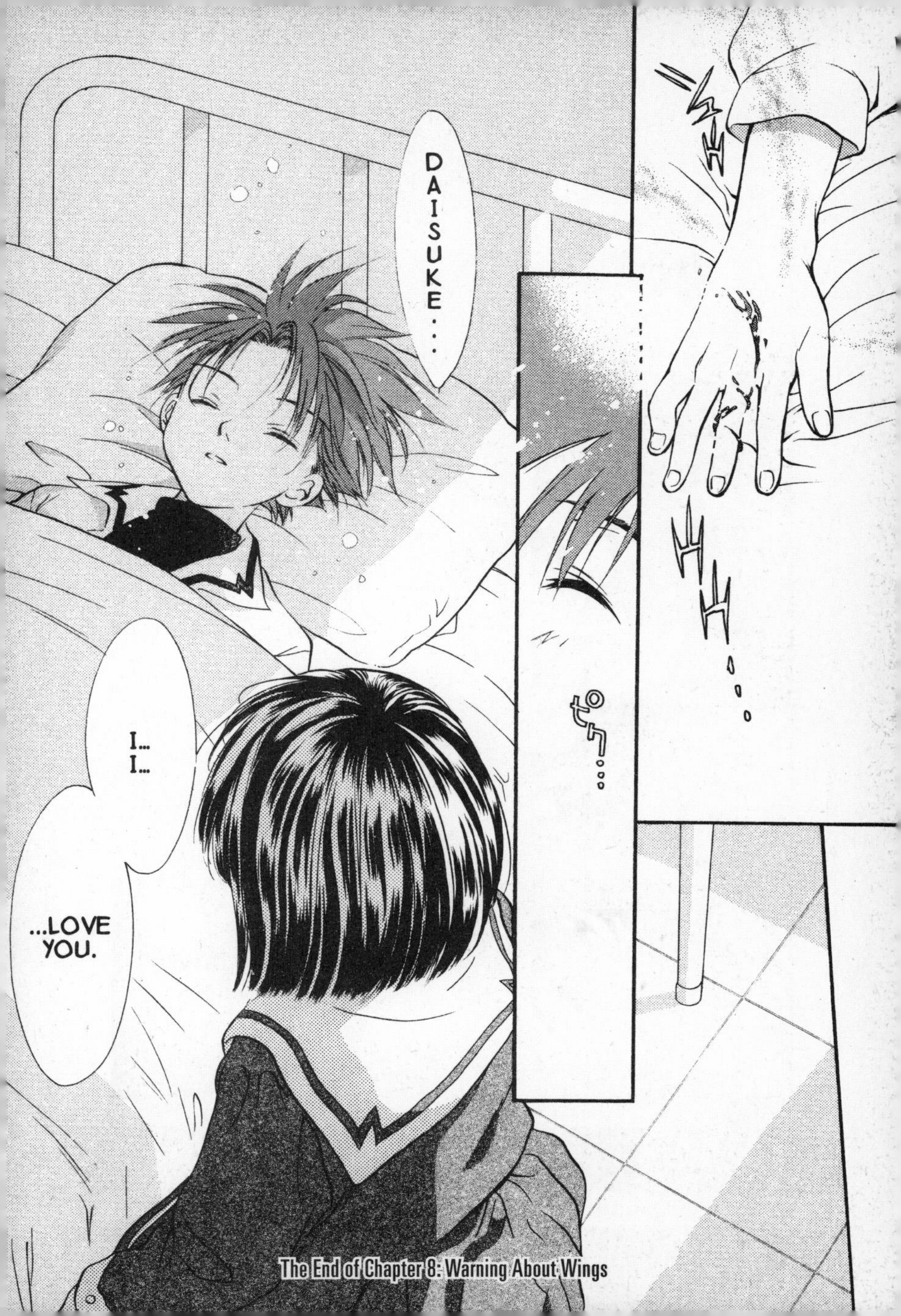
ピク…
DAISUKE...
I... I...
...LOVE YOU.

The End of Chapter 8: Warning About Wings

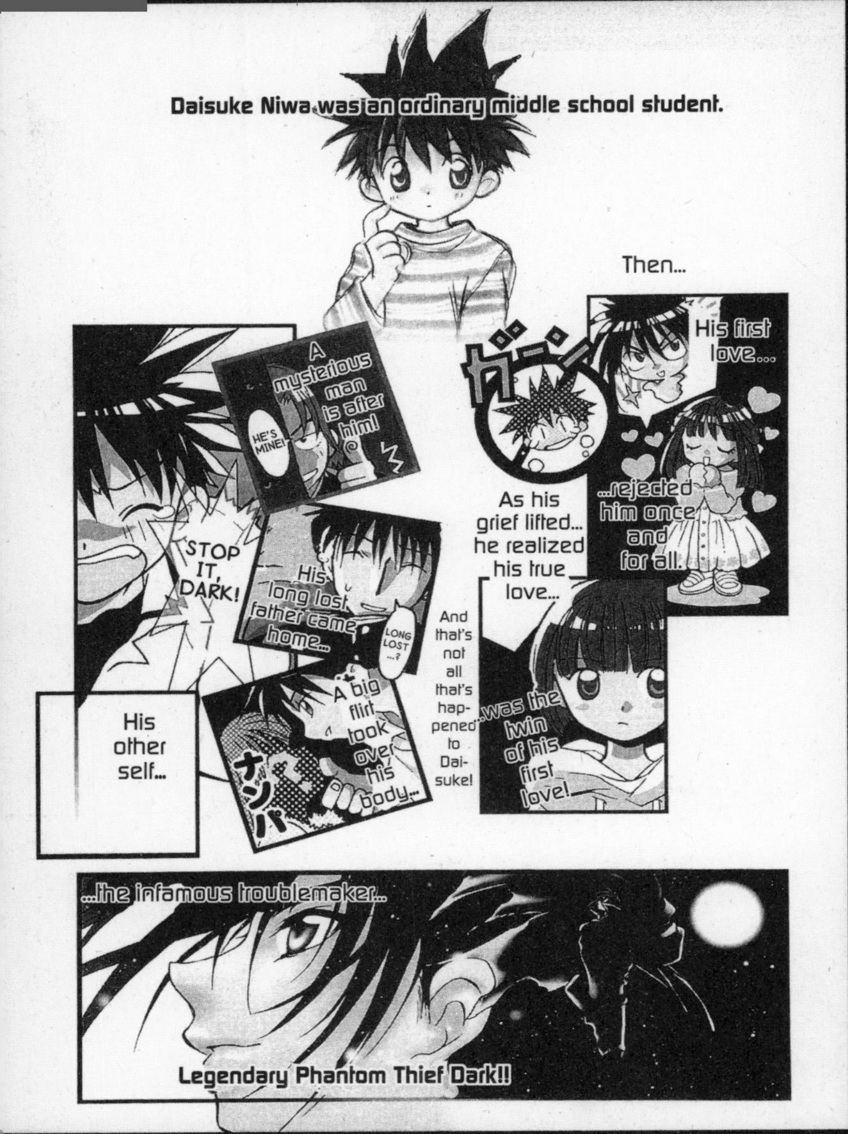
Daisuke Niwa was an ordinary middle school student.
Then...
His first love...
ガーン
...rejected him once and for all.
As his grief lifted... he realized his true love...
...was the twin of his first love!
A mysterious man is after him!
HE'S MINE!
His long lost father came home...
LONG LOST ...?
STOP IT, DARK!
A big flirt took over his body...
ナンパ
And that's not all that's happened to Daisuke!
His other self...
...the infamous troublemaker...
Legendary Phantom Thief Dark!!

9

Chapter 9: Warning About a Mask

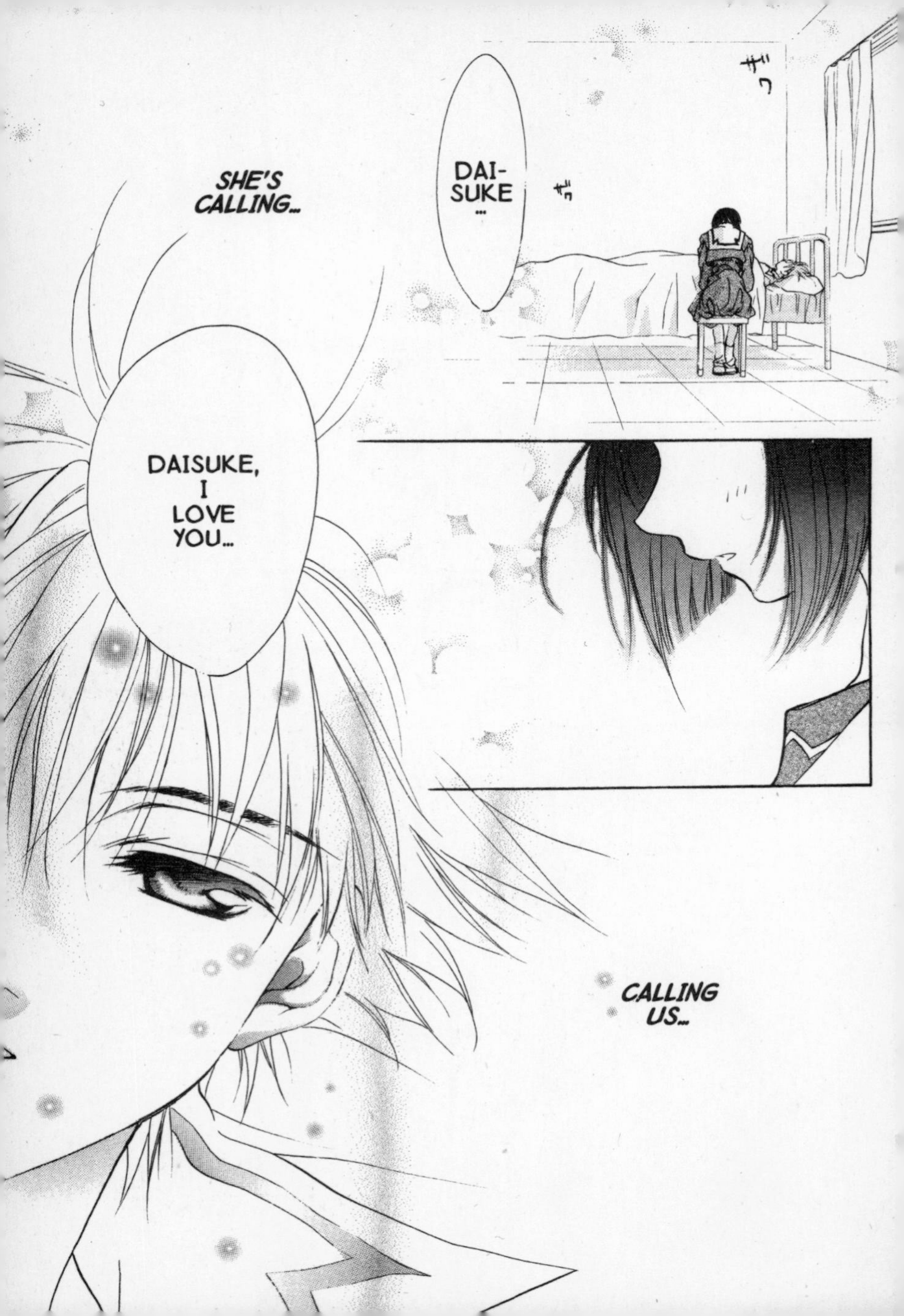
DAI-SUKE...
SHE'S CALLING...
DAISUKE, I LOVE YOU...
CALLING US...

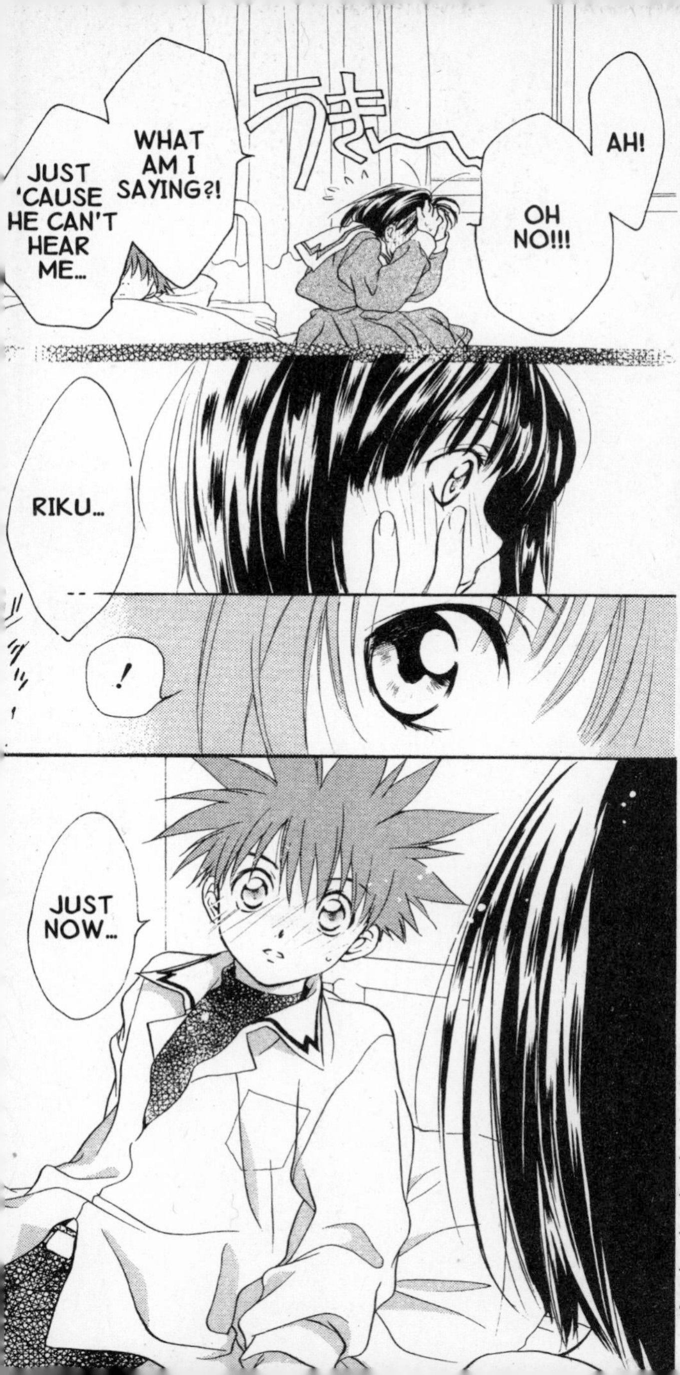
AH!
OH NO!!!
うき〜
WHAT AM I SAYING?!
JUST 'CAUSE HE CAN'T HEAR ME...
RIKU...
!
JUST NOW...

NO.1

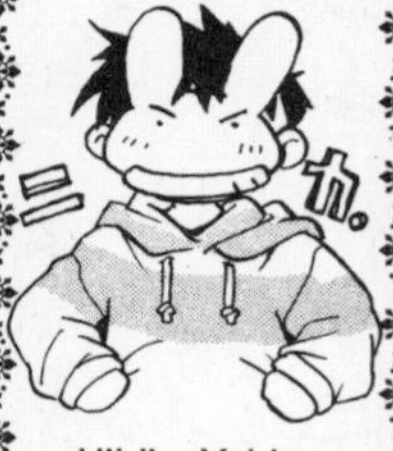
ニカ。

Hi! I'm Yukiru Sugisaki. Finally, volume 3 of DNAngel! This is the first time I've written anything to you in one of these spaces... I hope you don't mind! So...a lot of people have asked me why I'm always wearing my rabbit mask. Well...that's a very good question! I don't really know!! Somehow, I feel more comfortable wearing it... (Weird, I know...) And no, I don't wear it in real life!! I hope you didn't think I did!! I guess maybe you can think of it as...an expression of the power of a rabbit lover. (Luckily, there seem to be a lot of rabbit lovers!♡) To be continued...

② Go!

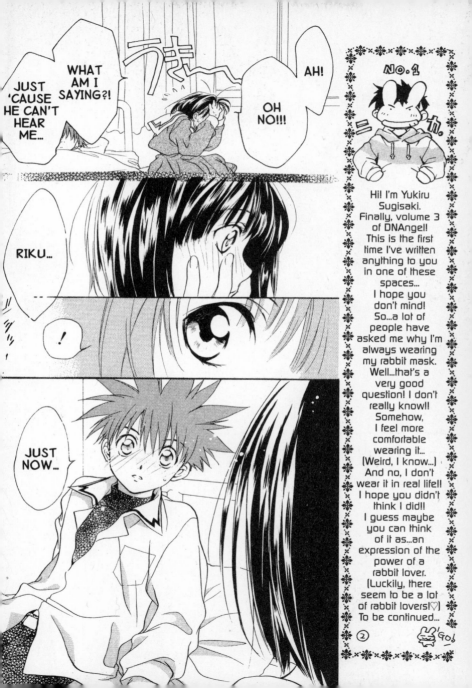

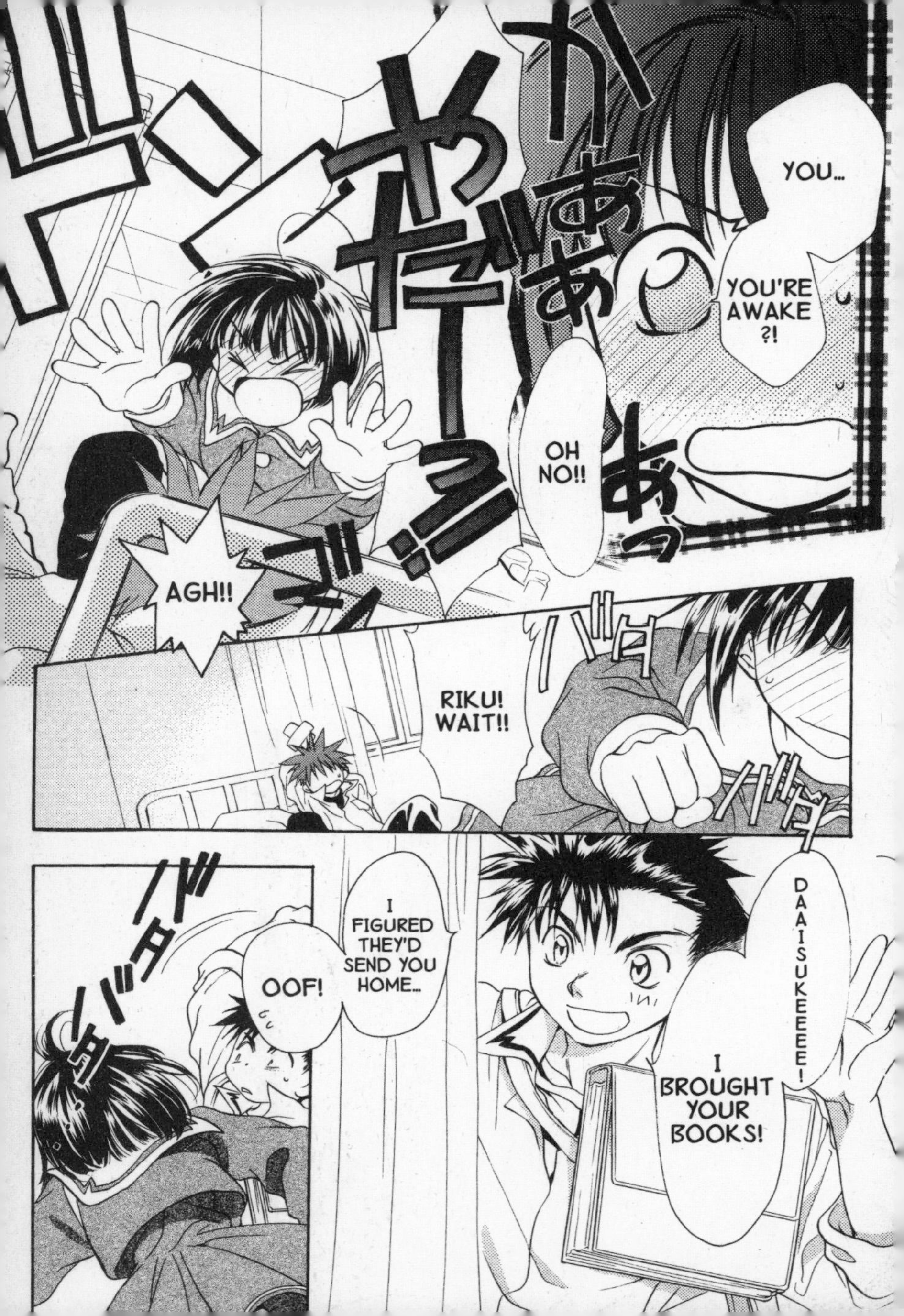
YOU...
YOU'RE AWAKE ?!
OH NO!!
AGH!!
RIKU! WAIT!!
DAAISUKEEEEE!
I BROUGHT YOUR BOOKS!
I FIGURED THEY'D SEND YOU HOME...
OOF!

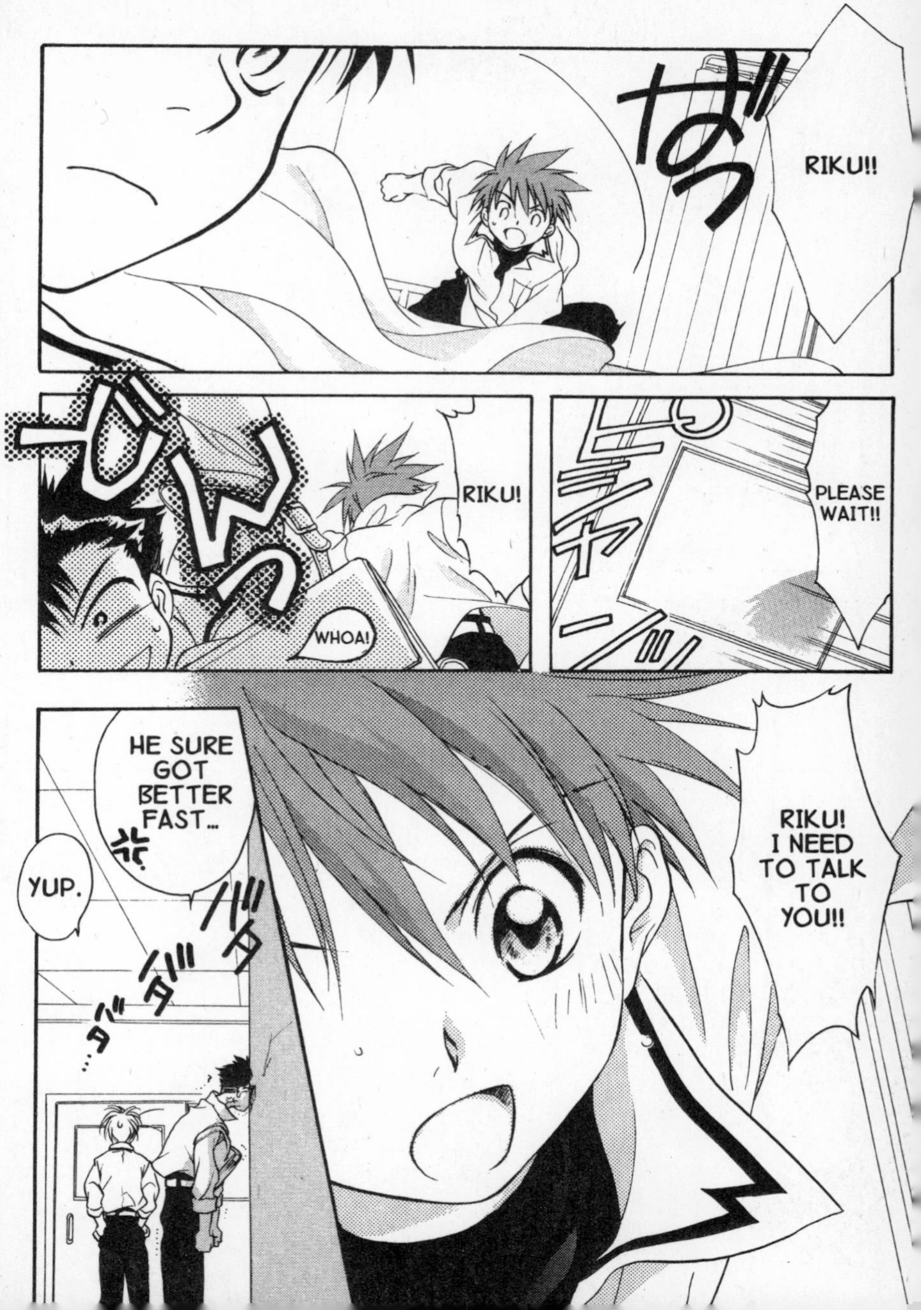
RIKU!!
PLEASE WAIT!!
RIKU!
WHOA!
RIKU! I NEED TO TALK TO YOU!!
HE SURE GOT BETTER FAST...
YUP.

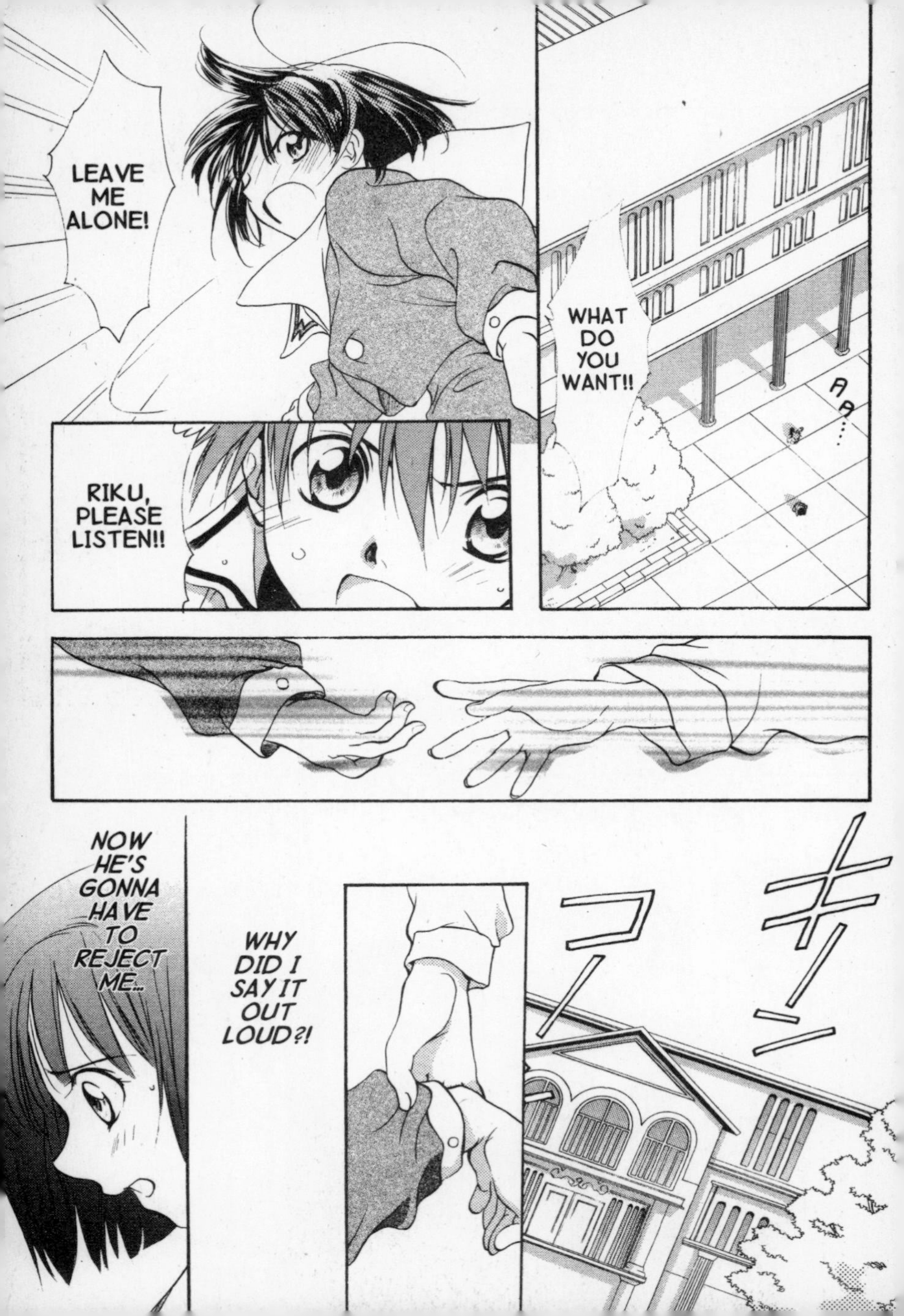
WHAT DO YOU WANT!!
AA...
LEAVE ME ALONE!
RIKU, PLEASE LISTEN!!
WHY DID I SAY IT OUT LOUD?!
NOW HE'S GONNA HAVE TO REJECT ME...

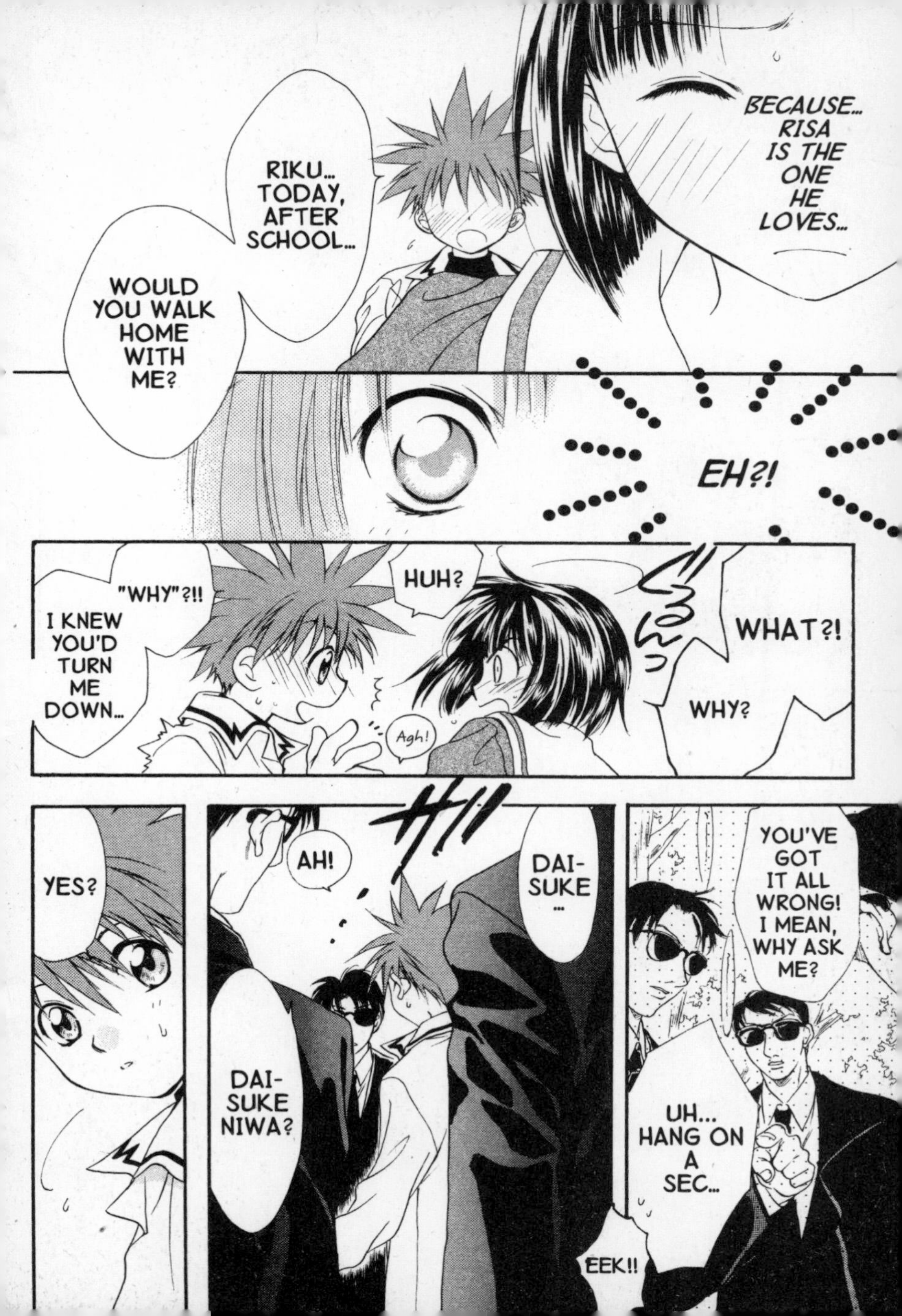
BECAUSE... RISA IS THE ONE HE LOVES...
RIKU... TODAY, AFTER SCHOOL...
WOULD YOU WALK HOME WITH ME?
EH?!
WHAT?!
WHY?
HUH?
Agh!
"WHY"?!! I KNEW YOU'D TURN ME DOWN...
YOU'VE GOT IT ALL WRONG! I MEAN, WHY ASK ME?
UH... HANG ON A SEC...
EEK!!
DAI-SUKE ...
AH!
DAI-SUKE NIWA?
YES?

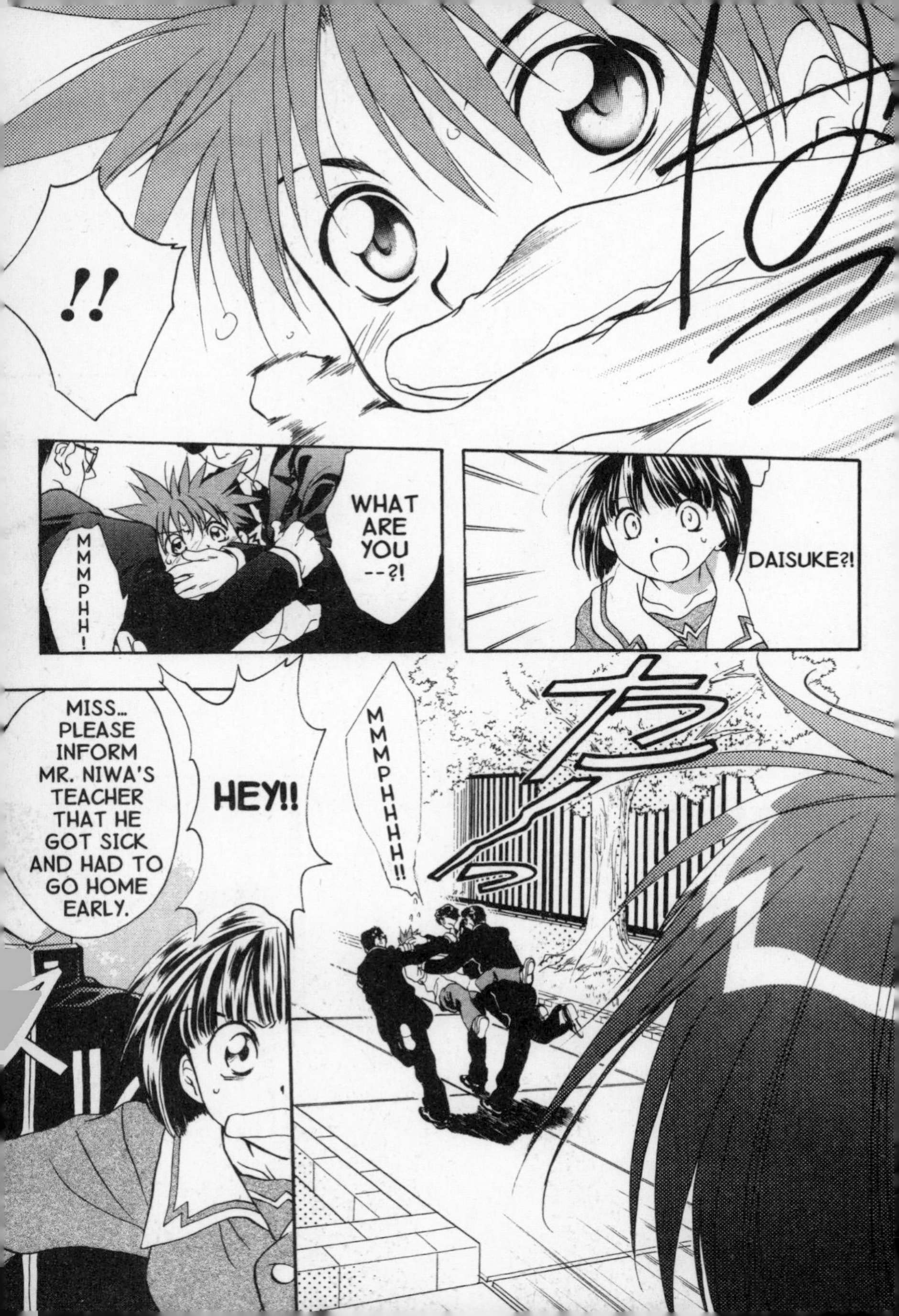

!!
DAISUKE?!
WHAT ARE YOU --?!
MMMPHH!
HEY!!
MMMPHHHHH!!
MISS... PLEASE INFORM MR. NIWA'S TEACHER THAT HE GOT SICK AND HAD TO GO HOME EARLY.

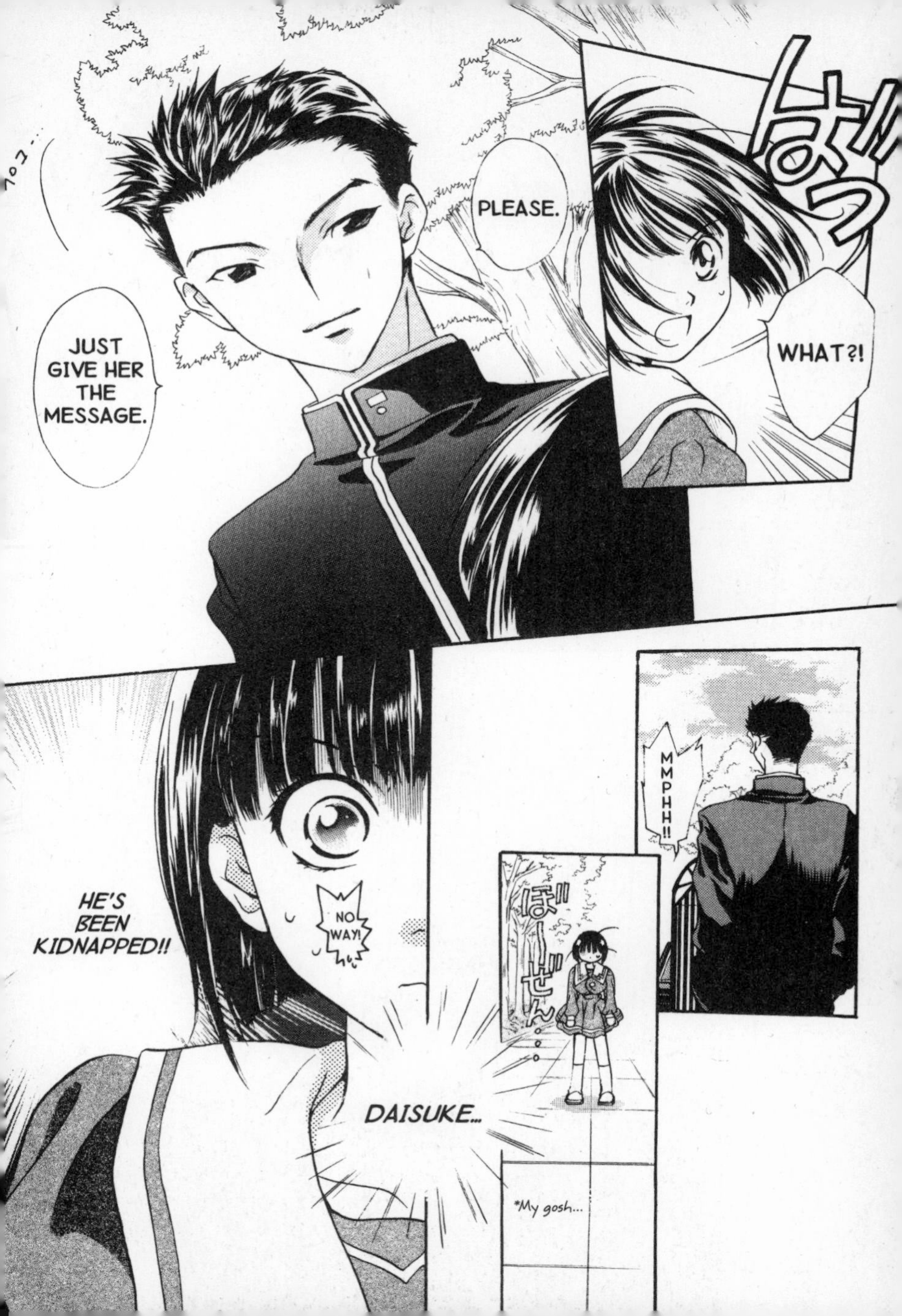

はっ!!
WHAT?!
PLEASE.
フッ…
JUST GIVE HER THE MESSAGE.
MMPHH!!
ぼーぜん…
NO WAY!
HE'S BEEN KIDNAPPED!!
DAISUKE...
*My gosh...

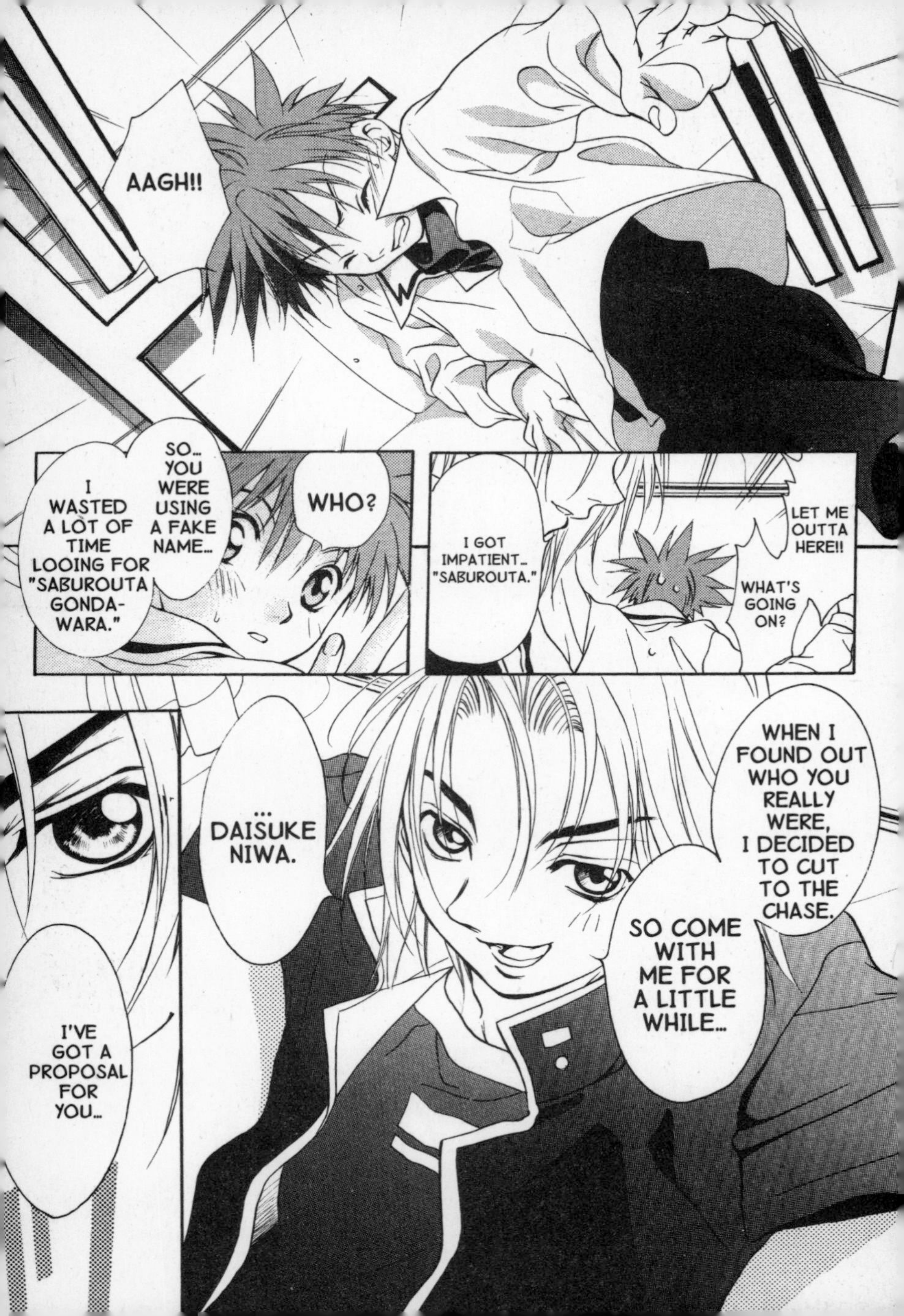
AAGH!!
LET ME OUTTA HERE!!
WHAT'S GOING ON?
I GOT IMPATIENT... "SABUROUTA."
WHO?
SO... YOU WERE USING A FAKE NAME...
I WASTED A LOT OF TIME LOOING FOR "SABUROUTA GONDA-WARA."
WHEN I FOUND OUT WHO YOU REALLY WERE, I DECIDED TO CUT TO THE CHASE.
SO COME WITH ME FOR A LITTLE WHILE...
...DAISUKE NIWA.
I'VE GOT A PROPOSAL FOR YOU...

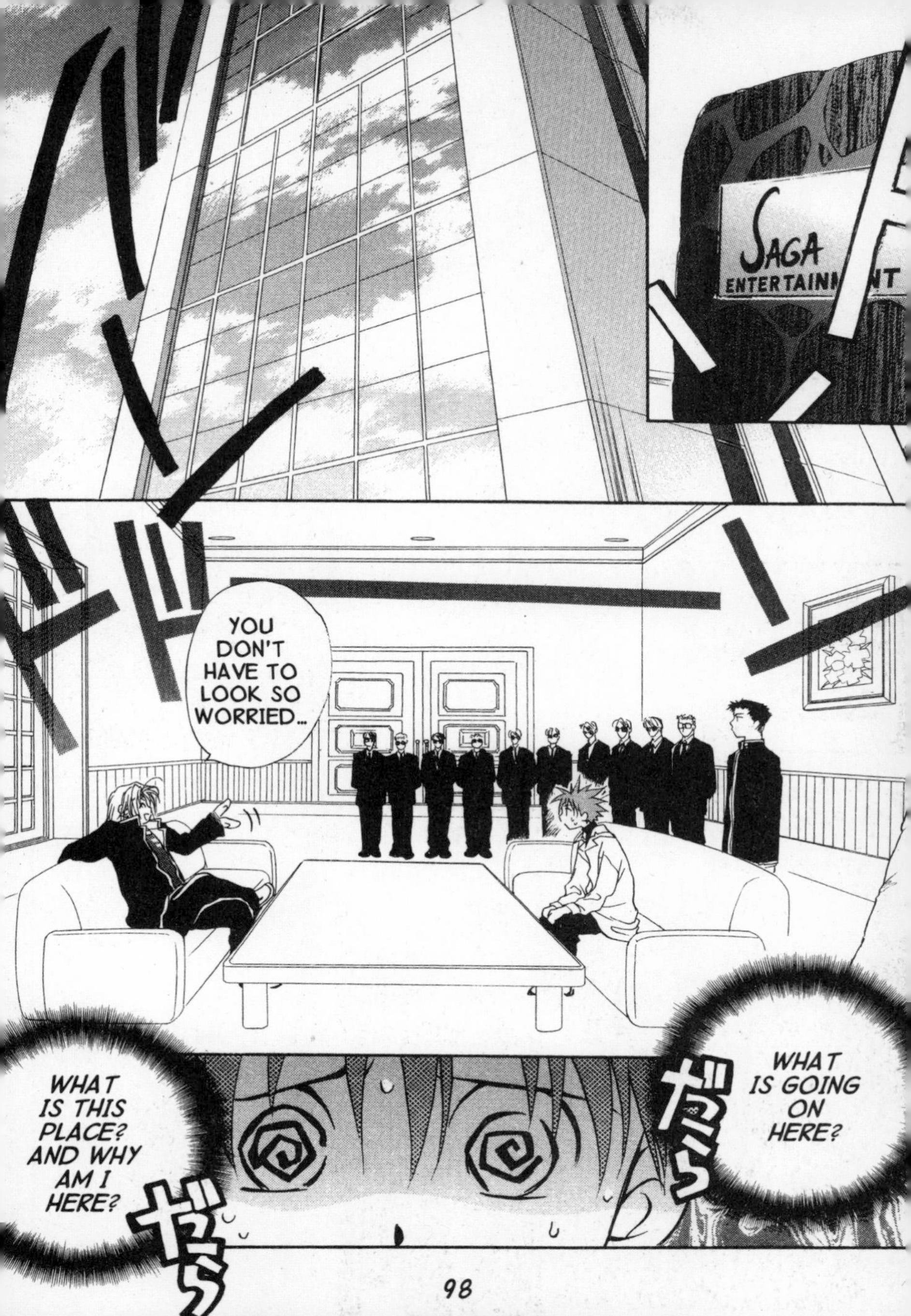
SAGA
ENTERTAINM NT
YOU DON'T HAVE TO LOOK SO WORRIED...
WHAT IS GOING ON HERE?
だら
WHAT IS THIS PLACE? AND WHY AM I HERE?
だら

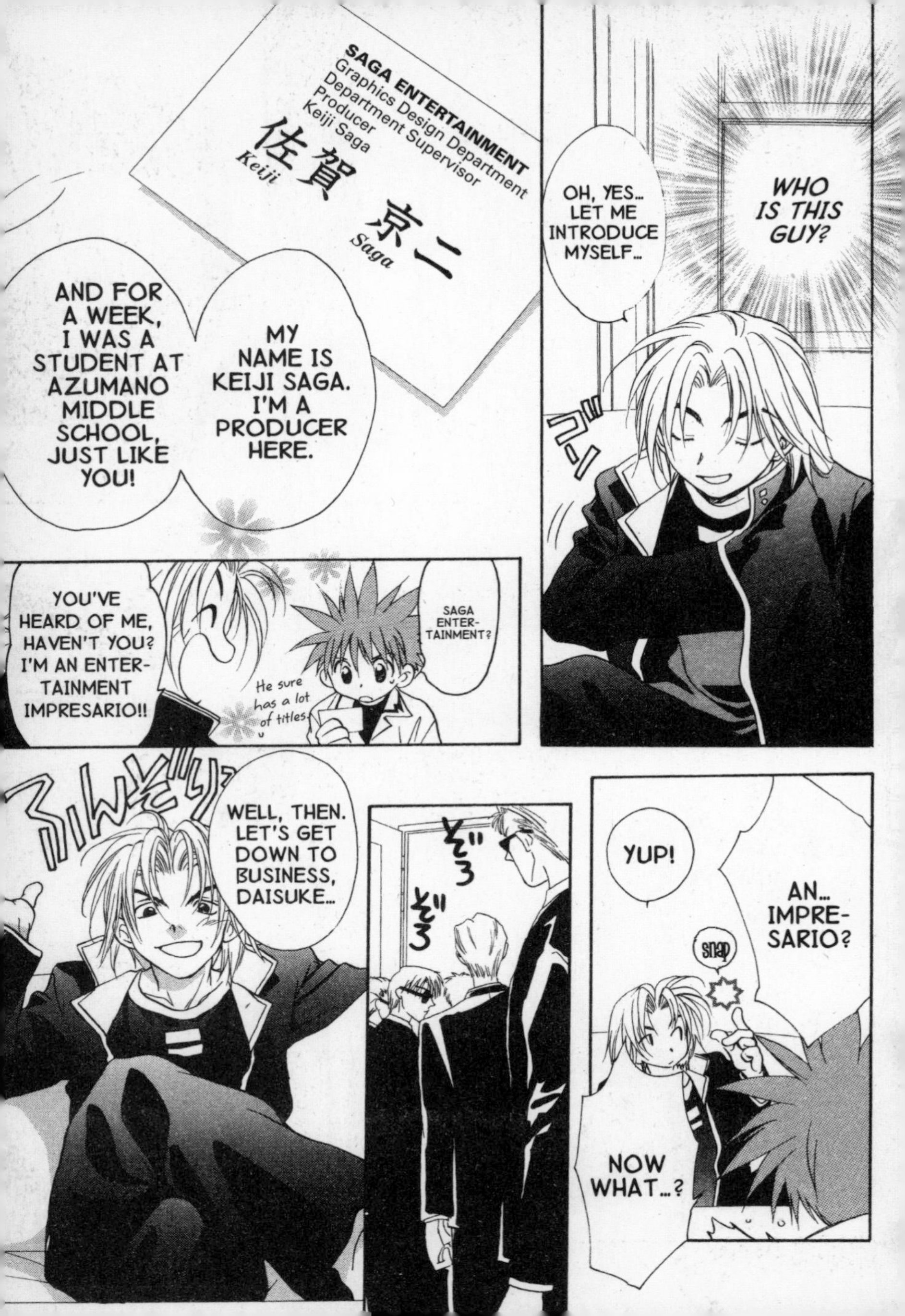

WHO IS THIS GUY?
OH, YES... LET ME INTRODUCE MYSELF...
SAGA ENTERTAINMENT
Graphics Design Department
Department Supervisor
Producer
Keiji Saga
佐賀 京二
Keiji Saga
MY NAME IS KEIJI SAGA. I'M A PRODUCER HERE.
AND FOR A WEEK, I WAS A STUDENT AT AZUMANO MIDDLE SCHOOL, JUST LIKE YOU!
SAGA ENTER-TAINMENT?
He sure has a lot of titles.
YOU'VE HEARD OF ME, HAVEN'T YOU? I'M AN ENTER-TAINMENT IMPRESARIO!!
AN... IMPRE-SARIO?
YUP!
snap
NOW WHAT...?
ぞろ ぞろ
WELL, THEN. LET'S GET DOWN TO BUSINESS, DAISUKE...

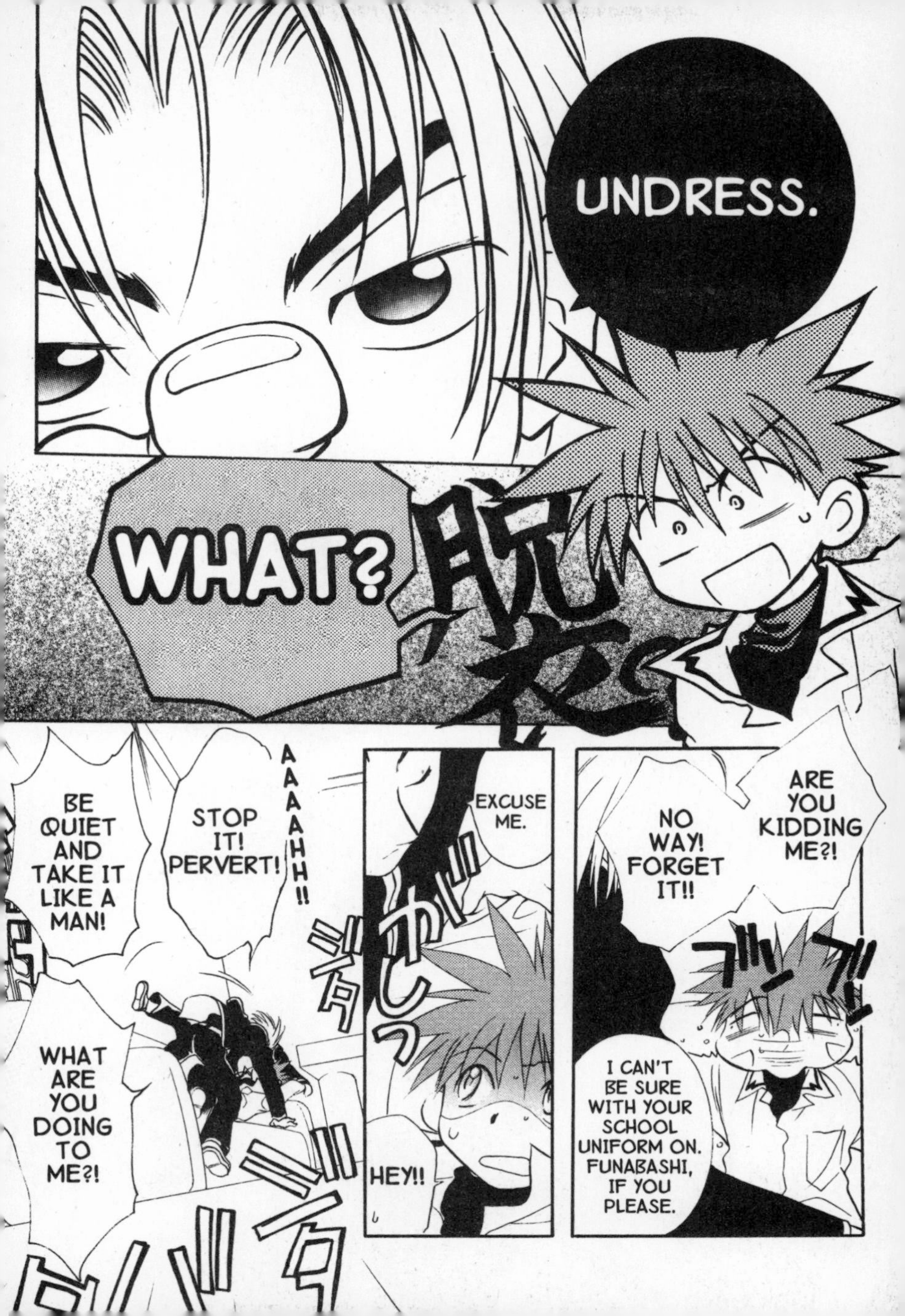
UNDRESS.
WHAT?
ARE YOU KIDDING ME?!
NO WAY! FORGET IT!!
I CAN'T BE SURE WITH YOUR SCHOOL UNIFORM ON. FUNABASHI, IF YOU PLEASE.
EXCUSE ME.
HEY!!
AAAAAHH!!
STOP IT! PERVERT!
BE QUIET AND TAKE IT LIKE A MAN!
WHAT ARE YOU DOING TO ME?!

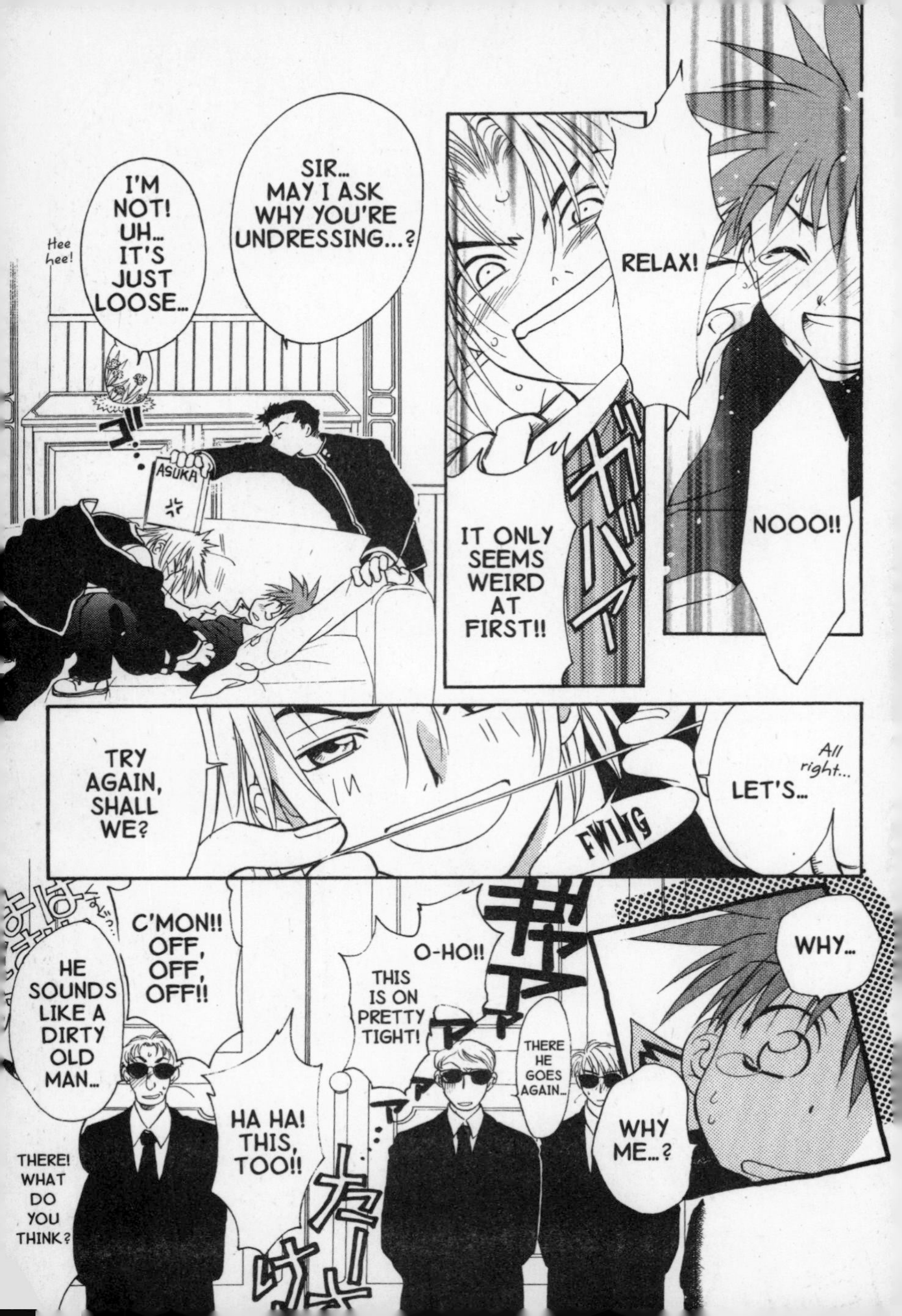
RELAX!
NOOO!!
IT ONLY SEEMS WEIRD AT FIRST!!
SIR... MAY I ASK WHY YOU'RE UNDRESSING...?
I'M NOT! UH... IT'S JUST LOOSE...
Hee hee!
ASUKA
All right...
LET'S...
FWING
TRY AGAIN, SHALL WE?
WHY...
WHY ME...?
O-HO!!
THIS IS ON PRETTY TIGHT!
THERE HE GOES AGAIN...
C'MON!! OFF, OFF, OFF!!
HA HA! THIS, TOO!!
HE SOUNDS LIKE A DIRTY OLD MAN...
THERE! WHAT DO YOU THINK?

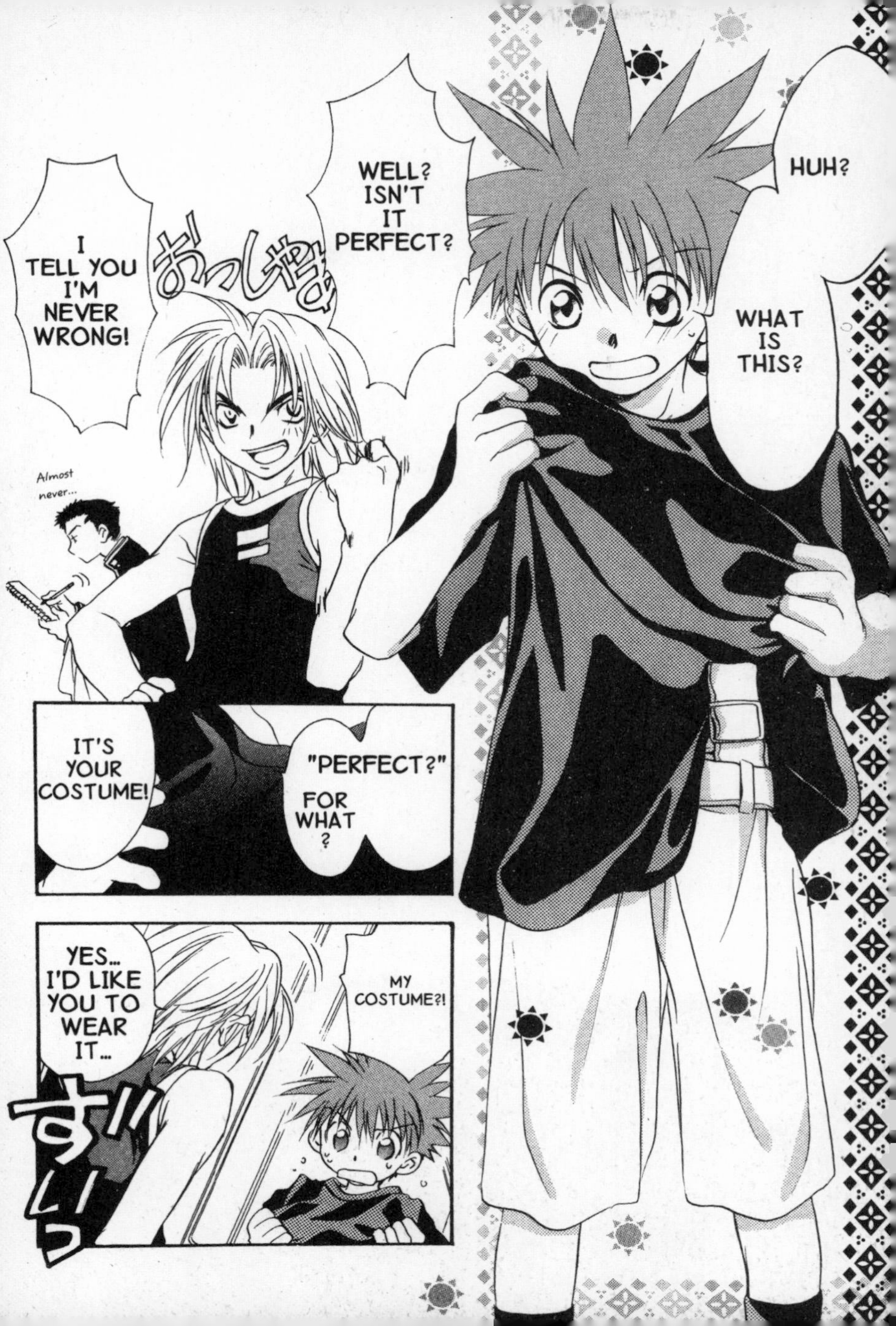
HUH?
WHAT IS THIS?
WELL? ISN'T IT PERFECT?
I TELL YOU I'M NEVER WRONG!
Almost never...
"PERFECT?" FOR WHAT?
IT'S YOUR COSTUME!
MY COSTUME?!
YES... I'D LIKE YOU TO WEAR IT...

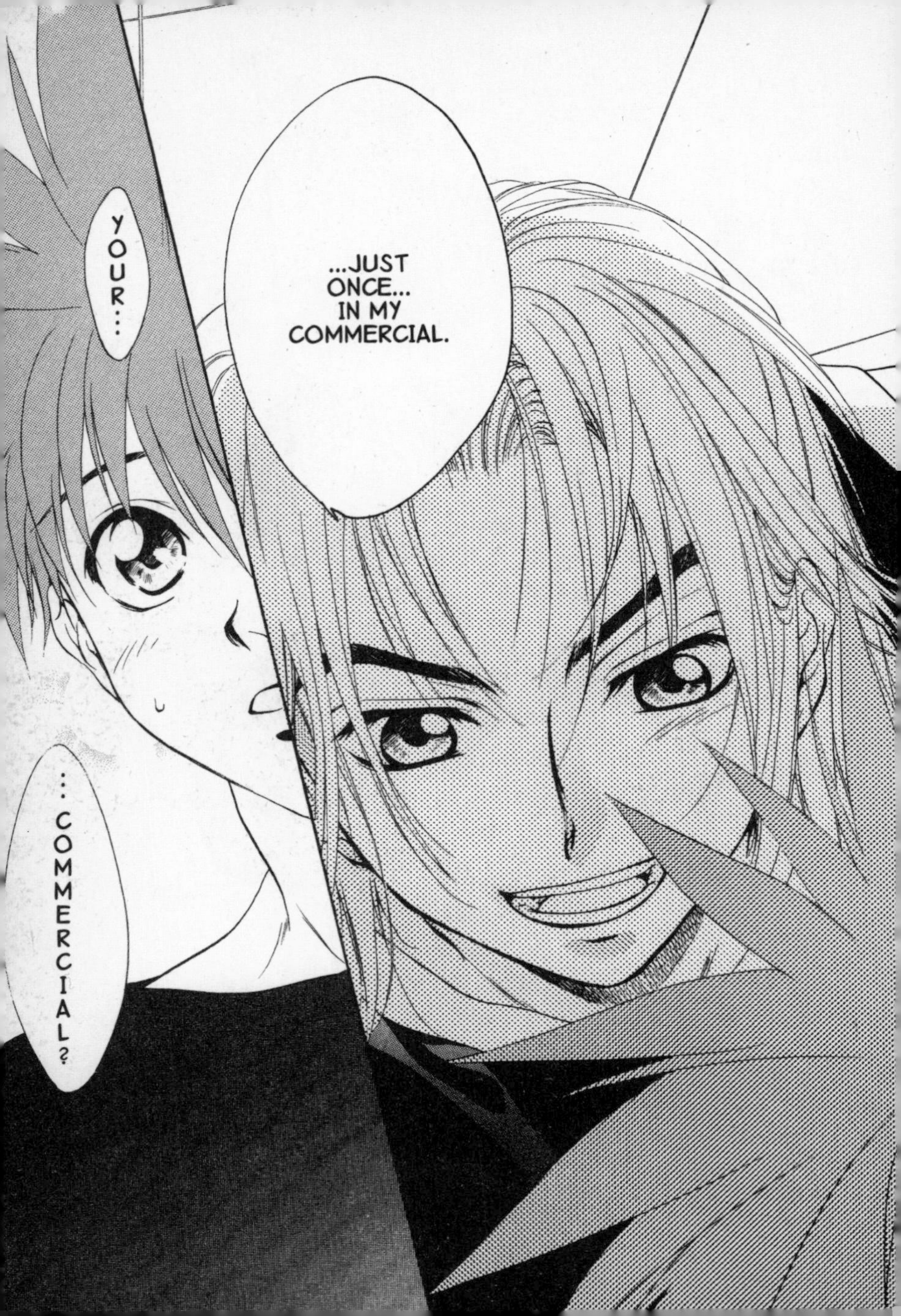
...JUST ONCE... IN MY COMMERCIAL.
YOUR...
...COMMERCIAL?

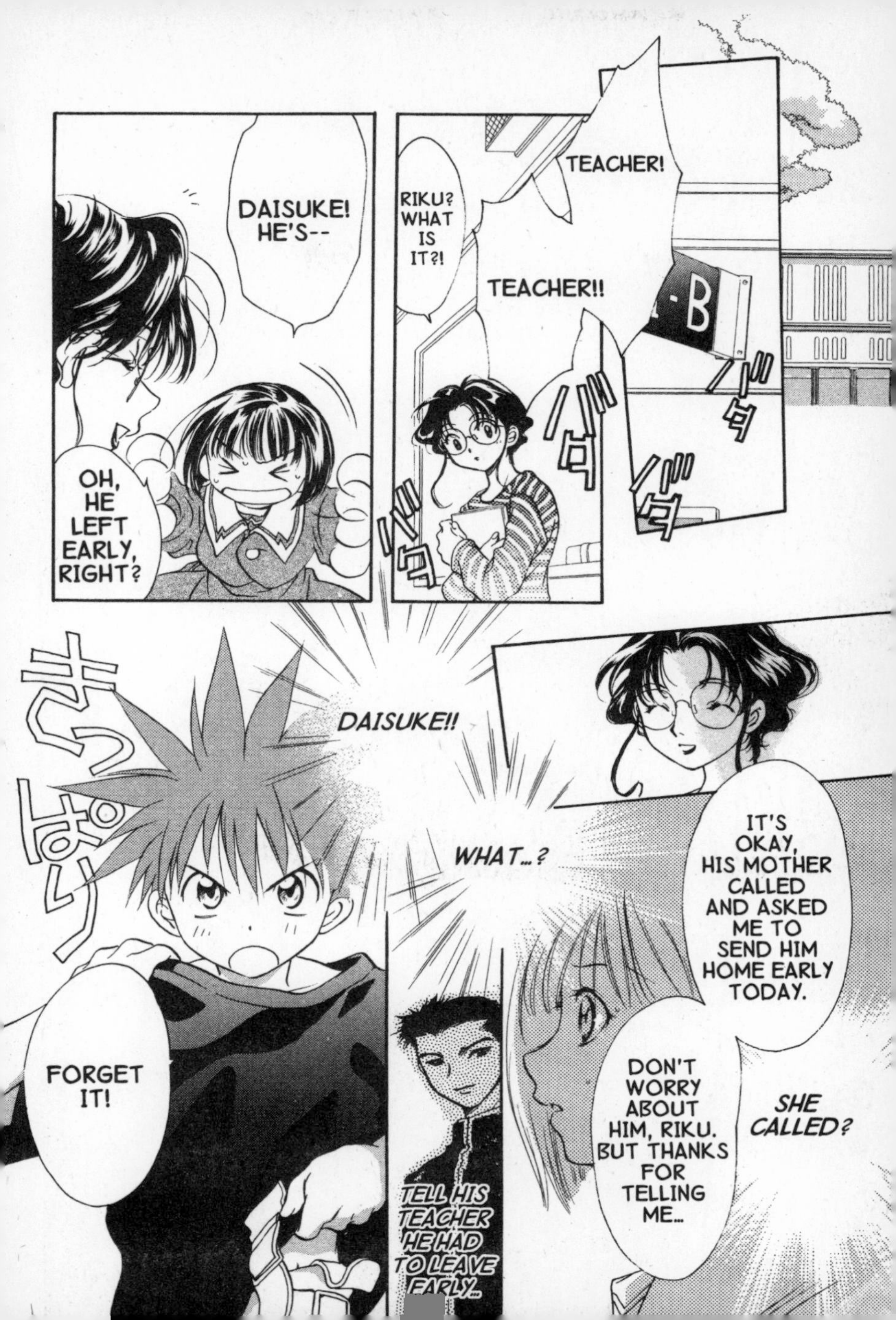
TEACHER!
TEACHER!!
RIKU? WHAT IS IT?!
DAISUKE! HE'S--
OH, HE LEFT EARLY, RIGHT?
IT'S OKAY, HIS MOTHER CALLED AND ASKED ME TO SEND HIM HOME EARLY TODAY.
DON'T WORRY ABOUT HIM, RIKU. BUT THANKS FOR TELLING ME...
SHE CALLED?
TELL HIS TEACHER HE HAD TO LEAVE EARLY...
WHAT...?
DAISUKE!!
きっぱり
FORGET IT!

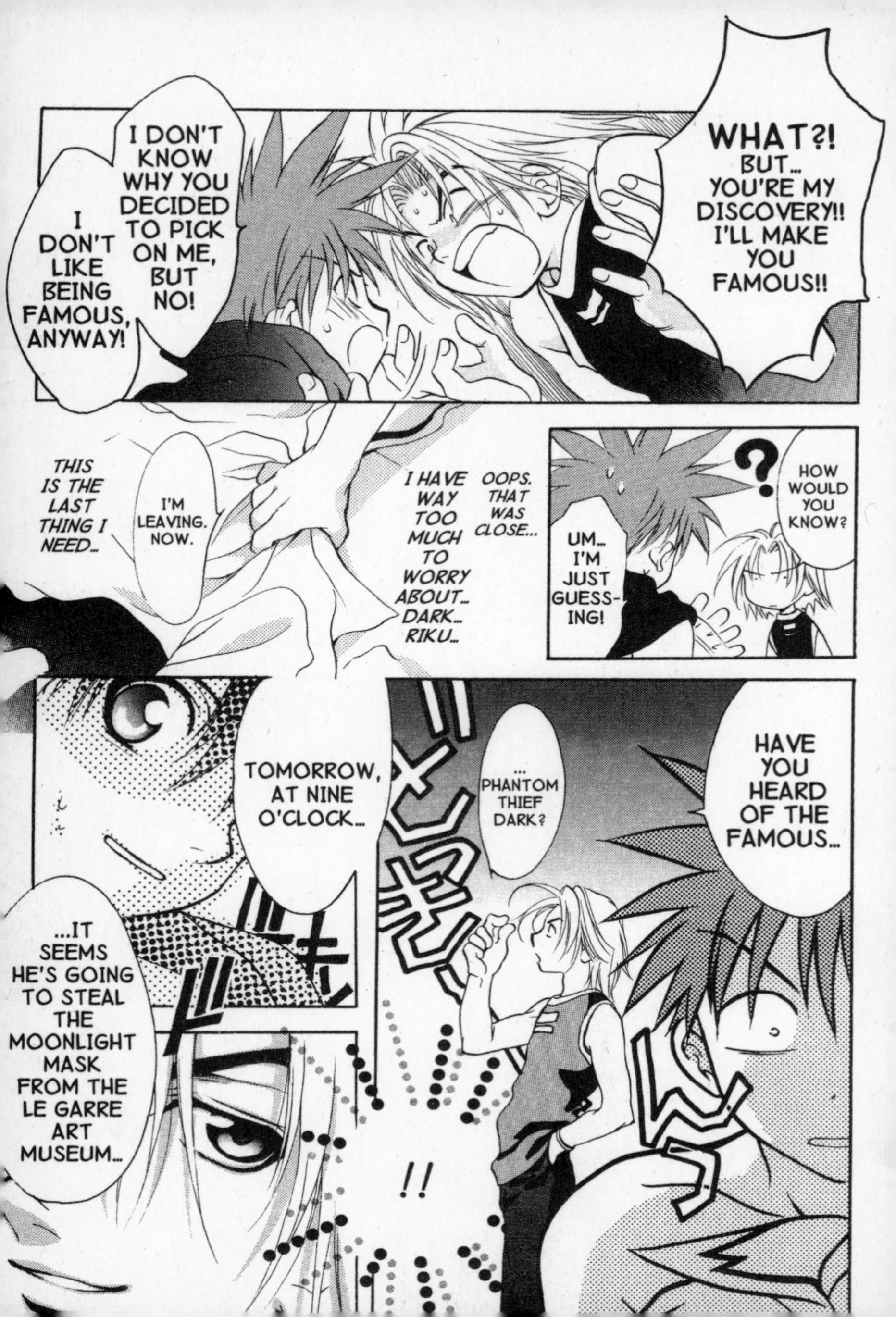
WHAT?! BUT... YOU'RE MY DISCOVERY!! I'LL MAKE YOU FAMOUS!!
I DON'T KNOW WHY YOU DECIDED TO PICK ON ME, BUT NO!
I DON'T LIKE BEING FAMOUS, ANYWAY!
HOW WOULD YOU KNOW?
UM... I'M JUST GUESSING!
OOPS. THAT WAS CLOSE...
I HAVE WAY TOO MUCH TO WORRY ABOUT... DARK... RIKU...
I'M LEAVING. NOW.
THIS IS THE LAST THING I NEED...
HAVE YOU HEARD OF THE FAMOUS...
...PHANTOM THIEF DARK?
!!
TOMORROW, AT NINE O'CLOCK...
...IT SEEMS HE'S GOING TO STEAL THE MOONLIGHT MASK FROM THE LE GARRE ART MUSEUM...

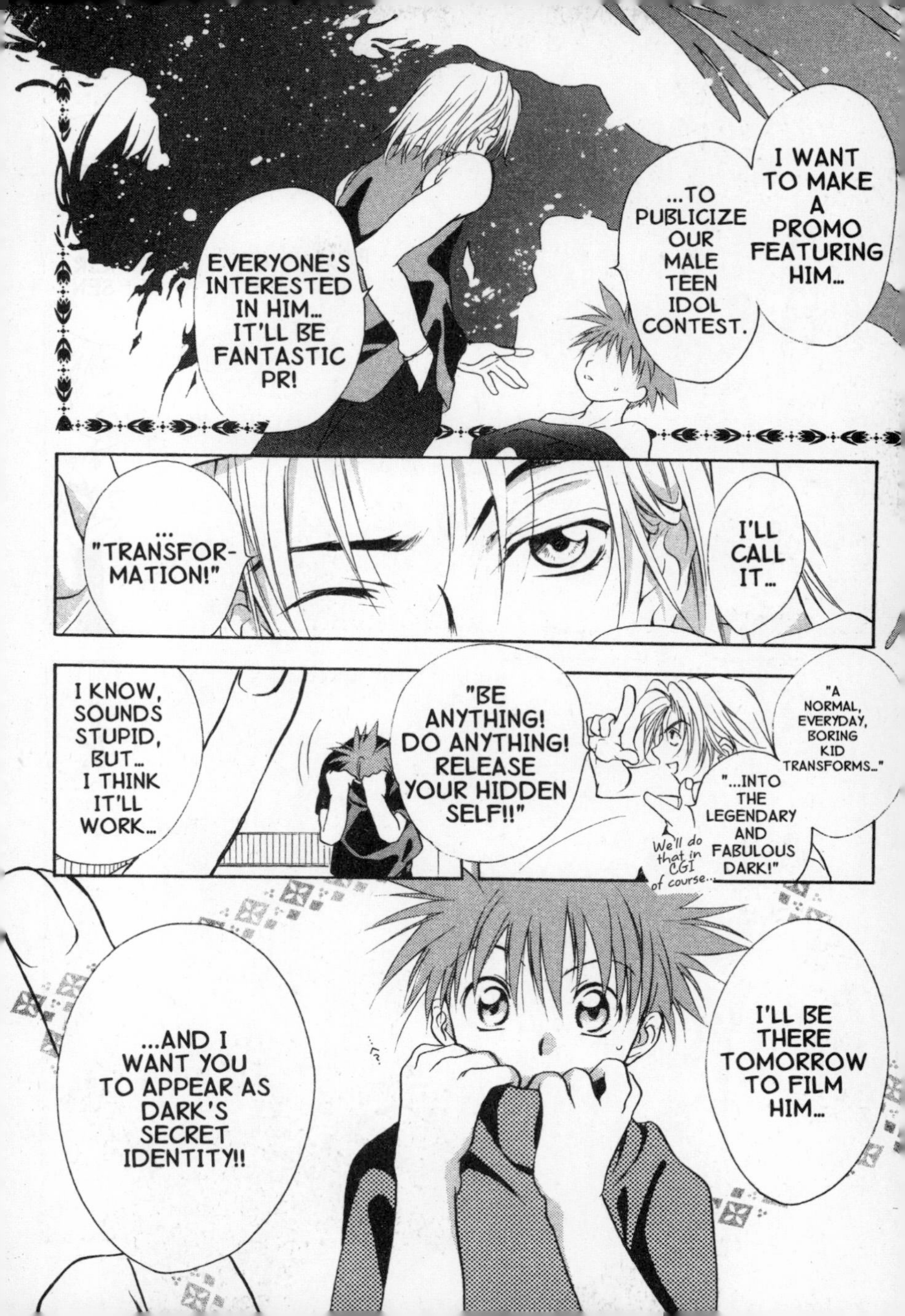
I WANT TO MAKE A PROMO FEATURING HIM...
...TO PUBLICIZE OUR MALE TEEN IDOL CONTEST.
EVERYONE'S INTERESTED IN HIM... IT'LL BE FANTASTIC PR!
I'LL CALL IT...
..."TRANSFORMATION!"
"A NORMAL, EVERYDAY, BORING KID TRANSFORMS..."
"...INTO THE LEGENDARY AND FABULOUS DARK!"
We'll do that in CGI of course...
"BE ANYTHING! DO ANYTHING! RELEASE YOUR HIDDEN SELF!!"
I KNOW, SOUNDS STUPID, BUT... I THINK IT'LL WORK...
I'LL BE THERE TOMORROW TO FILM HIM...
...AND I WANT YOU TO APPEAR AS DARK'S SECRET IDENTITY!!

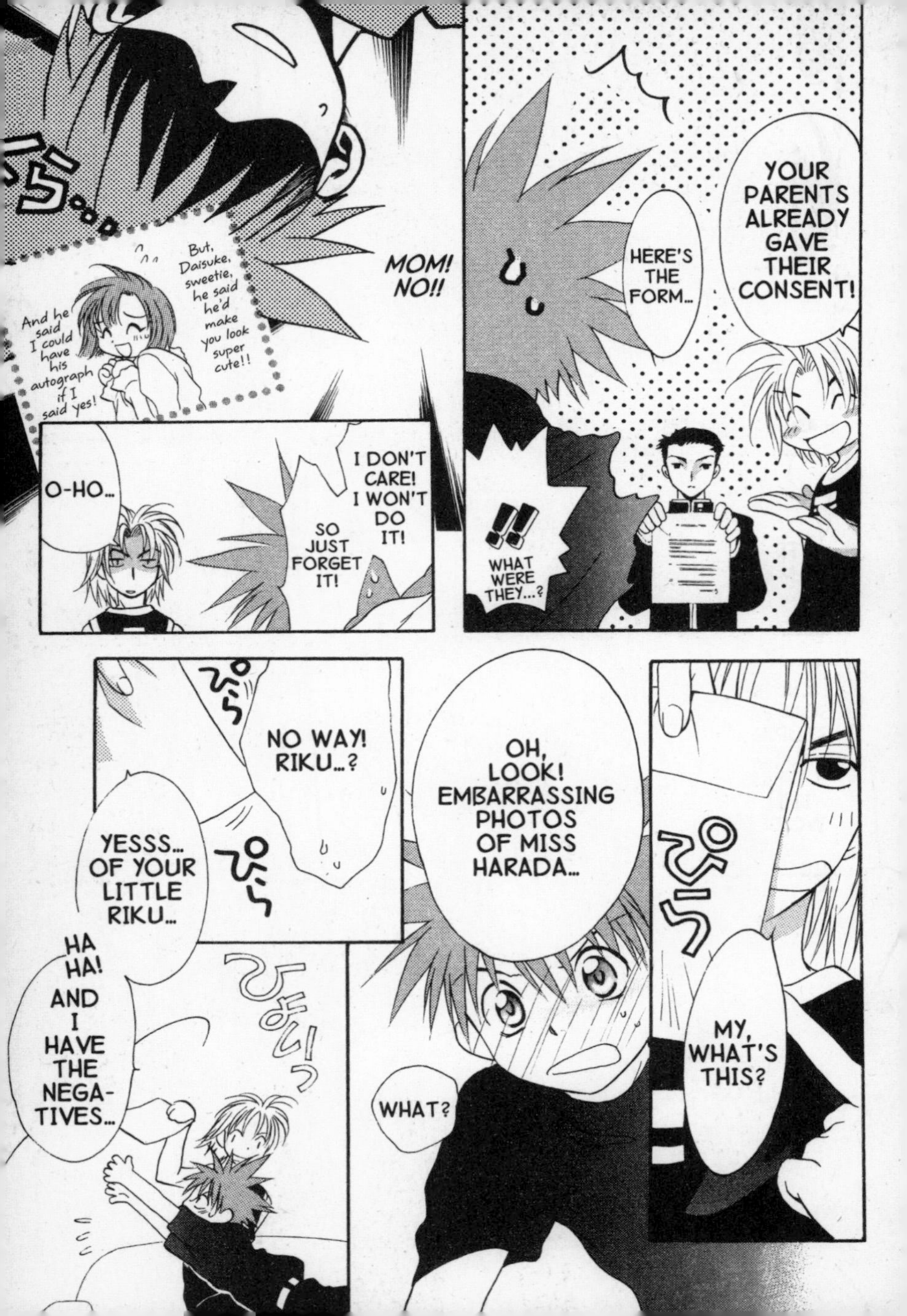
YOUR PARENTS ALREADY GAVE THEIR CONSENT!
HERE'S THE FORM...
WHAT WERE THEY...?
MOM! NO!!
But, Daisuke, sweetie, he said he'd make you look super cute!!
And he said I could have his autograph if I said yes!
I DON'T CARE! I WON'T DO IT!
SO JUST FORGET IT!
O-HO...
MY, WHAT'S THIS?
OH, LOOK! EMBARRASSING PHOTOS OF MISS HARADA...
WHAT?
NO WAY! RIKU...?
YESSS... OF YOUR LITTLE RIKU...
HA HA! AND I HAVE THE NEGATIVES...

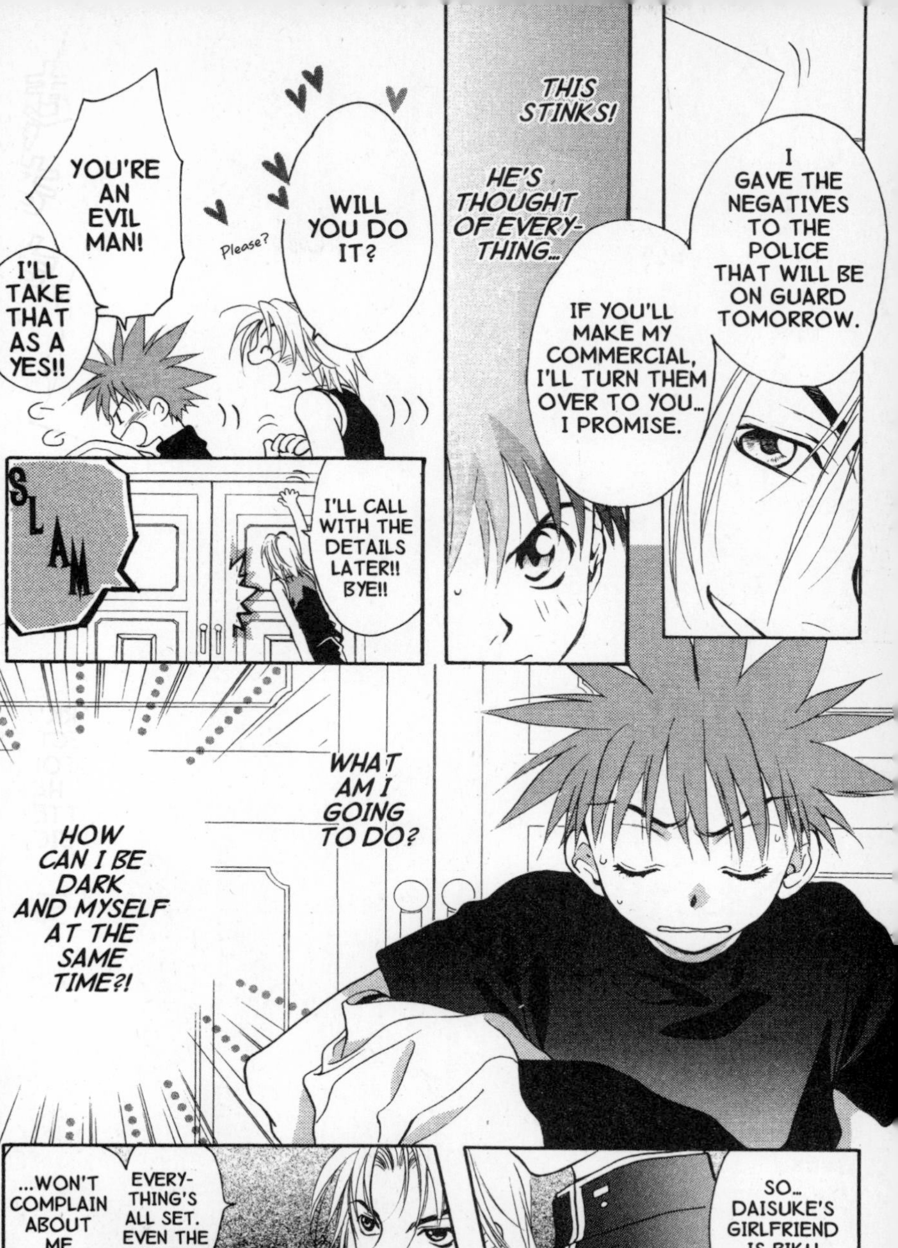
I GAVE THE NEGATIVES TO THE POLICE THAT WILL BE ON GUARD TOMORROW.
IF YOU'LL MAKE MY COMMERCIAL, I'LL TURN THEM OVER TO YOU... I PROMISE.
THIS STINKS!
HE'S THOUGHT OF EVERY-THING...
WILL YOU DO IT?
Please?
YOU'RE AN EVIL MAN!
I'LL TAKE THAT AS A YES!!
I'LL CALL WITH THE DETAILS LATER!! BYE!!
SLAM
WHAT AM I GOING TO DO?
HOW CAN I BE DARK AND MYSELF AT THE SAME TIME?!
SO... DAISUKE'S GIRLFRIEND IS RIKU HARADA...?
EVERY-THING'S ALL SET. EVEN THE POLICE...
...WON'T COMPLAIN ABOUT ME FILMING...

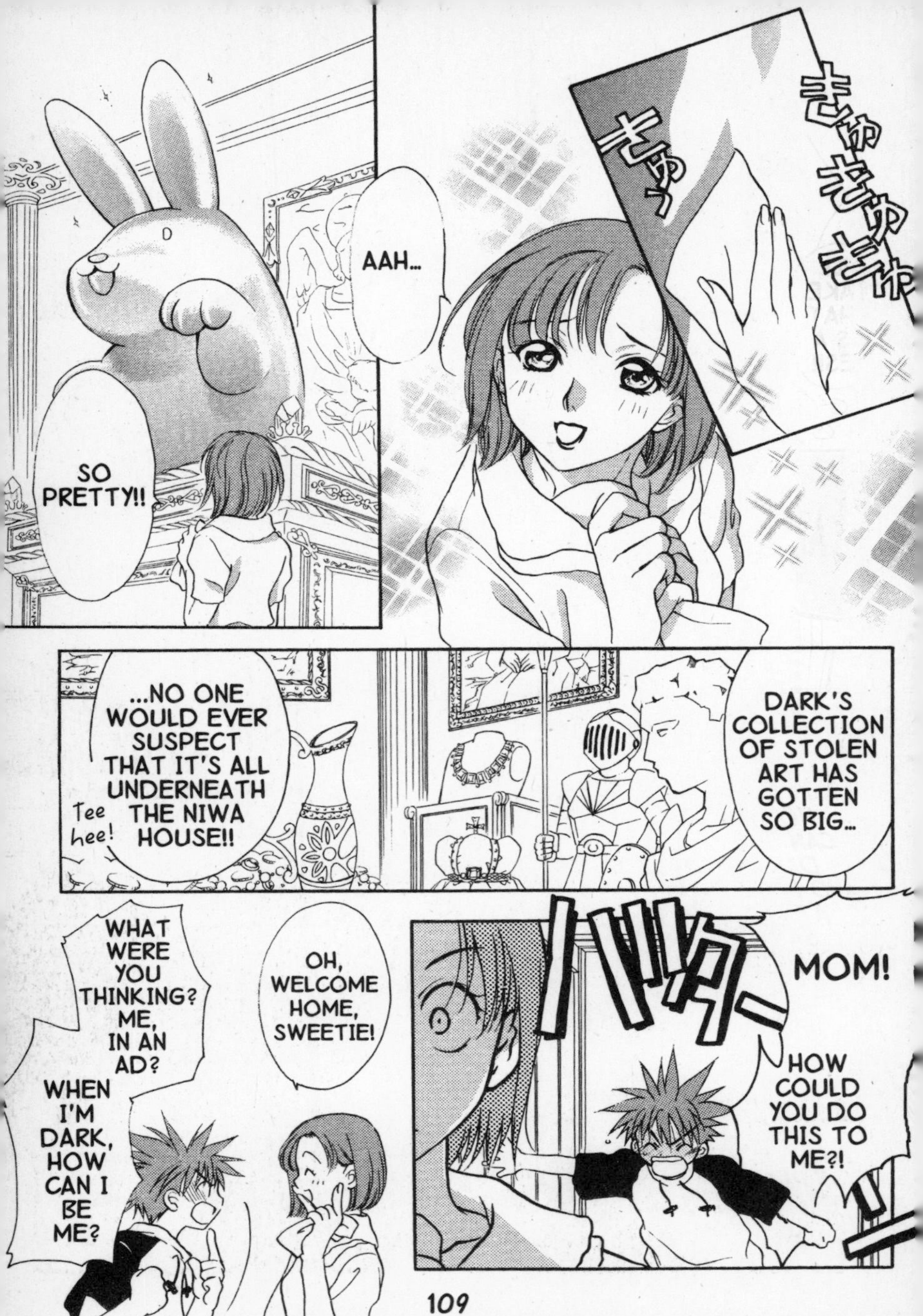

きゅきゅきゅ
きゅっ
AAH...
SO PRETTY!!
DARK'S COLLECTION OF STOLEN ART HAS GOTTEN SO BIG...
...NO ONE WOULD EVER SUSPECT THAT IT'S ALL UNDERNEATH THE NIWA HOUSE!!
Tee hee!
MOM!
HOW COULD YOU DO THIS TO ME?!
OH, WELCOME HOME, SWEETIE!
WHAT WERE YOU THINKING? ME, IN AN AD?
WHEN I'M DARK, HOW CAN I BE ME?

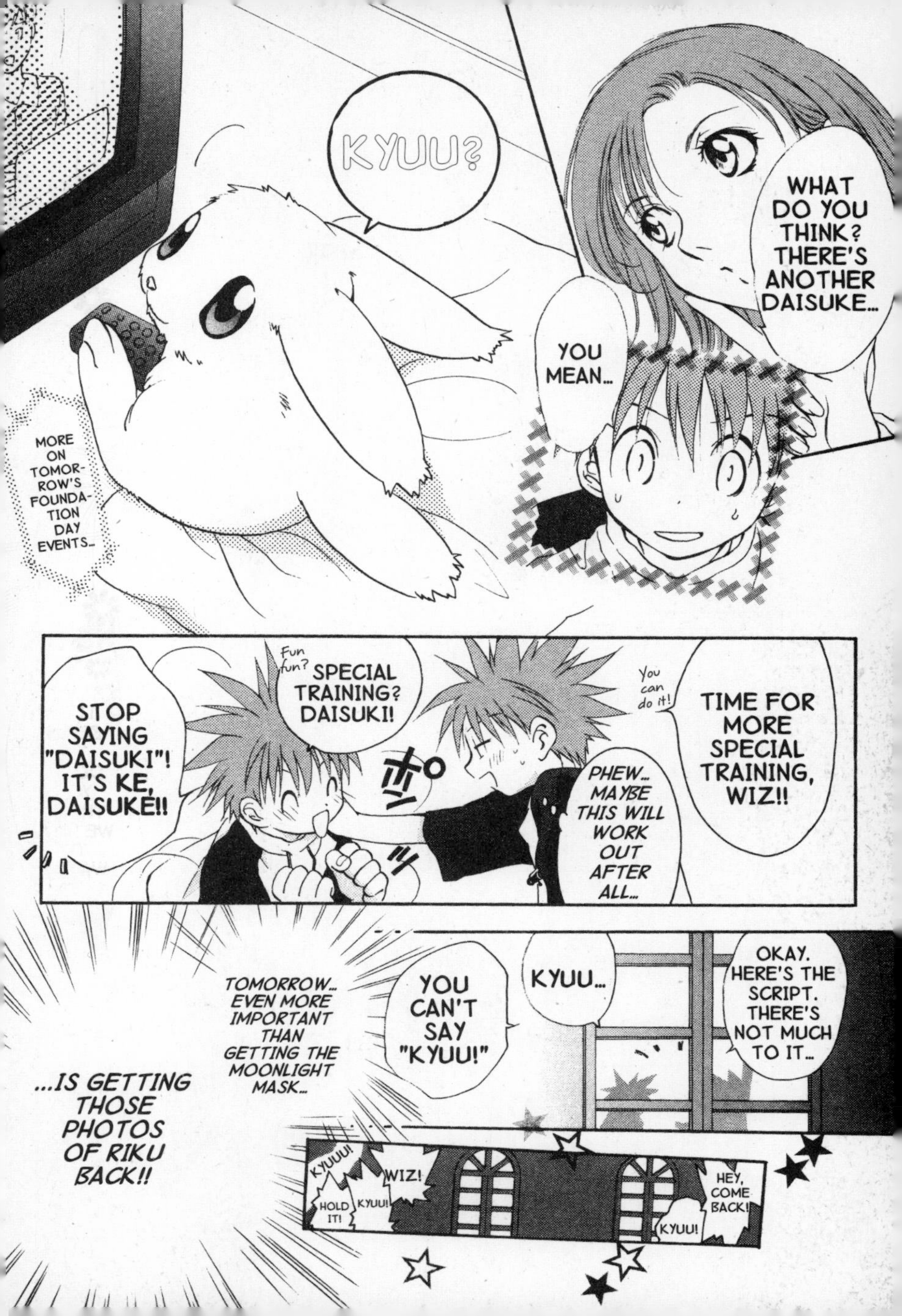
WHAT DO YOU THINK? THERE'S ANOTHER DAISUKE...
YOU MEAN...
KYUU?
MORE ON TOMORROW'S FOUNDATION DAY EVENTS...
TIME FOR MORE SPECIAL TRAINING, WIZ!!
You can do it!
PHEW... MAYBE THIS WILL WORK OUT AFTER ALL...
SPECIAL TRAINING? DAISUKI!
Fun fun?
STOP SAYING "DAISUKI"! IT'S KE, DAISUKE!!
OKAY. HERE'S THE SCRIPT. THERE'S NOT MUCH TO IT...
KYUU...
YOU CAN'T SAY "KYUU!"
TOMORROW... EVEN MORE IMPORTANT THAN GETTING THE MOONLIGHT MASK...
...IS GETTING THOSE PHOTOS OF RIKU BACK!!
HEY, COME BACK!
KYUU!
WIZ!
KYUUU!
KYUU!
HOLD IT!

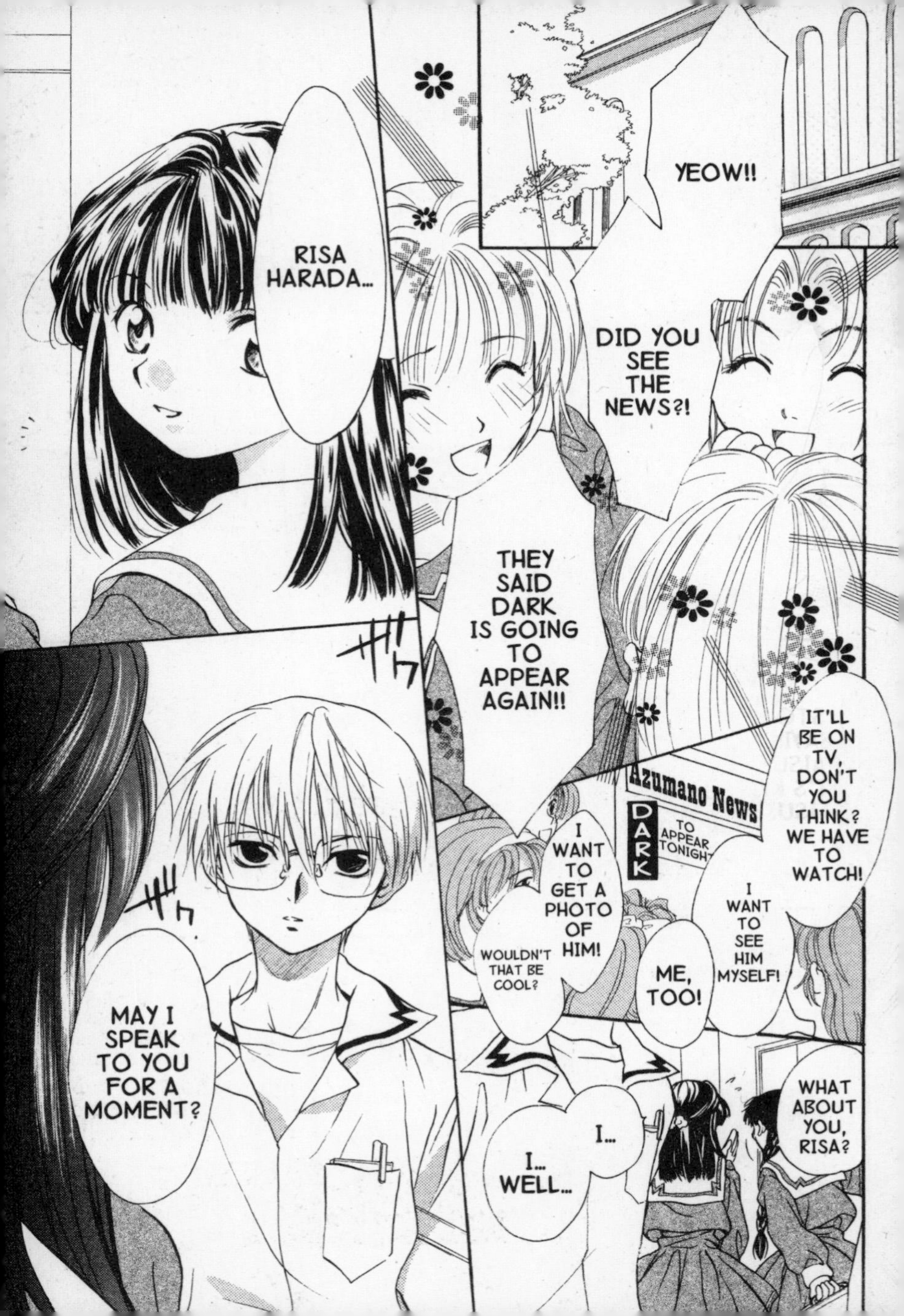

YEOW!!
DID YOU SEE THE NEWS?!
THEY SAID DARK IS GOING TO APPEAR AGAIN!!
RISA HARADA...
IT'LL BE ON TV, DON'T YOU THINK? WE HAVE TO WATCH!
Azumano News
DARK
TO APPEAR TONIGHT
I WANT TO SEE HIM MYSELF!
ME, TOO!
I WANT TO GET A PHOTO OF HIM!
WOULDN'T THAT BE COOL?
WHAT ABOUT YOU, RISA?
I...
I... WELL...
MAY I SPEAK TO YOU FOR A MOMENT?

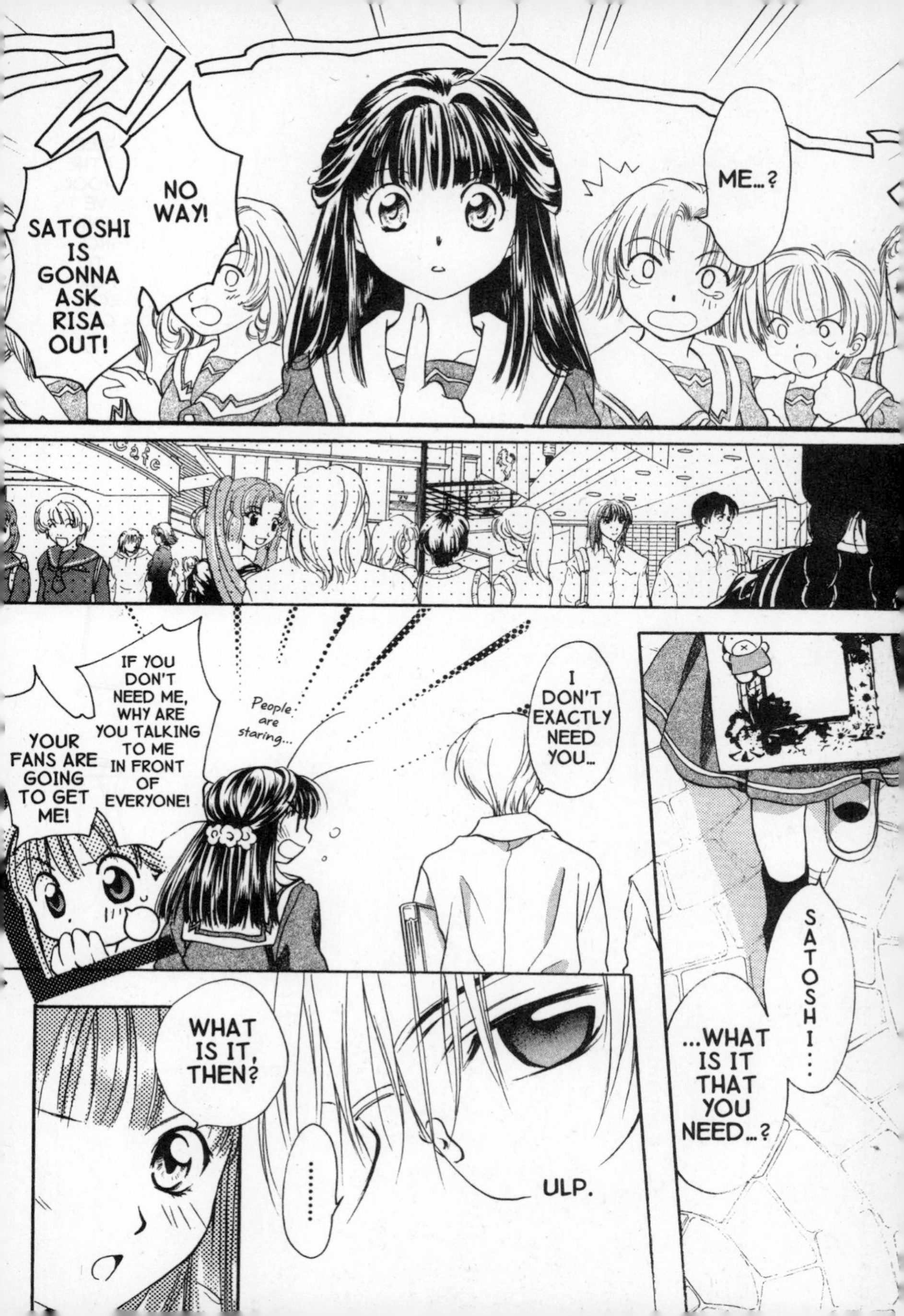
ME...?
NO WAY!
SATOSHI IS GONNA ASK RISA OUT!
SATOSHI...
I DON'T EXACTLY NEED YOU...
People are staring...
IF YOU DON'T NEED ME, WHY ARE YOU TALKING TO ME IN FRONT OF EVERYONE!
YOUR FANS ARE GOING TO GET ME!
...WHAT IS IT THAT YOU NEED...?
ULP.
......
WHAT IS IT, THEN?

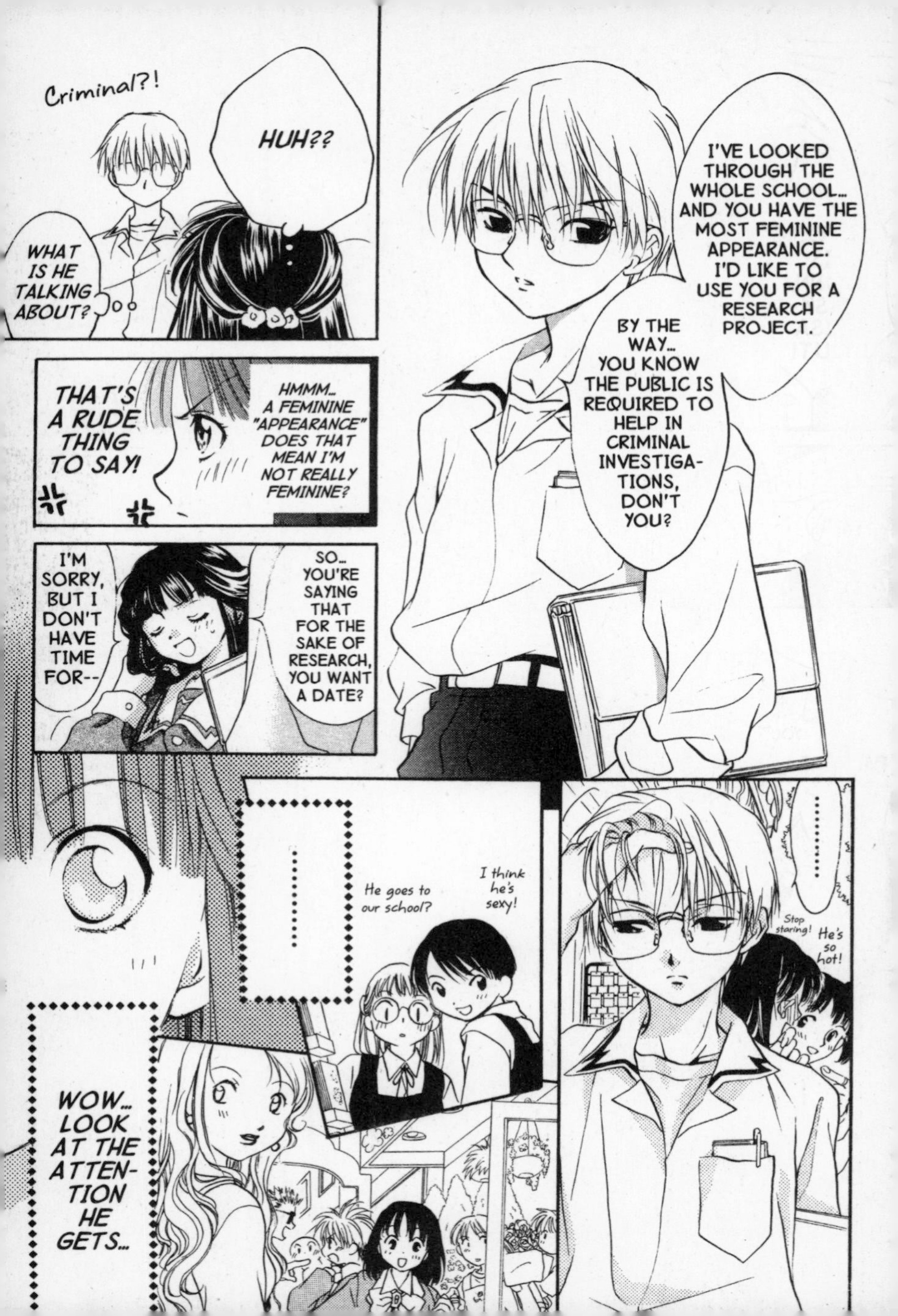
I'VE LOOKED THROUGH THE WHOLE SCHOOL... AND YOU HAVE THE MOST FEMININE APPEARANCE. I'D LIKE TO USE YOU FOR A RESEARCH PROJECT.
BY THE WAY... YOU KNOW THE PUBLIC IS REQUIRED TO HELP IN CRIMINAL INVESTIGA-TIONS, DON'T YOU?
HUH??
Criminal?!
WHAT IS HE TALKING ABOUT?
HMMM... A FEMININE "APPEARANCE" DOES THAT MEAN I'M NOT REALLY FEMININE?
THAT'S A RUDE THING TO SAY!
SO... YOU'RE SAYING THAT FOR THE SAKE OF RESEARCH, YOU WANT A DATE?
I'M SORRY, BUT I DON'T HAVE TIME FOR--
......
Stop staring!
He's so hot!
I think he's sexy!
He goes to our school?
......
WOW... LOOK AT THE ATTENTION HE GETS...

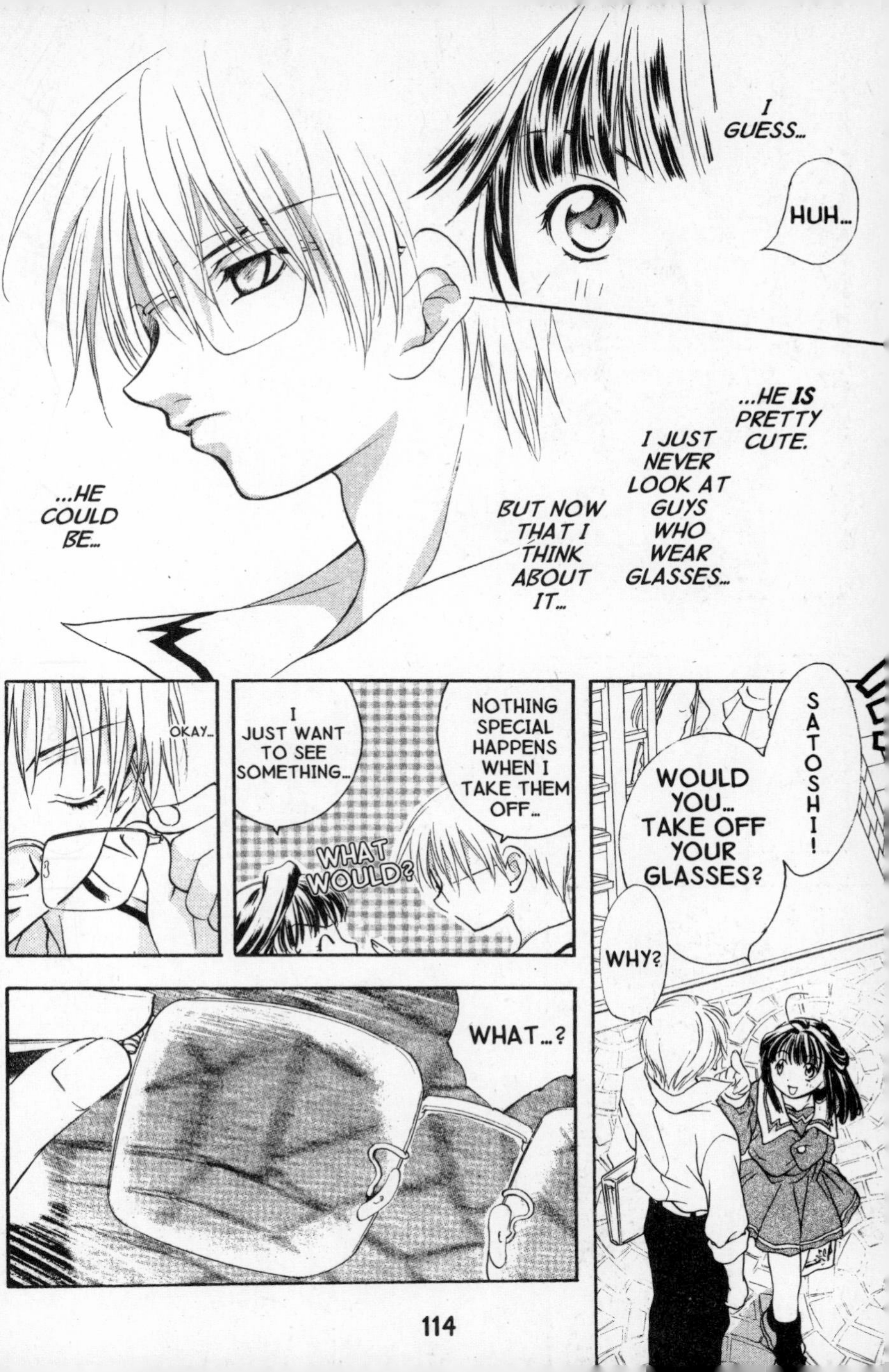

I GUESS...
HUH...
...HE IS PRETTY CUTE.
I JUST NEVER LOOK AT GUYS WHO WEAR GLASSES...
BUT NOW THAT I THINK ABOUT IT...
...HE COULD BE...
SATOSHI!
WOULD YOU... TAKE OFF YOUR GLASSES?
WHY?
NOTHING SPECIAL HAPPENS WHEN I TAKE THEM OFF...
I JUST WANT TO SEE SOMETHING...
WHAT WOULD?
OKAY...
WHAT...?

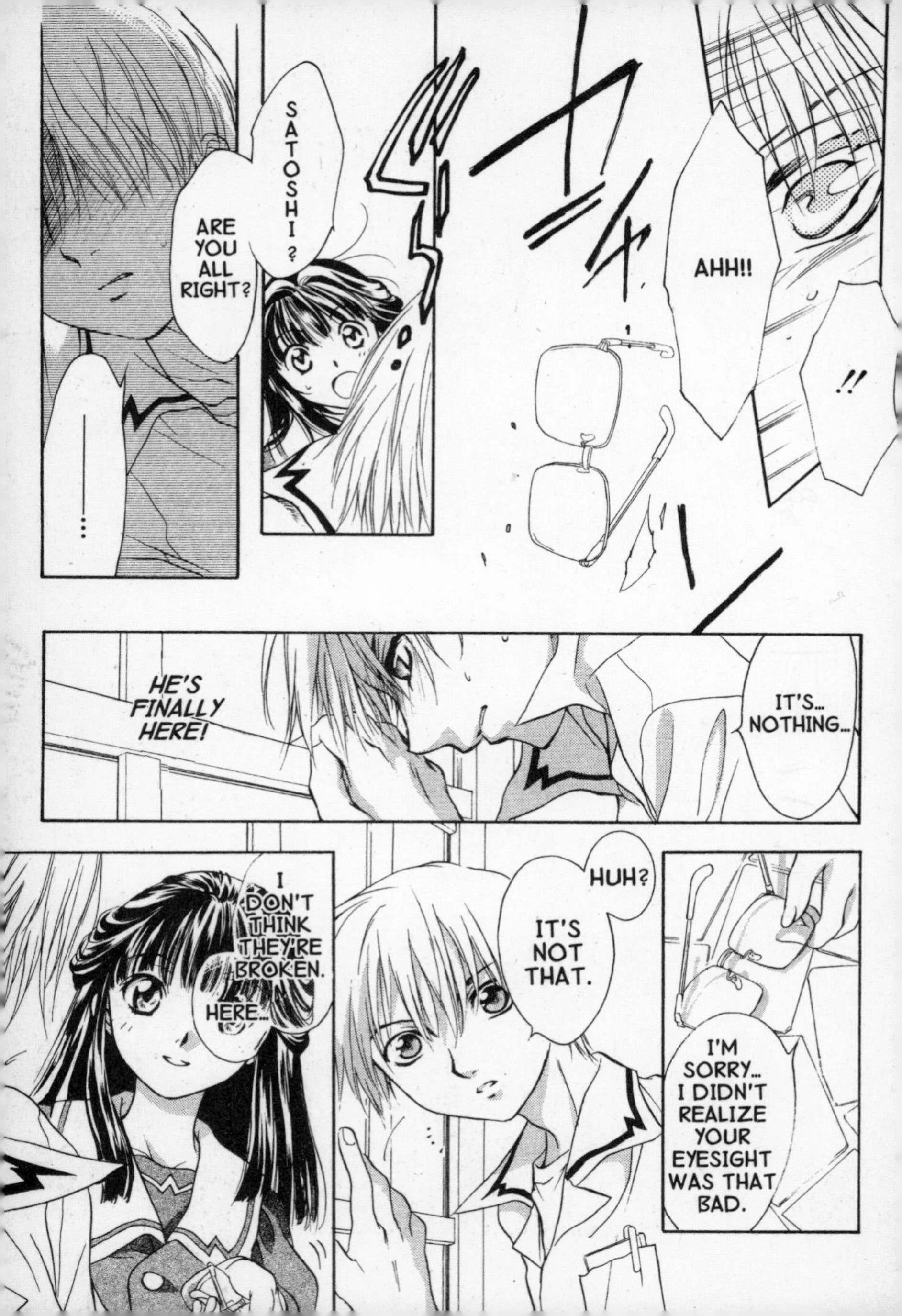
AHH!!
!!
SATOSHI?
ARE YOU ALL RIGHT?
......
IT'S... NOTHING...
HE'S FINALLY HERE!
I'M SORRY... I DIDN'T REALIZE YOUR EYESIGHT WAS THAT BAD.
HUH?
IT'S NOT THAT.
I DON'T THINK THEY'RE BROKEN.
HERE...

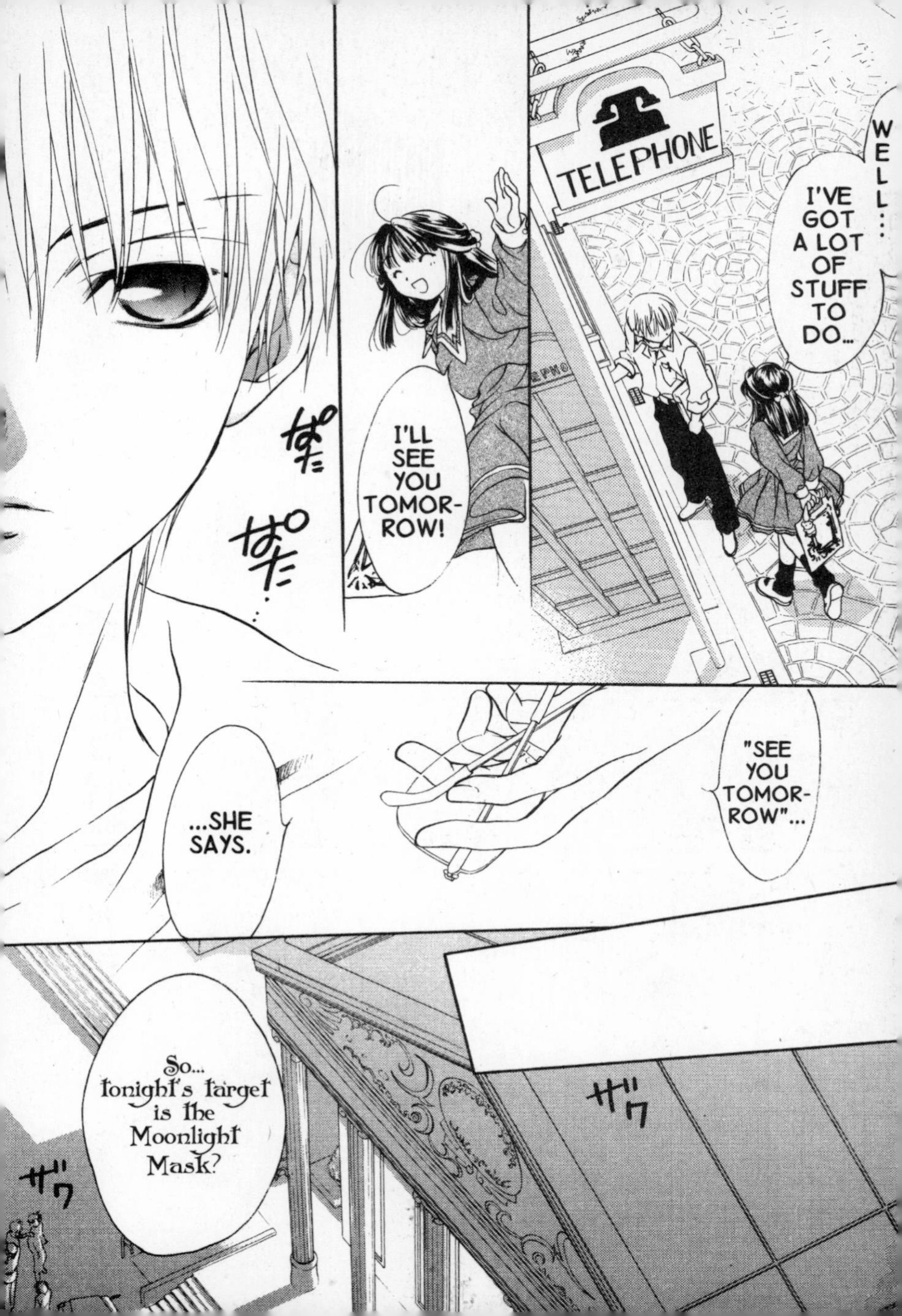
TELEPHONE
WELL... I'VE GOT A LOT OF STUFF TO DO...
I'LL SEE YOU TOMORROW!
ぱた
ぱた...
"SEE YOU TOMORROW"...
...SHE SAYS.
ザワ
So... tonight's target is the Moonlight Mask?
ザワ

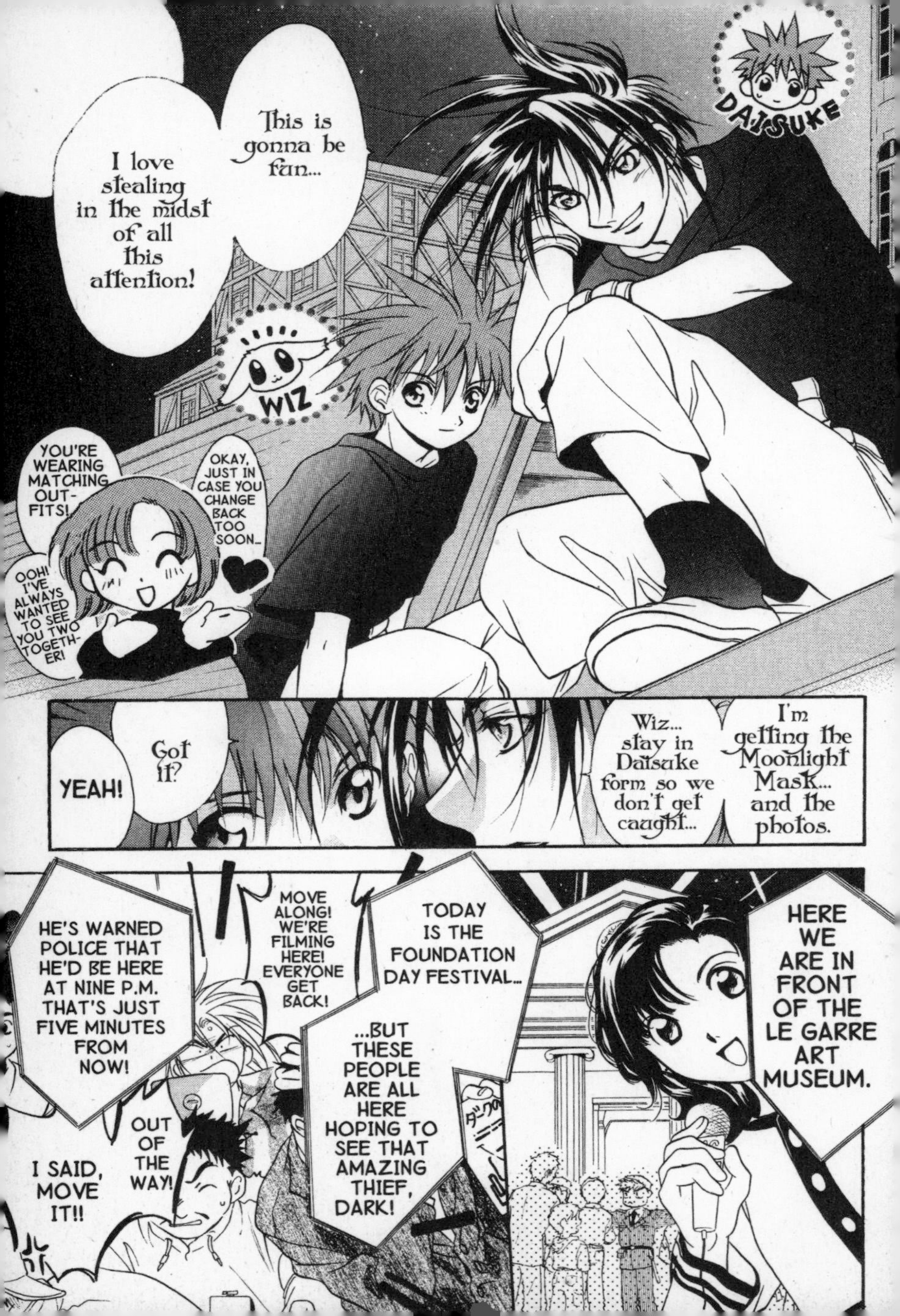
DAISUKE
This is gonna be fun...
I love stealing in the midst of all this attention!
WIZ
OKAY, JUST IN CASE YOU CHANGE BACK TOO SOON...
YOU'RE WEARING MATCHING OUT-FITS!
OOH! I'VE ALWAYS WANTED TO SEE YOU TWO TOGETH-ER!
I'm getting the Moonlight Mask... and the photos.
Wiz... stay in Daisuke form so we don't get caught...
Got it?
YEAH!
HERE WE ARE IN FRONT OF THE LE GARRE ART MUSEUM.
TODAY IS THE FOUNDATION DAY FESTIVAL...
...BUT THESE PEOPLE ARE ALL HERE HOPING TO SEE THAT AMAZING THIEF, DARK!
MOVE ALONG! WE'RE FILMING HERE! EVERYONE GET BACK!
HE'S WARNED POLICE THAT HE'D BE HERE AT NINE P.M. THAT'S JUST FIVE MINUTES FROM NOW!
OUT OF THE WAY!
I SAID, MOVE IT!!

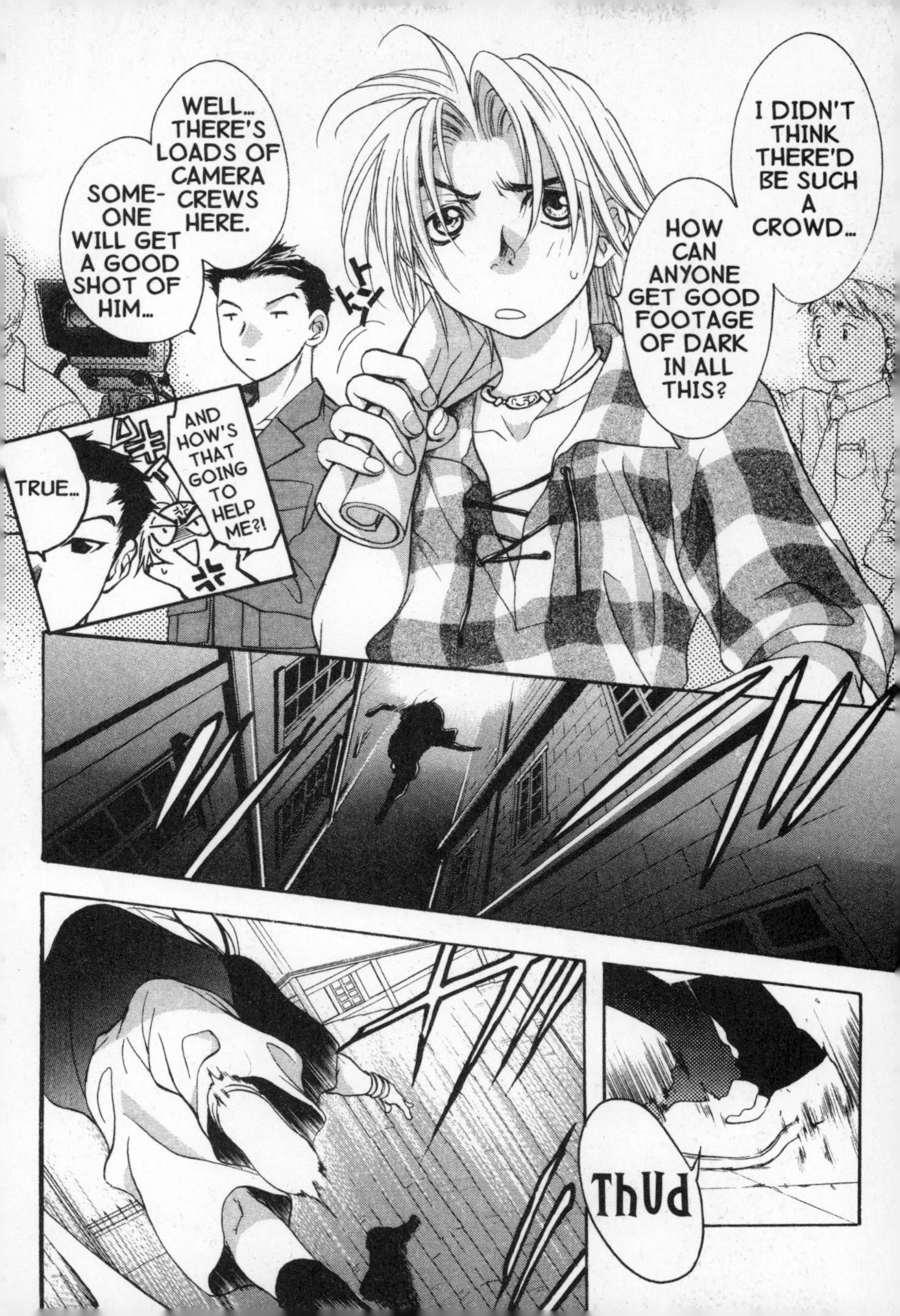
I DIDN'T THINK THERE'D BE SUCH A CROWD...
HOW CAN ANYONE GET GOOD FOOTAGE OF DARK IN ALL THIS?
WELL... THERE'S LOADS OF CAMERA CREWS HERE.
SOME-ONE WILL GET A GOOD SHOT OF HIM...
AND HOW'S THAT GOING TO HELP ME?!
TRUE...
ThUd

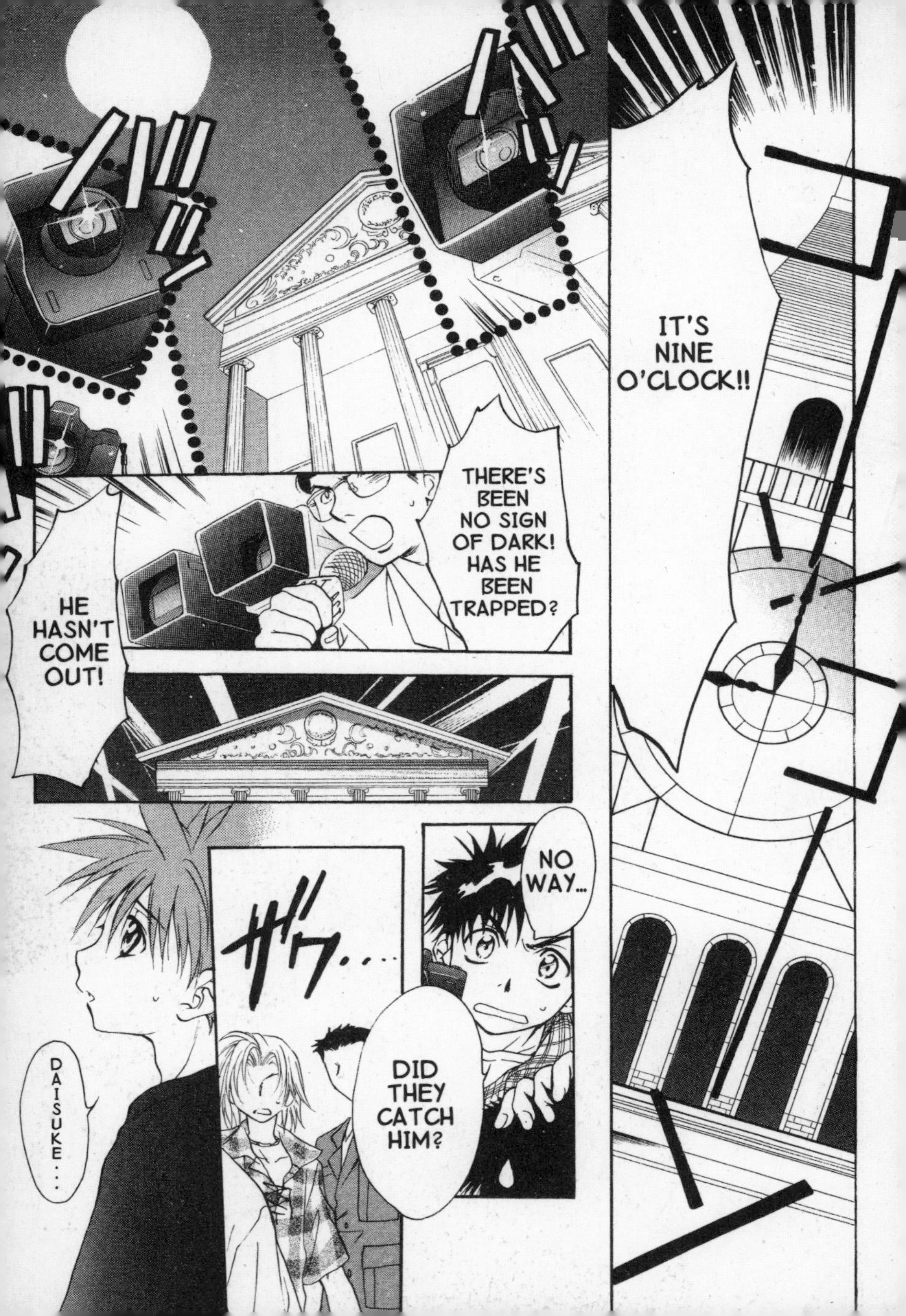
IT'S NINE O'CLOCK!!
THERE'S BEEN NO SIGN OF DARK! HAS HE BEEN TRAPPED?
HE HASN'T COME OUT!
NO WAY...
ザワ...
DID THEY CATCH HIM?
DAISUKE...

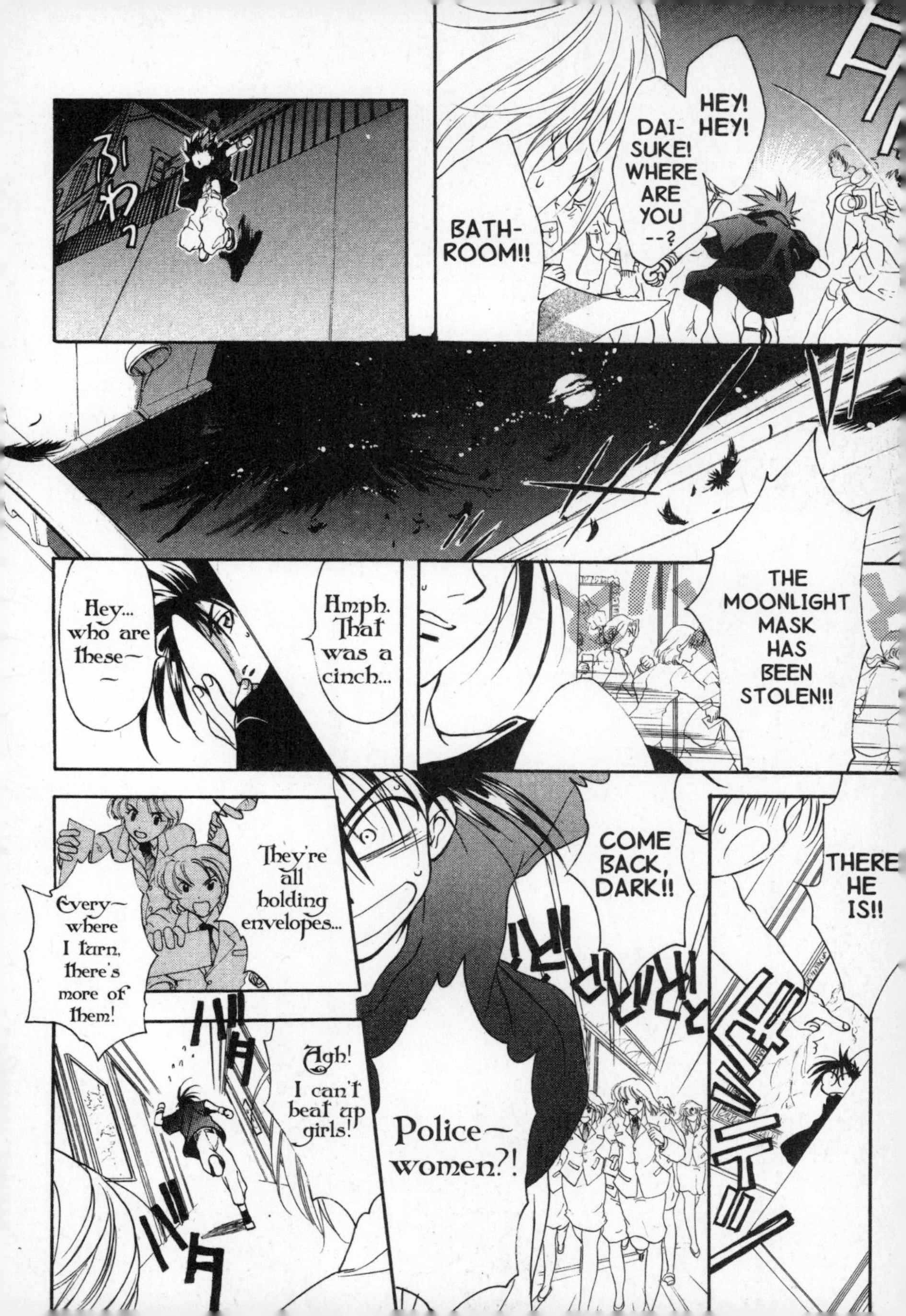
HEY! HEY!
DAI-SUKE! WHERE ARE YOU --?
BATH-ROOM!!
ふわっ
THE MOONLIGHT MASK HAS BEEN STOLEN!!
Hmph. That was a cinch...
Hey... who are these~~
THERE HE IS!!
COME BACK, DARK!!
They're all holding envelopes...
Every~where I turn, there's more of them!
Agh! I can't beat up girls!
Police~women?!

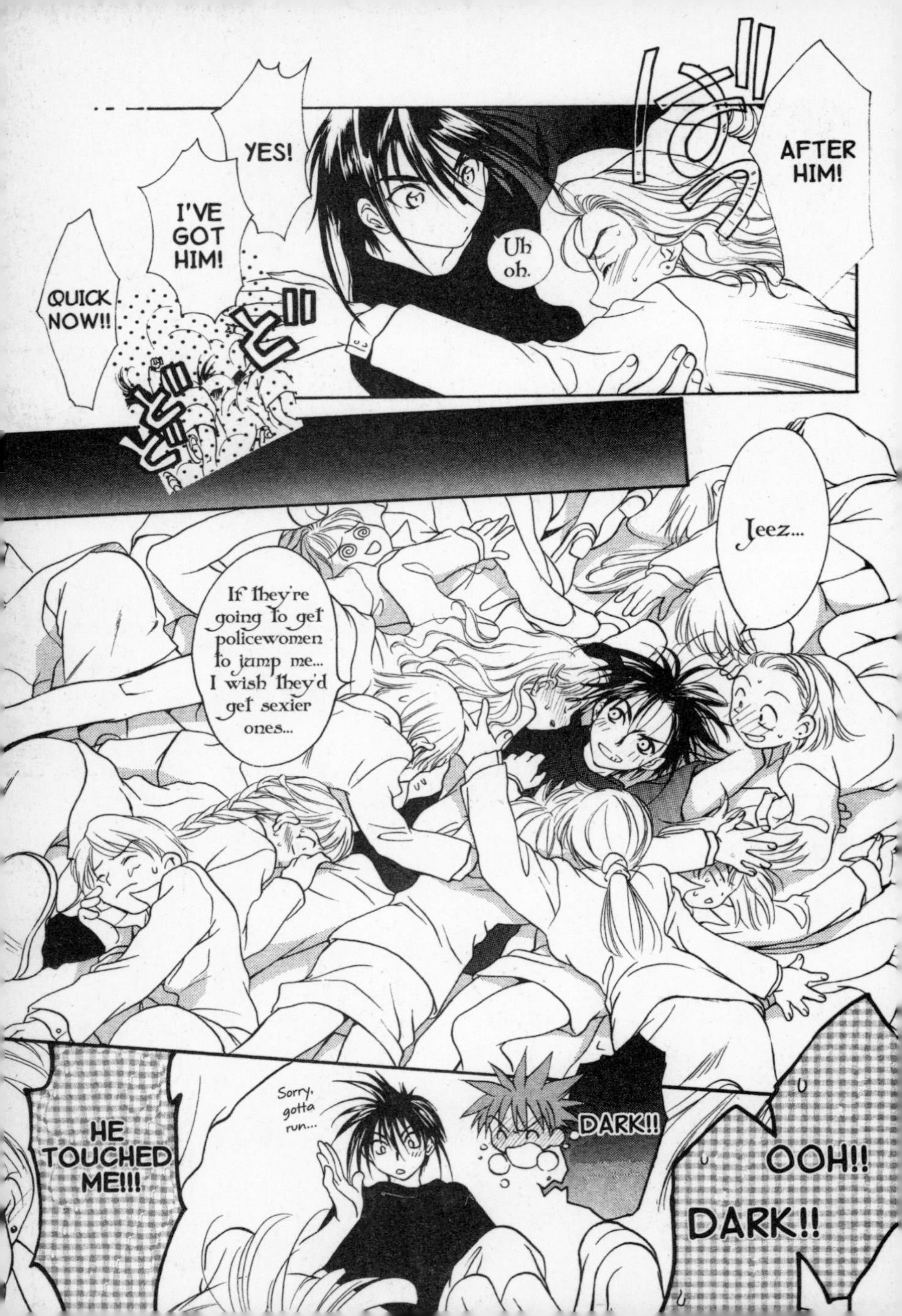
AFTER HIM!
Uh oh.
YES!
I'VE GOT HIM!
QUICK NOW!!
Jeez...
If they're going to get policewomen to jump me... I wish they'd get sexier ones...
OOH!! DARK!!
DARK!!
Sorry, gotta run...
HE TOUCHED ME!!!

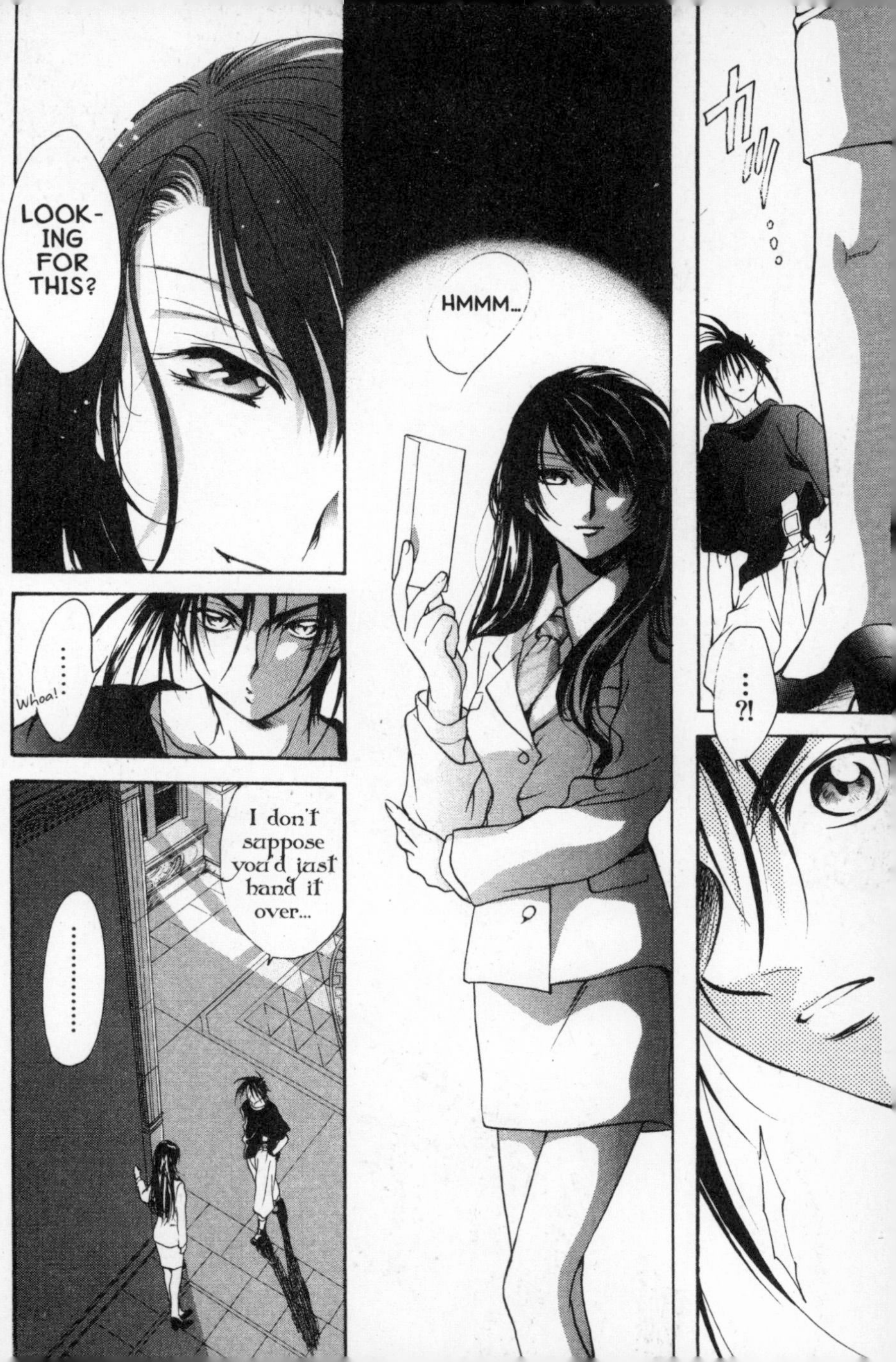

カッ
...?!
HMMM...
LOOKING-ING FOR THIS?
......
Whoa!
I don't suppose you'd just hand it over...
....

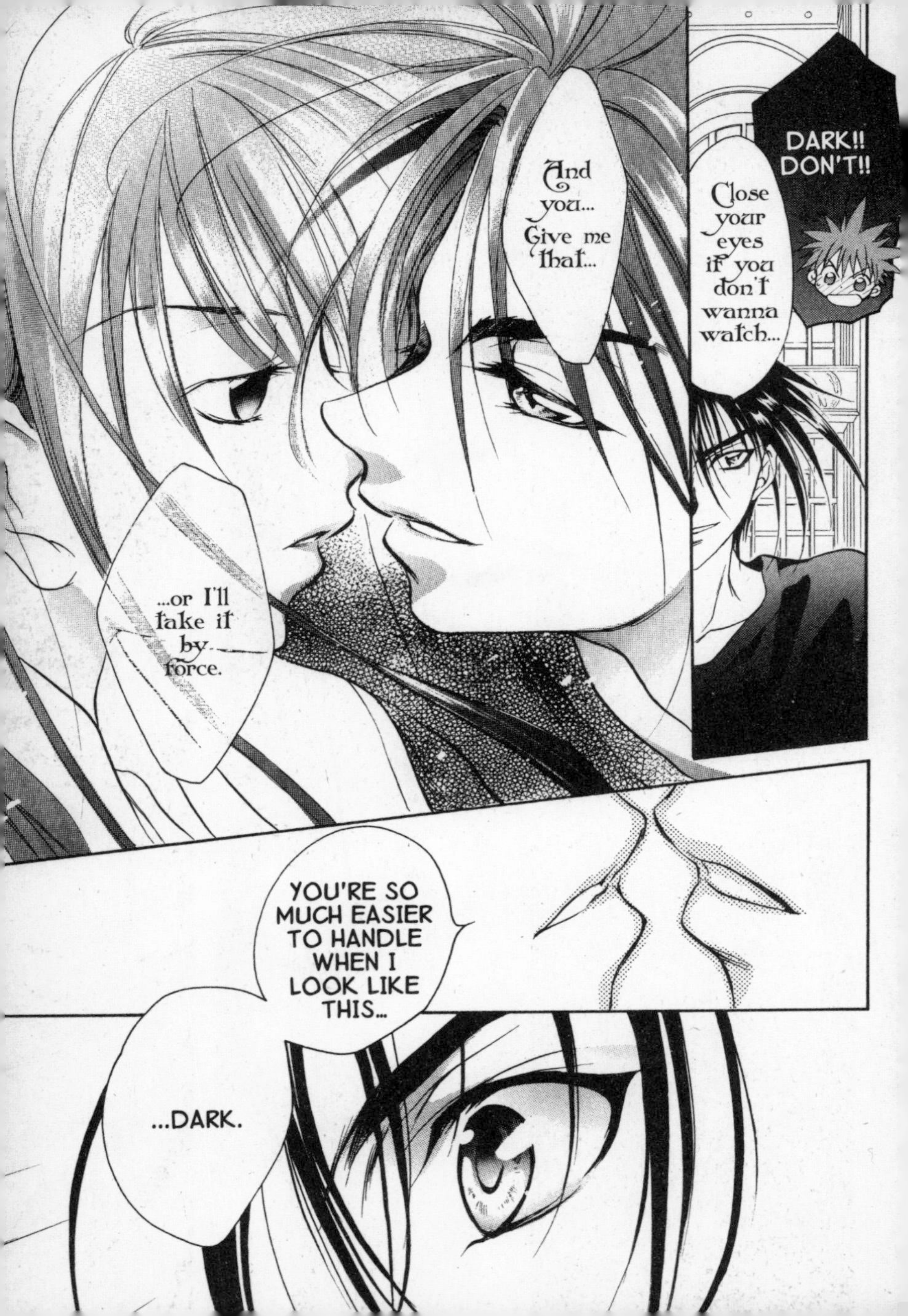
DARK!! DON'T!!
Close your eyes if you don't wanna watch...
And you... Give me that...
...or I'll take it by force.
YOU'RE SO MUCH EASIER TO HANDLE WHEN I LOOK LIKE THIS...
...DARK.

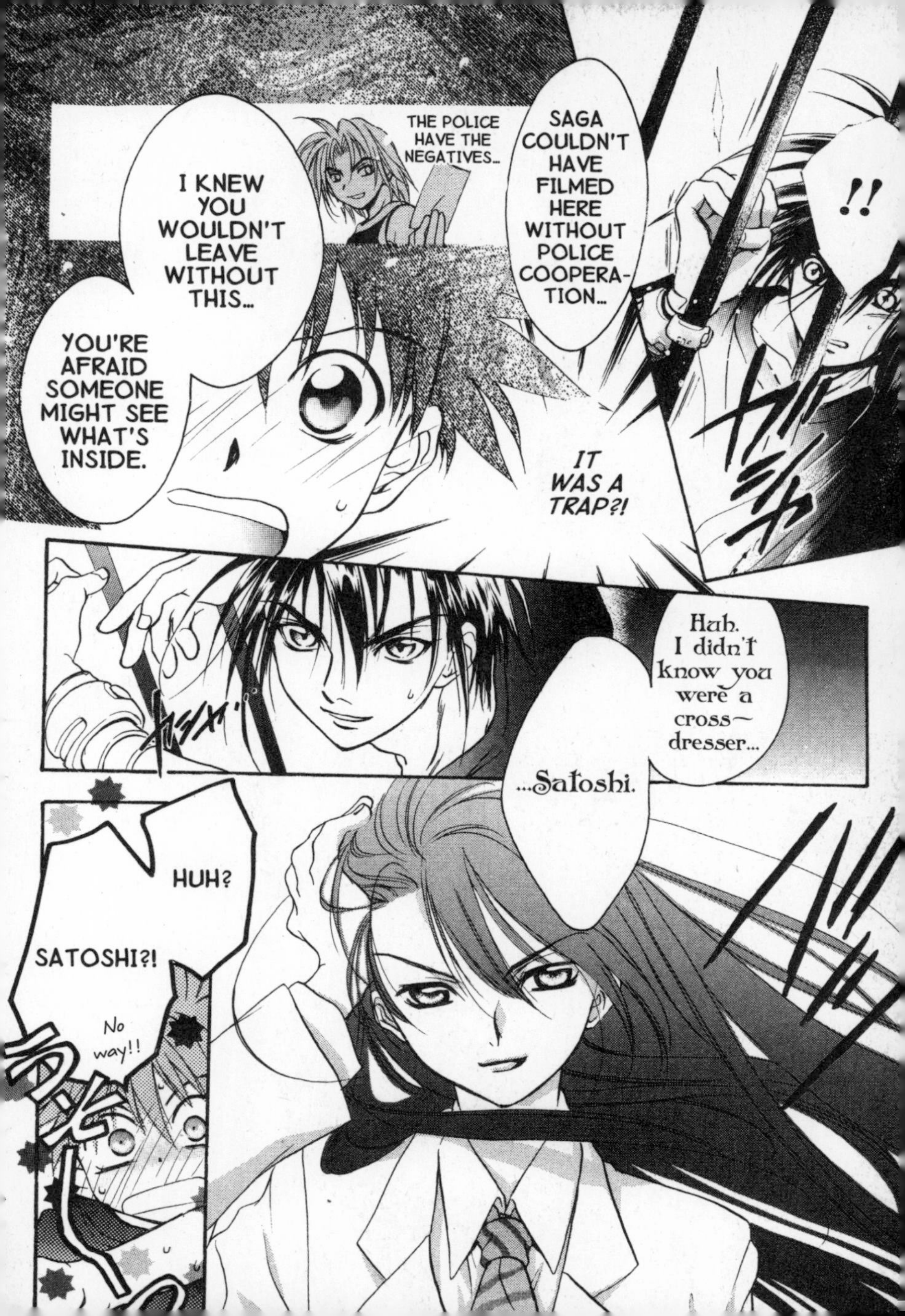
!!
SAGA COULDN'T HAVE FILMED HERE WITHOUT POLICE COOPERATION...
THE POLICE HAVE THE NEGATIVES...
I KNEW YOU WOULDN'T LEAVE WITHOUT THIS...
YOU'RE AFRAID SOMEONE MIGHT SEE WHAT'S INSIDE.
IT WAS A TRAP?!
Huh. I didn't know you were a cross-dresser...
...Satoshi.
HUH?
SATOSHI?!
No way!!

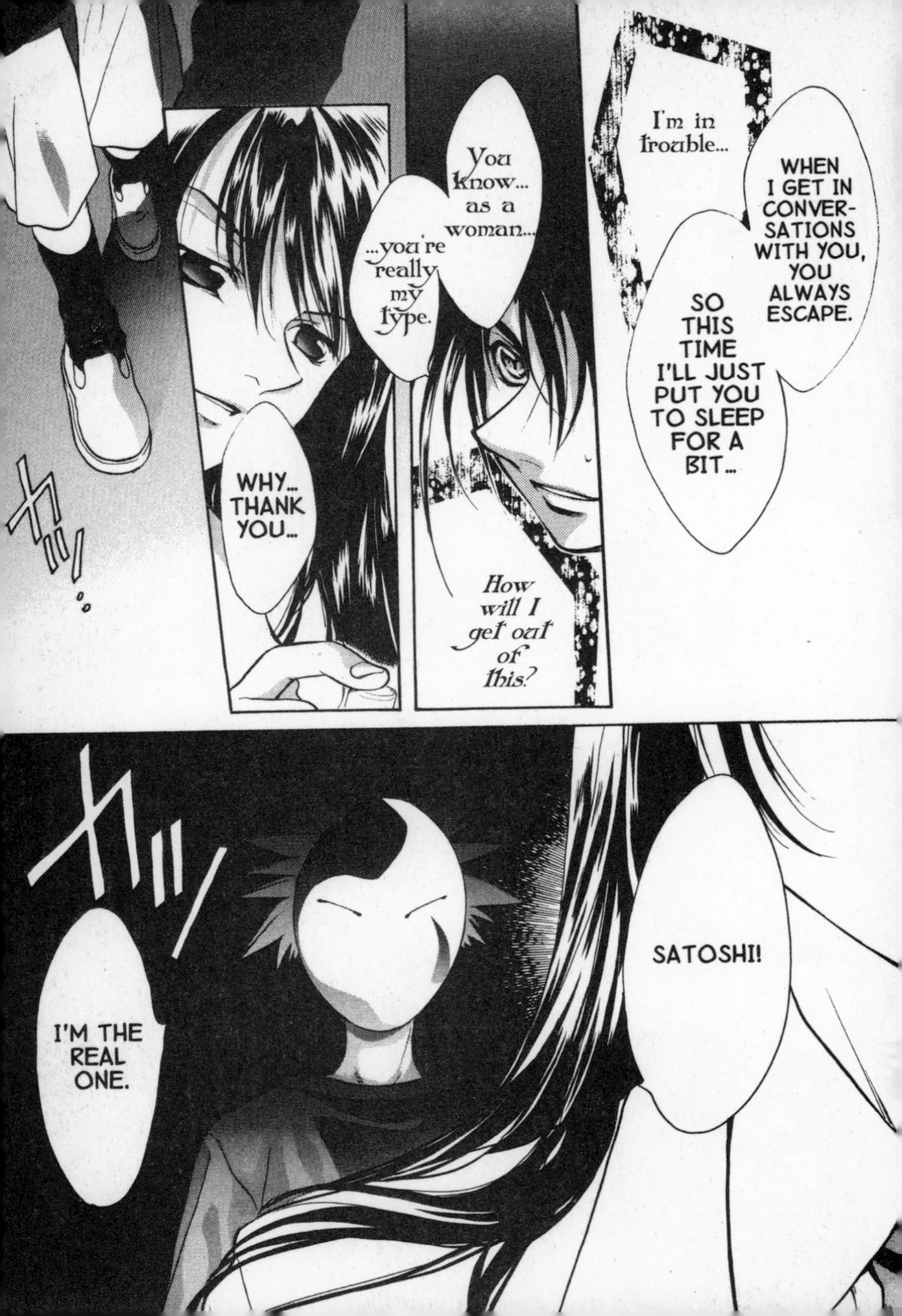
I'm in trouble...
WHEN I GET IN CONVERSATIONS WITH YOU, YOU ALWAYS ESCAPE.
SO THIS TIME I'LL JUST PUT YOU TO SLEEP FOR A BIT...
How will I get out of this?
You know... as a woman...
...you're really my type.
WHY... THANK YOU...
SATOSHI!
I'M THE REAL ONE.

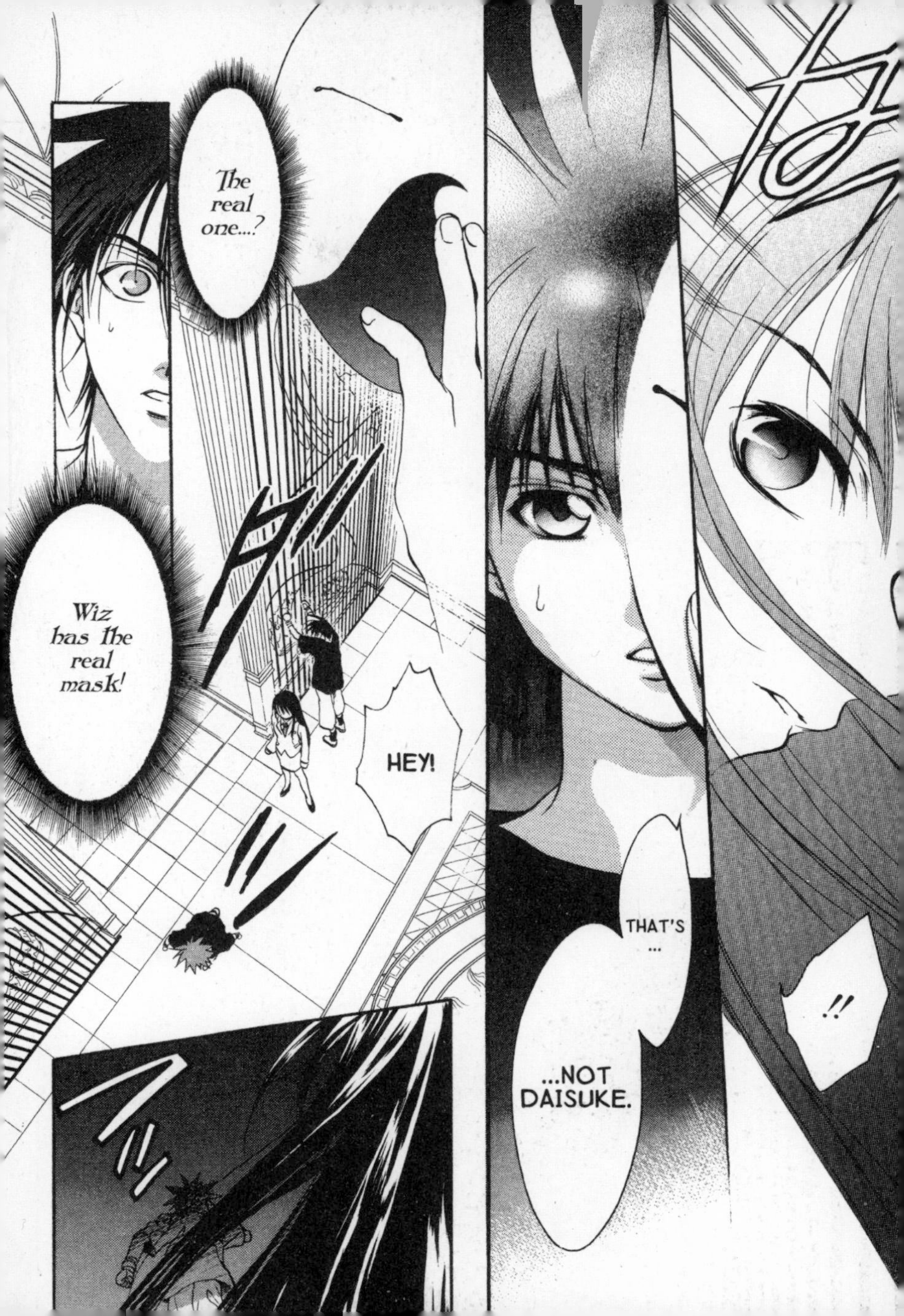
!!
THAT'S ...
...NOT DAISUKE.
The real one...?
Wiz has the real mask!
HEY!

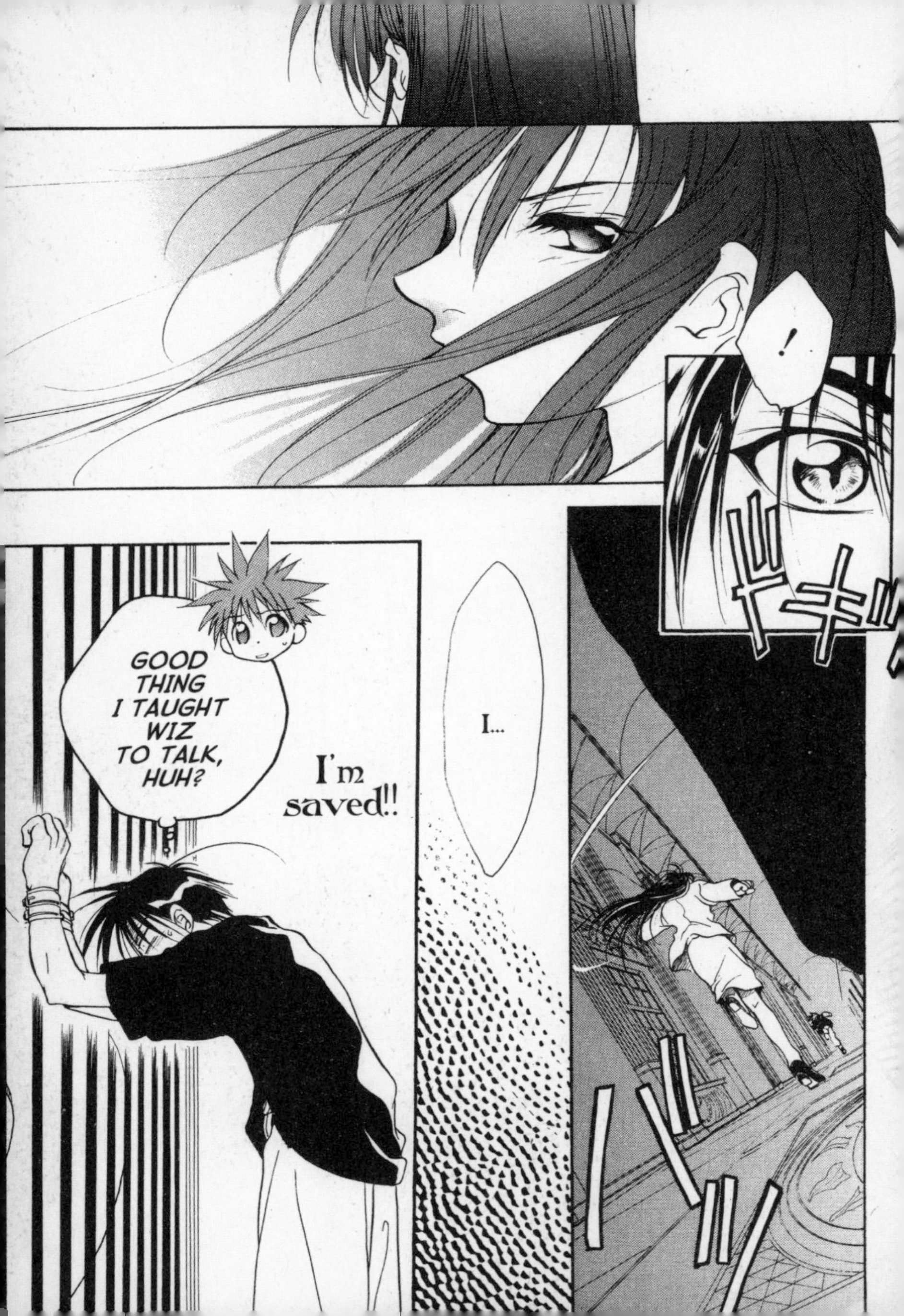
!
I...
GOOD THING I TAUGHT WIZ TO TALK, HUH?
I'm saved!!

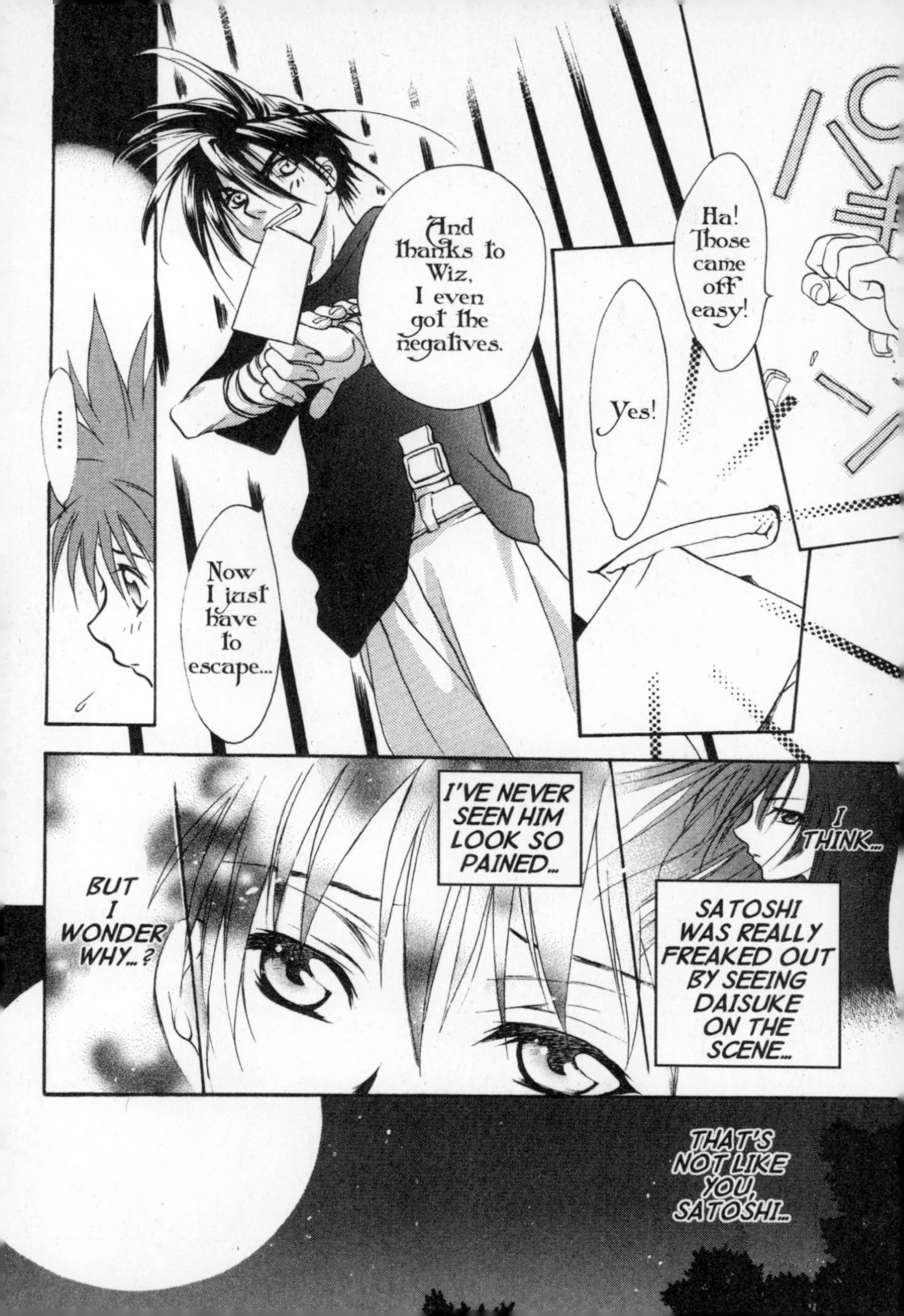
Ha! Those came off easy!
Yes!
And thanks to Wiz, I even got the negatives.
Now I just have to escape...
......
I THINK...
SATOSHI WAS REALLY FREAKED OUT BY SEEING DAISUKE ON THE SCENE...
I'VE NEVER SEEN HIM LOOK SO PAINED...
BUT I WONDER WHY...?
THAT'S NOT LIKE YOU, SATOSHI...

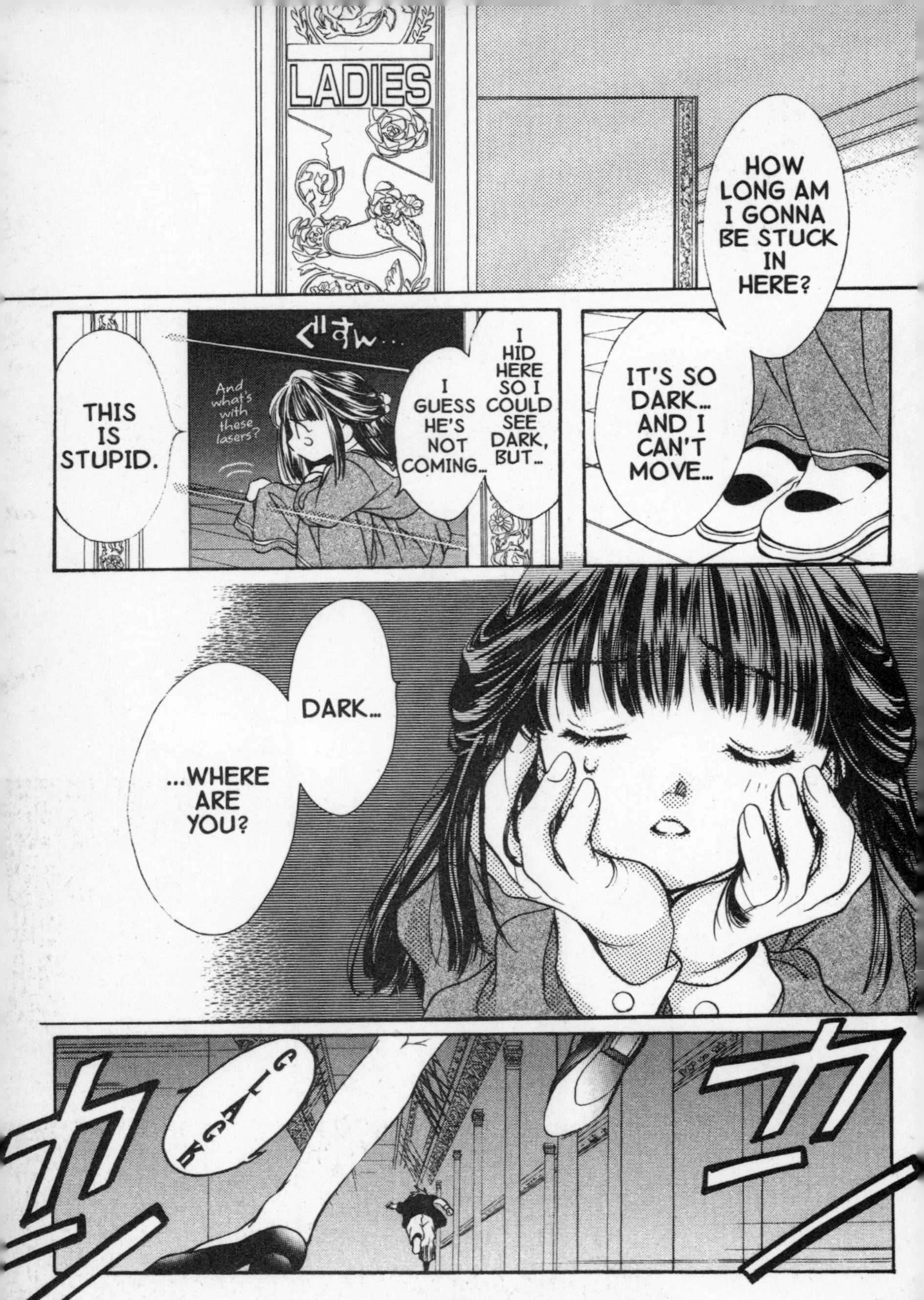
LADIES
HOW LONG AM I GONNA BE STUCK IN HERE?
IT'S SO DARK... AND I CAN'T MOVE...
I HID HERE SO I COULD SEE DARK, BUT...
I GUESS HE'S NOT COMING...
ぐすん...
And what's with these lasers?
THIS IS STUPID.
DARK...
...WHERE ARE YOU?
CLACK

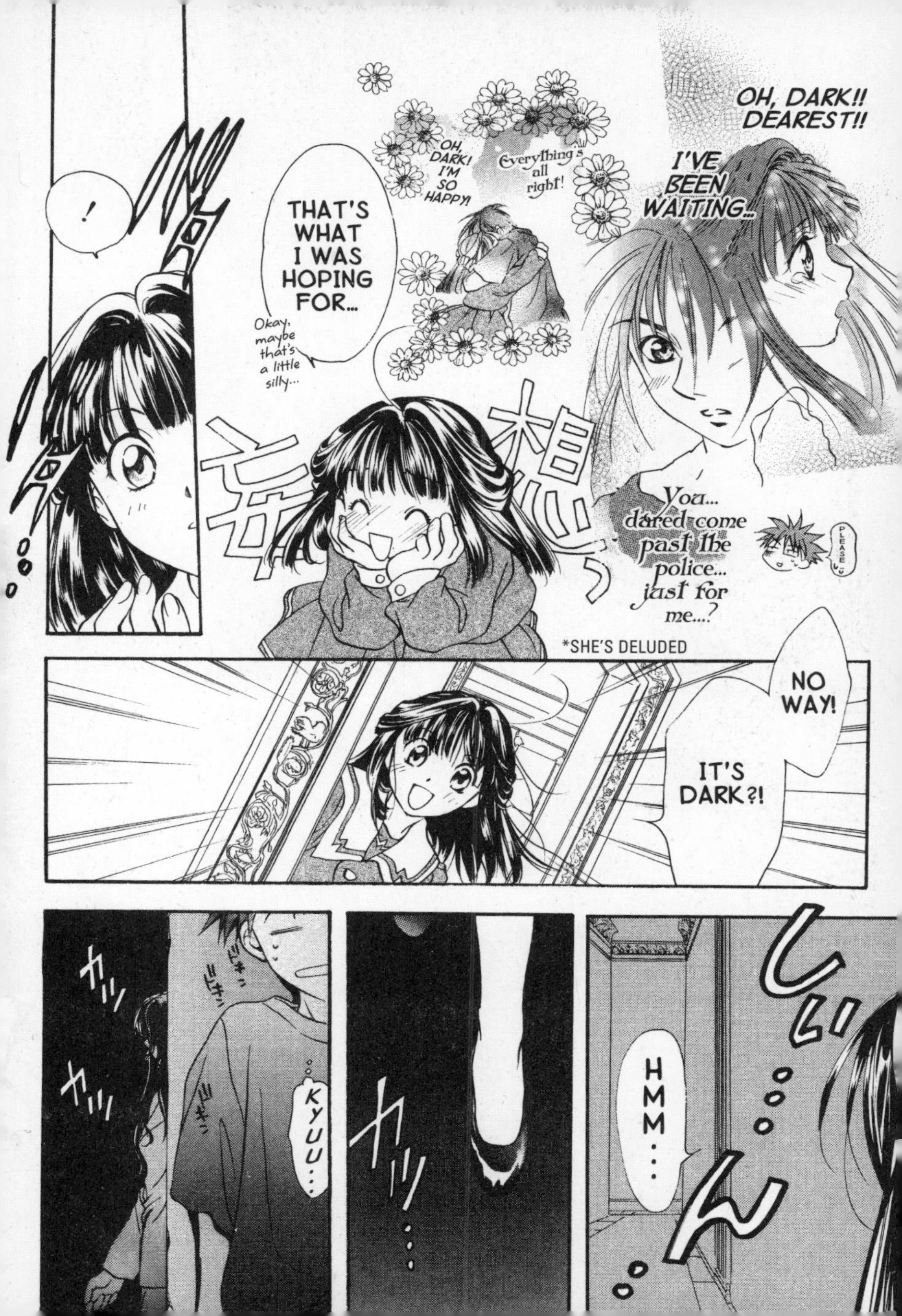
OH, DARK!! DEAREST!!
I'VE BEEN WAITING...
You... dared come past the police... just for me...?
PLEASE
OH, DARK! I'M SO HAPPY!
Everything's all right!
THAT'S WHAT I WAS HOPING FOR...
Okay, maybe that's a little silly...
!
*SHE'S DELUDED
NO WAY!
IT'S DARK?!
HMM...
KYUU...

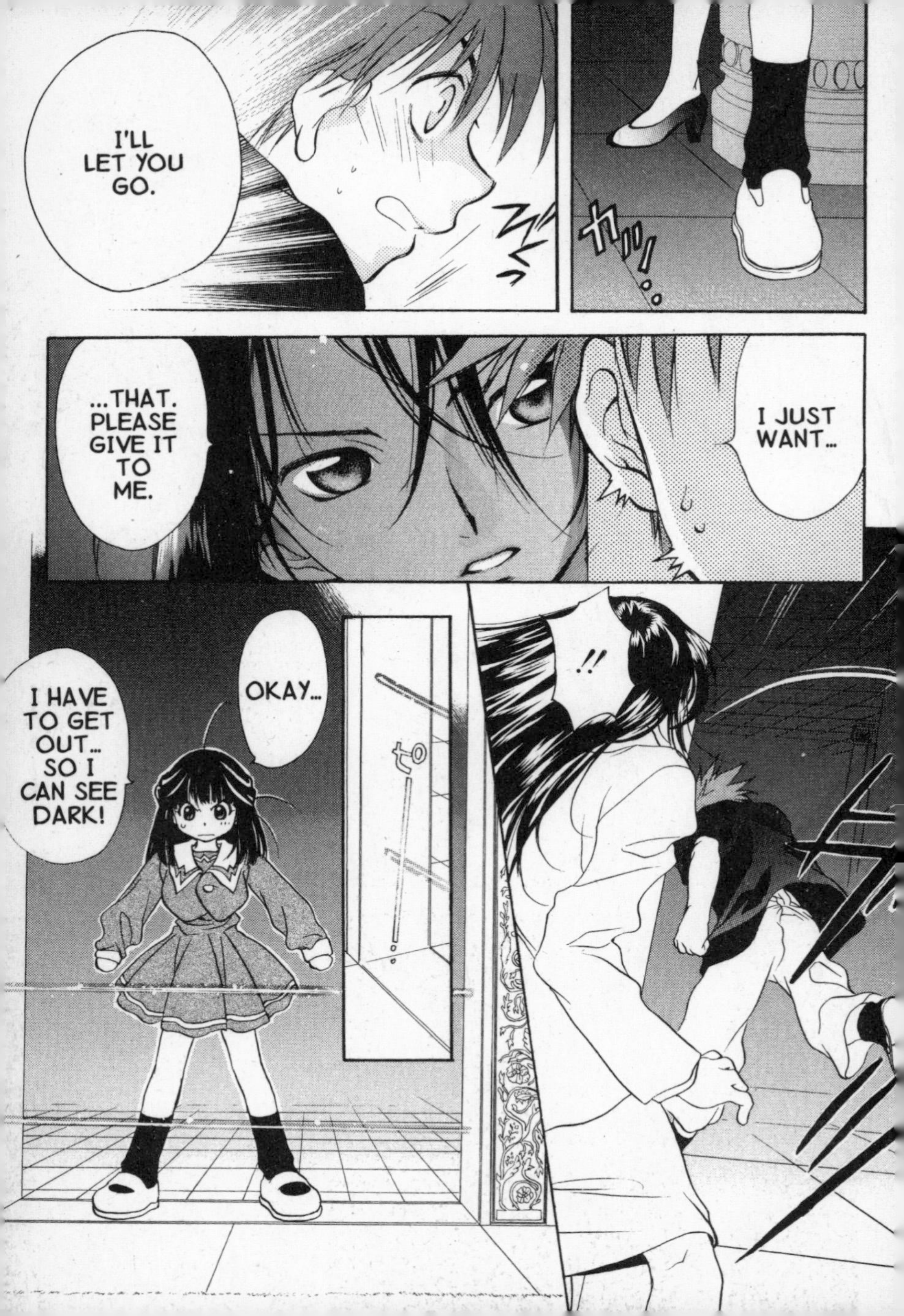

I'LL LET YOU GO.
I JUST WANT...
...THAT. PLEASE GIVE IT TO ME.
!!
OKAY...
I HAVE TO GET OUT... SO I CAN SEE DARK!

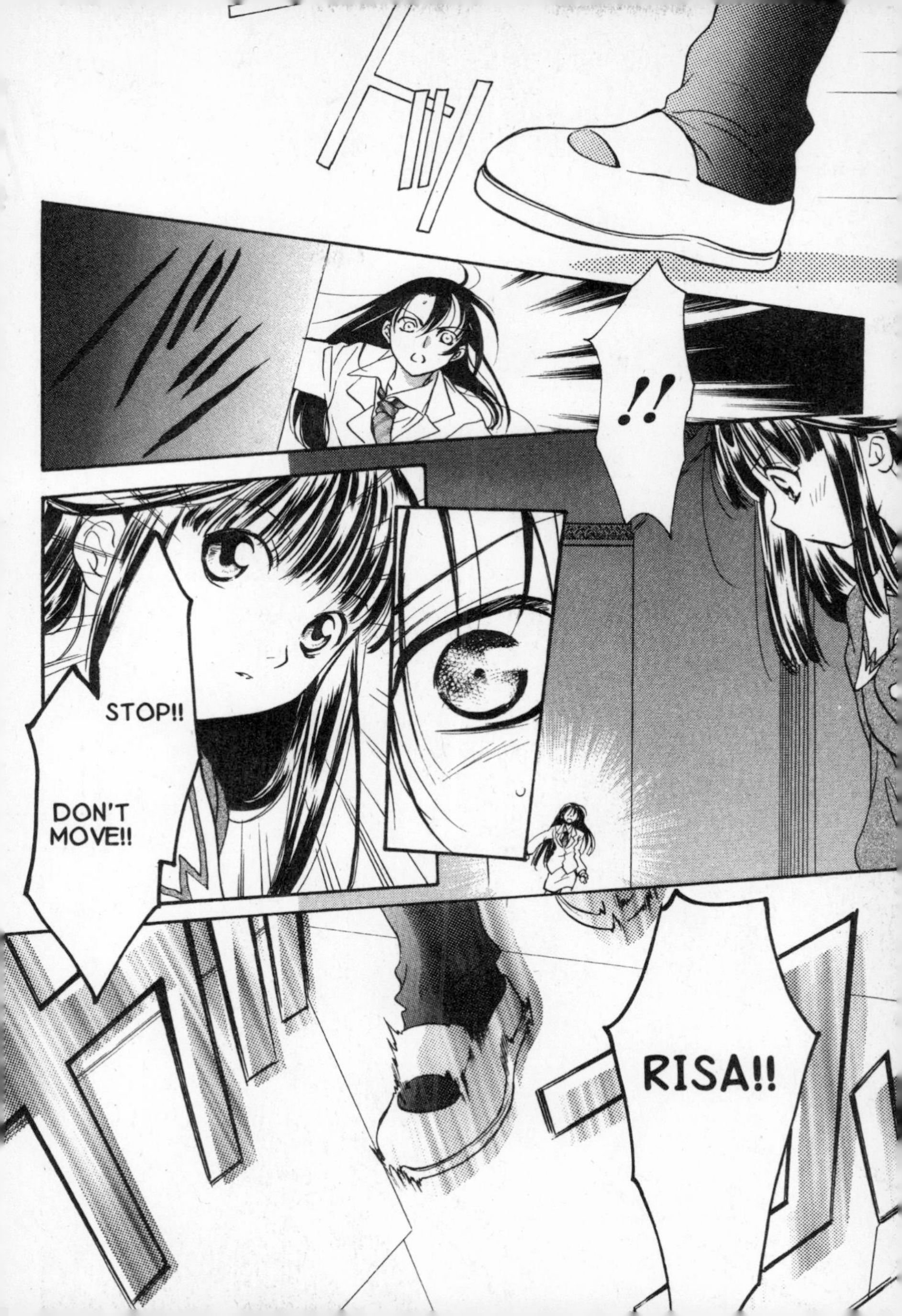
!!
STOP!!
DON'T MOVE!!
RISA!!

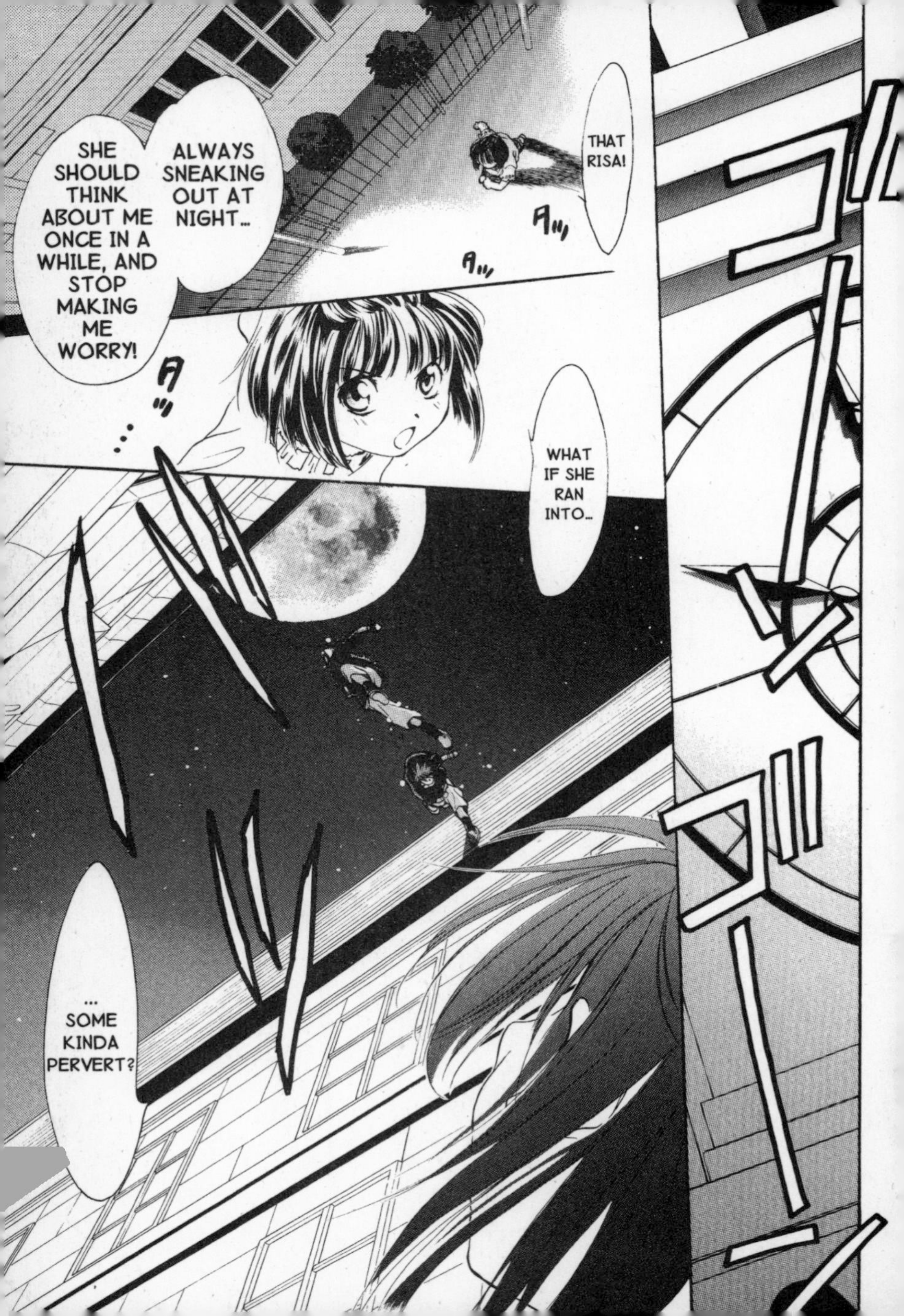

THAT RISA!
ALWAYS SNEAKING OUT AT NIGHT...
SHE SHOULD THINK ABOUT ME ONCE IN A WHILE, AND STOP MAKING ME WORRY!
WHAT IF SHE RAN INTO...
... SOME KINDA PERVERT?

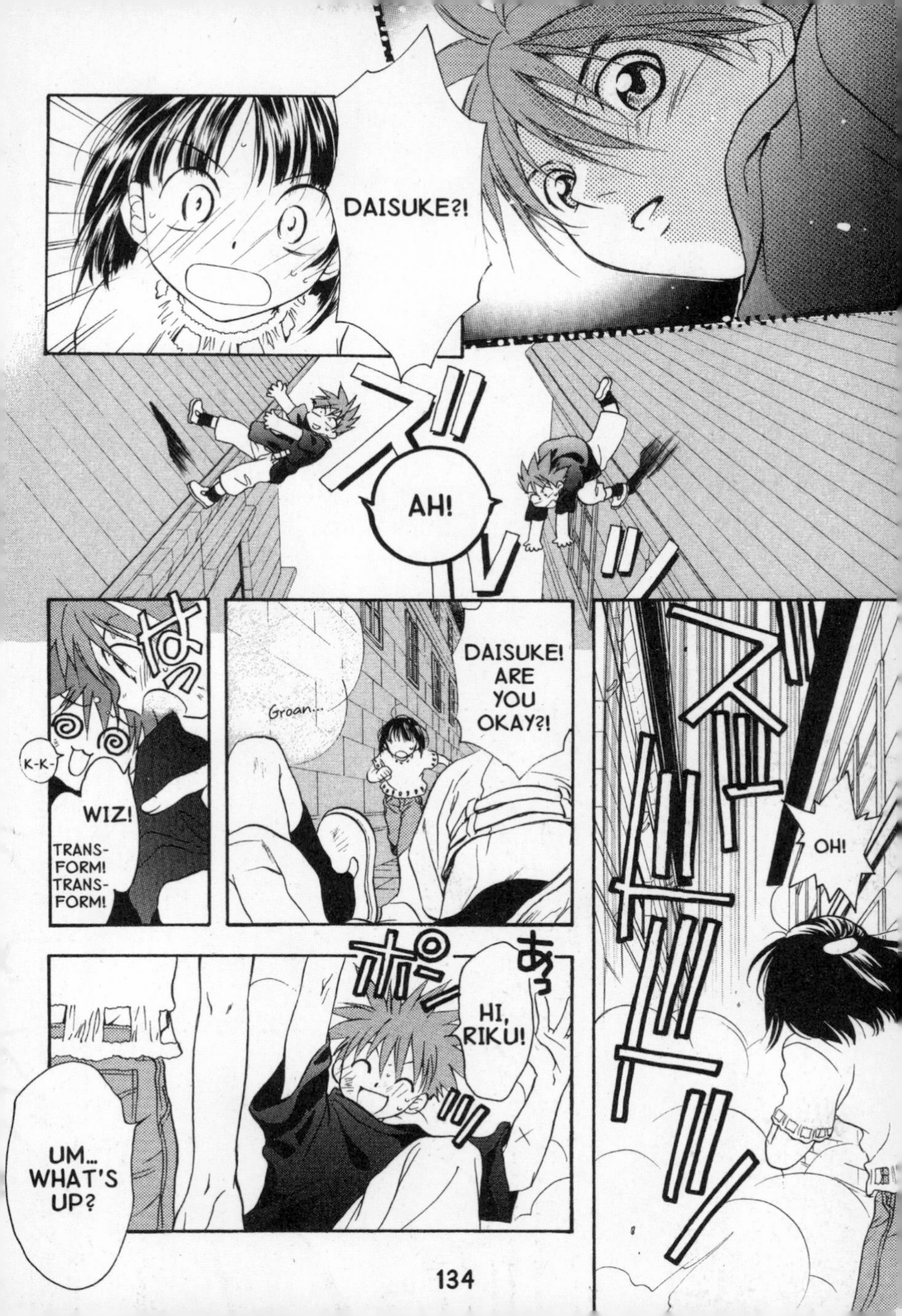
DAISUKE?!
AH!
OH!
DAISUKE! ARE YOU OKAY?!
Groan...
なっ
K-K-
WIZ!
TRANSFORM! TRANSFORM!
あっ
HI, RIKU!
UM... WHAT'S UP?

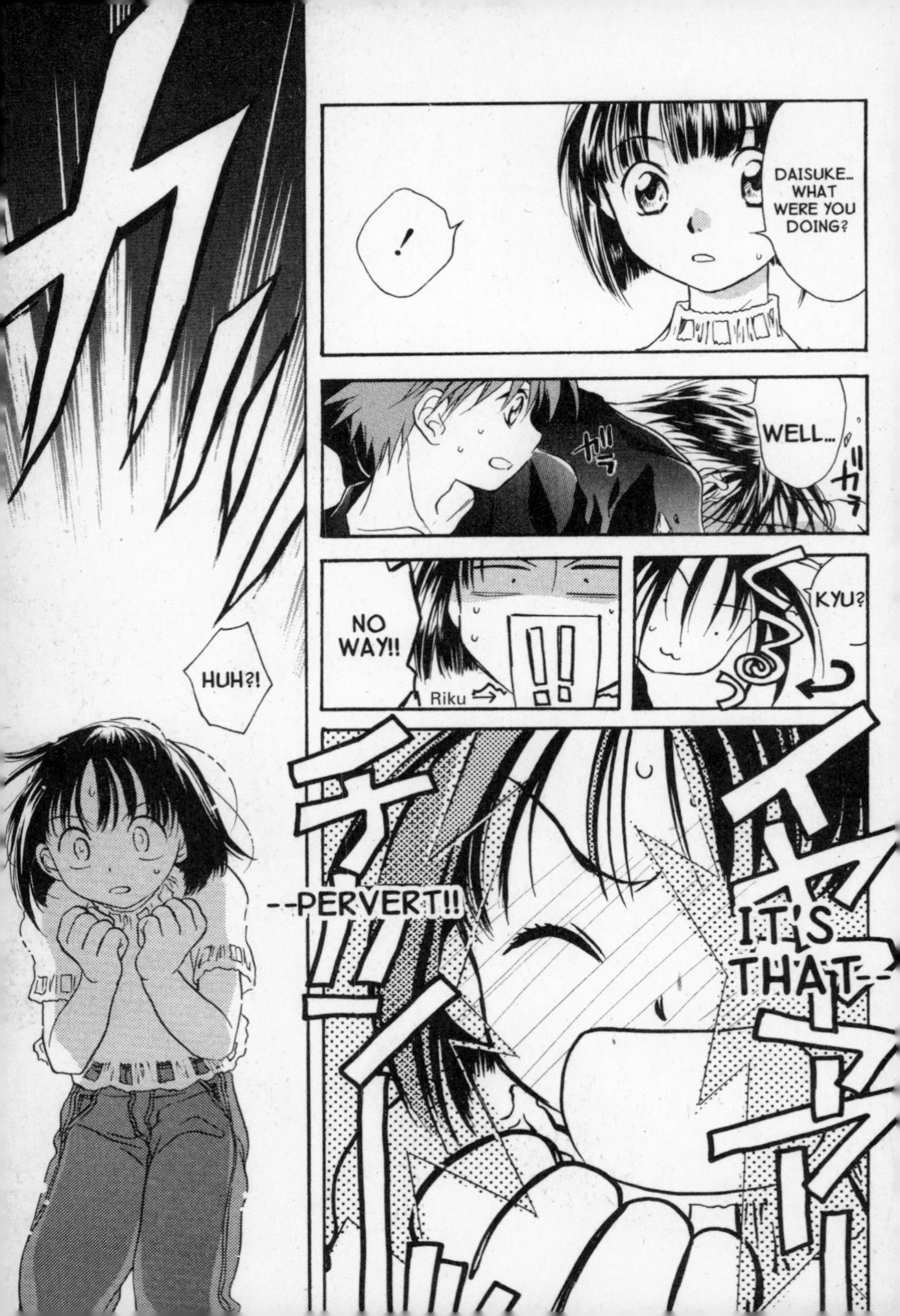
DAISUKE... WHAT WERE YOU DOING?
!
WELL...
KYU?
NO WAY!!
Riku
HUH?!
IT'S THAT--
--PERVERT!!

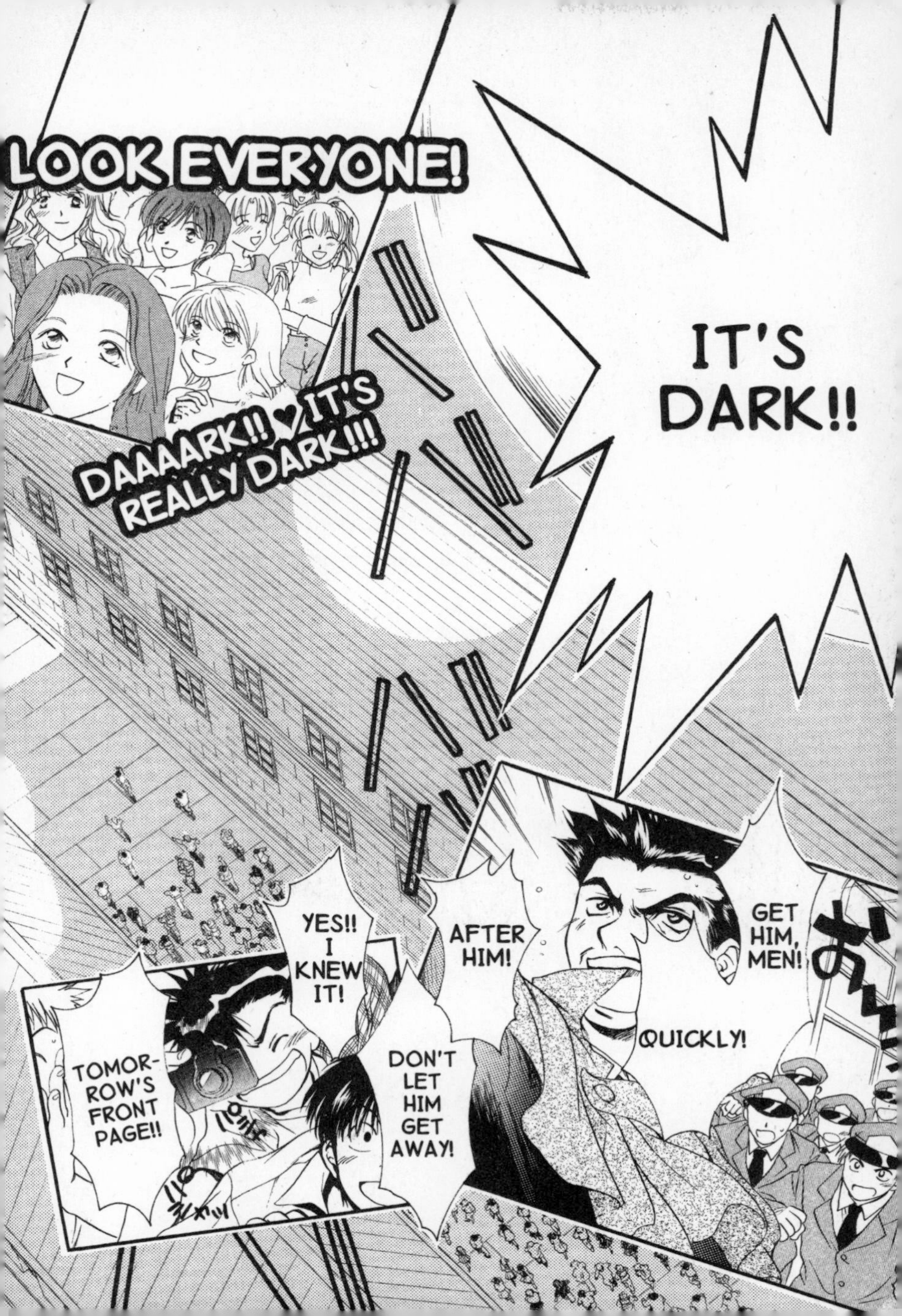
IT'S DARK!!
LOOK EVERYONE!
DAAAARK!! ♥ IT'S REALLY DARK!!!
GET HIM, MEN!
QUICKLY!
AFTER HIM!
DON'T LET HIM GET AWAY!
YES!! I KNEW IT!
TOMORROW'S FRONT PAGE!!

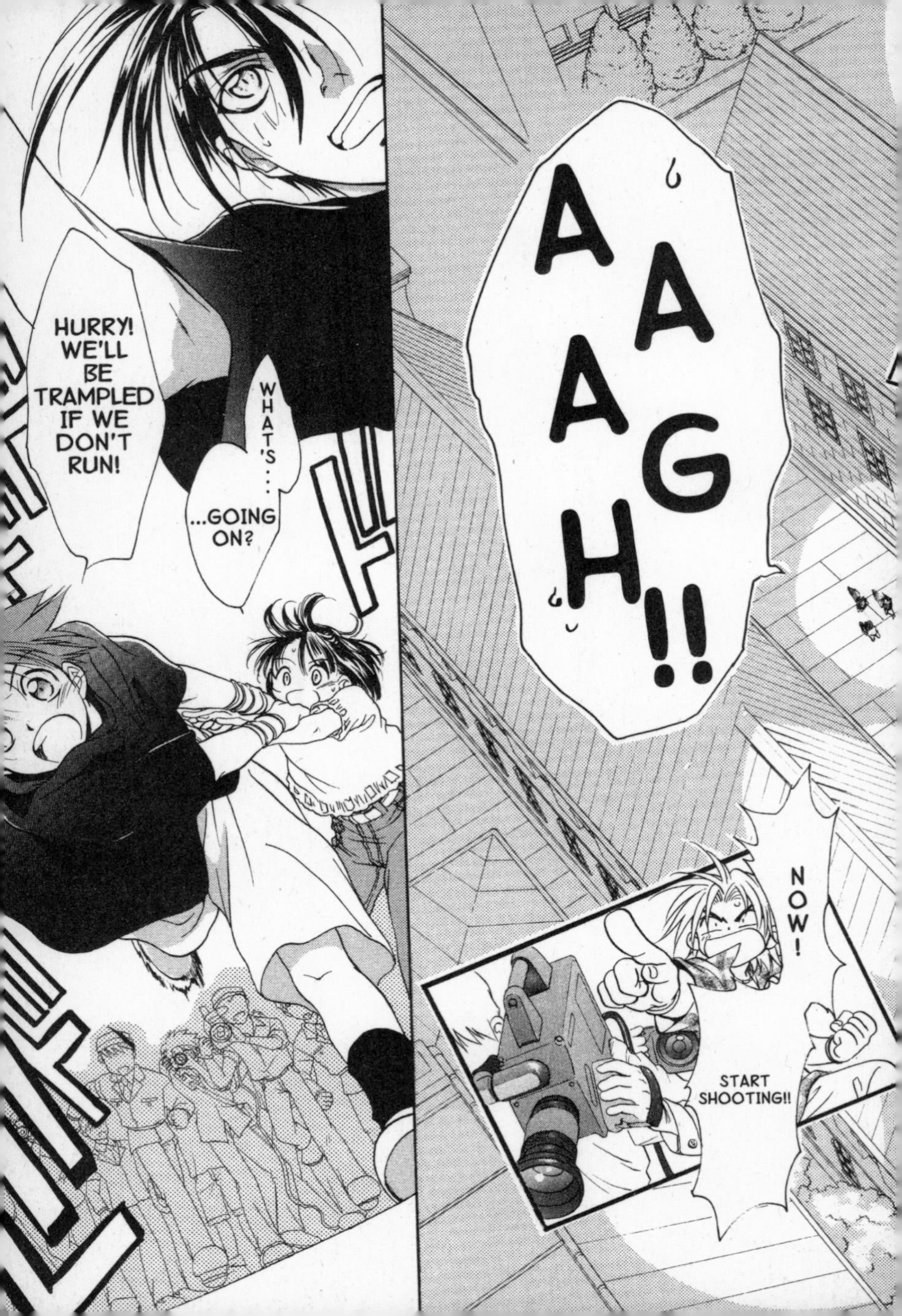
AAAGH!!
NOW!
START SHOOTING!!
WHAT'S...
...GOING ON?
HURRY! WE'LL BE TRAMPLED IF WE DON'T RUN!

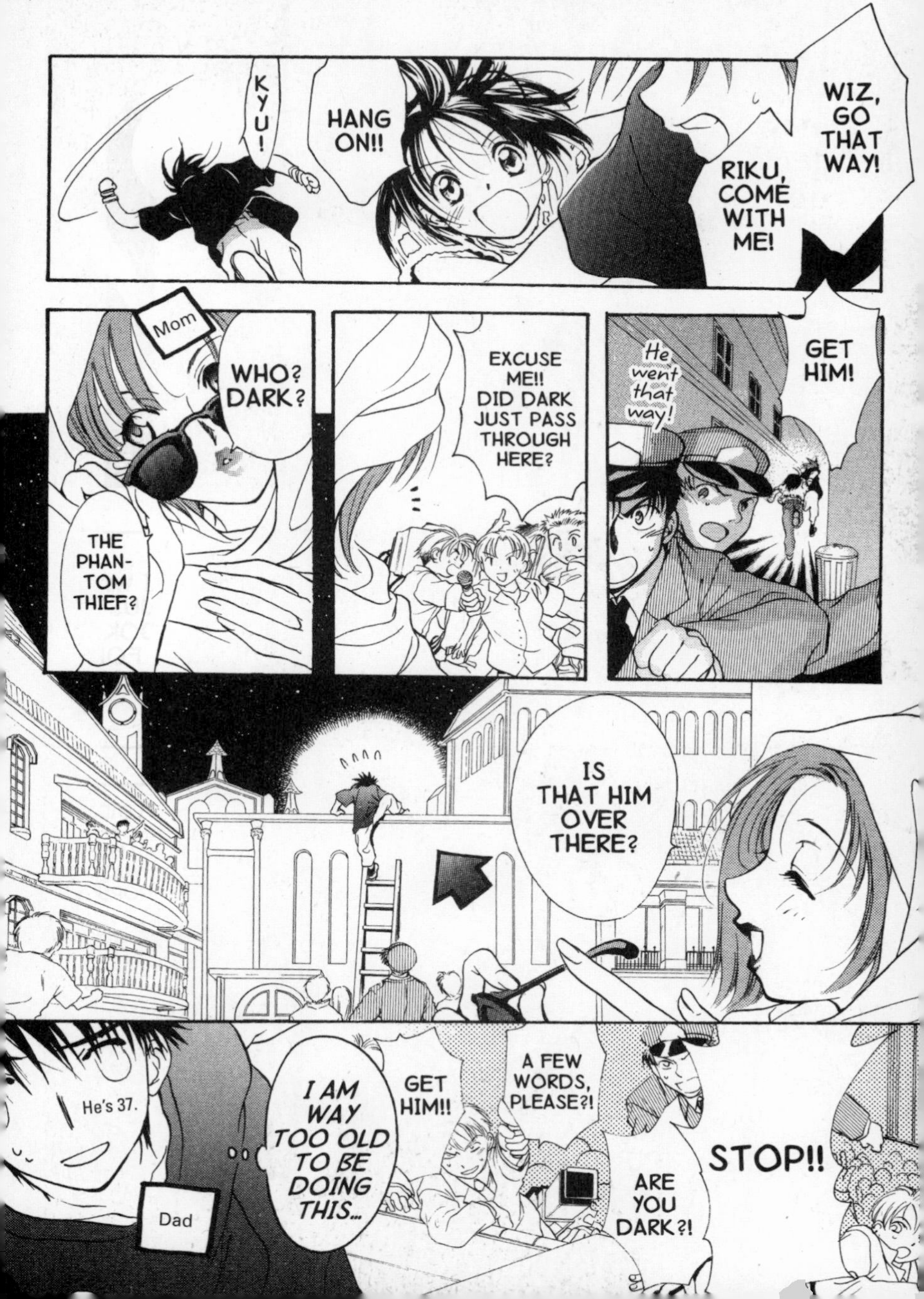
WIZ, GO THAT WAY!
RIKU, COME WITH ME!
HANG ON!!
KYU!
GET HIM!
He went that way!
EXCUSE ME!! DID DARK JUST PASS THROUGH HERE?
Mom
WHO? DARK?
THE PHAN-TOM THIEF?
IS THAT HIM OVER THERE?
STOP!!
ARE YOU DARK?!
A FEW WORDS, PLEASE?!
GET HIM!!
I AM WAY TOO OLD TO BE DOING THIS...
He's 37.
Dad

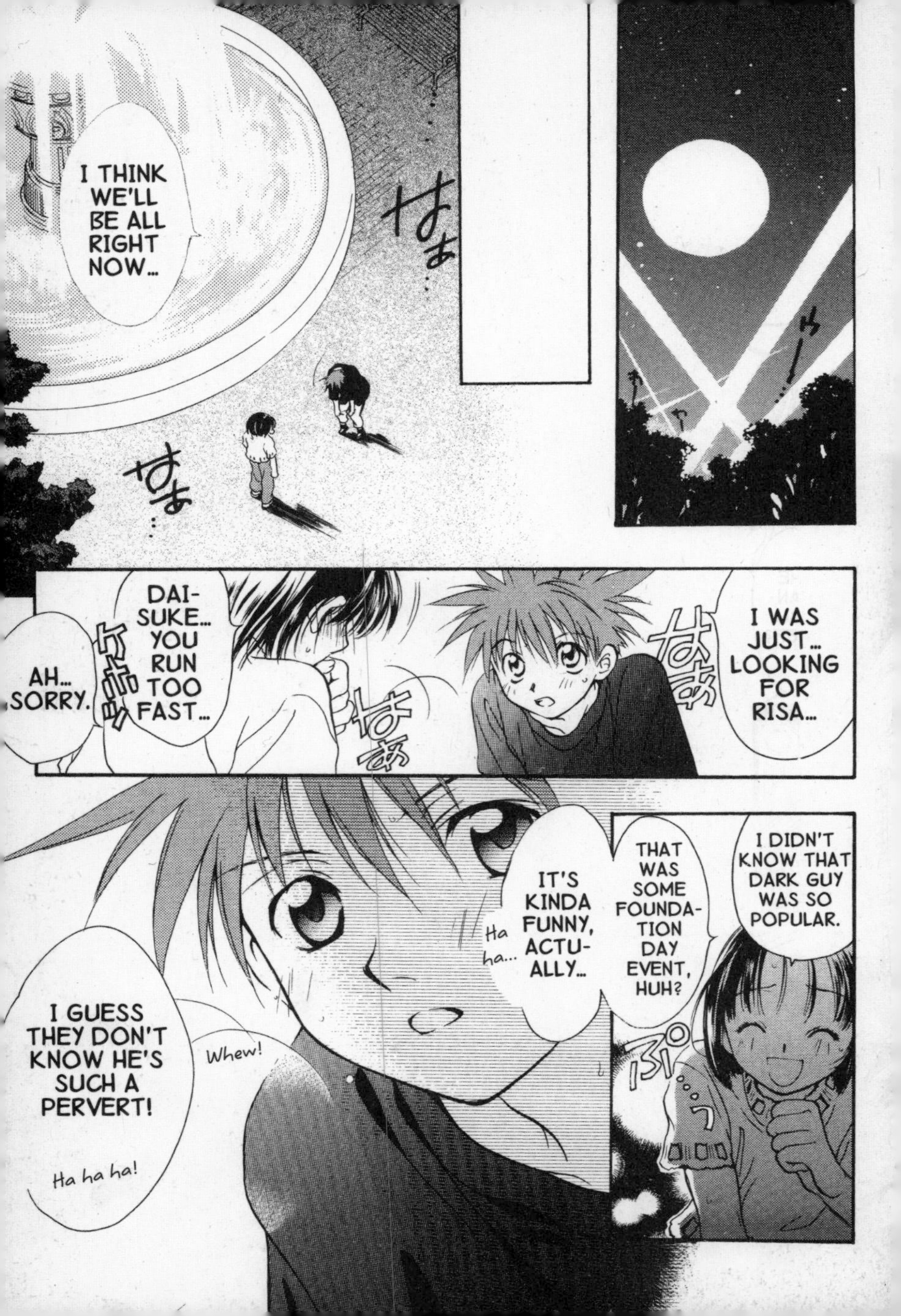

I THINK WE'LL BE ALL RIGHT NOW...
I WAS JUST... LOOKING FOR RISA...
DAI-SUKE... YOU RUN TOO FAST...
AH... SORRY.
I DIDN'T KNOW THAT DARK GUY WAS SO POPULAR.
THAT WAS SOME FOUNDA-TION DAY EVENT, HUH?
IT'S KINDA FUNNY, ACTU-ALLY...
Ha ha...
I GUESS THEY DON'T KNOW HE'S SUCH A PERVERT!
Whew!
Ha ha ha!

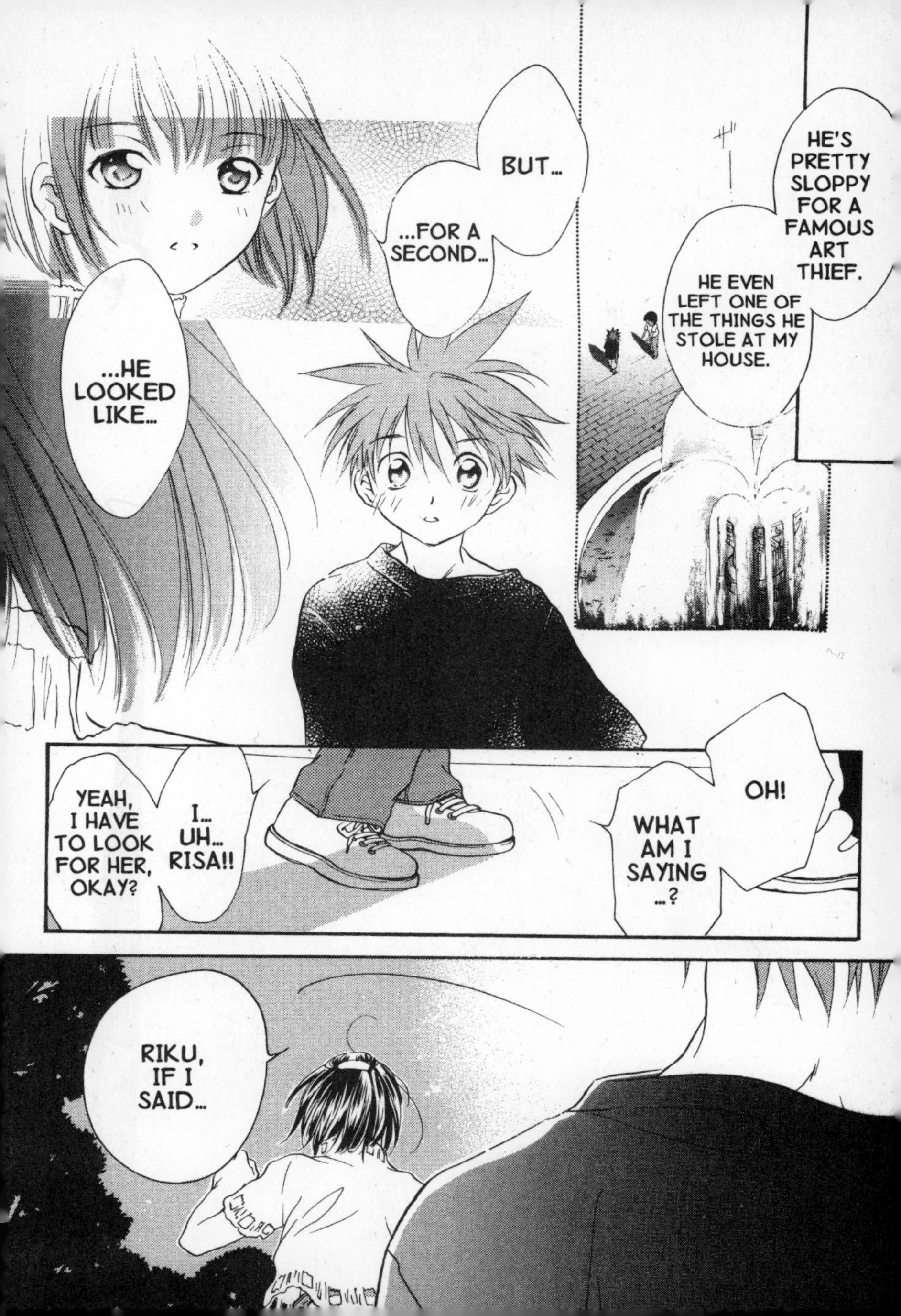
HE'S PRETTY SLOPPY FOR A FAMOUS ART THIEF.
HE EVEN LEFT ONE OF THE THINGS HE STOLE AT MY HOUSE.
BUT...
...FOR A SECOND...
...HE LOOKED LIKE...
OH!
WHAT AM I SAYING ...?
I... UH... RISA!!
YEAH, I HAVE TO LOOK FOR HER, OKAY?
RIKU, IF I SAID...

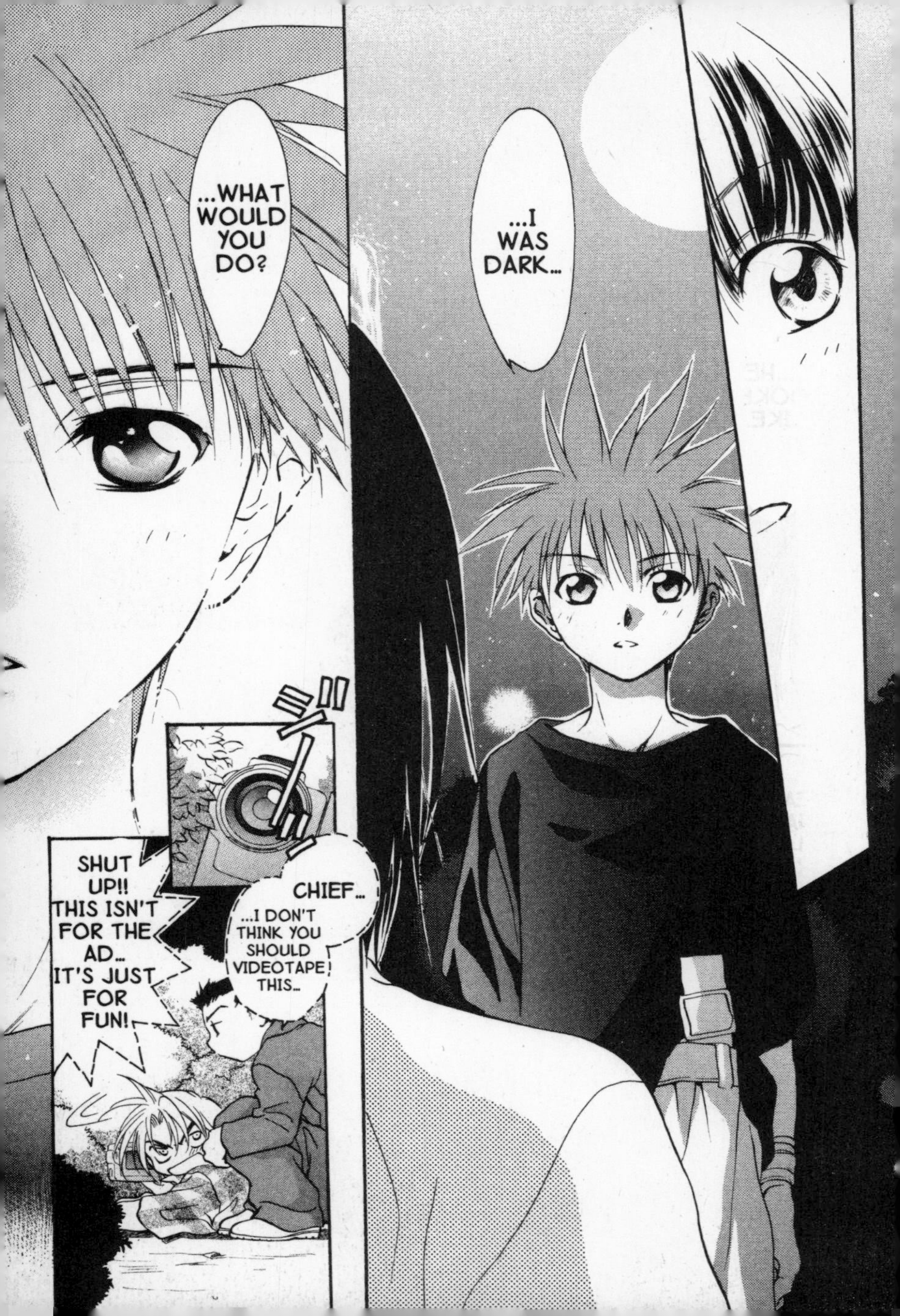
...I WAS DARK...
...WHAT WOULD YOU DO?
CHIEF... ...I DON'T THINK YOU SHOULD VIDEOTAPE THIS...
SHUT UP!! THIS ISN'T FOR THE AD... IT'S JUST FOR FUN!

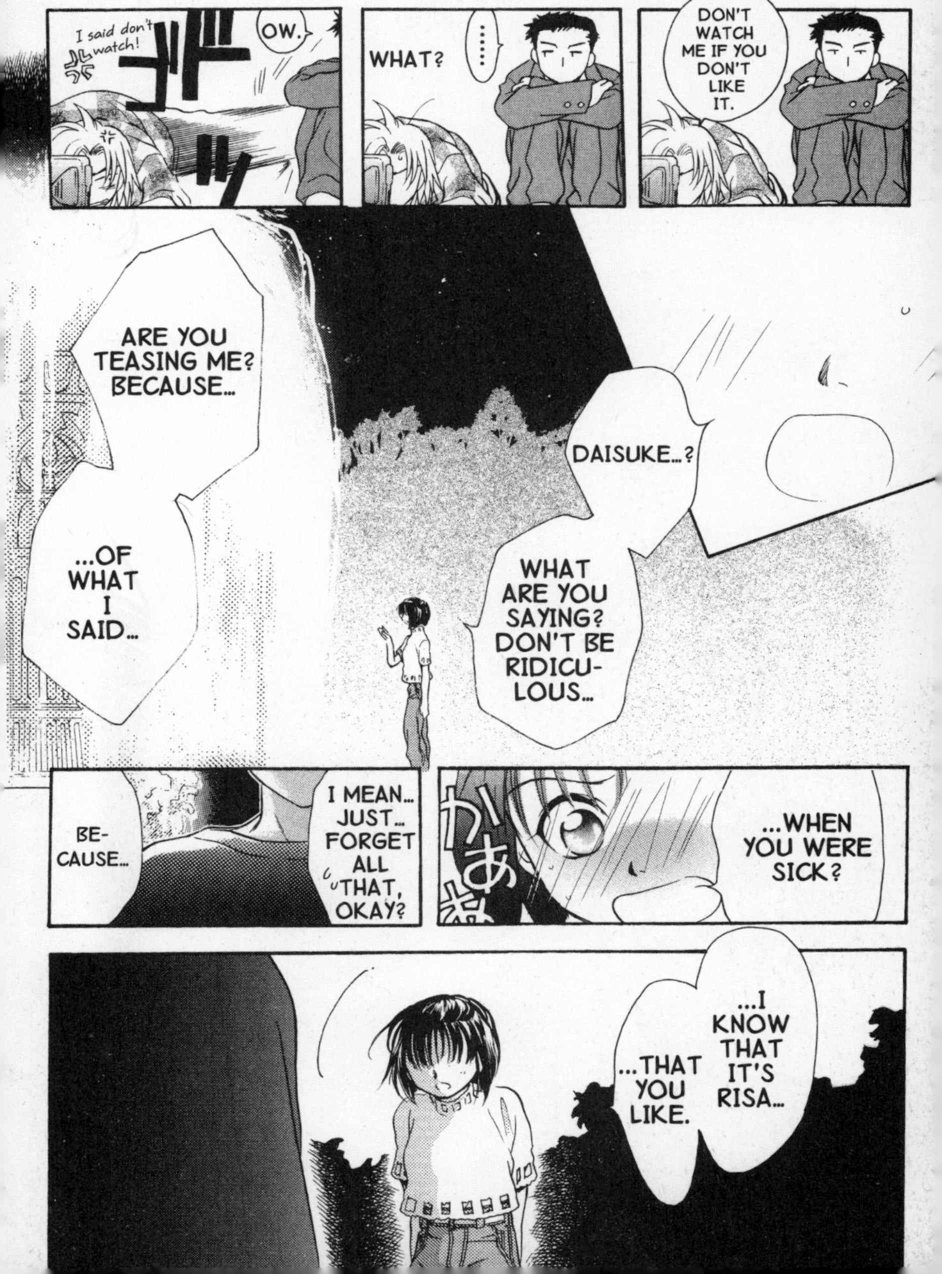
DON'T WATCH ME IF YOU DON'T LIKE IT.
......
WHAT?
OW.
I said don't watch!
DAISUKE...?
WHAT ARE YOU SAYING? DON'T BE RIDICULOUS...
ARE YOU TEASING ME? BECAUSE...
...OF WHAT I SAID...
...WHEN YOU WERE SICK?
I MEAN... JUST... FORGET ALL THAT, OKAY?
BE-CAUSE...
...I KNOW THAT IT'S RISA...
...THAT YOU LIKE.

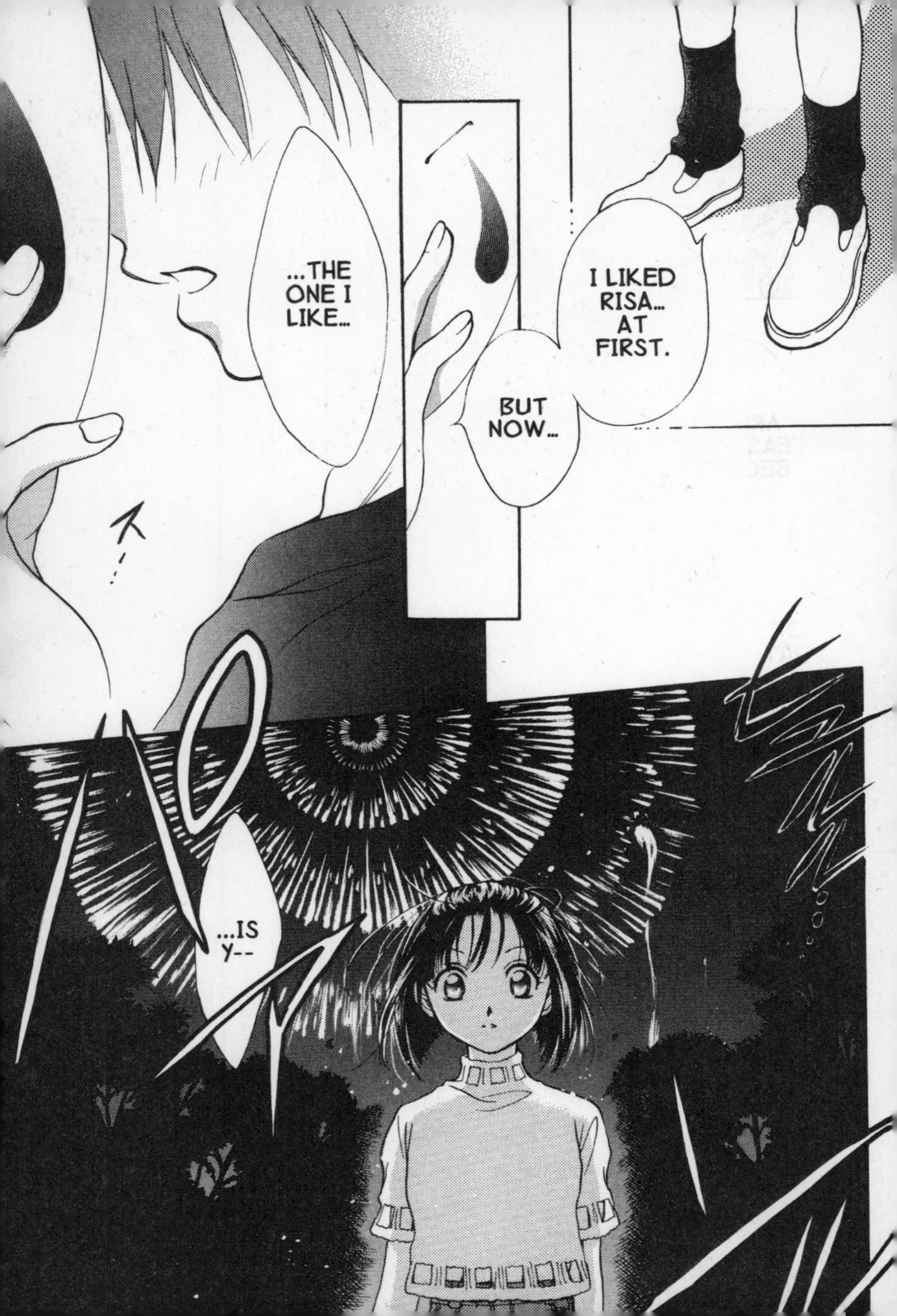
I LIKED RISA... AT FIRST.
BUT NOW...
...THE ONE I LIKE...
...IS Y--

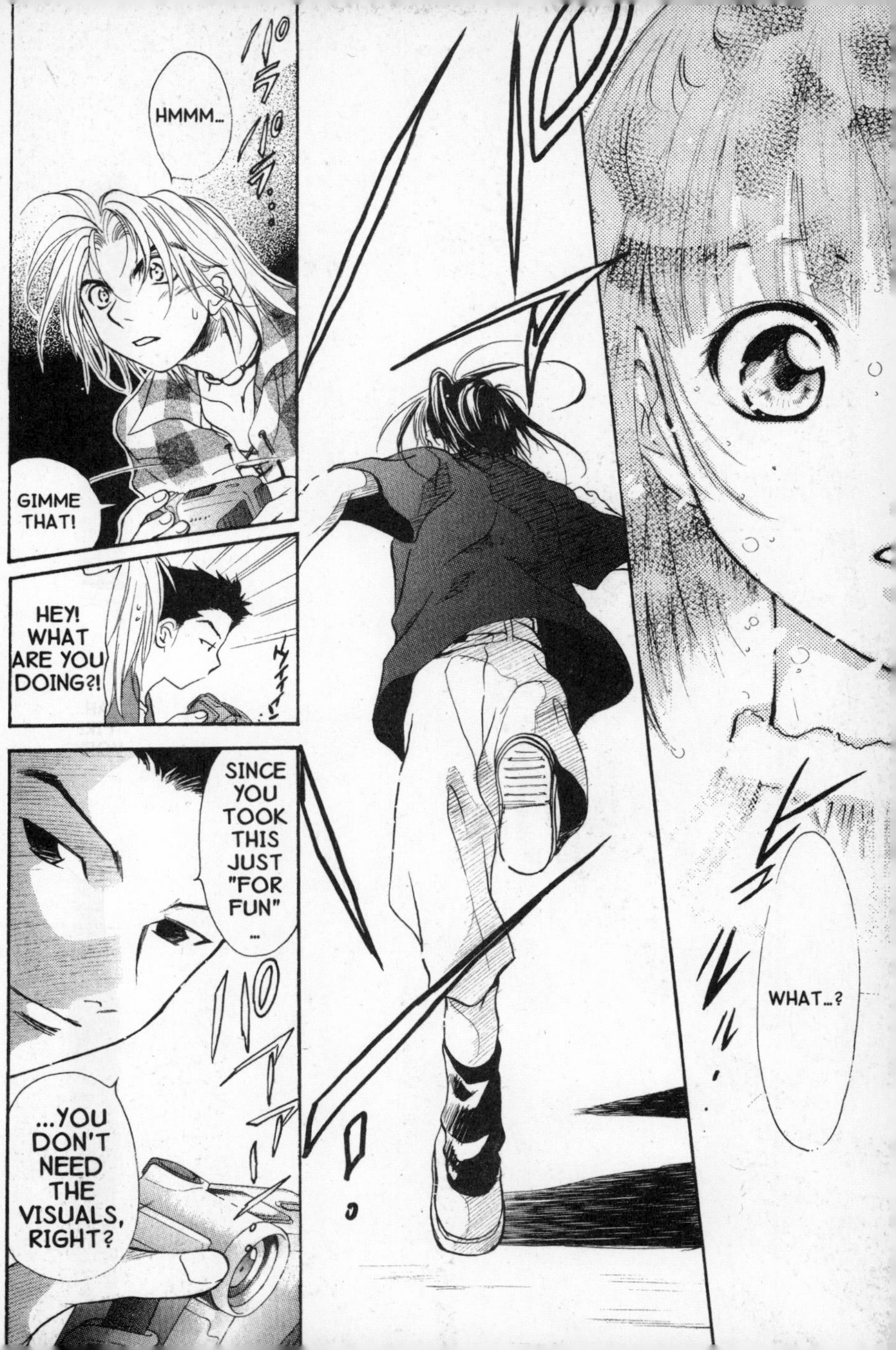
WHAT...?
HMMM...
GIMME THAT!
HEY! WHAT ARE YOU DOING?!
SINCE YOU TOOK THIS JUST "FOR FUN"...
...YOU DON'T NEED THE VISUALS, RIGHT?

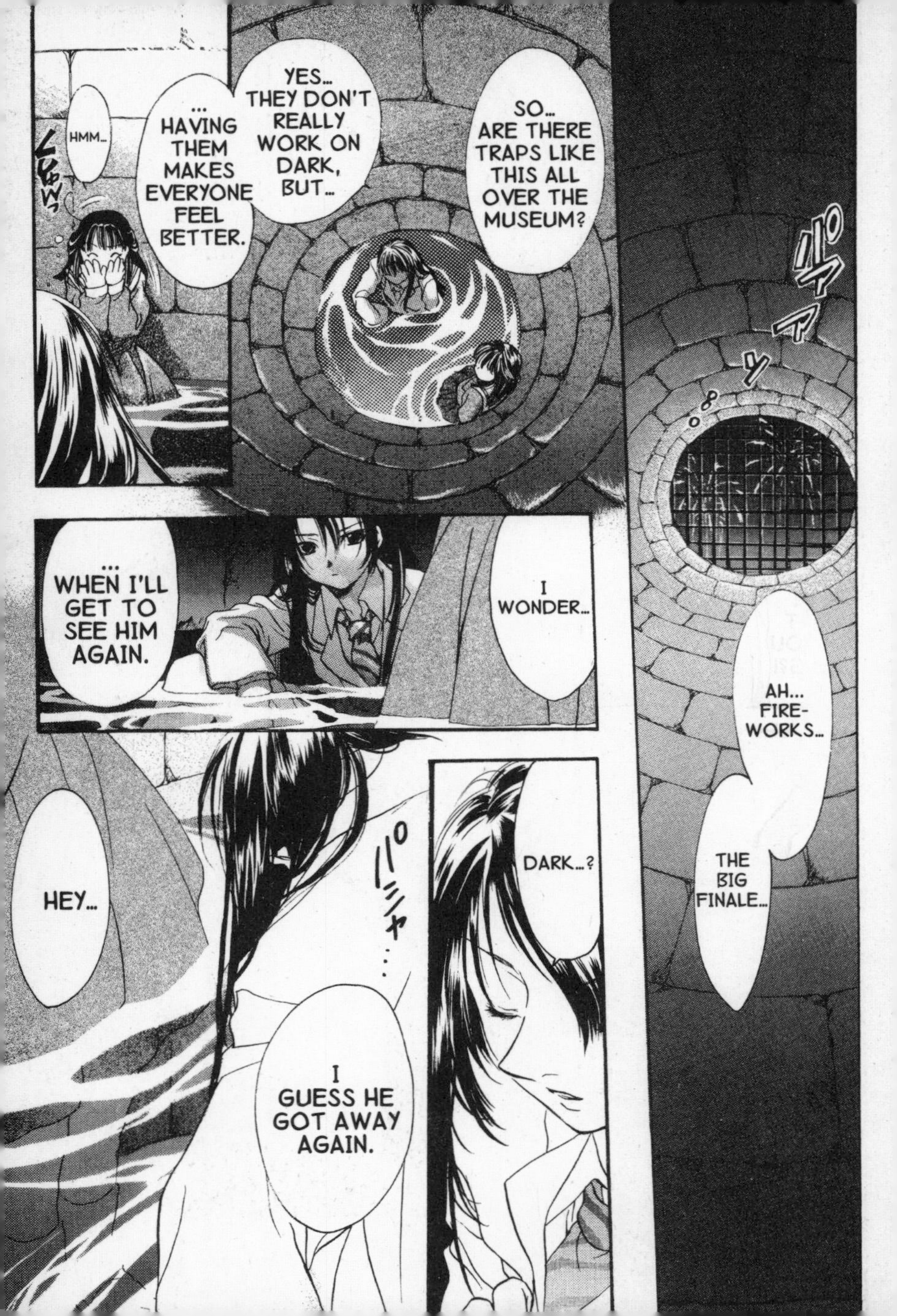
AH... FIRE-WORKS...
THE BIG FINALE...
SO... ARE THERE TRAPS LIKE THIS ALL OVER THE MUSEUM?
YES... THEY DON'T REALLY WORK ON DARK, BUT...
...HAVING THEM MAKES EVERYONE FEEL BETTER.
HMM...
I WONDER...
...WHEN I'LL GET TO SEE HIM AGAIN.
DARK...?
HEY...
I GUESS HE GOT AWAY AGAIN.

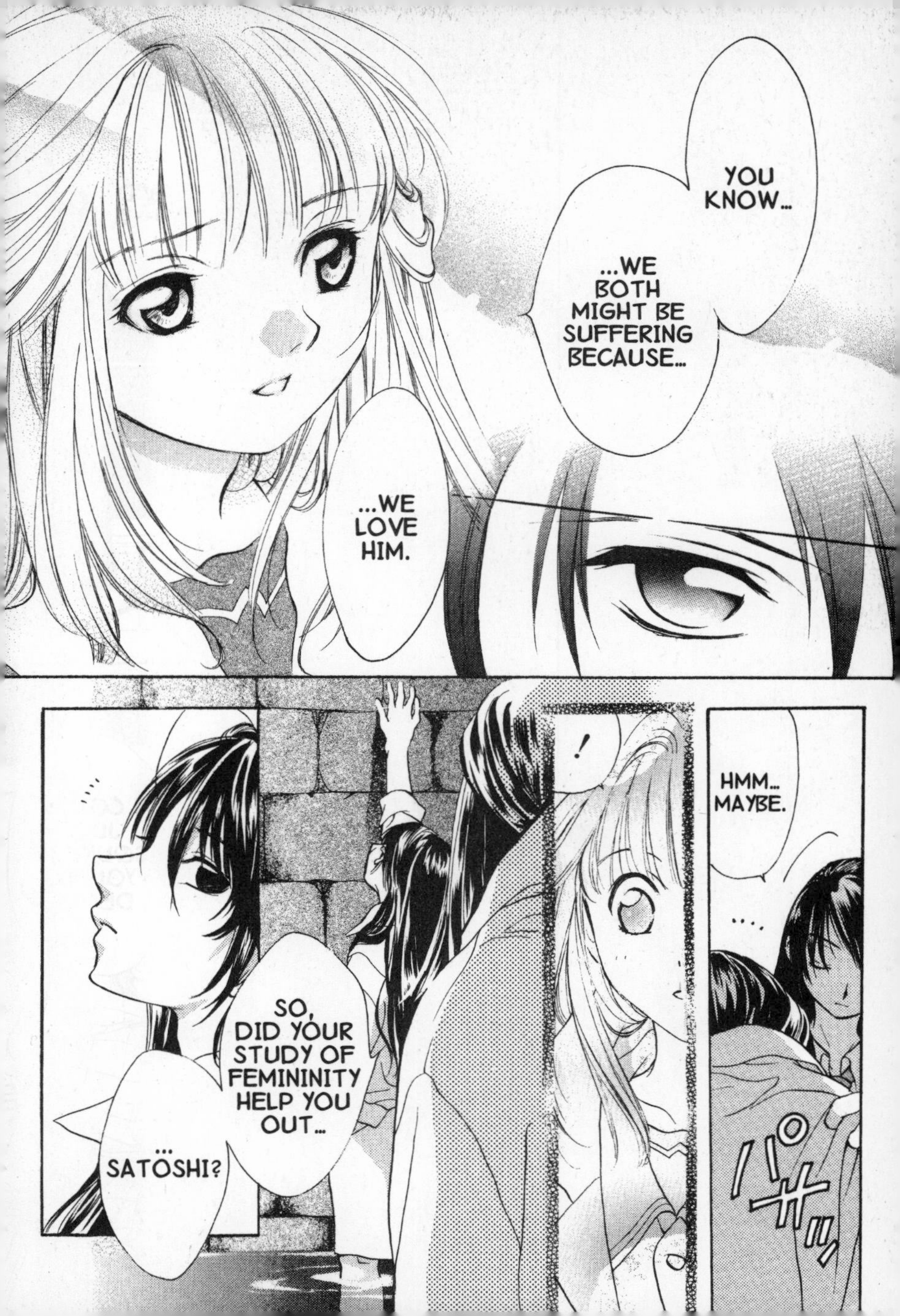
YOU KNOW...
...WE BOTH MIGHT BE SUFFERING BECAUSE...
...WE LOVE HIM.
HMM... MAYBE.
...
パサッ
!
...
SO, DID YOUR STUDY OF FEMININITY HELP YOU OUT...
... SATOSHI?

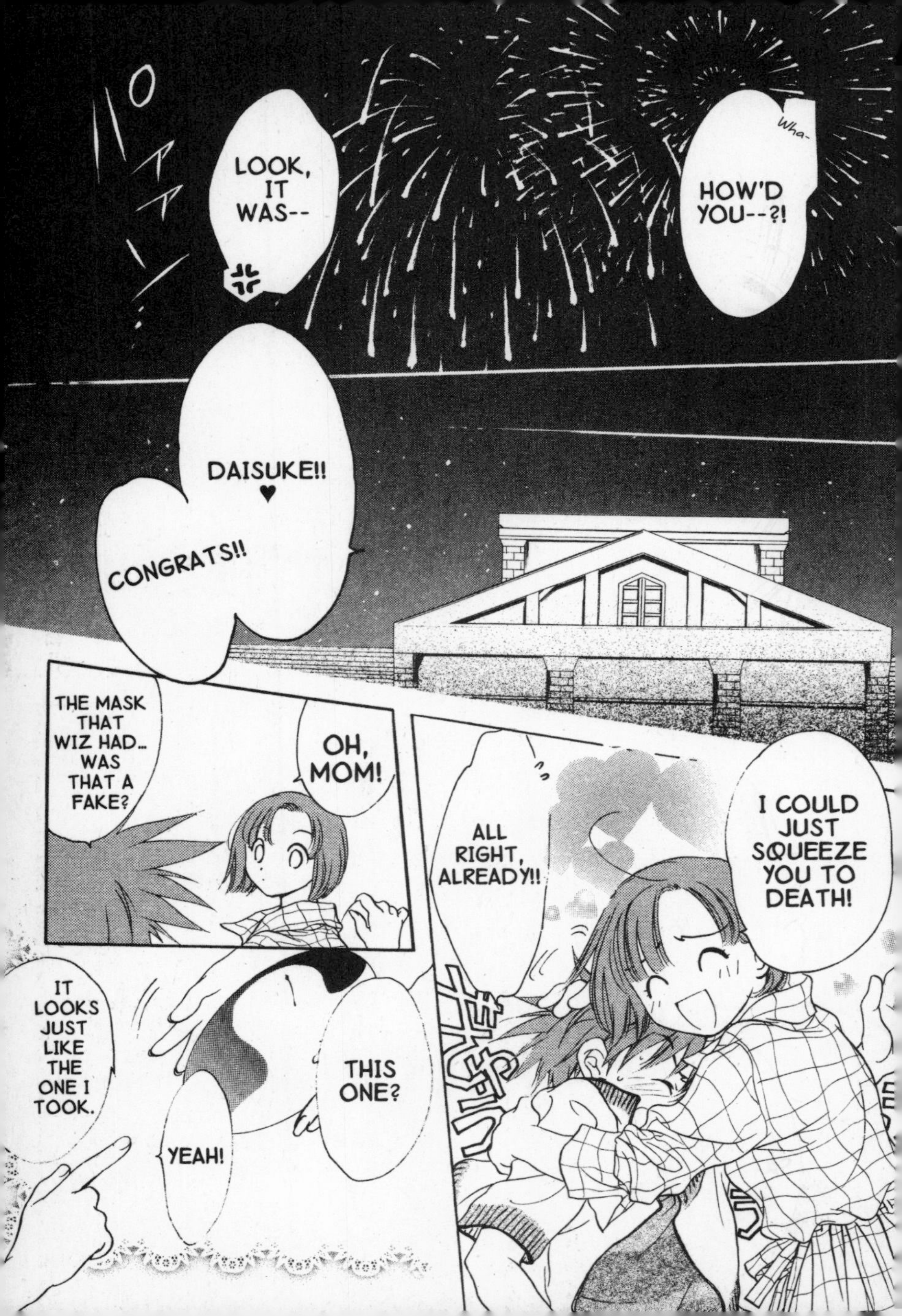
Wha-
HOW'D YOU--?!
LOOK, IT WAS--
DAISUKE!! ♥
CONGRATS!!
I COULD JUST SQUEEZE YOU TO DEATH!
ALL RIGHT, ALREADY!!
OH, MOM!
THE MASK THAT WIZ HAD... WAS THAT A FAKE?
THIS ONE?
YEAH!
IT LOOKS JUST LIKE THE ONE I TOOK.

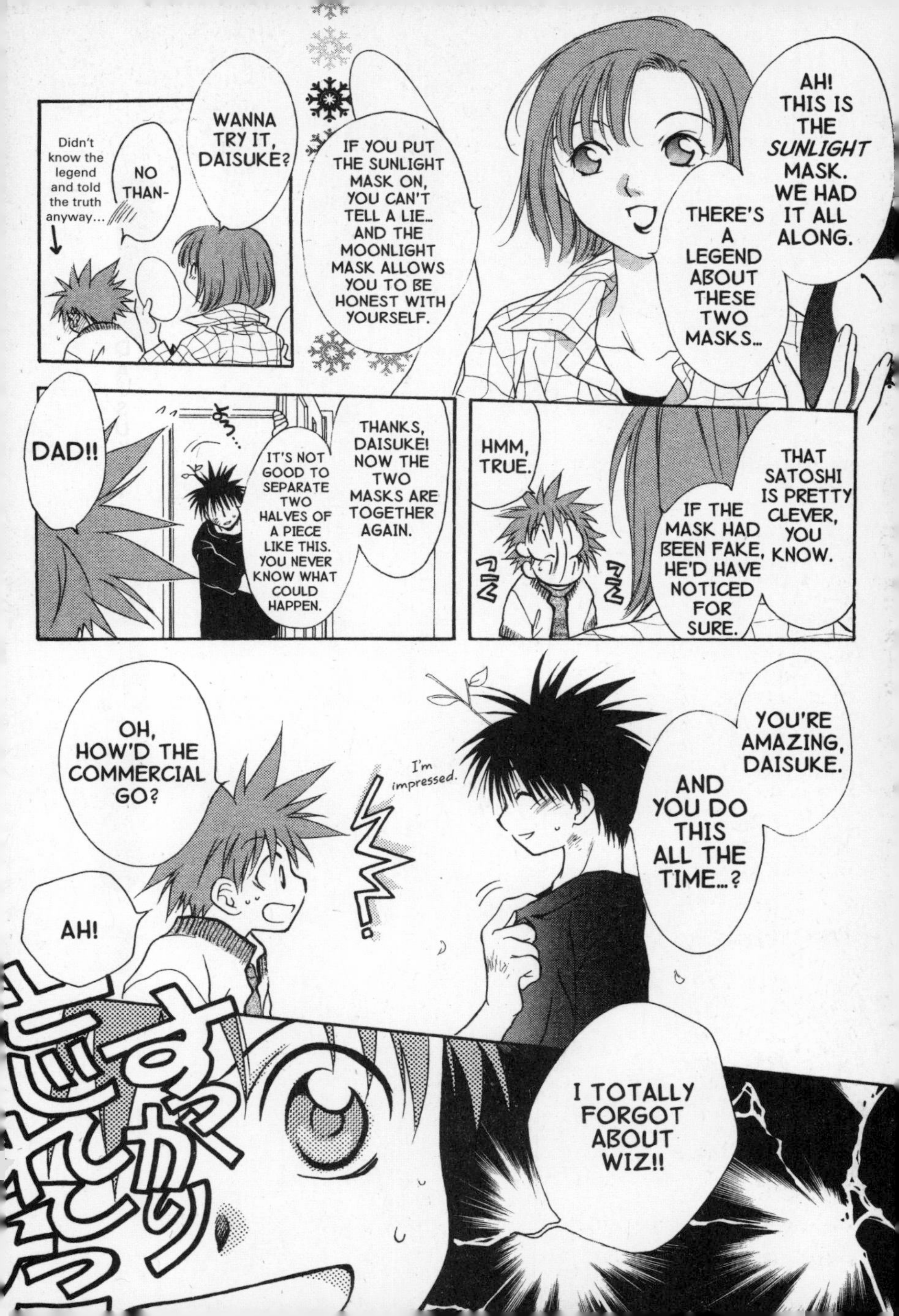
AH! THIS IS THE *SUNLIGHT* MASK. WE HAD IT ALL ALONG.
THERE'S A LEGEND ABOUT THESE TWO MASKS...
IF YOU PUT THE SUNLIGHT MASK ON, YOU CAN'T TELL A LIE... AND THE MOONLIGHT MASK ALLOWS YOU TO BE HONEST WITH YOURSELF.
WANNA TRY IT, DAISUKE?
NO THAN-
Didn't know the legend and told the truth anyway...
THAT SATOSHI IS PRETTY CLEVER, YOU KNOW.
IF THE MASK HAD BEEN FAKE, HE'D HAVE NOTICED FOR SURE.
HMM, TRUE.
THANKS, DAISUKE! NOW THE TWO MASKS ARE TOGETHER AGAIN.
IT'S NOT GOOD TO SEPARATE TWO HALVES OF A PIECE LIKE THIS. YOU NEVER KNOW WHAT COULD HAPPEN.
DAD!!
YOU'RE AMAZING, DAISUKE.
AND YOU DO THIS ALL THE TIME...?
I'm impressed.
OH, HOW'D THE COMMERCIAL GO?
AH!
I TOTALLY FORGOT ABOUT WIZ!!

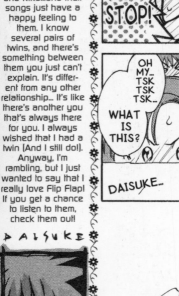

NO. 2

Another thing people ask is, what do I listen to when I'm drawing DNAngel? Lately, I've been listening to a pop group called Flip Flap while I draw. They're a pair of identical-twin girls named Aiko and Yuko...so they're kind of like Risa and Riku...and their songs just have a happy feeling to them. I know several pairs of twins, and there's something between them you just can't explain. It's different from any other relationship... It's like there's another you that's always there for you. I always wished that I had a twin (And I still do!). Anyway, I'm rambling, but I just wanted to say that I really love Flip Flap! If you get a chance to listen to them, check them out!

DAISUKE

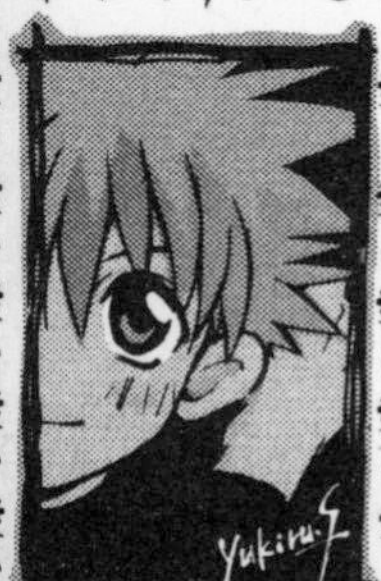
Yukiru S

PS: See my interview in back!

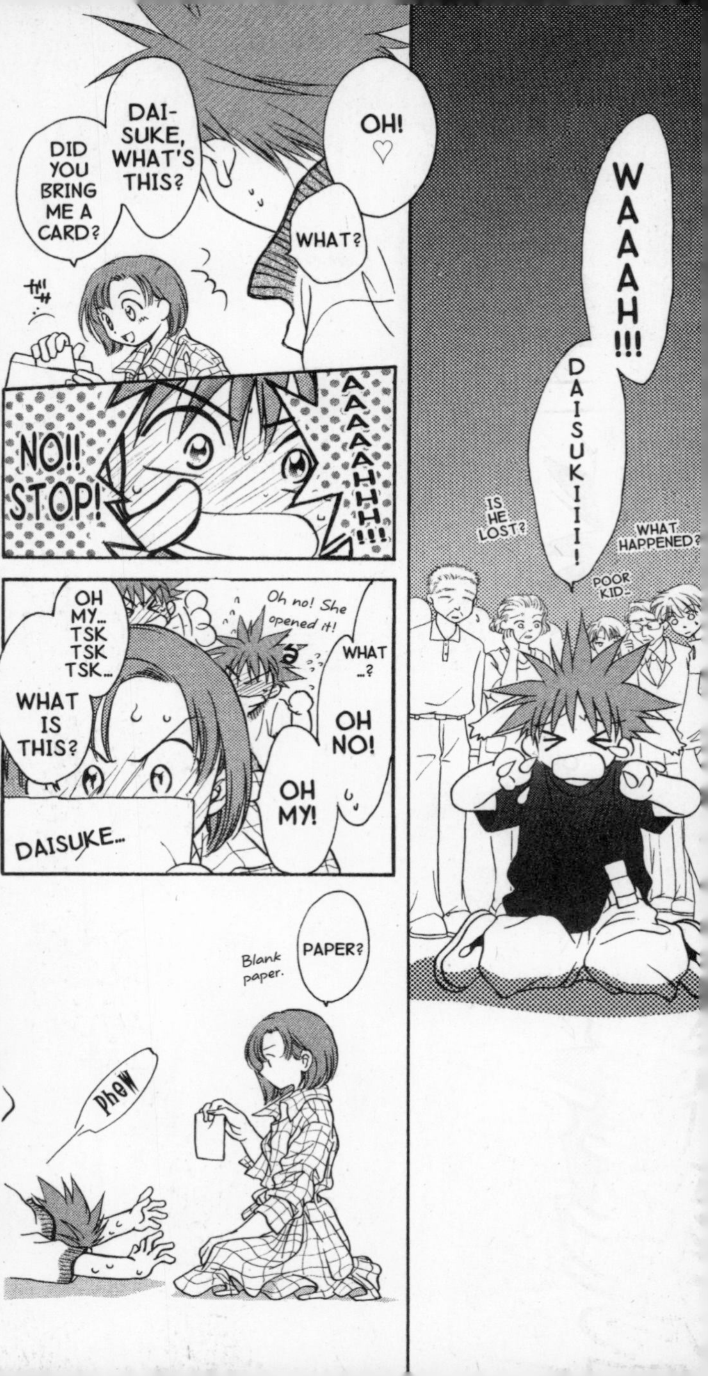
WAAAAH!!!
DAISUKIIII!
IS HE LOST?
WHAT HAPPENED?
POOR KID...
OH! ♡
WHAT?
DAI-SUKE, WHAT'S THIS?
DID YOU BRING ME A CARD?
AAAAAAHHH!!!
NO!! STOP!
Oh no! She opened it!
WHAT ...?
OH NO!
OH MY!
OH MY... TSK TSK TSK...
WHAT IS THIS?
DAISUKE...
PAPER?
Blank paper.
Phew

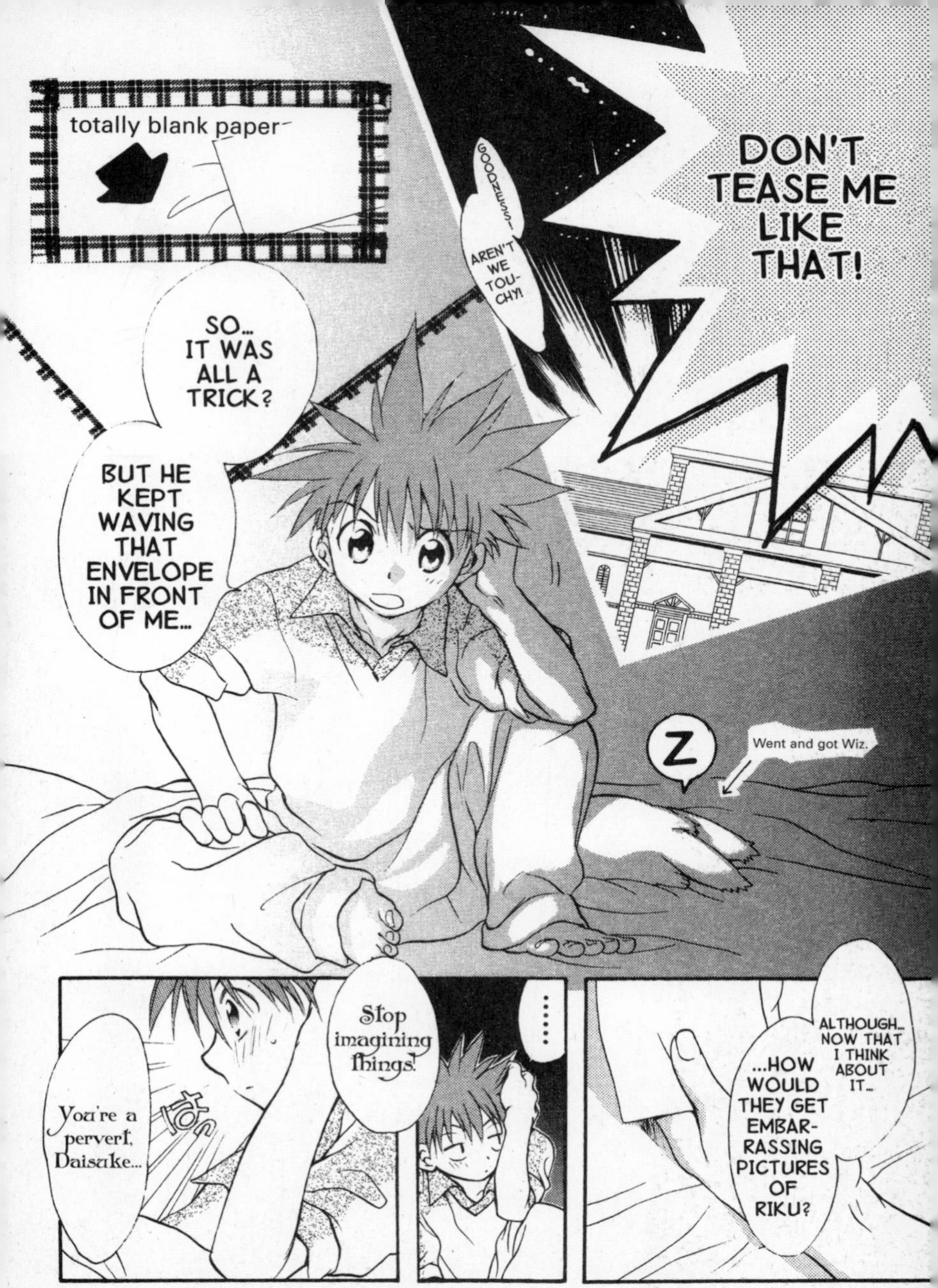
DON'T TEASE ME LIKE THAT!
GOODNESS! AREN'T WE TOUCHY!
totally blank paper
SO... IT WAS ALL A TRICK?
BUT HE KEPT WAVING THAT ENVELOPE IN FRONT OF ME...
Z
Went and got Wiz.
ALTHOUGH... NOW THAT I THINK ABOUT IT...
...HOW WOULD THEY GET EMBARRASSING PICTURES OF RIKU?
......
Stop imagining things!
You're a pervert, Daisuke...

CHAPTER 9

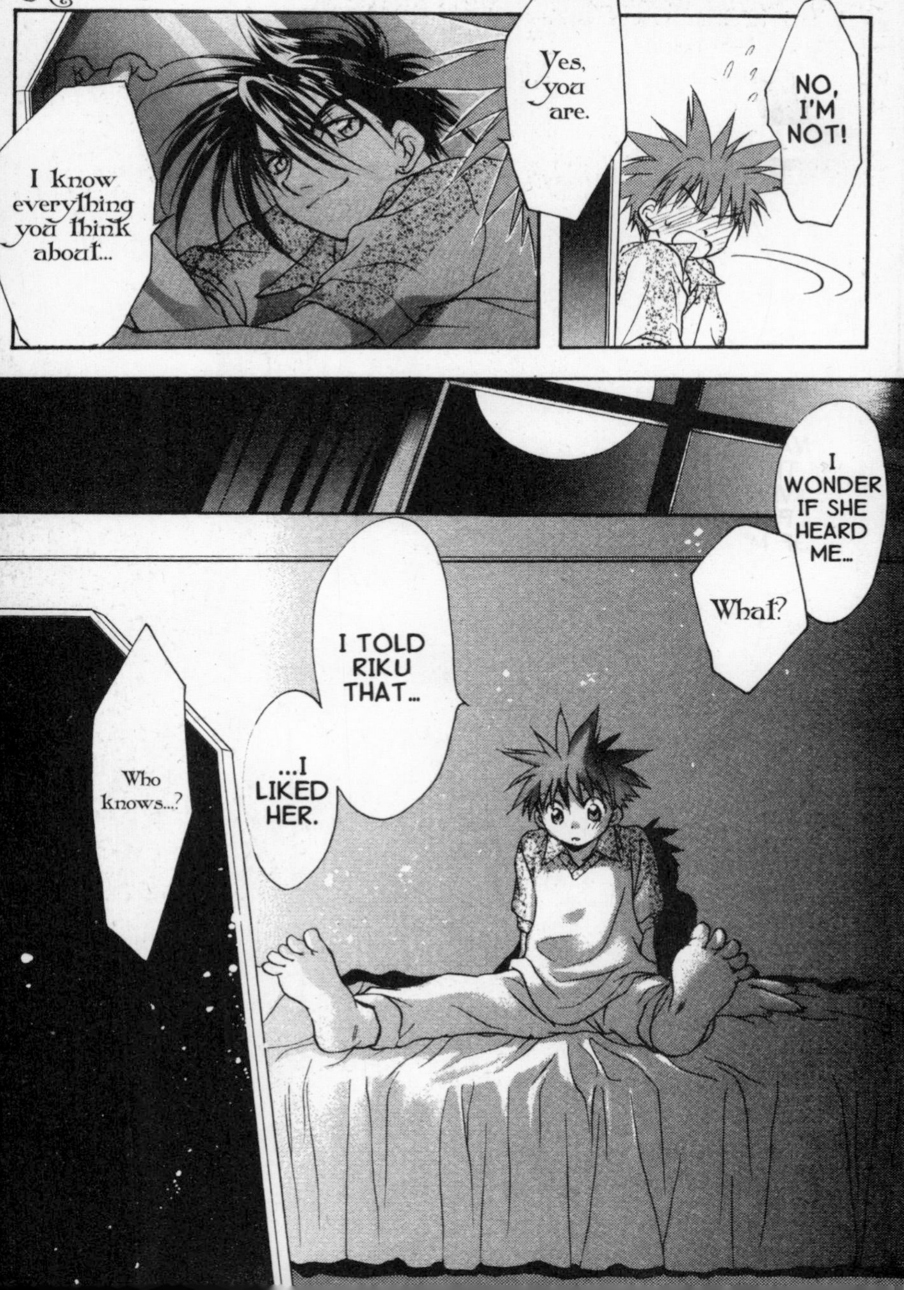
NO, I'M NOT!
Yes, you are.
I know everything you think about...
I WONDER IF SHE HEARD ME...
What?
I TOLD RIKU THAT...
...I LIKED HER.
Who knows...?

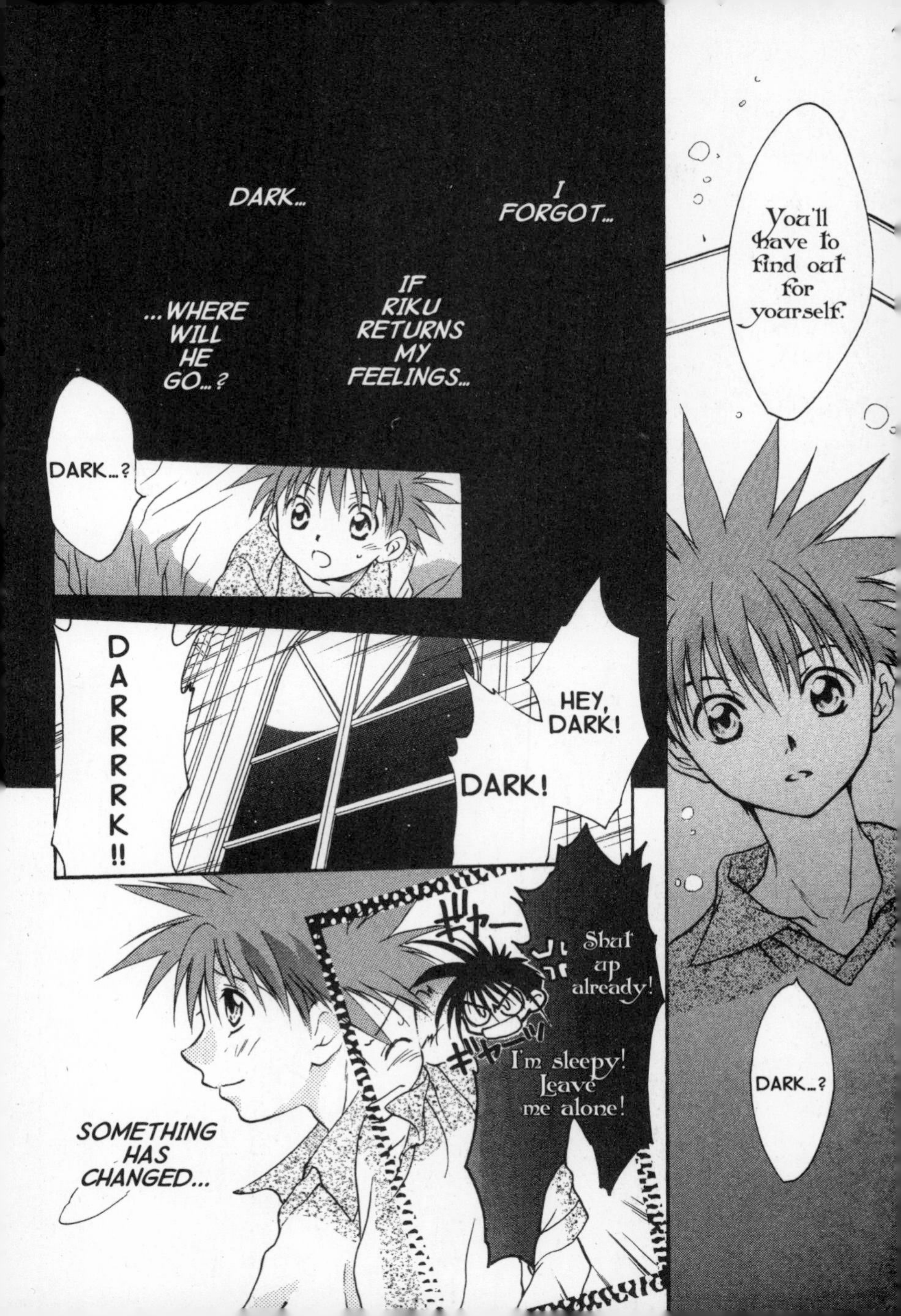
You'll have to find out for yourself.
DARK...?
I FORGOT...
DARK...
IF RIKU RETURNS MY FEELINGS...
...WHERE WILL HE GO...?
DARK...?
HEY, DARK!
DARK!
DARRRRRK!!
ギャー
Shut up already!
ギャー
I'm sleepy! Leave me alone!
SOMETHING HAS CHANGED...

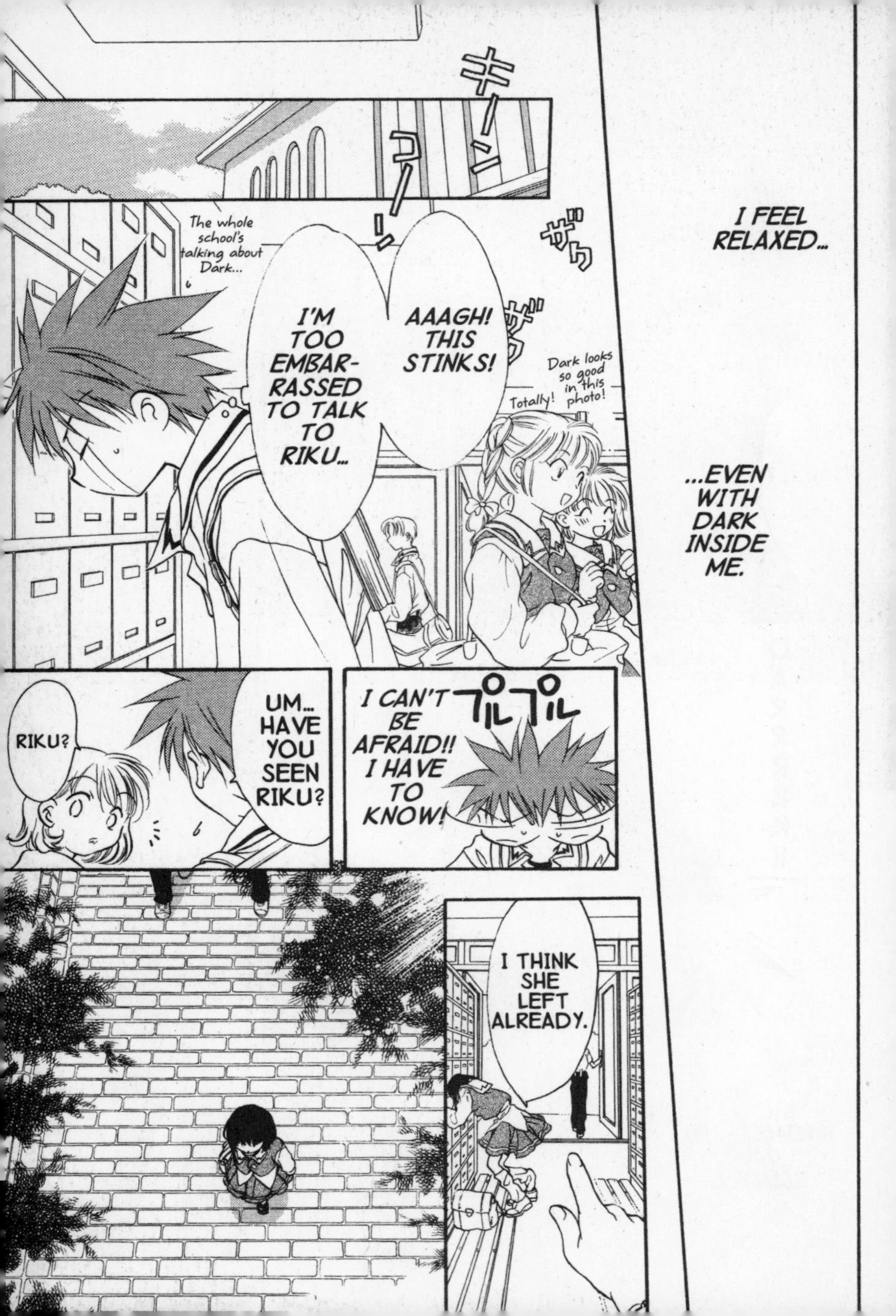

I FEEL RELAXED...
...EVEN WITH DARK INSIDE ME.
キーンコーン
ざわ ざわ
AAAGH! THIS STINKS!
I'M TOO EMBARRASSED TO TALK TO RIKU...
The whole school's talking about Dark...
Dark looks so good in this photo!
Totally!
I CAN'T BE AFRAID!! I HAVE TO KNOW!
プルプル
UM... HAVE YOU SEEN RIKU?
RIKU?
I THINK SHE LEFT ALREADY.

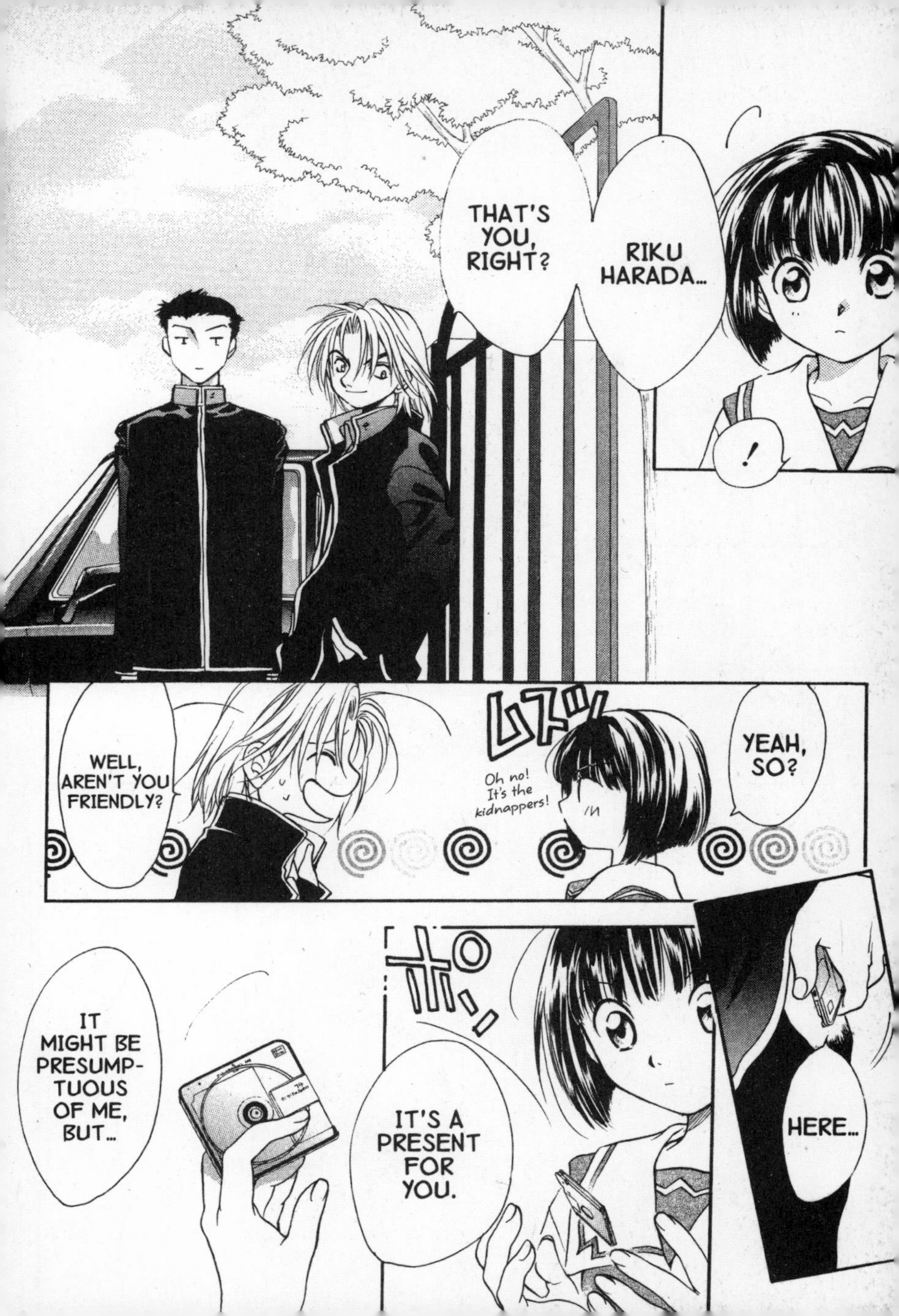
RIKU HARADA...
THAT'S YOU, RIGHT?
!
YEAH, SO?
ムスッ
Oh no! It's the kidnappers!
WELL, AREN'T YOU FRIENDLY?
HERE...
ポッ
IT'S A PRESENT FOR YOU.
IT MIGHT BE PRESUMPTUOUS OF ME, BUT...

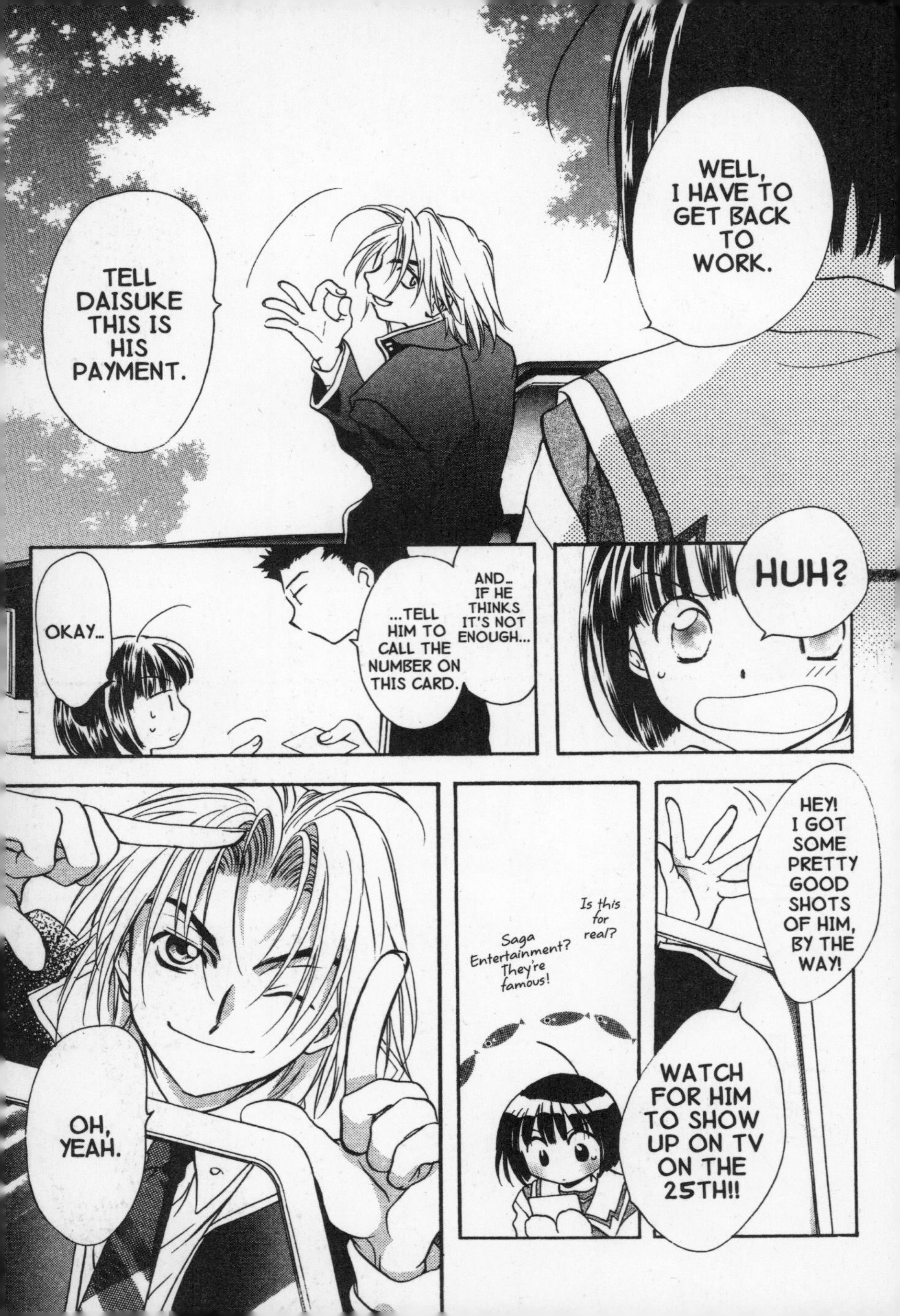
WELL, I HAVE TO GET BACK TO WORK.
TELL DAISUKE THIS IS HIS PAYMENT.
HUH?
AND.. IF HE THINKS IT'S NOT ENOUGH...
...TELL HIM TO CALL THE NUMBER ON THIS CARD.
OKAY...
HEY! I GOT SOME PRETTY GOOD SHOTS OF HIM, BY THE WAY!
WATCH FOR HIM TO SHOW UP ON TV ON THE 25TH!!
Is this for real?
Saga Entertainment? They're famous!
OH, YEAH.

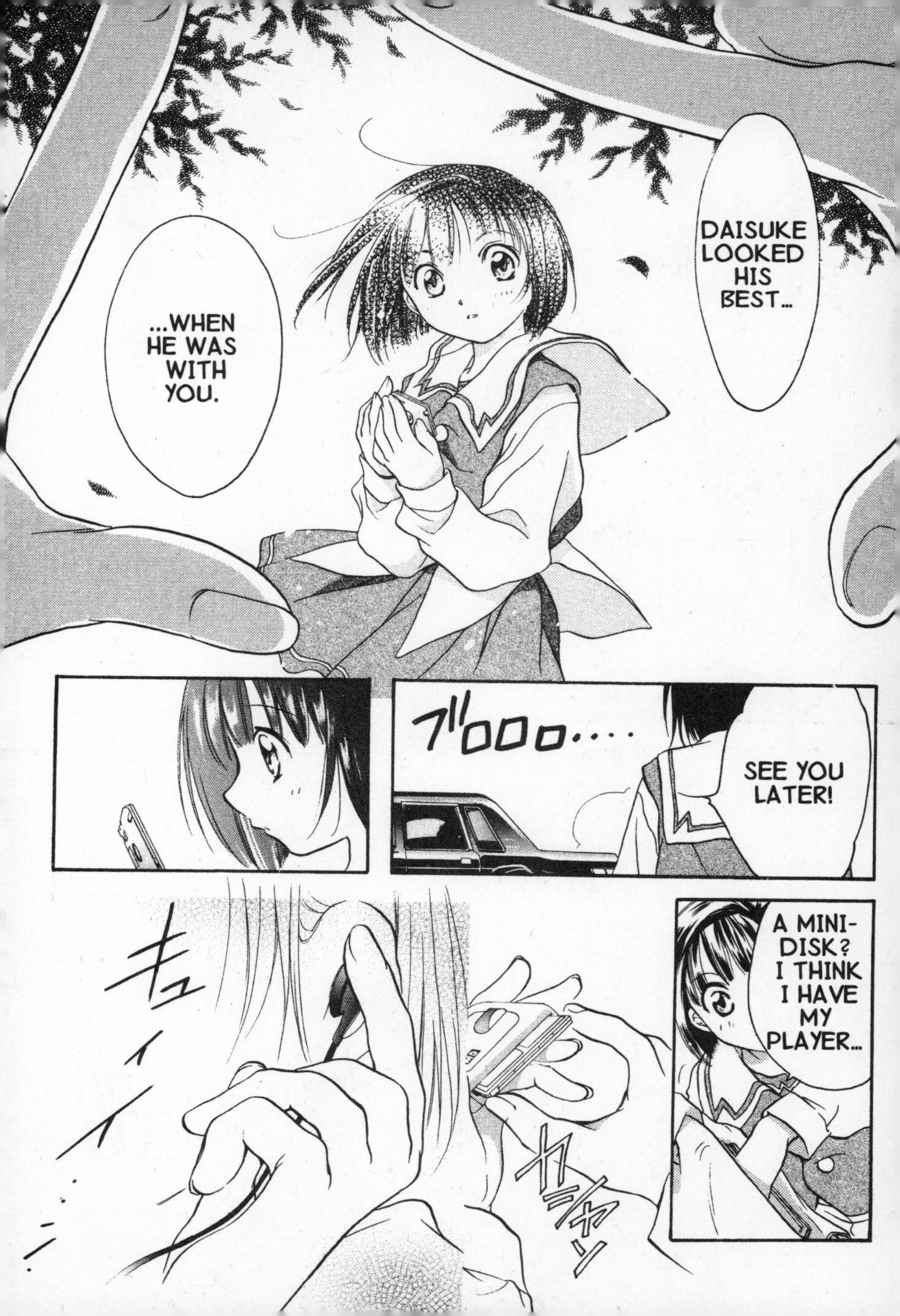
DAISUKE LOOKED HIS BEST...
...WHEN HE WAS WITH YOU.
SEE YOU LATER!
A MINI-DISK? I THINK I HAVE MY PLAYER...

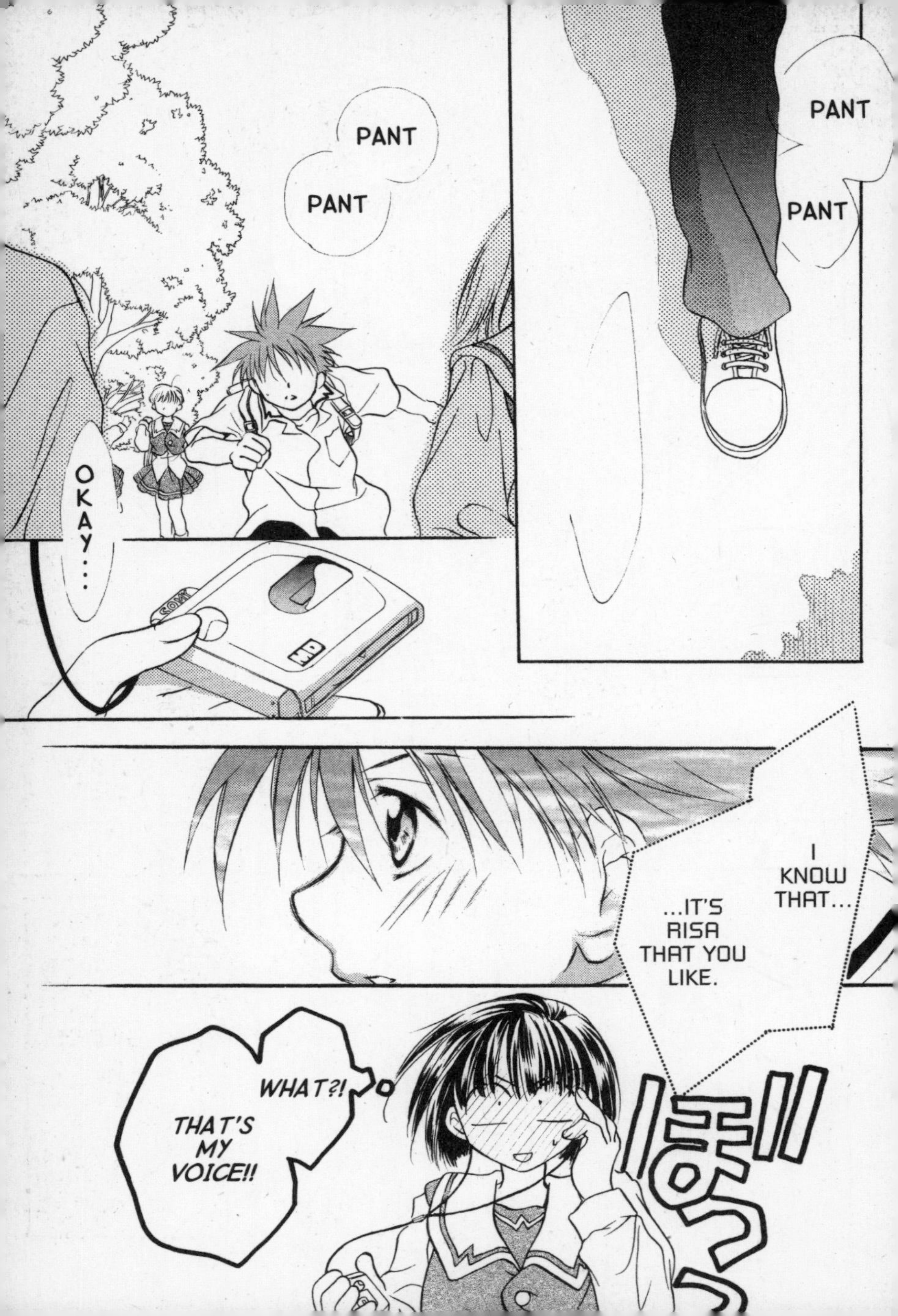
PANT
PANT
PANT
PANT
OKAY...
I KNOW THAT...
...IT'S RISA THAT YOU LIKE.
WHAT?!
THAT'S MY VOICE!!

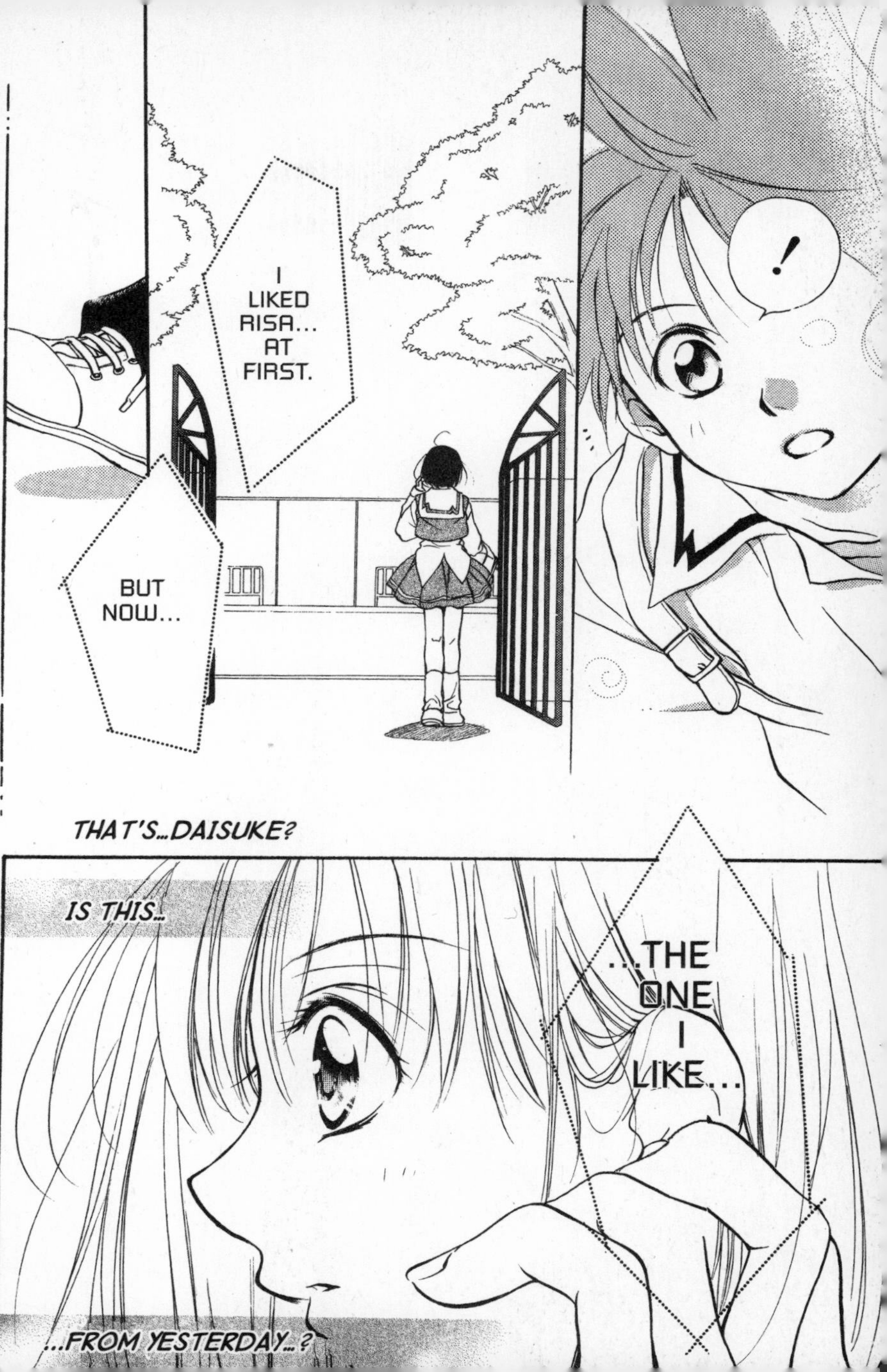
!
I LIKED RISA... AT FIRST.
BUT NOW...
THAT'S...DAISUKE?
IS THIS...
...THE ONE I LIKE...
...FROM YESTERDAY...?

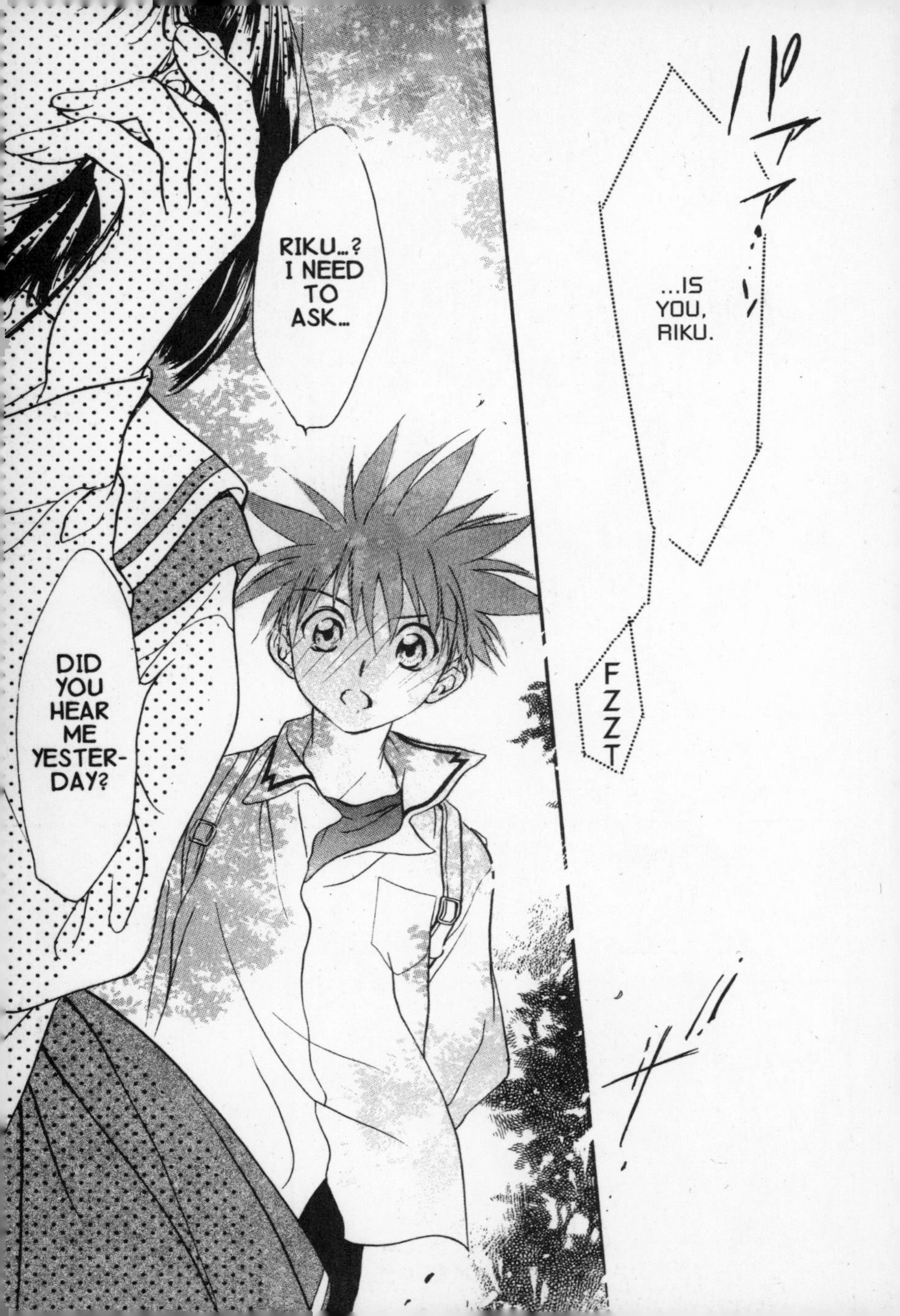
...IS YOU, RIKU.
FZZT
RIKU...? I NEED TO ASK...
DID YOU HEAR ME YESTER-DAY?

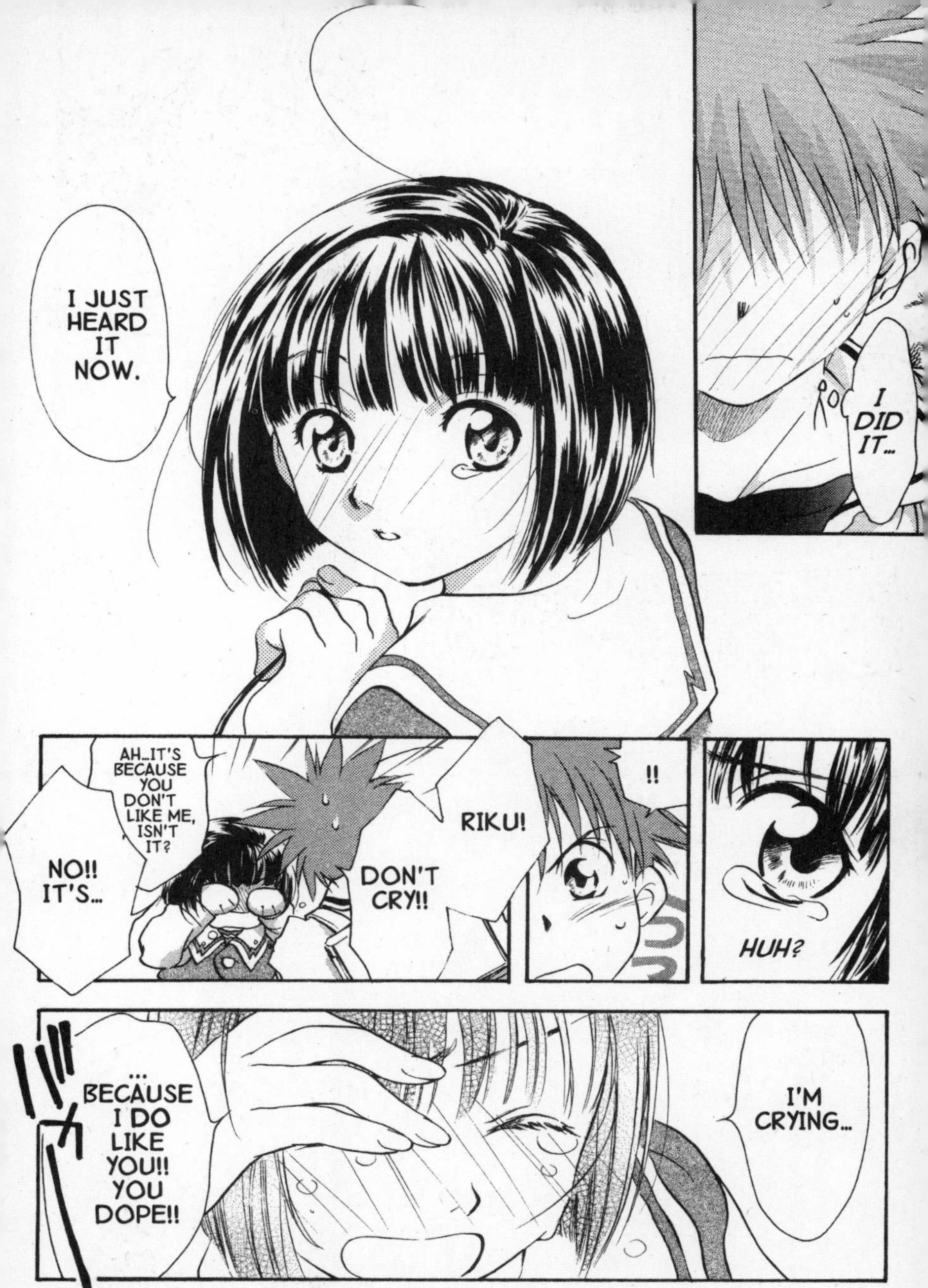

I DID IT...
I JUST HEARD IT NOW.
HUH?
!!
RIKU!
DON'T CRY!!
AH...IT'S BECAUSE YOU DON'T LIKE ME, ISN'T IT?
NO!! IT'S...
I'M CRYING...
...BECAUSE I DO LIKE YOU!! YOU DOPE!!

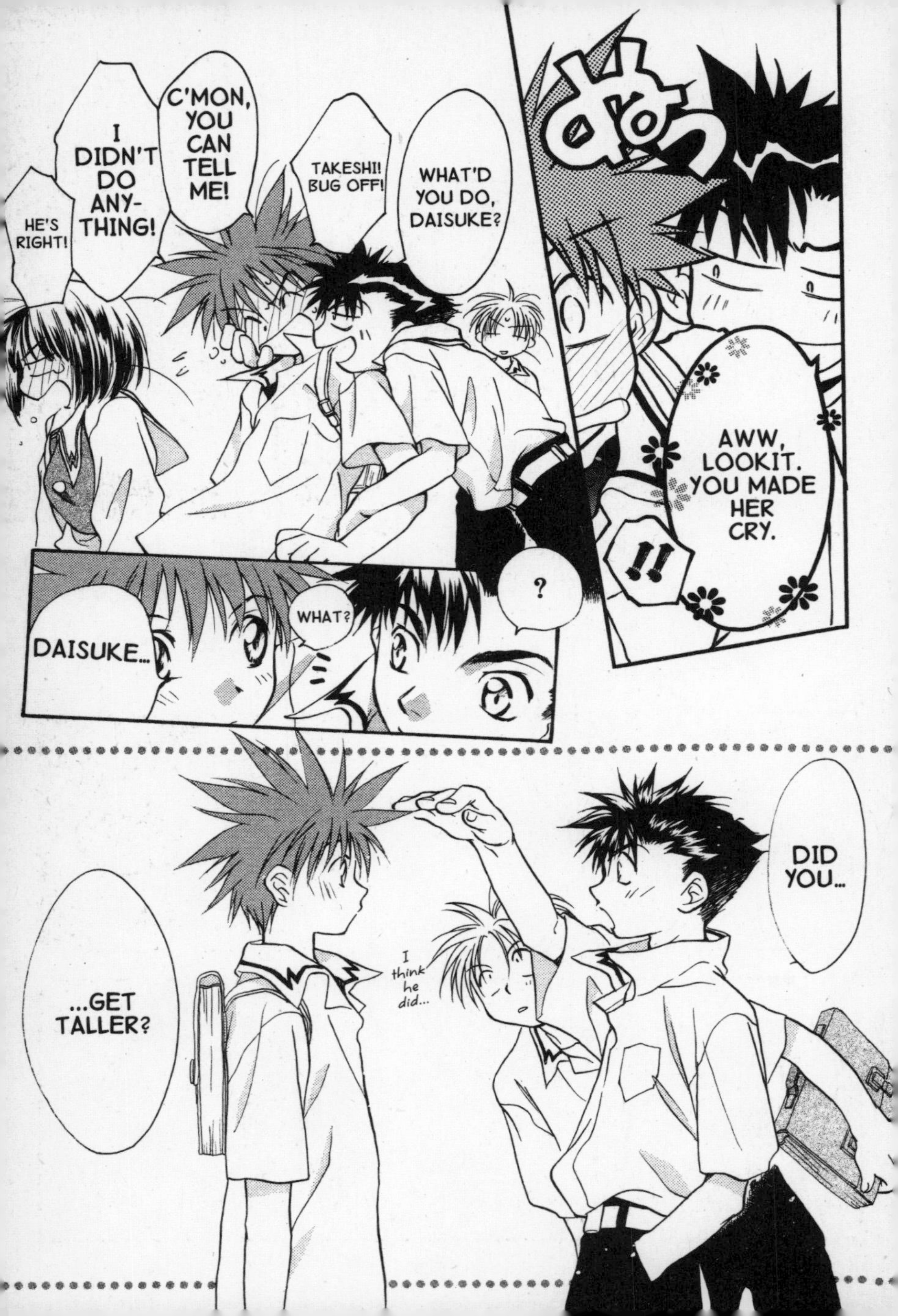
AWW, LOOKIT. YOU MADE HER CRY.
!!
WHAT'D YOU DO, DAISUKE?
TAKESHI! BUG OFF!
C'MON, YOU CAN TELL ME!
I DIDN'T DO ANY-THING!
HE'S RIGHT!
?
WHAT?
DAISUKE...
DID YOU...
I think he did...
...GET TALLER?

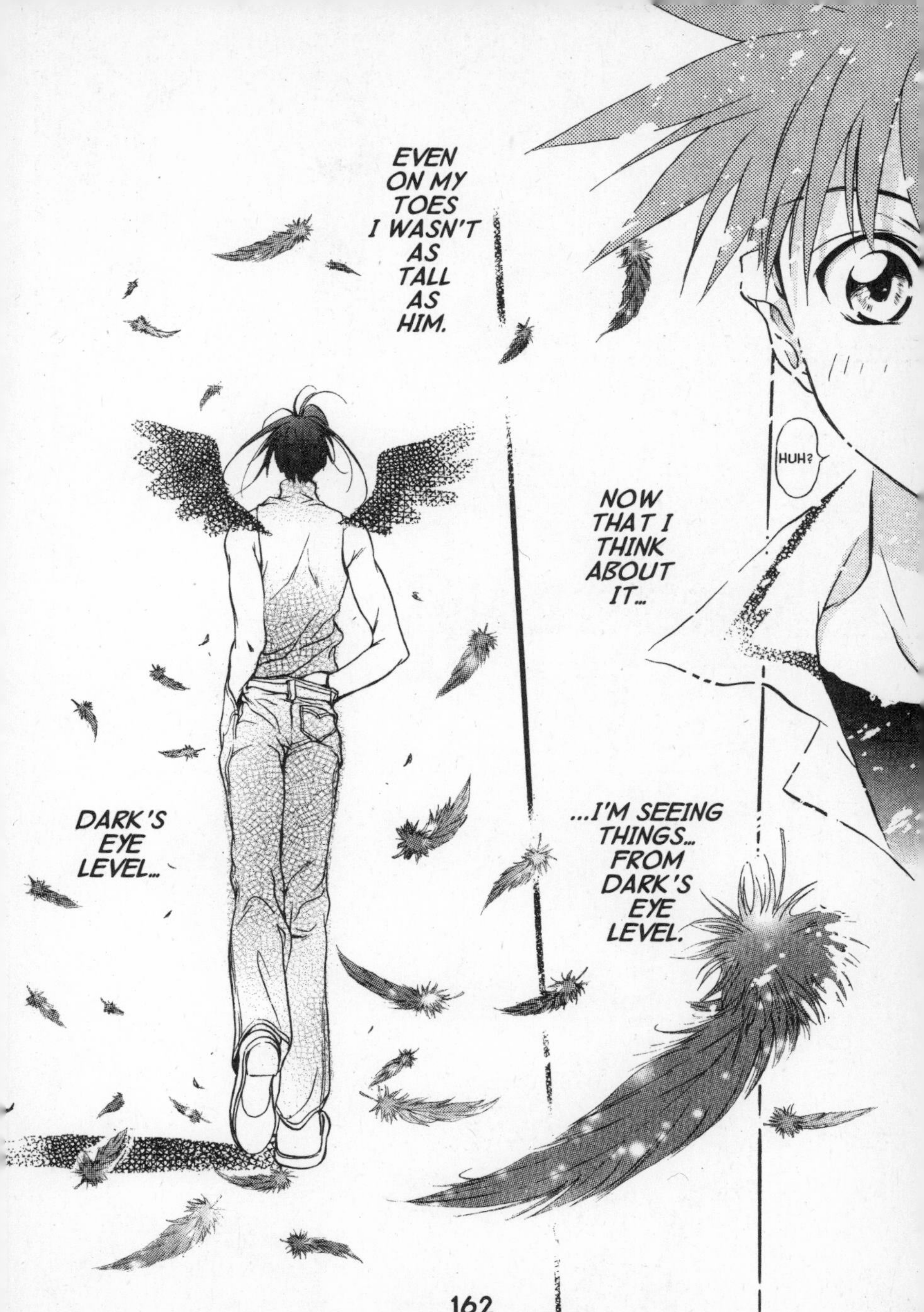
HUH?
NOW THAT I THINK ABOUT IT...
...I'M SEEING THINGS... FROM DARK'S EYE LEVEL.
EVEN ON MY TOES I WASN'T AS TALL AS HIM.
DARK'S EYE LEVEL...

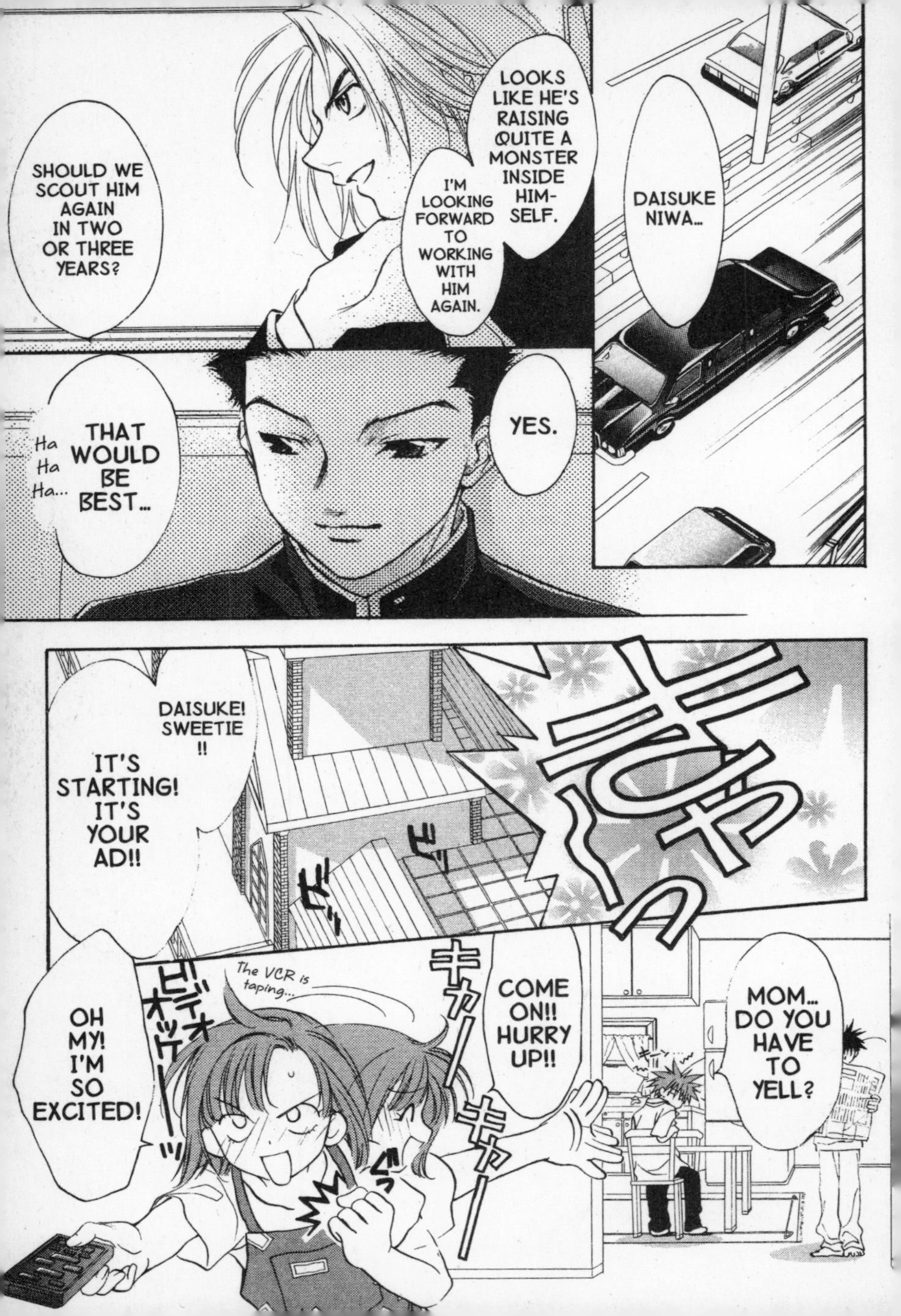
DAISUKE NIWA...
LOOKS LIKE HE'S RAISING QUITE A MONSTER INSIDE HIMSELF.
I'M LOOKING FORWARD TO WORKING WITH HIM AGAIN.
SHOULD WE SCOUT HIM AGAIN IN TWO OR THREE YEARS?
YES.
THAT WOULD BE BEST...
Ha Ha Ha...
DAISUKE! SWEETIE!!
IT'S STARTING! IT'S YOUR AD!!
MOM... DO YOU HAVE TO YELL?
COME ON!! HURRY UP!!
The VCR is taping...
OH MY! I'M SO EXCITED!

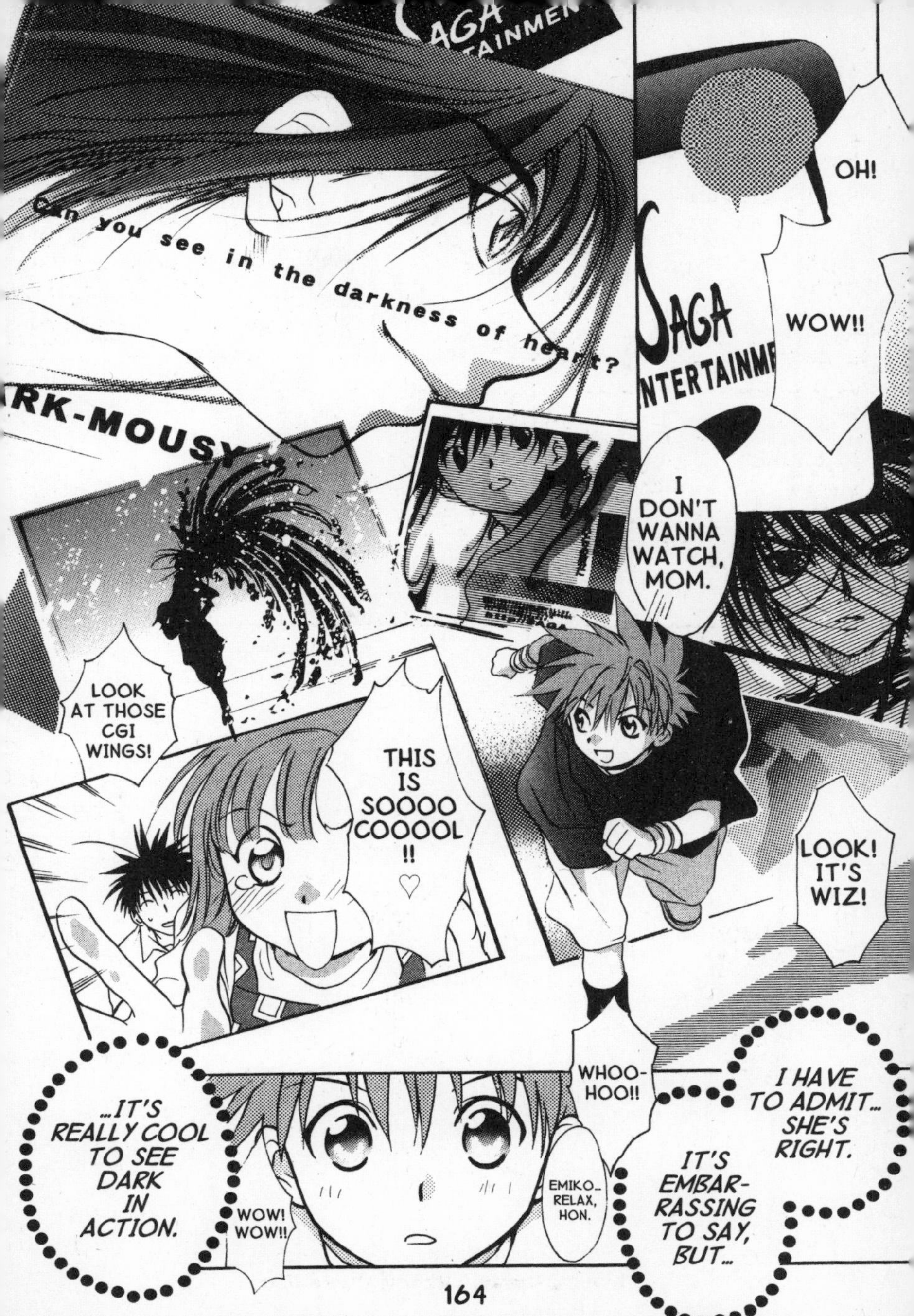

SAGA
OH!
WOW!!
I DON'T WANNA WATCH, MOM.
Can you see in the darkness of heart?
RK-MOUSY
LOOK! IT'S WIZ!
THIS IS SOOOO COOOOL !! ♡
LOOK AT THOSE CGI WINGS!
I HAVE TO ADMIT... SHE'S RIGHT.
IT'S EMBAR-RASSING TO SAY, BUT...
WHOO-HOO!!
EMIKO... RELAX, HON.
WOW! WOW!!
...IT'S REALLY COOL TO SEE DARK IN ACTION.

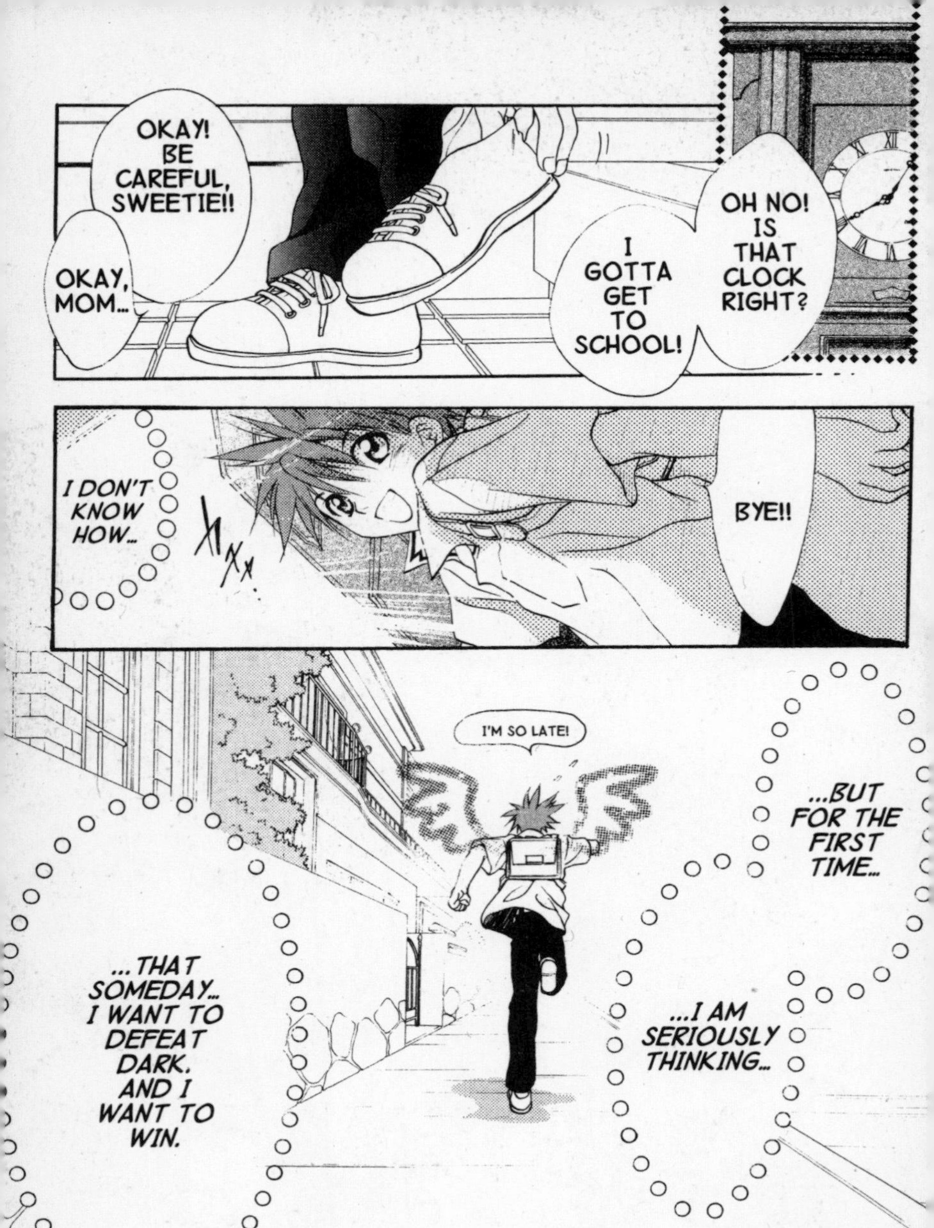
OH NO! IS THAT CLOCK RIGHT?
I GOTTA GET TO SCHOOL!
OKAY! BE CAREFUL, SWEETIE!!
OKAY, MOM...
BYE!!
I DON'T KNOW HOW...
I'M SO LATE!
...BUT FOR THE FIRST TIME...
...I AM SERIOUSLY THINKING...
...THAT SOMEDAY... I WANT TO DEFEAT DARK. AND I WANT TO WIN.

The End of Chapter 9: Warning About a Mask

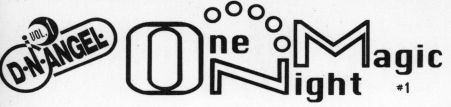

D·N·ANGEL VOL. 1

One Night Magic #1

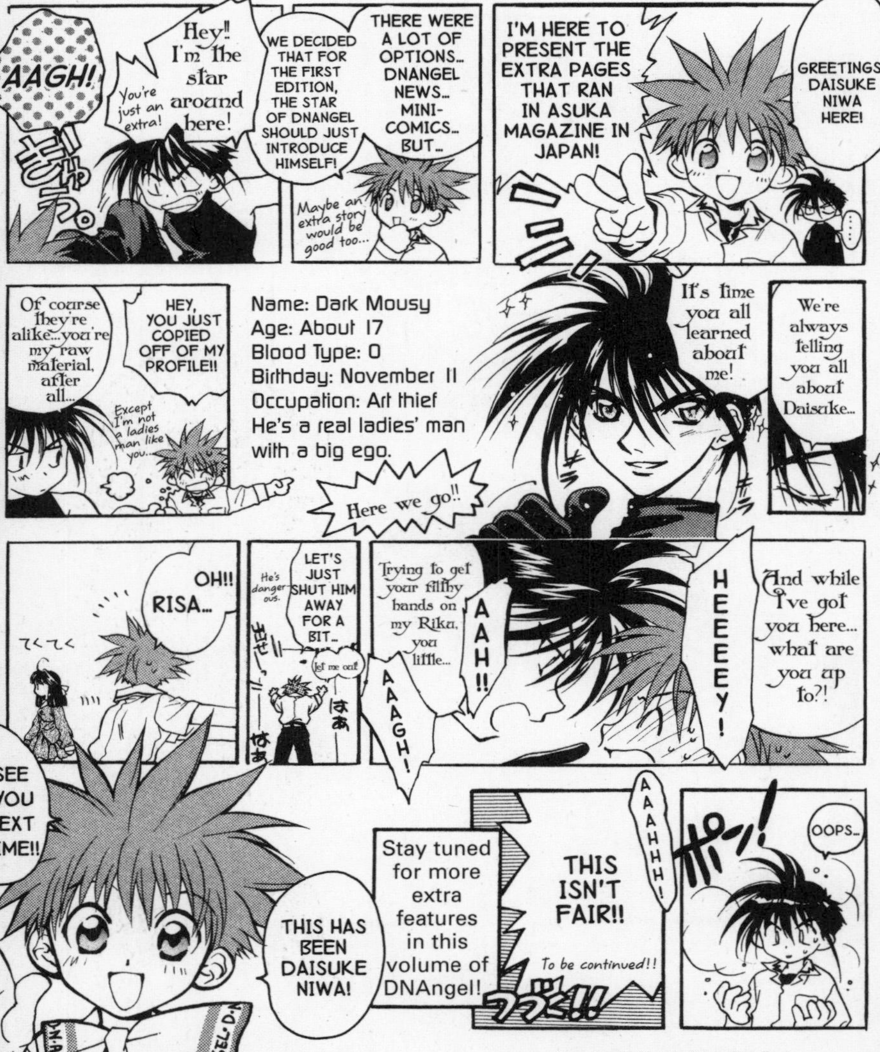
GREETINGS! DAISUKE NIWA HERE!
I'M HERE TO PRESENT THE EXTRA PAGES THAT RAN IN ASUKA MAGAZINE IN JAPAN!
...
THERE WERE A LOT OF OPTIONS... DNANGEL NEWS... MINI-COMICS... BUT...
WE DECIDED THAT FOR THE FIRST EDITION, THE STAR OF DNANGEL SHOULD JUST INTRODUCE HIMSELF!
Maybe an extra story would be good too...
Hey!! I'm the star around here!
You're just an extra!
AAGH!
We're always telling you all about Daisuke...
It's time you all learned about me!
Here we go!!
Name: Dark Mousy
Age: About 17
Blood Type: O
Birthday: November 11
Occupation: Art thief
He's a real ladies' man with a big ego.
HEY, YOU JUST COPIED OFF OF MY PROFILE!!
Of course they're alike...you're my raw material, after all...
Except I'm not a ladies man like you...
And while I've got you here... what are you up to?!
HEEEEEY!
Trying to get your filthy hands on my Riku, you little...
AAH!!
AAAGH!
LET'S JUST SHUT HIM AWAY FOR A BIT...
He's danger-ous.
Let me out!
はあ
はあ
OH!! RISA...
てくてく
OOPS...
AAAHHH!
THIS ISN'T FAIR!!
To be continued!!
Stay tuned for more extra features in this volume of DNAngel!
THIS HAS BEEN DAISUKE NIWA!
SEE YOU NEXT TIME!!

One Night Magic #1 -- The End

One Magic Night

VOL. 2 D・N・ANGEL

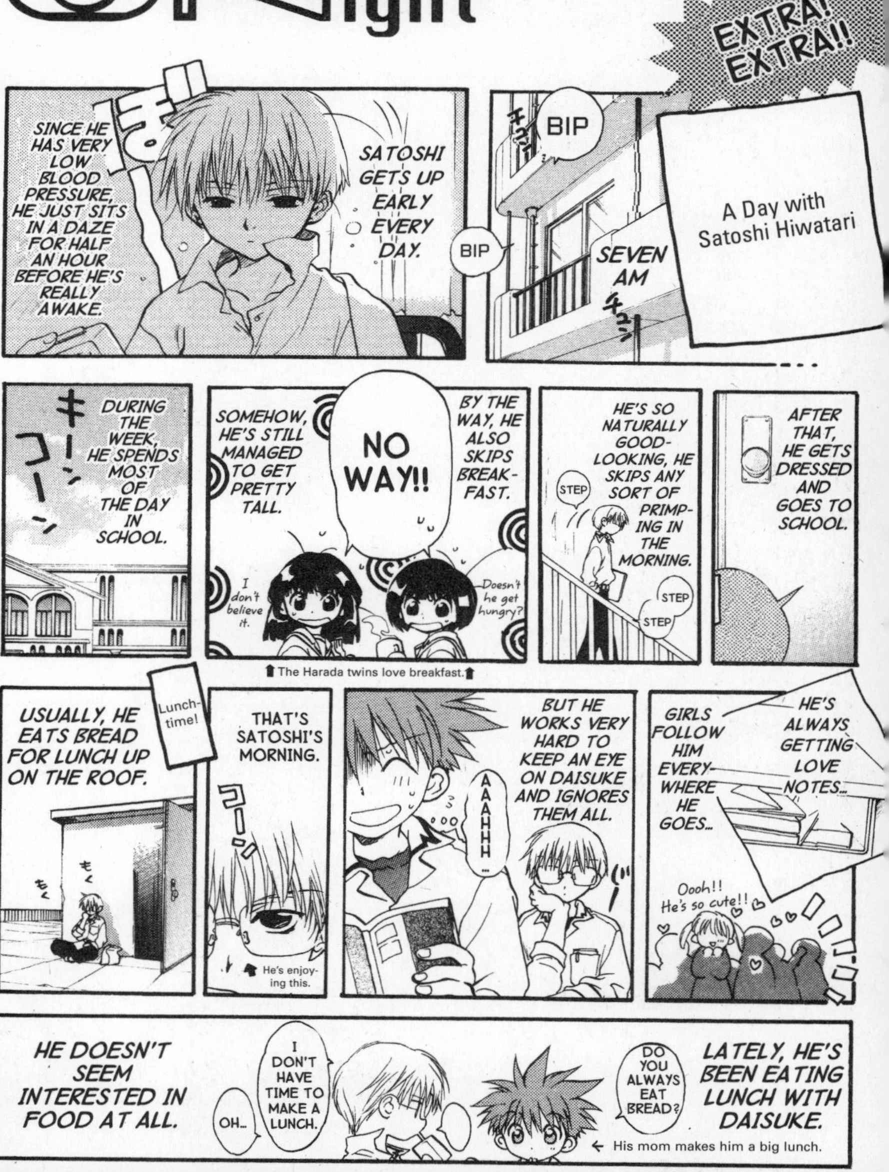
EXTRA! EXTRA!!
A Day with Satoshi Hiwatari
SEVEN AM
BIP
BIP
SATOSHI GETS UP EARLY EVERY DAY.
SINCE HE HAS VERY LOW BLOOD PRESSURE, HE JUST SITS IN A DAZE FOR HALF AN HOUR BEFORE HE'S REALLY AWAKE.
AFTER THAT, HE GETS DRESSED AND GOES TO SCHOOL.
HE'S SO NATURALLY GOOD-LOOKING, HE SKIPS ANY SORT OF PRIMPING IN THE MORNING.
STEP
STEP
STEP
BY THE WAY, HE ALSO SKIPS BREAKFAST.
NO WAY!!
SOMEHOW, HE'S STILL MANAGED TO GET PRETTY TALL.
Doesn't he get hungry?
I don't believe it.
The Harada twins love breakfast.
DURING THE WEEK, HE SPENDS MOST OF THE DAY IN SCHOOL.
GIRLS FOLLOW HIM EVERYWHERE HE GOES...
HE'S ALWAYS GETTING LOVE NOTES...
Oooh!! He's so cute!!
BUT HE WORKS VERY HARD TO KEEP AN EYE ON DAISUKE AND IGNORES THEM ALL.
AAAHHH...
THAT'S SATOSHI'S MORNING.
He's enjoying this.
Lunch-time!
USUALLY, HE EATS BREAD FOR LUNCH UP ON THE ROOF.
LATELY, HE'S BEEN EATING LUNCH WITH DAISUKE.
DO YOU ALWAYS EAT BREAD?
His mom makes him a big lunch.
I DON'T HAVE TIME TO MAKE A LUNCH.
OH...
HE DOESN'T SEEM INTERESTED IN FOOD AT ALL.

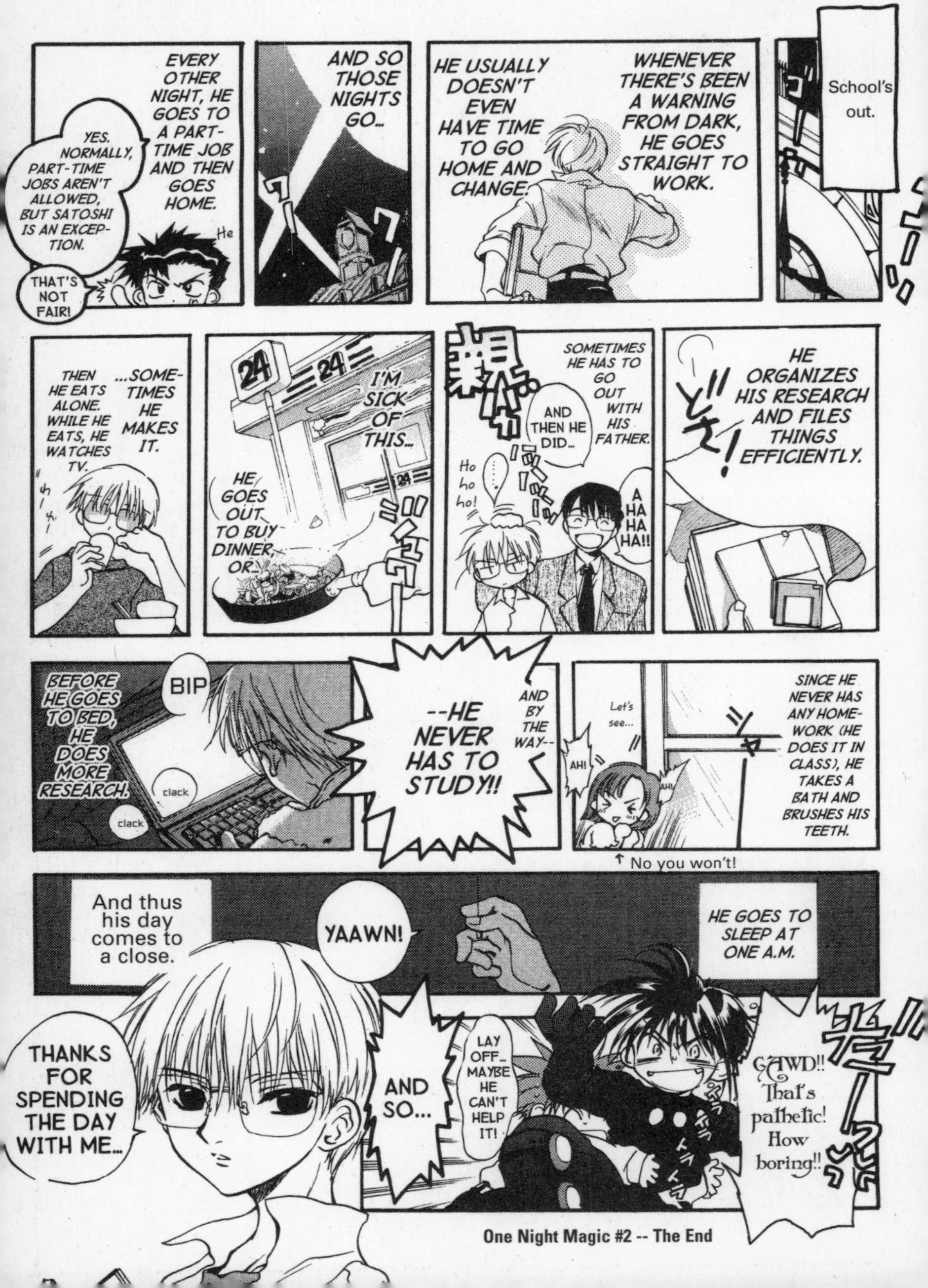
School's out.
WHENEVER THERE'S BEEN A WARNING FROM DARK, HE GOES STRAIGHT TO WORK.
HE USUALLY DOESN'T EVEN HAVE TIME TO GO HOME AND CHANGE.
AND SO THOSE NIGHTS GO...
EVERY OTHER NIGHT, HE GOES TO A PART-TIME JOB AND THEN GOES HOME.
YES. NORMALLY, PART-TIME JOBS AREN'T ALLOWED, BUT SATOSHI IS AN EXCEPTION.
He
THAT'S NOT FAIR!
HE ORGANIZES HIS RESEARCH AND FILES THINGS EFFICIENTLY.
SOMETIMES HE HAS TO GO OUT WITH HIS FATHER.
A HA HA HA!!
Ho ho ho!
AND THEN HE DID...
I'M SICK OF THIS...
HE GOES OUT TO BUY DINNER, OR...
...SOMETIMES HE MAKES IT.
THEN HE EATS ALONE. WHILE HE EATS, HE WATCHES TV.
SINCE HE NEVER HAS ANY HOMEWORK (HE DOES IT IN CLASS), HE TAKES A BATH AND BRUSHES HIS TEETH.
Let's see...
AH!
AH!
No you won't!
AND BY THE WAY--
--HE NEVER HAS TO STUDY!!
BEFORE HE GOES TO BED, HE DOES MORE RESEARCH.
BIP
clack
clack
HE GOES TO SLEEP AT ONE A.M.
YAAWN!
And thus his day comes to a close.
GAWD!! That's pathetic! How boring!!
LAY OFF... MAYBE HE CAN'T HELP IT!
AND SO...
THANKS FOR SPENDING THE DAY WITH ME...

One Night Magic #2 -- The End

D·N·ANGEL VOL. 3

One Night Magic

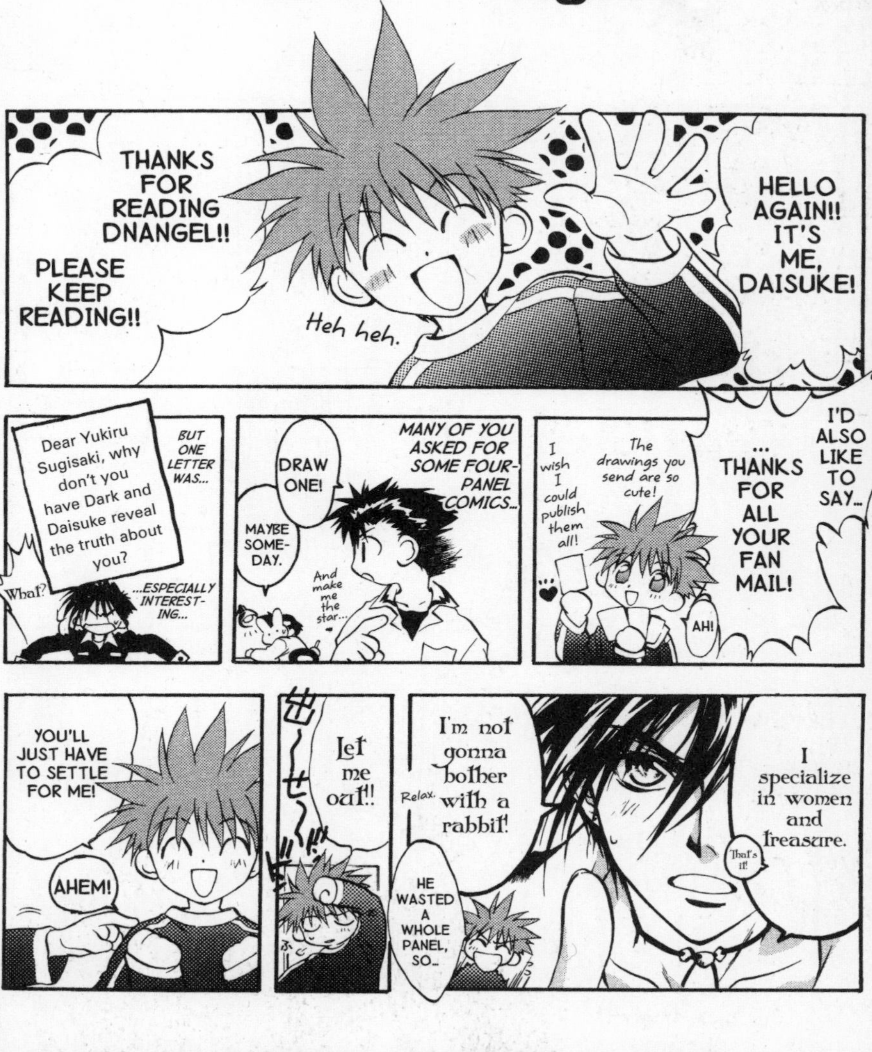

HELLO AGAIN!! IT'S ME, DAISUKE!
Heh heh.
THANKS FOR READING DNANGEL!!
PLEASE KEEP READING!!
I'D ALSO LIKE TO SAY...
...THANKS FOR ALL YOUR FAN MAIL!
AH!
The drawings you send are so cute!
I wish I could publish them all!
MANY OF YOU ASKED FOR SOME FOUR-PANEL COMICS...
DRAW ONE!
MAYBE SOME-DAY.
And make me the star...
BUT ONE LETTER WAS...
Dear Yukiru Sugisaki, why don't you have Dark and Daisuke reveal the truth about you?
...ESPECIALLY INTEREST-ING...
What?
I specialize in women and treasure.
That's it!
I'm not gonna bother with a rabbit!
Relax.
HE WASTED A WHOLE PANEL, SO...
Let me out!!
YOU'LL JUST HAVE TO SETTLE FOR ME!
AHEM!

Watching soap operas.

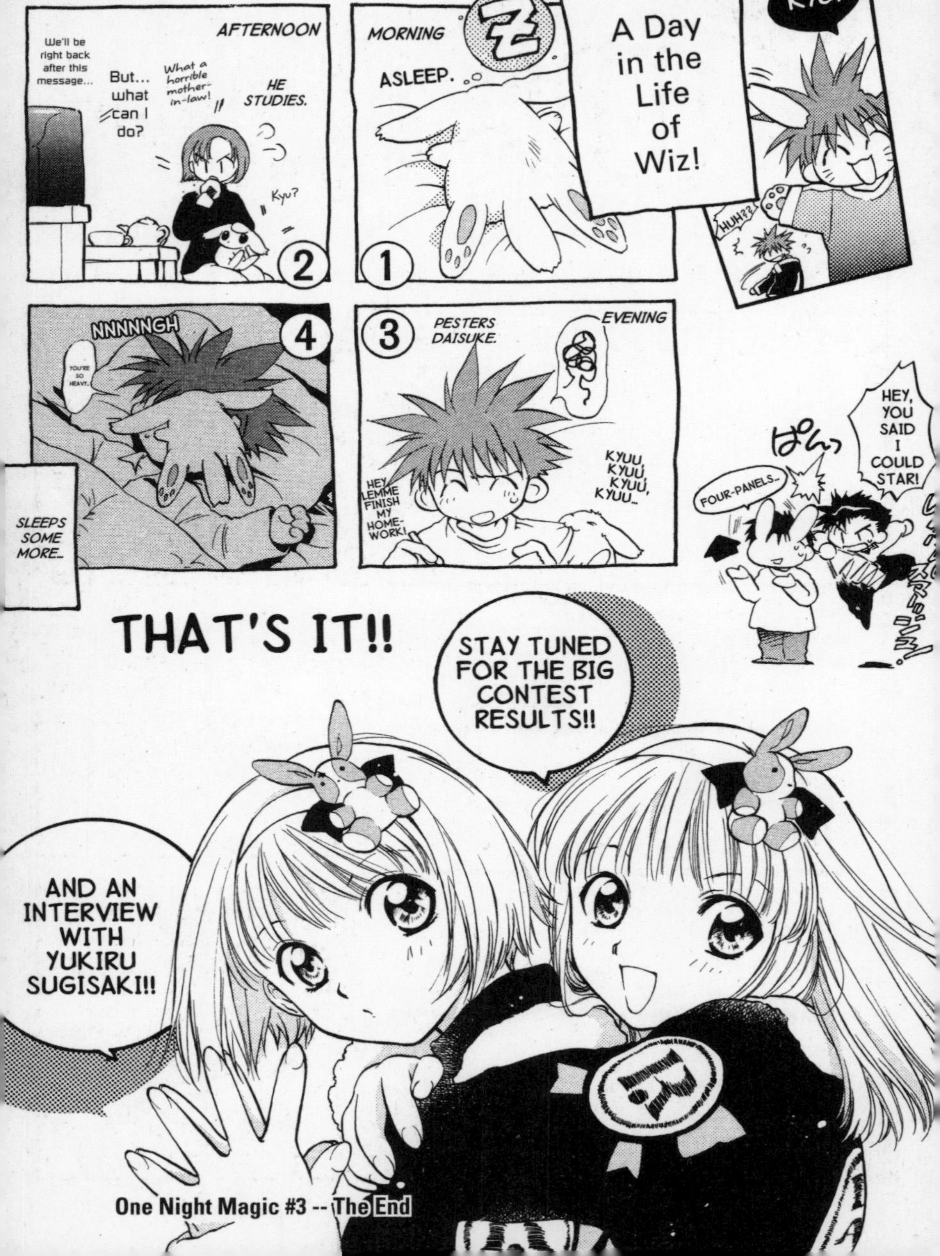

KYU!
HUH???
A Day in the Life of Wiz!
1
MORNING
ASLEEP.
2
AFTERNOON
HE STUDIES.
What a horrible mother-in-law!
But... what can I do?
We'll be right back after this message...
Kyu?
3
EVENING
PESTERS DAISUKE.
KYUU, KYUU, KYUU, KYUU...
HEY, LEMME FINISH MY HOME-WORK!
4
NNNNNGH
YOU'RE SO HEAVY...
SLEEPS SOME MORE...
HEY, YOU SAID I COULD STAR!
FOUR-PANELS...
THAT'S IT!!
STAY TUNED FOR THE BIG CONTEST RESULTS!!
AND AN INTERVIEW WITH YUKIRU SUGISAKI!!!
One Night Magic #3 -- The End

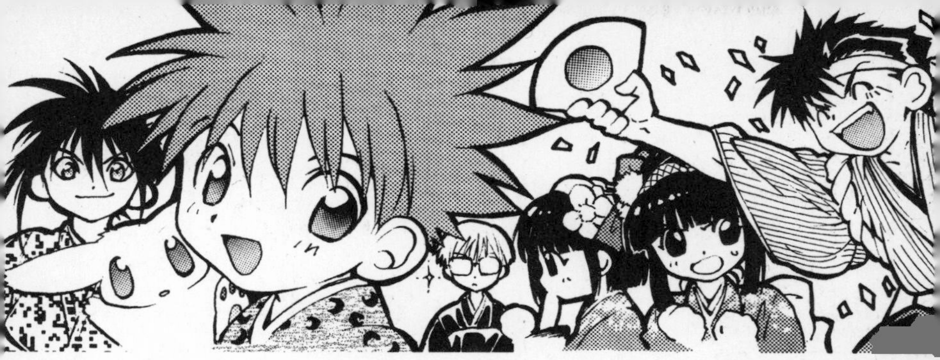

PRESENTING READER REQUESTS!!

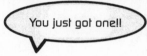

Here's a list of our top requests!! When will they be granted? Wait and see!

You just got one!!

1: We want DNAngel four-panel comic strips!

Don't we all?

2: We'd like to see profiles of all the characters.

3: A contest to see who's most popular!

4: I want to see them all when they were little!

5: I want to see Daisuke's father!

Other requests:

+ Can we see all their bedrooms?
+ I want a list of every thing Dark has stolen!
+ How about seeing what Daisuke's training was like when he was little?
+ I want to see Daisuke's grandpa transform!
+ How about a show-down between Risa and Riku?

Please note: Wishes 3 & 5 have also already been granted!

Thanks for all your input! ♥

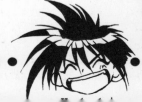

D·N·ANGEL

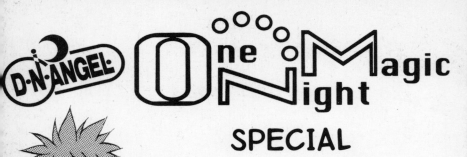

One Night Magic SPECIAL

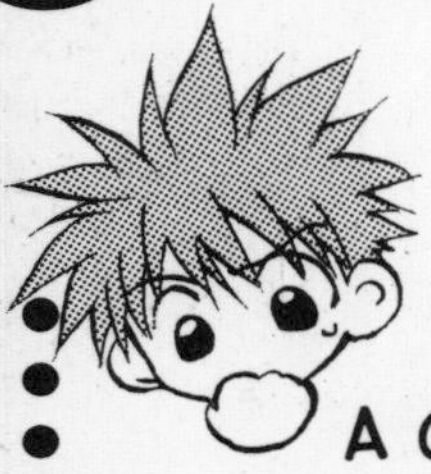

TAKESHI SAEHARA'S INTERVIEW

A Q&A FOR YUKIRU SUGISAKI

TAKESHI TOOK SOME OF YOUR TOP QUESTIONS AND SURPRISED YUKIRU SUGISAKI WITH AN INTERVIEW!

Q: Does Daisuke do well in school?
Sugisaki: He's about an average student. His strength is language (Japanese and English) and his weakness is math.
Takeshi: He's totally average.
Q: What does Dark do inside Daisuke when he isn't transformed?
Sugisaki: If he's awake, he sees and hears whatever Daisuke does. Sometimes he's scheming and planning...but mostly he sleeps.
Q: When the very first Niwa transformed into Dark...what did he look like?
Sugisaki: Hmm...that's a tough one...I think Dark probably looks the same every time.
Takeshi: What a cop-out! You don't know, do you?
Sugisaki: Hey! All I know is he was really handsome...
Q: What kind of food can Satoshi cook? And what kind of girl does he like?
Satoshi: I can make Kansai-style soba and deep-fried tofu. I like girls who look good in kimonos and don't have many secrets.
Sugisaki: What about looks?
Satoshi: As long as she's decent-looking, I don't care.
Takeshi: Satoshi, are you really a middle-school student?
Q: How old is Wiz? Is it a boy or a girl? Who were its parents?
Sugisaki: He's over a hundred years old, and he's a boy. His parents were rabbits...sort of.
Takeshi: "Sort of"? What do you mean by that?!
Daisuke: Umm... His true nature will stay secret...for now anyway.

One Night's Magic SPECIAL -- The End

The First DNAngel Character Popularity Contest Results!

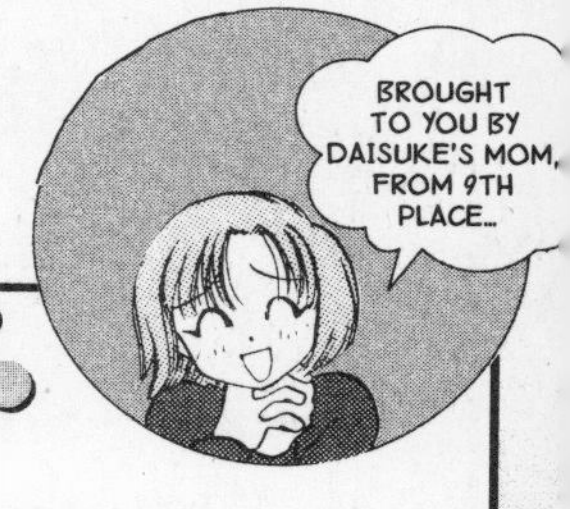
BROUGHT TO YOU BY DAISUKE'S MOM, FROM 9TH PLACE...

1

Daisuke Niwa, with 2852 votes

My little boy!! His adorable smile makes everyone swoon. I'm so glad he beat Dark in the popularity contest! ♥

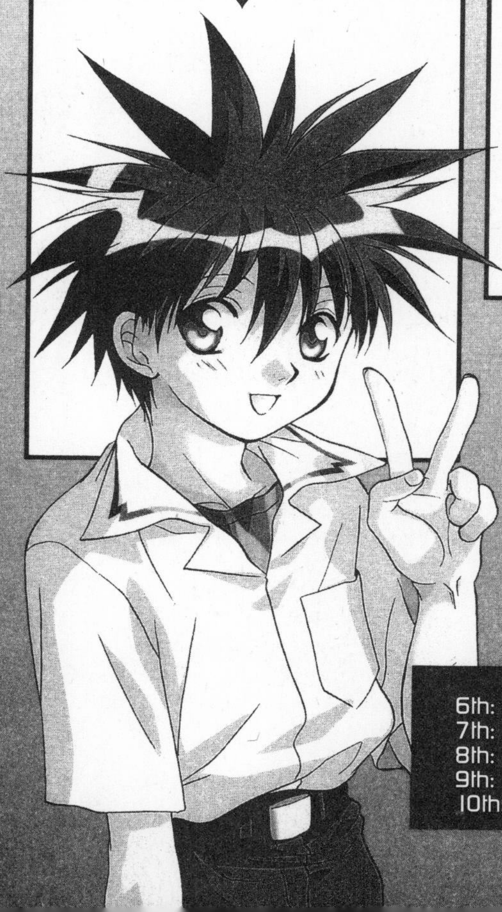

5

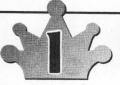

Wiz, with 897 votes

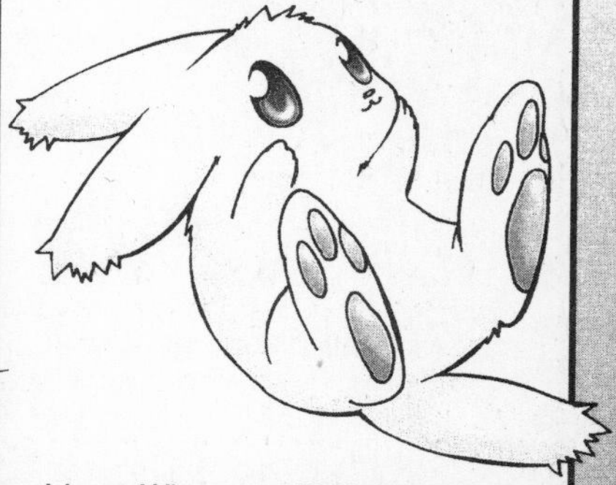

I love Wiz, myself! He's cute and fluffy and you can always count on him!! ♥

Thanks to everyone who voted! I was so happy to see all of your postcards.. and I can't believe how high you all ranked Wiz! And Keiji...he's hardly appeared and he still made tenth place!! Ha ha ha!

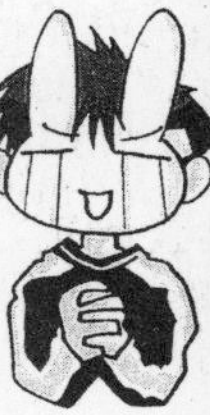

6th: Takeshi Saehara... 158 votes
7th: Risa Harada... 146 votes
8th: Kosuke Niwa... 111 votes
9th: Emiko Niwa... 59 votes
10th: Keiji Saga... 45 votes

D•N•ANGEL

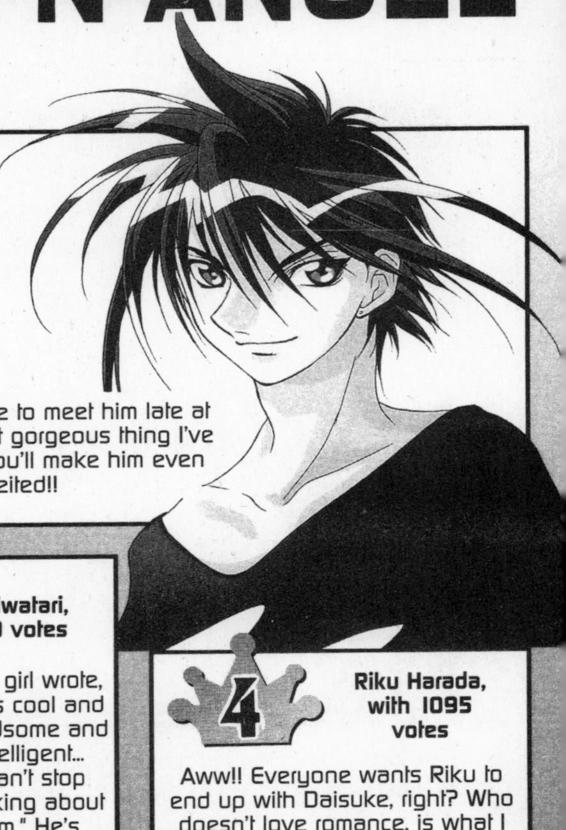

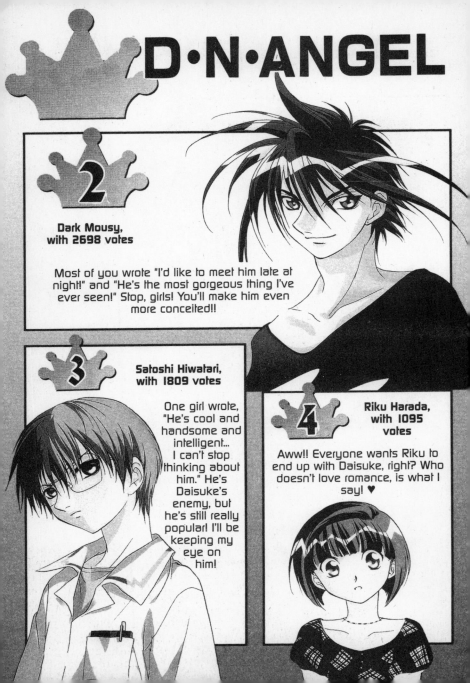

2

Dark Mousy, with 2698 votes

Most of you wrote "I'd like to meet him late at night!" and "He's the most gorgeous thing I've ever seen!" Stop, girls! You'll make him even more conceited!!

3

Satoshi Hiwatari, with 1809 votes

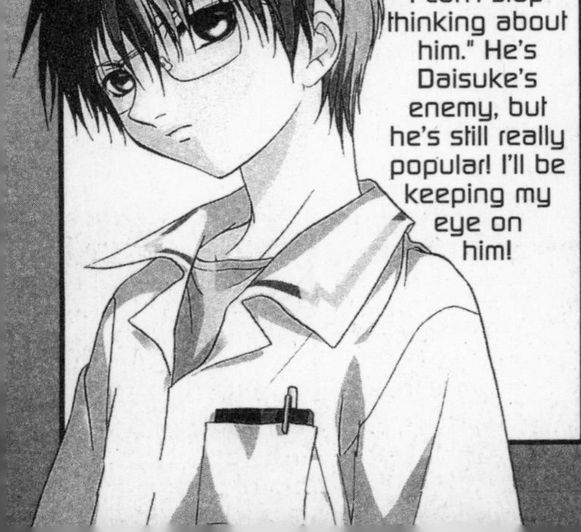

One girl wrote, "He's cool and handsome and intelligent... I can't stop thinking about him." He's Daisuke's enemy, but he's still really popular! I'll be keeping my eye on him!

4

Riku Harada, with 1095 votes

Aww!! Everyone wants Riku to end up with Daisuke, right? Who doesn't love romance, is what I say! ♥

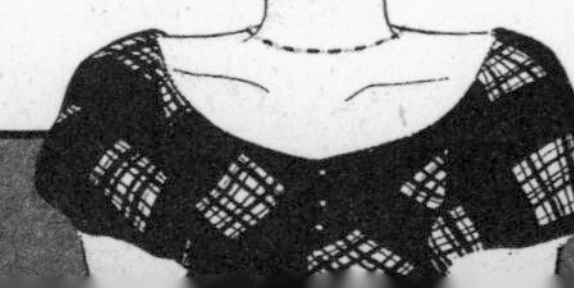

D·N·ANGEL

THINGS TO COME...

When a mysterious young woman takes an interest in Dark's next target, Takeshi makes it his mission to protect the item and win her heart. But does the aspiring news hound know where the ethereal beauty's best interests really lie? And it seems that the tenacious young Satoshi has a new weapon in his arsenal against the Phantom Thief. Will the boy genius finally capture the elusive Dark? And do Satoshi and Daisuke have more in common than anyone would have ever possibly imagined?

Be here for D.N. Angel volume 4!